D1260686

London under attack

London under attack

The Report of the Greater London Area War Risk Study Commission

Commissioners

Anne Ehrlich
S. William Gunn
J. Stuart Horner
John Marshall Lee
Peter Sharfman
Frank von Hippel

Rapporteur

Robin Clarke

Basil Blackwell

© South Bank Polytechnic 1986

First published 1986

Basil Blackwell Ltd
108 Cowley Road, Oxford OX4 1JF, UK

Basil Blackwell Inc.
432 Park Avenue South, Suite 1503,
New York, NY 10016, USA

All rights reserved. Except for the quotation of short passages for the purposes of criticism and review, no part of this publication may be reproduced, stored in a retrieval system, or transmitted, in any form or by any means, electronic, mechanical, photocopying, recording or otherwise, without the prior permission of the publisher.

Except in the United States of America, this book is sold subject to the condition that it shall not, by way of trade or otherwise, be lent, re-sold, hired out, or otherwise circulated without the publisher's prior consent in any form of binding or cover other than that in which it is published and without a similar condition including this condition being imposed on the subsequent purchaser.

British Library Cataloguing in Publication Data
London under attack : the report of the
GLAWARS Commission.
1. Nuclear warfare – Case studies
2. London (England) – Bombardment
I. Ehrlich, Anne H. II. Clarke, Robin
III. GLAWARS Commission
355′.0217 U263

ISBN 0-631-15018-8
ISBN 0-631-15044-7 Pbk

Typeset by Oxford Publishing Services, Oxford
Printed in Great Britain by Billing and Sons Ltd, Worcester

Contents

List of Tables

List of tables in the appendices

List of Figures

Acknowledgements

The Commissioners wish to thank the following people for making this report possible.

We are particularly grateful to Robin Clarke, the Rapporteur, who did an outstanding job in translating the Commission's ideas into the English language under a very tight schedule.

Without the help of Sue Roberts, GLAWARS Project Manager, and Graham Tubb, GLAWARS Research Manager, the Commission would have been unable to complete its task on time. They attended to the organization of the Commissioners' meetings and the letting of research contracts with meticulous attention to detail. They also prepared five of the seven appendices.

Thanks are also due to the 44 GLAWARS researchers, many of whom completed Herculean tasks of analysis working against almost impossible deadlines. Because they are too numerous to mention by name here, the complete list of researchers is included in Appendix 3.

Finally, we wish to thank Mrs Delia Buckle for administering the GLAWARS contract for the Greater London Council and Dr Robert Chilton for supervising it at the South Bank Polytechnic.

A. E.
S. W. G.
J. S. H.
J. M. L.
P. S.
F. v. H.

Enfield
Barnet
Harrow
Haringey
Waltham
Forest
Redbridge
Havering
Hillingdon
Brent
Camden
Islington
Hackney
Newham
Barking
Tower
Hamlets
City
Westminster
Kens. & Chels
Hammersmith
Ealing
Greenwich
Southwark
Hounslow
Bexley
Lambeth
Wandsworth
Lewisham
Richmond
upon
Thames
Kingston
upon
Thames
Merton
Bromley
Sutton
Croydon
GLC boundary
Inner London
boundary
0
km
10

Overview

This report is divided into three parts. The first assesses the likelihood of an attack on London in the near future and describes the forms that such an attack might take. The second examines the effects these attacks would have on London. And the third analyses the implications of these attacks for civil defence.

The main conclusions of the report are as follows.

1. The probability of any form of attack on or affecting the Greater London area during the next few years is extremely low.
2. A major war scare is less unlikely, and could have a profound effect on London, effectively bringing it to a halt even before an attack was launched.
3. Any attack on the UK would be likely to start with the use of conventional weapons against military targets. The use of chemical or biological weapons against London is considered extremely unlikely.
4. If nuclear weapons were ever used, attempts to restrict their use to military targets would be likely to fail. Should this happen, London would be destroyed.
5. The two most severe attacks considered assume that 65 and 90 megatons (Mt) of nuclear weapons would fall on the UK, with about 5 and 10 Mt on London. At least 85 per cent of Londoners would be killed or seriously injured. A nuclear winter would be likely to set in, effectively paralysing British agriculture for one or even two years. It would take London's pre-attack house-building industry more than 185 years to rebuild London's homes.
6. Even a much less severe attack, involving 31 Mt on the UK, of which only 1.35 Mt would fall on London, would destroy about one-third of the city. As a result, London might enter a spiral of decline from which it would never recover.
7. In the less likely event of a nuclear attack restricted to specific

military targets, London would survive, although regions in the west and north-west of London might be heavily damaged.

8 Civil defence must be planned to deal with specific threats. In both the UK and the US, the public is sceptical about civil defence because governments have refused to admit that civil defence would be ineffective against substantial nuclear attacks. However, no civil defence programme will work unless it receives popular support.

9 All forms of civil defence would be useless against heavy nuclear attacks. The GLC or its successor should therefore restrict its civil defence planning to deal principally with a war scare, conventional attack or the much less likely contingency of a small nuclear attack.

10 Civil defence measures that might mitigate the effects of these contingencies include an extended concept of land-use planning, a public information programme, improved communications, the provision of food and medical reserves, and plans for food rationing, the evacuation of high-risk areas in London, and the manning of essential and emergency services before and after attack.

Background to the study

The Greater London Area War Risk Study (GLAWARS) was commissioned by the Greater London Council (GLC) in 1984. The need for it arose from the Civil Defence Regulations 1983 which placed additional responsibilities on local authorities for civil defence. As a result, the GLC is now required by law to make civil defence plans; provide five emergency centres to control action in the event of an attack; train GLC and borough council staff for civil defence; take part in civil defence training exercises organized by the government; and organize a volunteer system for civil defence.

The requirements of some parts of the Civil Defence Regulations 1983 are quite detailed. They include surveys to identify buildings suitable for shelters, the provision of a rescue service for people trapped in damaged buildings, plans for disposing of dead bodies after an attack, and provision of a service for distributing food after an attack. All plans are to be capable of being implemented within 7 days, and their most vital elements within 48 hours.

In order to meet these responsibilities, the GLC requested additional information from the Home Office about the planning assumptions on which London's civil defence should be based. The information needed concerned the likely scale and nature of an attack on or affecting the

Greater London area. The Home Office declined to provide this information. After taking legal advice, the GLC sought expert opinion from a team of scientists, military experts and disaster relief specialists who were then appointed as GLAWARS Commissioners. The South Bank Polytechnic was contracted to conduct the study, which was to investigate the nature, extent and effects of possible hostile attacks on or affecting the Greater London area, and the effectiveness of possible defence measures. The terms of reference of GLAWARS are included in Appendix 1, and biographical details of the Commissioners are to be found in Appendix 2.

The Commissioners carried out most of their work during 1984 and 1985. To assist them in their studies, they commissioned extensive research on the issues involved, most of which was conducted between January and November 1985. In all, 44 authors were involved in the preparation of 33 separate research papers (see Appendix 3). Together, these represent the most detailed analysis ever made of the consequences of attack on a major city.

This report is based largely on the findings of the GLAWARS researchers. Their papers, however, do not necessarily reflect the views of the GLAWARS Commissioners; nor are all the research results included in this report.

While individual Commissioners might have expressed some sections of the report in differing ways, the report does not include any minority dissenting views. It is a consensus view of the GLAWARS Commissioners which was reached after intensive discussion but without any major difficulties.

Summary of the study

The military threat

It is very unlikely that either the UK or London will be subjected to attack by a nation or alliance in the near future. Should such an attack occur, however, the threat would be from a war in which three types of weapon – conventional, chemical and biological, and nuclear – might be used. To the limited extent that such a threat exists at all, it is from the Warsaw Pact countries. The possibility that any other nation or alliance could or would attack the UK can be discounted.

It is very unlikely that such a war would involve the use of either chemical or biological weapons (CBW). These currently appear to offer few military advantages over the use of conventional or nuclear weapons. The effects of attacks with CBW were therefore excluded from the study.

A future war is likely to start with the use of conventional weapons against military targets. Because the survival of both sides would be threatened if such a war escalated to the use of nuclear weapons, intensive efforts would be made to terminate the war or to restrict its conduct to the use of conventional weapons. The Commission's view is that these efforts would probably fail. The war would then escalate to a nuclear phase.

GLAWARS was required to identify the form and weight of possible future attacks affecting the London area. Because the pursuit of a nuclear war would involve acts of irrational behaviour that defy reasoned analysis, it is impossible for GLAWARS fully to discharge its responsibility to identify all the military scenarios that could affect London. The Commission does not pretend to knowledge to which neither it, nor anyone else, has access.

On the other hand, examination of the weapons available to the Warsaw Pact, and of what is currently known of the strategic plans of the major powers, suggests that some outcomes of such a war are more likely than others. This evidence suggests that if nuclear weapons were ever used, attempts would be made to restrict this use to military targets. It is possible that these attempts might succeed.

The Commission believes, however, that it is much more likely that these attempts would fail. In the chaos that would surround the first use of nuclear weapons, the temptation to depart from planned strategies and to release an orgy of destruction in the hope of preventing retaliation would be high. The Commission considers this outcome to be substantially more likely than the chance of being able to fight a 'limited' nuclear war and then terminate it before industrial and urban areas were targeted.

On the basis of these considerations, the Commission constructed a series of six possible contingencies around which to conduct its studies. Within some of these contingencies, it elaborated more detailed scenarios that identified the number and nature of the weapons used, and the targets that would be attacked. These scenarios also included assumptions about which weapons failed to detonate and which missed their targets due to malfunction. These contingencies and scenarios are summarized in Table 1.

The scenarios outlined in Table 1 were used to calculate the effects on London. To do this, a simplifying assumption had to be made: that all the weapons in each scenario would be exploded more or less simultaneously. In reality, this would be most unlikely, and the effects of nuclear attacks are therefore likely to be more severe than those described in this report.

The fact that weapons would not be exploded simultaneously in reality also has important psychological implications. Londoners could never know which weapon was the last in an attack – in a nuclear war, it is never possible to sound an 'all clear'. Nor, after the heavier attacks, would there be any means of negotiating a peace. There may therefore

Table 1 GLAWARS contingencies and scenarios

Contingency	Type of target	Weapons used	Weight of attack
A: Continued non-belligerence	–	–	–
B: War scare	–	–	–
C: Non-nuclear attacks	a) Military b) London's services	Conventional only	Not assessed in detail but probably a few tens of aircraft loads
D: Nuclear attacks on nuclear targets			
Scenario 1	UK or UK-based nuclear capabilities	Bombers, carrying nuclear bombs and air-to-surface missiles	8.0 Mt on UK (38 weapons), London escapes damage
Scenario 2	As above, plus military command and control centres	As above	13.0 Mt on UK (56 weapons) including 2 Mt on London (7 weapons)
E: Nuclear attacks on nuclear targets, and on UK naval and air power			
Scenario 3	Nuclear and non-nuclear military targets	SS-20 missiles, each carrying three 150-kt warheads	31.05 Mt on UK (207 weapons), including 1.35 Mt on London (9 weapons)
F: Nuclear attacks on military, industrial and urban targets			
Scenario 4	Military and industrial targets	SS-20 missiles, and submarine-launched missiles with 1-Mt warheads	65.05 Mt on UK (241 weapons), including 5.35 Mt on London (13 weapons)
Scenario 5	Military, industrial and urban targets	As above, but with an extra 32 1-Mt warheads	90.05 Mt on UK (266 weapons), including 10.35 Mt on London (18 weapons)

be no means of knowing when either a nuclear attack or a nuclear war has ended.

In addition to the weapons included in Table 1, it is likely that, from scenario 2 on, one or more exo-atmospheric nuclear explosions would be included to generate an electromagnetic pulse (EMP) that would disable most communications systems in the UK (few of which are hardened to withstand the effects of EMP).

It is also important to relate attacks on the UK to what might be happening elsewhere in Europe and in the United States. If large-scale nuclear attacks were also occurring there, a nuclear winter would be likely to result. Its severity would depend largely on the size and character of these attacks. It is assumed by GLAWARS that scenarios 1, 2 and 3 are associated with a global nuclear exchange of about 3000 megatons (Mt). Scenarios 4 and 5 are associated with an exchange of about 6500 Mt.

A major nuclear attack on the UK (contingency F) could well result in much higher levels of attack than are assumed in this report (the largest of which amounts to 90 Mt on the UK). Most previous studies have assumed attacks of about 200 Mt or more to strike the UK. It is a major finding of the Commission that much smaller attacks than were previously assumed would effectively destroy both the UK and London. Scenario 5 would kill or injure half the population of the UK, and 97 per cent of Londoners. The capital would be reduced to rubble. There is therefore no point in studying even larger attacks.

Effects on London

The effects of these contingencies on London, in particular the five nuclear attack scenarios, were studied in great detail. Computer models were used to assess casualties in the UK and in London, and damage to buildings, agriculture, and essential and emergency services. Studies were also made of the psychological effects, impact on the health services, long-term effects on health, the effects of a nuclear winter on the biosphere, and of the social, economic and political repercussions of the attacks. Only when all these effects are considered cumulatively can anything like a true picture be drawn of the likely consequences for London. Furthermore, many of these effects are mutually reinforcing: for example, destruction of hospitals and medical supplies, the onset of a nuclear winter, and lack of food due to damaged agriculture would all greatly decrease the chances of the injured recovering.

1. Contingency A: continued non-belligerence. The GLAWARS Commission believes that the current state of uneasy peace – best described as 'non-belligerence' – between the UK and Warsaw Pact countries is likely to continue. However, because the peace is uneasy, the next most likely contingency is one of war scare.

2. Contingency B: war scare. As part of its research, GLAWARS commissioned a study of Londoners' views of nuclear war (see Appendix 5). This revealed that during a war scare, surprisingly high numbers of Londoners would protest, some violently, against the prospect of the UK becoming involved in a war. Furthermore, many would try to stock up with food, decide not to work and attempt to leave London.

It is therefore a major finding of this report that a war scare could paralyse London, even before an attack were launched. There would be widespread panic and confusion, a scramble to acquire food, a mass exodus from the capital, and the desertion of most workers from their jobs, whether or not these were in the public services and whether or not they were vital to the running of the city.

3. Contingency C: non-nuclear attacks. The Commission identified two possibilities: attacks with conventional weapons on military targets and similar attacks on London's services.

There are few military targets in the London area, and nearly all of them are confined to the west and north-west perimeters of the city. Attacks on them with conventional weapons would affect Londoners in those areas, and improvements in existing rescue, fire, ambulance and medical services in the affected areas would help curtail loss of life.

The second possibility is that London might be severely disrupted if a conventional attack were mounted on London's services. The accuracy of modern weapons is such that it might be possible to destroy key facilities connected with London's water, energy and transport systems with only a few tens of aircraft delivering air-to-ground missiles. The Commission was unable to estimate the probability of such an attack, which would depend on the Soviet view of the extent to which disrupting London's civilian economy would reduce the UK's contribution to NATO, the operational accuracy of Soviet weapons, and a Soviet assessment of the chance that the UK, unable to mount conventional attacks on Moscow, would therefore escalate the war to a nuclear phase. The Commission nevertheless wishes to draw attention to the civil defence implications of this scenario.

4. Contingency D: nuclear attacks on nuclear targets. Scenario 1 would produce about 860,000 casualties in the UK but none in London. Even so, there would be light damage to buildings in the west of London, and power supplies would be likely to be interrupted in some areas for at least a period. The population would not know whether more attacks were likely, and whether they would include London, so many of those who had not already done so would probably try to leave the city. This would have severe effects on London's services, such as transport and the supply of water and electricity. Commuters would find great difficulty in getting to work, and many of the city's offices would close. Few people would even try to get to work until they could be sure their families were safe from further attacks. Although physically undamaged, the city would thus be severely disrupted. How long it took to recover would depend on the situation elsewhere in the UK and abroad. The fact that nuclear weapons had been exploded on the UK, and the country's expensive posture of nuclear deterrence had failed, would be likely to have severe political repercussions.

Scenario 2 would have much more severe effects. Some 2.76 million people would be killed or injured in the UK, including nearly 1 million in London. This level of casualties would totally overwhelm all rescue and health systems. Many Londoners would try to leave the city, by foot if necessary. By the end of the third day, the uninjured would be waiting, in considerable fear, to be bombed, and the injured would be waiting in apathy, bewilderment and misery to die. Their fate would probably be sealed by the lack of food and medical treatment, and the spread of infectious disease caused by at least a partial breakdown of the water and sewerage systems.

About 350,000 dwellings – 13 per cent of London's total – would be demolished, and a further 134,000 would be structurally damaged. The boroughs of Hillingdon and Harrow would be totally devastated; more than two-thirds of all homes in Hounslow would be destroyed, as would about one-third of the houses in Barnet, Brent, Ealing and Richmond. In addition, fires would rage in all these areas, and might spread inwards towards the city centre. Most fires would be left to extinguish themselves except in areas where radiation levels were low enough to allow firemen safe access. About a third of London's fire stations would be destroyed or damaged by blast.

The overall result is that a very small nuclear attack, confined to four targets in west and north-west London, would render a quarter of the city's housing uninhabitable. Windows would be broken in at least 80 per cent of the houses left standing. Overall, the number of houses destroyed in London would be 50 per cent greater than in the whole of the UK during the whole of World War 2. It would take one or two years to clear rubble from London's roads and railway lines, and a further 6–10 years to improvise repairs to the houses left standing. Even if London's house-building industry were completely undamaged, and all materials remained easily available, it would take a further 30 years to rebuild the destroyed housing stock. In reality, with the building industry also damaged and materials in short supply, it would take far longer.

If an exo-atmospheric detonation were included in this scenario, the effects of EMP would be to knock out most communications systems. In addition, electronic controls, computers and computer tapes would be damaged. As a result, gas and electricity would be likely to be cut off for at least 72 hours, and probably much longer, even in undamaged areas. The water supply system to the west of London would also be seriously damaged by blast, and it is possible that the banks of the Thames would be breached at Staines, leading to flooding. About 40 per cent of London telephone exchanges would be damaged or destroyed, and the telephone system put out of action. Around a third of all radio masts in London would be damaged or destroyed by blast, leading to a major loss of communications in the public services.

Within 100 km of London, agriculture would be severely damaged, with 25–30 per cent losses in most farming categories. Pigs and poultry, however, would suffer more severely: disruptions in power supplies would cause more than 50 per cent losses. Outside London, transport systems would be severely damaged and there would be little chance of food being imported into the capital for some time. As normal London food stocks would last for only a few days, there would either be a severe shortage of food in London, or its supply would become non-existent. This would force many people to try to move out of the capital.

Economic life in London would be totally disrupted for a period of at least two years. Recovery would depend on the speed of recovery elsewhere in the UK but it would lag behind it because of the nature of the services – mostly tertiary – that London provides. In the heavily damaged boroughs, recovery would be very much slower, taking decades; indeed, these areas would be unlikely to be rebuilt in their previous form at all. For London as a whole, recovery would be unlikely to mean a return to pre-attack conditions, though London would continue to exist. The impact of scenario 2 on London might be roughly comparable to that of either the Great Fire or the Plague.

5. Contingency E: nuclear attacks on UK sea and air power. There is a decisive difference between scenarios 2 and 3. Not only would the damage be considerably increased in scenario 3, but it would be more widely spread. Because so many more weapons would be used, the chance of accidental damage due to malfunction would be greatly increased. For this reason, scenario 3 includes the explosion of a bomb designed for Heathrow which due to malfunction lands on Hampstead.

This would produce enormous damage to the city centre. A likely result would be that the city entered a spiral of decline from which it might never recover.

This scenario produces 8.3 million casualties in the UK, with nearly 1.5 million in London (23 per cent of the population). Immediately after the initial attack, there would be nearly three-quarters of a million corpses to dispose of. A third of London's housing – some 800,000 homes – would be rendered uninhabitable, with roughly ten times as many houses destroyed in a few minutes as in six years during World War 2. The bomb on Hampstead, falling on a densely populated area of the city, would make three boroughs uninhabitable and two others largely so. In Westminster, 80 per cent of homes would be uninhabitable. Fires would rage throughout much of London. It would take 15–20 years just to clear the rubble from London's roads and railways, and to improvise repairs to those houses left standing. The cost of repair and reconstruction for all London's buildings would amount to at least £35,000 million (in 1983 prices).

After scenario 3, London's services would be essentially out of action. Three-quarters of London's transport nodes, for example, would be damaged or destroyed. London transportation would simply stop. There would be no public supplies of gas, electricity or water.

Within 100 km of London, agriculture would be badly damaged, with cattle losses of around 50 per cent; barely 10 per cent of pigs and poultry would survive. A nuclear winter could follow and, if the attack occurred during the summer, this could bring temperatures down to around freezing point, in effect turning summer into winter. There could be periods of greatly increased darkness and abnormally high precipitation. If a severe nuclear winter occurred, regardless of season, at least one year's agricultural harvest, and possibly two years', would be basically lost. One result would be that essentially no food would enter London.

Although regional command centres would, in theory, remain fairly intact, they would probably not be connected to a functioning political and social system. They would not, therefore, be able to command and control it. London would cease to function as an economic system, and virtually no one would go to work or have work to go to. The best that could be hoped for would be that groups would eventually form to look after their own interests. In a functional sense, most of the population would not have a government, and would be concerned only with finding water, food and shelter for their families.

In the immediate aftermath of the war, it is possible that London would be abandoned. This could happen simply because the survivors themselves moved out or as a result of a decision to re-establish the seat of government elsewhere. It is also possible that the rest of the country would refuse to provide either food or assistance for a region where the principal economic function – the provision of tertiary services – would be of little use in a long-term recovery programme. Instead of growing, as it has for some 2000 years, the city might then enter an indefinite period of decline.

London's ultimate fate would depend on whether outside help were available for reconstruction, as it was, for example, for Hiroshima after World War 2. This seems unlikely. At best, it would take decades for London to recover as a functioning system. When, and if, it did, it would not resemble the pre-war capital. London might subsequently become a minor city, with the country's capital and the seat of government both located in a less damaged area.

6. Contingency F: nuclear attacks on military, industrial and urban targets. The outcomes of scenarios 4 and 5 are less ambiguous. In both, more than 85 per cent of Londoners would be killed or injured. More than 90 per cent of homes would be uninhabitable, and there would be no essential services, and no prospects of services. In 25 of London's 33 boroughs, more than 75 per cent of dwellings would be destroyed in scenario 4. In scenario 5, only Bromley would escape with less than 75 per cent damage, and even there only 8000 homes would still have their walls and roofs intact. This is all that would remain of London's buildings. Fires would force virtually all survivors to flee, if they could. Those that remained would be unlikely to survive for long; they would be cold, probably injured, diseased, hungry, thirsty, homeless and isolated. Furthermore, their problems would be greatly compounded by the nuclear winter that would probably follow.

In scenarios 4 and 5, London would be reduced to rubble. The city would be abandoned, and would not recover.

Civil defence

The GLAWARS Commission identified two important principles of civil defence: civil defence measures must be planned to deal with specific threats; and no civil defence programme can work unless it receives popular support.

Civil defence programmes in both the UK and the United States have proved unpopular for two reasons. First, their existence appears to admit the possibility that the expensive, and in some quarters unpopular, doctrine of nuclear deterrence may fail. Secondly, both governments, unlike some others in Europe, have refused to acknowledge that affordable civil defence measures would be ineffective against substantial nuclear attacks. This has led to widespread public scepticism about civil defence in both countries.

Countries such as Switzerland and Sweden acknowledge that no forms of civil defence could protect their populations against direct nuclear attack. Their civil defence plans are designed only to reduce casualties in the event of nuclear attacks on neighbouring areas or of conventional or small-scale nuclear attacks on military targets.

In contrast, UK civil defence is currently planned as a flexible response designed to mitigate the effects of *all* forms of attack. The Commission regards this as an essentially unworkable philosophy because civil defence measures are usually effective only if they are planned to deal with specific threats. The UK consistently refuses to suggest likely patterns of attack or to identify likely military targets. Unless it does so, the Commission believes, civil defence in the UK is likely to be of marginal use and its cost effectiveness to remain extremely limited.

The GLAWARS Commission believes that UK civil defence planners must concede that if London's civilian population were deliberately targeted, or even if a series of major nuclear attacks were mounted against nearby military installations, civil defence measures would be of little or no relevance. The Commission's view is that the Greater London Council, or its successor, should therefore restrict its civil defence planning to deal principally with a war scare, conventional attack and the much less likely contingency of small-scale nuclear attacks against military targets.

There are two types of civil defence measure: those designed to save lives before and during an attack; and those designed to save life after an attack. The Commission points out that the latter, which include rescue services and the training of volunteers in rescue and first aid, can contribute far less to public survival in the event of nuclear attack than the former. They should be regarded as a second string in civil defence, as they are in both Sweden and Switzerland.

A war scare is the most likely of the GLAWARS contingencies and could have profound effects on London. Among the measures that could improve the situation during a war scare are plans for the manning of emergency and essential services, a public information programme that provided realistic information about the likely effects of a war and about which areas in London would be at high risk, the introduction of food rationing, stockpiling of food and medical reserves, and improved communications.

The Commission does not believe that large-scale evacuation plans for London would be either workable or effective. It did, however, consider the possibility of local evacuation, within London, of the boroughs most at risk in the west and north-west of the city. A population of about 1 million people would be involved. The Commission concludes that such evacuation schemes merit further study. Because millions of Londoners would try to move out of the city during a war scare, or following an attack, the Commission believes that Londoners should in any case be supplied with specific information about the location of military targets within the London area. This information might help guide those who chose to move of their own accord to potentially safer areas.

The Commission also considered the possibility of providing blast shelters for Londoners. To do so would take several decades and cost at least £250 per head, assuming that the cost of Swedish blast shelters provides a realistic comparison. Such a plan would probably be considered too expensive. Furthermore, recent evidence suggests that conflagrations following nuclear attacks might well be so extensive that many of those in the shelters would either die of asphyxiation or heat, or be trapped in them as nearby buildings collapsed. In any case, a shelter programme, whether of blast or fall-out shelters, would be of little use in saving lives in the long term after a major nuclear attack; most survivors would subsequently succumb to the combined effects of cold, starvation, disease and lack of medical care.

A cheaper alternative might be to provide blast shelters only for London's high-risk areas. Calculations carried out for GLAWARS by the Swedish Civil Defence Administration suggest that in scenario 2 such shelters would reduce casualties by about two-thirds. However, these calculations do not take recent evidence about the extent of conflagrations into account. Although such a plan would save some lives in the event of a conventional or a small nuclear attack, more detailed studies of cost effectiveness would be needed to decide whether this was a viable option, particularly in view of the very low probability accorded to a small nuclear attack.

The civil defence measures considered by the Commission as potentially useful for the contingencies of a war scare, a conventional attack or a small nuclear attack are: a realistic public information programme, improved communications, the stockpiling of food and medical reserves, and plans for food rationing and the emergency manning of essential services.

Two additional measures were also suggested as meriting further study to deal with these contingencies: local evacuation schemes, and the idea of an expanded concept of land-use planning, in which facilities such as hospitals and potential community centres would in future be deliberately sited away from military targets.

In conclusion, the report quotes one of the GLAWARS researchers who described the prospect facing those who initially survived a nuclear war as follows: 'Survival will be fear, exhaustion, disease, pain and long, lonely misery'. Avoiding a nuclear war, the report concludes, is still the only way of avoiding such a fate.

1

The Military Threat

This report deals with the consequences for London of the United Kingdom becoming involved in a future war. The effects that such a war would have on London and Londoners raise difficult questions about what could be done, if anything, to minimize damage to the city and its inhabitants, and facilitate reconstruction.

These questions can be answered only if assumptions are made about the nature of such a future war. Who is the potential enemy? What would the enemy hope to achieve by attacking the UK? What, in particular, would the enemy hope to gain by attacking London? With what weapons is such a war likely to be fought? And what are the likely patterns of attack? These questions are the subject of Part 1 of the GLAWARS report.

The UK's military resources are substantial; it possesses both nuclear and sophisticated conventional weapons. It is highly unlikely, therefore, to be successfully attacked by any state that is not a major power. (Acts by terrorist groups, because they are likely to produce only isolated and limited damage, are not included in the study.) Any future conflict is therefore likely to hinge on the nuclear weapons available to either or both sides.

This does not necessarily mean that nuclear weapons will be used in such a conflict. But it does mean that their existence will certainly determine the conduct of the hostilities to a marked degree. For this reason, the analyses that follow stem from what is known or assumed of the current military strategies of the major powers.

These strategies envisage that a future war would probably start with the use of conventional weapons. Attempts would undoubtedly be made by both sides to limit action to these weapons. If these attempts were to fail, the war would enter a nuclear phase. Again, attempts would probably be made to limit the use of nuclear weapons – for example, to restrict their use to specific military targets. If these attempts were also to fail, nuclear weapons might be more widely used.

There is also the possibility that chemical and biological weapons might be used.

The threat to the UK, therefore, is not from three different types of war but from one kind of war in which any or all of three different types of weapons might be used in different phases. The use of conventional, chemical and biological, and nuclear weapons is analysed within this context. Technical details of the nature and effects of these weapons are included in Appendix 6.

1.1 The problem of prediction

Predicting the future is hazardous. Predicting the precise course of a future war is especially so. The GLAWARS Commission believes that war between nuclear states would be the greatest act of folly yet perpetrated by the human species. Pursuing such a war would involve acts of irrational behaviour which defy reasoned analysis. In this sense, it is impossible for GLAWARS fully to discharge its responsibility to identify the military scenarios that could give rise to attacks affecting London, and to describe the pattern and weight of those attacks. No one knows what form such a war would take; furthermore, no one will ever know until, and if, it happens. It would be highly improper for the Commission to pretend to knowledge to which neither it, nor anyone else, has access.

On the other hand, there are ways of thinking about the issues that have critical implications for civil defence planning. GLAWARS was created as an aid to civil defence planning and, early on in its deliberations, it reached an important conclusion: civil defence can have value only to the extent that it plans to deal with specific contingencies.

For the reasons given above – that the future is essentially unknowable – current Home Office civil defence plans are based on a "flexible" response, intended to deal with any contingency that may arise. Such a stance, of course, avoids the necessity of making predictions about the nature of future attacks. It is certainly true that, as the Home Office puts it

> The Government is not party to the military planning of potential aggressors and the Government guidance on planning assumptions deliberately avoids spurious precision about the scale of an attack or the targets that will be chosen.
>
> (Home Office 1985)

This approach to planning, however, leads to a civil defence policy that is no policy at all – one that is dispersed, dilute and inconsistent.

There are some forms of attack against which any form of civil defence would clearly be useless. To prepare for them is a waste of resources. Other forms of attack might create a real need for civil defence. Preparations to deal with such attacks might make sense if undertaken on the explicit premise that they were a hedge against an admittedly improbable contingency, not as preparation for 'the' form which a war would take. Moreover, the existing requirement to plan for civil defence against both conventional and nuclear attacks leads to major conflicts in priorities, with no guidance on how to resolve them. A similar conflict exists between the goals of protecting a civilian population against attack and of ensuring that survivors can continue to survive and begin to rebuild their society. These conflicts cannot be eliminated, but the first stage in dealing rationally with them is to acknowledge that they exist.

One of the costs of the Home Office decision to plan a "flexible" response is that current civil defence policies lack credibility and public support. During its work, GLAWARS commissioned a survey of Londoners' attitudes to nuclear war and civil defence (referred to in the rest of this report as the GLAWARS survey; some of the results of the survey are included in Appendix 5). To the question "Overall, how well prepared do you think the authorities are to help people survive after a nuclear attack on London?", nearly half (48 per cent) of Londoners replied "not at all prepared", although only 21 per cent felt that nothing could be done. Only 1.5 per cent of those interviewed felt that the authorities were "very well prepared" (Loizos and Marsh 1986).

These issues are explored in more detail in Part 3, where specific civil defence policies and measures are reviewed. Their relevance here is that any assessment of a civil defence measure must take account of three factors:

1 the probability that it will be needed;
2 its likely effectiveness when required; and
3 its cost.

It follows that any civil defence measure that is extremely unlikely to be required, is highly ineffective or is extremely expensive can be ignored. The implications of these conclusions are also examined in Part 3. The first factor – probability – is, however, the basic issue to be considered in assessing the military threat.

Two approaches are possible. A great deal is publicly known about the military dispositions and strategies of the major nuclear powers, and something is known about their targeting policies. The first approach, therefore, is to assess at least the initial objectives and targets of any hostile state or pact attempting to attack the UK. The Commission rejects the conclusion that these are essentially unknowable; on the contrary, it is certainly possible to distinguish what, in the event of war, is highly improbable, what is possible, and what is probable. In a study of this kind, it would be wholly unreasonable to ignore, for any reason, the abundant public evidence that exists of the likely approach of the major powers to the conduct of war.

However, a second approach is also necessary to allow for the probability that, in the chaos of a nuclear war, events will get out of hand. Attempts to prevent escalation may fail and such will be the pressures on those engaged in hostilities that carefully considered war plans may even be dispensed with altogether.

No set of plans can embrace all possibilities. Weather conditions, the prior course of hostilities and the mix of forces remaining on both sides would all affect the sort of attacks that could be carried out. Leaders determined on a nuclear attack but awaiting optimum conditions might find their hands forced by evidence that the other side was preparing for an attack. An attack following one by the enemy would inevitably be improvised to some degree, simply because of the loss of key capabilities, changes in the enemy force structure, the disruption of command and control systems, and so on (Bracken 1983).

The attacks on Hiroshima and Nagasaki are instructive. The attack on Hiroshima went according to plan. But the weather was poor for the second attack and an observation plane failed to make its rendezvous. Three runs were made against the primary target, Kokura, without a sighting. As the second target, Niigata, was now beyond range, an attempt was made to bomb Nagasaki, the lowest priority target. After one run, the bomb was dropped through a hole in the cloud cover, exploding some 2 km from the target.

It is hard to imagine the nightmare that would follow the decision to launch a nuclear attack. However, it is not hard to imagine the feelings of desperation that would be inevitable in the minds of all political and military leaders when they realized that the long-held doctrine of nuclear deterrence had finally failed. These leaders would be instantly engaged in a battle for the survival of their entire countries. The decisions they made would be reached under enormous stress and there is documented evidence that this can lead to breakdown (Williams 1986). Such extremes of human conduct do not lend themselves to prediction, and the temptation to depart from planned strategies and to release an orgy of destruction in the hope of preventing retaliation would be high. On balance, the Commission considers this outcome to be substantially more likely than the chance of being able to fight a 'limited' nuclear war and terminate it before civilization was destroyed.

As Williams (1986) writes

> A war in Europe would be full of confusion and uncertainty, with neither NATO governments nor the Soviet Union having full control over events. Furthermore, the potential for misunderstanding, breakdowns in communication, and miscalculation is enormous. These occurrences are all the more likely because of the conditions under which decisions would have to be made. Decision making in national capitals would almost certainly be in the hands of small groups of key individuals, who would have to make choices on the basis of inadequate information, against a background of rapidly moving events. The stress on the group would be intense and, as previous studies of crisis behaviour have shown, intense stress can have a profoundly debilitating effect on the ability of group members to make analytical assessments and sound judgements about the impact of choices they make. Indeed, during the Cuban missile crisis at least two members of the US decision-making team were overcome by stress. A war in Europe would generate much higher levels of stress and for longer periods. The consequences of this would be to inject even greater uncertainty into the evolving situation.

These conclusions are echoed by what Londoners feel. The GLAWARS survey revealed that "exactly two-thirds of Londoners believe the first attack will signal a total war that no-one will be able to stop and one-third retains a belief that the destruction visited by the first few bombs will force both sides to pause and perhaps find a different solution to the conflict" (Loizos and Marsh 1986).

On the basis of these considerations, GLAWARS formulated a set of six major contingencies that should be considered in civil defence planning. While it is not possible to make any precise evaluation of the probability of individual contingencies, it is possible to assess their relative probabilities. Before considering them in more detail, however, this report will deal with the question of identifying possible aggressors.

1.2 Potential sources of attack

In theory, London is vulnerable to nuclear attack from countries which are:

1 capable of obtaining their own nuclear weapons;
2 capable of delivering these nuclear weapons against London; and
3 potential enemies of the UK.

There are now five declared nuclear powers: China, France, the Soviet Union, the UK and the United States. In addition, India tested a nuclear device (ostensibly for peaceful purposes) in 1974; Israel is widely believed to have the capacity to assemble a nuclear weapon very quickly;

and South Africa may be in the process of acquiring such a capability. Other countries that may be in sight of a nuclear capability include Argentina, Brazil, Iraq, Pakistan, and the Republic of Korea. Yet others are capable of producing nuclear weapons if they so desired (and some so desire but lack the wherewithal). In all cases, actual proximity to nuclear status is a matter of dispute. The construction of nuclear weapons is not as easy as is often assumed.

One further possibility is that a state could buy or steal nuclear weapons from another power. The Commission considered the possibility of stealing nuclear weapons to be currently extremely unlikely. Very few nations now possess nuclear weapons and they have taken stringent security measures not only to safeguard them but also to prevent their accidental detonation. Nor could any country currently buy a nuclear weapon – though if there were substantial nuclear weapons proliferation in the future, this situation could change.

It is possible to conceive of circumstances in which UK forces might be vulnerable to nuclear attack while the UK mainland remained secure – for example, a second Falklands War with a nuclear Argentina, or an intervention in the Middle East after one of the local powers had obtained nuclear weapons. For the UK itself to be attacked, the attacker must either own long-range bombers or missiles, or be able to deploy shorter-range systems on carriers or submarines. More unorthodox methods of delivery, such as a trawler carrying a nuclear device entering a port, cannot be precluded but they are inherently unreliable and lack utility for deterrence or other peace-time purposes.

The other four declared nuclear powers all have the ability to attack the UK, although in the case of China this is limited. None of the other possible nuclear weapons states has any obvious means of delivering nuclear weapons against the UK. As can be seen from Figure 1, the UK's geographical position means that weapons systems with ranges of well over 1500 km would be needed by any non-Warsaw Pact country planning to attack the UK. No near-nuclear state is within 3000 km but two, Iraq and Israel, are within 5000 km.

Attacks by either on the UK seem extraordinarily unlikely. Furthermore, Israel has no long-range bombers. Iraq is reported to own seven *TU-22 Blinders* and eight *TU-16 Badgers*, built by the Soviet Union in the early 1960s and late 1950s respectively. Their respective ranges of 2800 and 2400 km would not enable them to attack the UK even if they had reason to do so. (Libya also owns seven *TU-22 Blinders*, which could theoretically reach the UK on a bombing mission; however, Libya is nowhere near a nuclear weapons capability.)

Of the four established nuclear powers, France and the United States are allies and can be discounted as potential enemies. This leaves China and the Soviet Union. China has a handful of inter-continental ballistic

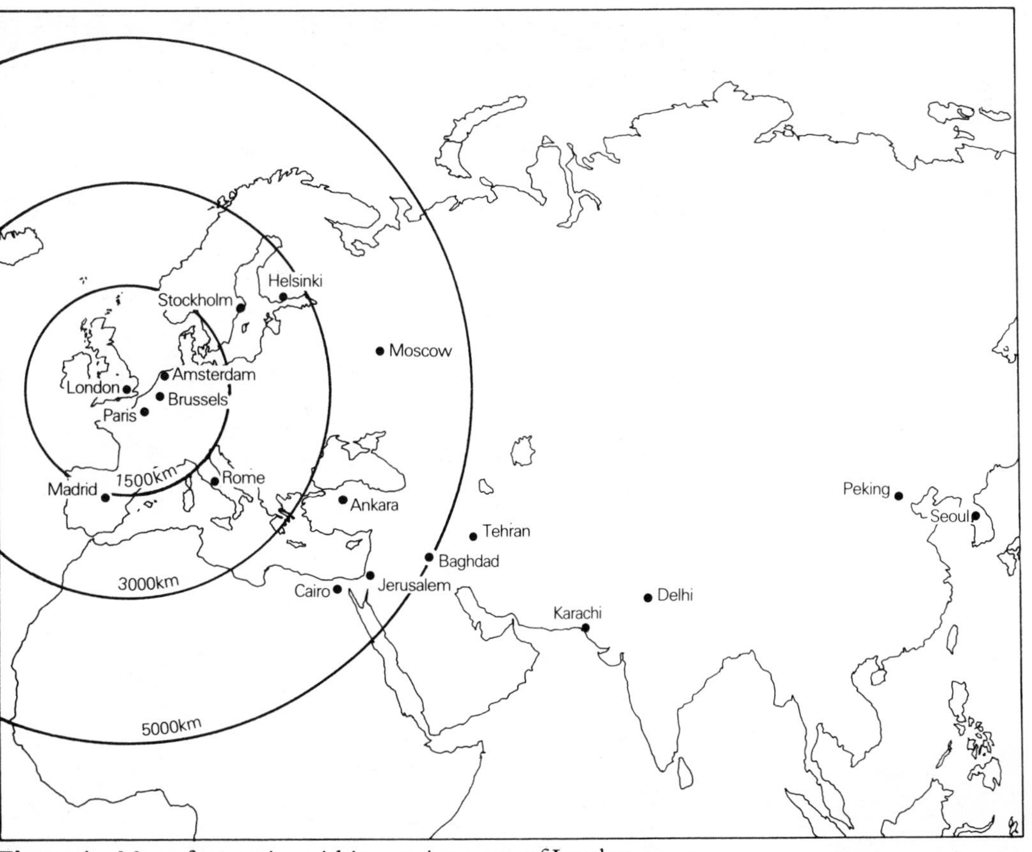

Figure 1 Map of countries within certain ranges of London

missiles, with ranges between 8800 and 11,200 km, and one submarine capable of launching ballistic missiles. Theoretically, China could just attack the UK. However, given that the UK has the means of retaliation and that there are currently no serious political differences between the UK and China, it is hard to imagine why China should attempt to attack the UK. Thus the Warsaw Pact countries are the only serious source of a nuclear attack on the UK. This conclusion accords with the current judgement of the UK government.

Terrorist attacks, regardless of the nature of the weapons used, were excluded by the terms of reference of the study.

1.3 The six contingencies

GLAWARS had little difficulty in identifying the most likely contingency in the near future: that the current state of uneasy peace will continue. The probability that this will happen is much greater than the probability that the UK will become involved in any sort of war with the Warsaw Pact. This conclusion accords well with the views of Londoners. The GLAWARS survey revealed that 50 per cent of Londoners were certain that the UK would not be attacked with nuclear weapons in the next five years; 25 per cent were certain that such an attack would not occur within 20 years.

This contingency is referred to as continued non-belligerence, for reasons that relate to the probabilities of other contingencies. It was felt inappropriate to describe current relations between NATO and Warsaw Pact countries as peaceful. On the contrary, the two pacts are bound into an antagonistic relationship marked by deep mutual mistrust and the knowledge that each side could certainly destroy the other.

If such a situation is allowed to continue indefinitely, the future is likely to be marked by periods of high tension between the two pacts. The next most likely contingency is therefore identified as one of war scare, a condition which might or might not result in overt hostilities. War scares lead to panic, and one of GLAWARS' major findings is that civil defence could do a great deal to lessen the chance of such a panic and help ensure that the London system did not break down even if no war took place (or was declared) – which is a serious possibility. Current civil defence plans do not appear to deal with this possibility as vigorously as they might.

Should the war scare end in hostilities, it is likely that the war would begin with the use of non-nuclear weapons – conventional, chemical or biological. This is current strategy within both NATO and the Warsaw Pact. The Commission considers this contingency as the most likely form of overt hostility between the two pacts. Such a war would not necessarily include an attack on the UK. However, the Commission also recognizes that a non-nuclear war between the pacts could well turn nuclear, in which case the UK would almost certainly be attacked.

The Commission assessed the probabilities of these different forms of war as follows: the most likely is a conventional attack followed by a nuclear exchange; the next most likely is conventional attack not followed by nuclear exchange; and the least likely is a nuclear exchange with no conventional phase.

Three nuclear contingencies were then considered. The first assumes that current strategic plans to limit nuclear warfare prevail, and that the only targets attacked in the UK would be nuclear capabilities, and command and control centres (whether those of UK forces or of US forces stationed in the UK). In this situation, London would escape very severe physical damage. Whether the city would survive in any meaningful sense would depend not on the physical effects of the war but on the social, economic and political repercussions that ensued.

The second nuclear contingency is that both nuclear and non-nuclear military installations in the UK are targeted. While still limited, this would involve a substantially larger attack on the UK and would create considerable damage in London. So many weapons would now be involved that the effects on London become more difficult to anticipate because the chances of a weapon exploding on London in error would be much increased. The effects of one such error would be sufficient to decide London's fate. At this level, major effects of the explosions on the climate would also become likely; even low-level nuclear winter effects could significantly increase darkness and reduce temperatures, at least temporarily and for intermittent periods. As the discussion in Part 2 shows, it seems unlikely that London would ever recover from such an attack.

The final nuclear contingency assumes that industrial and urban centres would also be targeted. By this stage, attempts to limit the nuclear war would have failed. London would be obliterated beyond hope of recovery. The political and economic survival of the United Kingdom and even of Western Europe would be in doubt. It is a major finding of GLAWARS that this degree of damage would be inflicted by substantially lower levels of attack than those that have been assumed to occur in most UK defence exercises and other studies.

The two most destructive scenarios considered in this report involve the explosion of about 65 and 90 Mt on the UK. Both would devastate London and the UK. Most other studies have assumed attacks of about 200 Mt. The Commission did not consider it necessary to examine the effects of attacks at this level, though it acknowledges that they could occur, because their effects could not be distinguished from those produced by attacks of less than half this size.

The six GLAWARS contingencies can thus be summarized as follows:

Contingency	*Weapons used*	*Type of target*
A	continued non-belligerence	–
B	war scare	–
C	non-nuclear	military installations, possibly civilian infra-structure
D	nuclear	nuclear weapon sites and related targets
E	nuclear	nuclear and non-nuclear military targets
F	nuclear	as above, plus urban and industrial targets

Before considering each contingency in more detail, some more general comments are in order. A future war could involve all six contingencies, starting with A and ending with F. Or the war could terminate at any intermediate stage. However, once contingency D, that of nuclear attack, were reached, momentous decisions would have been taken and the world would never be the same again. Although D might be described as 'limited', the damage created at even this low level of nuclear attack would vastly exceed anything so far experienced in British history. Even in the lightest imaginable attack, more explosive would fall on the UK alone than was used in the whole of World War 2 – and it could fall within a matter of hours.

Another important qualification is that such a war might not be limited to a few hours. In this case, the results would be worse. If nuclear attacks continued to occur, damage, panic, confusion and the difficulties of rescue work would all be greatly compounded. The scenarios for nuclear attack described later all assume that the weapons are delivered within a few hours. This is a simplifying assumption which is unlikely to be true. The consequences of these attacks, which are described in Part 2, are therefore optimistic. In fact, throughout this report, GLAWARS has applied a consistent philosophy of making optimistic assumptions wherever unresolvable doubts occur. In other words, the effects of nuclear attacks would certainly be as severe as is stated later, but would probably be considerably more so.

A nuclear war, it must be stressed, would bear little resemblance to World War 2. Two myths in particular need to be destroyed. The first, perpetuated by Home Office literature, assumes that at some point after a nuclear attack an all clear would be sounded. In the very unlikely event that the UK communications network and the whole of the UK early warning system remained completely undamaged, the population could expect, at most, a few minutes warning of the arrival of the second wave of nuclear missiles. No all clear could be sounded because of the possibility that further missiles could arrive at any time. A similar state of affairs occurred during the rocket attacks on London at the end of World War 2, and had a damaging psychological effect on those exposed to it. As each day passed without further nuclear attack, the probability that further attacks would not occur would increase but it might be weeks or even months before the survivors could assume that the attacks were over. Throughout this period it would be most unlikely that any systematic measures directed at recovery would be taken. The situation would be infinitely worse if, in fact, sporadic further attacks – or even the threat of further attacks – occurred.

The second myth is that a formal peace would be declared so that hostilities could come to an official end, victor and vanquished could be identified, and post-war reconstruction could begin. In a devastated post-nuclear landscape, national leaders would lack both the power and the means of communication with which to negotiate a peace. No elected government could survive the knowledge that the policy of deterrence had finally failed and that the nuclear threshold might be crossed again at any time. All of its energies would be taken up by attempts to re-establish its authority and credibility with its own citizens. This uncertain state could well continue indefinitely, creating insuperable problems for those responsible for civil defence. One of the most terrifying consequences of a nuclear war is that there may be no way of knowing when it has ended.

1.4 Contingency A: continued non-belligerence

The probability that there will be no overt hostilities between NATO and the Warsaw Pact in the foreseeable future is very high. This is far more likely than any other eventuality.

However, there is an important paradox to be explained when assessing the chances of war. Over the past decade or so, the nature of nuclear weapons has changed dramatically. The weapons produced today are generally smaller and much more accurate. This has led many critics to argue that the danger of nuclear war has increased. They claim that politicians may well view the new breed of nuclear weapons as more usable and useful than the massive, multi-megaton weapons of the

1950s and 1960s. The concept of a limited nuclear war has thus been more widely discussed. Furthermore, it is also argued that the temptation to make a pre-emptive strike is now greater because the improved accuracy of the new weapons has increased the chances of being able to eliminate the enemy's nuclear arsenal.

The paradox is that, while this has been happening, political and military leaders in both East and West seem, in fact, to have distanced themselves yet further from the idea of nuclear war. Instead of nuclear weapons being pushed increasingly to the fore in international crises, the reverse has happened: there is a marked reluctance to give any major crisis a nuclear dimension or to create a situation where the two superpowers might confront each other directly (Blechman and Kaplan 1978). The current trend in strategic thinking, in both East and West, is to reduce dependence on nuclear weapons because of an awareness of the enormous damage inherent in their use. This is demonstrated in President Reagan's expressed desire to render nuclear weapons "impotent and obsolete", international calls for no first use agreements, proposals to improve conventional forces, and the emphasis on nuclear weapons reductions in arms control talks. (In spite of this, of course, the numbers of nuclear weapons are still increasing.)

At its most basic level, the answer to the paradox may simply be that the more thought that is given to nuclear war, the more horrific the consequences appear. If this be true, thinking about the unthinkable does appear to have some merit.

There is also some concrete evidence that the worst predictions of humankind may not be fulfilled. During the past two decades, many possible scenarios were developed for a war between East and West. Most postulated a nuclear war arising from one specific event – such as the death of Tito, a war between major oil producers, a direct Soviet intervention in the Third World, the breakdown of arms control talks, the election of a hawkish US Administration or a popular mass movement in an East European state. In fact, all these events actually did occur during 1980 and 1981 without precipitating a war. It is therefore not unreasonable to hope that similar, perhaps more dramatic events could occur during the 1980s and 1990s without precipitating conflict.

None of these arguments, however, affects the chance of nuclear war starting unintentionally. Two situations must be distinguished. In the first, confusion and misunderstanding could initiate a chain of events that caused the war plans of the major powers to be put into effect. Political leaders could fail to sort the situation out in time, in spite of the numerous 'hot lines' that now exist. In this case, the war would proceed immediately to contingencies D, E or F.

The other situation is that a human or mechanical error caused one or a few nuclear weapons to be fired unintentionally, and one or several struck the UK. Such a catastrophe would be likely to be accompanied by frenzied communications between the powers involved, and offers of assistance from the offending nation. It would not necessarily result in hostilities. This possibility – one or a few nuclear weapons exploding during a time of non-belligerence – could therefore perhaps be held to contingency A. In time of tension or war scare (contingency B), the probability of unintentional firing triggering major exchanges – thus shifting the action to contingencies D, E or F – would be much greater.

The risk of either of these unintentional firings would be substantially greater in times of tension, contingency B, when government and military organizations were subjected to high stress, and brought to instant readiness, and when the tight controls and stringent safety measures governing nuclear weapons would consequently be tested to, and possibly beyond, their limits. The Commission rates the risk of unintentional firing occurring and escalating as highly unlikely in contingency A, but as a matter of great concern in contingency B.

The unintentional explosion of a single nuclear weapon, or of a very small number of weapons, has a number of civil defence implications because several effective and cheap measures could be taken to reduce casualties and panic. These measures would also be useful in dealing with some civil disasters, such as a major nuclear power accident. They would also be useful in the unlikely event that a single nuclear weapon were somehow secreted into this country, perhaps by boat, and exploded as an act of hostility which would defy definition as either terrorism or war. These implications are explored in Part 3.

1.5 Contingency B: war scare

Under its terms of reference, GLAWARS is required to address the question of "the length of warning time likely to be available between the time at which hostilities may be judged by the government to be inevitable . . . and the commencement of an actual attack on the territory of the United Kingdom".

The minimum warning time of a surprise attack is approximately three minutes (Home Office 1977) – this being the minimum time between detection of oncoming missiles by the UK Warning and Monitoring Organization and the arrival of the missiles. The maximum warning time (as defined above), and depending on circumstances, could be several months.

Warning time can therefore be defined only retrospectively: in any attack, the warning that was available would be known only after the attack had taken place. The question posed above is thus unanswerable. However, the issues involved have important implications for civil defence.

Although a surprise attack, a bolt from the blue, cannot be ruled out, the Commission considers this possibility extremely unlikely. The gains to an aggressor would be, at best, uncertain, the move would be fraught with danger and risk, and there would be little chance of the aggressor escaping UK nuclear retaliation. This GLAWARS conclusion agrees with the current view of the UK government (Home Office 1985).

Current UK civil defence plans assume that there will be at least one week's warning to implement the most important civil defence plans, and at least 48 hours to implement the most critical ones. While these assumptions do not appear unreasonable, consideration must be given to the factors that will weigh most heavily on the government in deciding whether to issue a warning, and on the likely behaviour of the population during times of mounting international tension.

Presumably, the government's highest priority would be to avert war, and it would then have to judge whether issuing a public warning would tend to deter an enemy attack or precipitate it. In most cases, the information it received would be ambiguous, and the more ambiguous it were, the worse the dilemma. The dilemma is whether issuing a warning, or declaring an emergency, would make matters worse or better. Extremely delicate issues of crisis management would be involved. Moreover, the government's focus would be likely to be not on preparations for civil defence but on preparations for defence itself. In the event of a major international crisis, government plans include widespread measures to take over civil institutions wherever appropriate (Campbell 1982 and 1985). If the crisis seemed likely to require the UK to reinforce NATO forces in Germany, then this would

> require the use of merchant ships, commercial aircraft, roads and railways. It would inevitably cause major disruption to the life of the country. Furthermore, the international crisis might be so severe as to precipitate a collapse of trade, leading to shortages of essential commodities.
>
> (Home Office 1984)

Such measures seem likely to be taken before civil defence is alerted (Home Office 1984 and Williams 1986). Indeed, the fact that civil defence was not alerted could be used as a signal to the enemy that war was not regarded as inevitable, and that the military preparations were no more than precautions.

A great deal of caution would be needed before initiating any measure which suggested that nuclear, or even non-nuclear, war was inevitable.

Any such measure would be likely to cause panic, and could well exacerbate the crisis. Plans to activate civil defence itself could be interpreted by the enemy as an indication that war was inevitable, and might thus play a role in precipitating the event which civil defence is designed to mitigate. During the 1962 Cuban missile crisis, the most recent major international crisis, the Home Secretary subsequently announced that "Civil defence could have been alerted at short notice at that time. It was, however, a specific decision by H. M. Government that no such steps should be taken in the crisis". As one commentator put it, "The government then consciously chose to do nothing, lest its actions be interpreted by the Soviet Union as war preparations" (de Kadt 1964).

The other horn of the dilemma is the danger of doing too little too late. In most cases, public knowledge of what is going on would be provided by the media, even though the government might have better sources of information (though, as Freedman (1986) comments, "the past performance of intelligence agencies as against the news media in such circumstances indicates that this advantage cannot be assumed"). Furthermore, media censorship of the type carried out in World War 2 is no longer thought to be practical. Although a recent government statement acknowledges the importance of the control of military information in war, and points to the need for "extensive guidance to editors", it argues that

> The government . . . does not believe that a system of home censorship similar to that which operated in the Second World War is practicable today. The totally different volume and nature of international communication mean that for practical purposes the country can no longer be enclosed in an "information net".
>
> (Ministry of Defence 1985)

The population would thus be likely to be aware of the gravity of the situation, whether or not the government provided any specific signals. How people in general, and Londoners in particular, would react depends greatly on circumstances. In the event of a surprise attack, for example, there is substantial evidence that the three-minute warning that would be issued by 8000 sirens in the UK would be largely ignored. In Oakland, California, in May 1955, air raid signals sounded and were widely recognized as the signal for an attack. However, 80 per cent of the population dismissed the warning (correctly) as a mistake (de Kadt 1964). In February 1984, an early warning siren sounded for 30 seconds at 6.30 a.m. in Coventry. Most people turned over and went back to sleep.

Similar behaviour has been observed in other studies of disaster warnings. As one authority puts it

> It is difficult to secure public acceptance of warning messages. People tend to seize on any vagueness, ambiguity, or incompatibility in the warning message that enables them to interpret the situation hopefully. They search for more information that will confirm, deny, or clarify the warning message, and often they continue to interpret signs of danger as familiar, normal events until it is too late to take effective precautions.
> (Fritz 1968)

Siren warnings, however, are likely to be taken more seriously if they are preceded by a period of high international tension. Even so, three minutes is a perilously short time in which to take evasive action from the effects of nuclear war. Running for shelter is the only option. The fact that warning time could be so short is an important justification of the UK 'stay put' civil defence policy. Mass evacuation is not only impossible to achieve in such a short time but could result in large numbers of people being caught in the open when the attack occurred. This would greatly increase the casualty rate.

In a period of rapidly worsening international relations, there is a further important reason why the government might delay issuing any formal warning: fear of public opposition to the use of nuclear weapons. Feelings about war, and nuclear war in particular, run high in many segments of the British population. Even the threat of war over Suez produced considerable public protest (Loizos and Marsh 1986). The GLAWARS survey revealed some surprisingly high figures about likely levels of protest in "the event that war seems likely in two weeks". About one-third of Londoners would be disposed to join mass demonstrations against UK involvement in such a war. A quarter would be disposed to use direct methods of protest, such as occupations and erecting street blockades. And 12 per cent would be prepared to consider using violent methods of protest – an option that previous research has shown to be limited to all but a handful of respondents. Although people do not necessarily behave in the event as they say they would in a poll, Loizos and Marsh (1986) comment

> These are exceptionally high figures. If translated into action, the authorities would be faced with political unrest of unmanageable proportions. Since the capital is an obvious site for such activity, these large numbers of Londoners who say they would take to the streets to dissuade the government from nuclear conflict would almost certainly be joined in huge number by like-minded citizens from elsewhere in Britain. It would be hard to characterize such people as a minority or as an enemy within. They would look like a majority . . . Official planning should take account of a strong likelihood that great numbers in London will oppose the war. They will be joined by others. To ignore such a potential for opposition would, from an official point of view, be the greatest unwisdom.

Protest apart, there is also ample evidence that Londoners "would increasingly take matters into their own hands" (Freedman 1986). The GLAWARS survey showed that in an emergency many would stock up with food, attempt to leave London and fail to report to work:

percentage of Londoners	'certain to stock up with food'	'would try to leave London'	'certain not to go to work'
	38%	35%	63% (of those in work)

These figures merit further comment. The numbers of people who would try to leave London, in spite of much repeated official advice to the contrary, are high. Furthermore, it is a poignant comment on current civil defence plans that those who spontaneously claimed to have read an official publication of advice to be followed in the event of an emergency were significantly more likely to try to leave London than those who had not (Loizos and Marsh 1986).

The survey revealed that, of those who have jobs, only 27 per cent in the public sector and 12 per cent in the private sector say they would wish to stay in London and that they even 'might' report for work. Of the 12 people in the survey who have instructions as part of their job as to what to do in an emergency, only 8 feel it likely they could do their job. Of the latter, only 3 would definitely elect to stay in London, and only 1 would definitely report to work.

The picture that emerges is that a war scare in London would produce widespread panic and confusion, extensive political protest, a scramble to acquire food stocks, a mass exodus of the population from the capital, and the desertion of most workers from their jobs, whether or not these were in the public services and whether or not they were vital to the continued running of the city.

The city would thus be effectively paralysed even before any attack against it was launched. This is a major finding of GLAWARS, and it has important implications for civil defence planning. These implications are discussed in Part 3.

1.6 Contingency C: non-nuclear attacks

At the beginning of the 1960s, most Soviet strategists assumed that any war would go nuclear almost immediately and that the first blow might well be decisive. This confirmed the popular view that a future war would start and probably end with a massive use of nuclear weapons. There has since been a gradual retreat from this view. By 1967, a much greater role had been allotted to conventional weapons, although nuclear weapons were still expected to be decisive. Over the following decade or so, attempts were made to develop a new strategy.

This strategy involved three stages:

1 the conventional stage during which one of the priority tasks for conventional forces was to attack and destroy as many of NATO's nuclear forces as possible;
2 nuclear attacks (always described by the Soviet Union as pre-empting the use of nuclear weapons by NATO) designed to remove surviving nuclear forces and then destroy major conventional forces; and
3 a mopping-up stage when conventional forces would remove remaining sources of resistance and then occupy enemy territory.

This strategy envisaged that the Soviet Union would use nuclear weapons to win a war once it was clear that war could not be avoided. Like all strategies, however, it depended on certain assumptions about the likely activities of the enemy. It depended on the Soviet Union pre-empting a NATO nuclear strike and on NATO not contemplating such a step until it had lost most of its nuclear forces. A second critical assumption was that Soviet territory would be respected as a sanctuary by NATO (especially the United States).

These assumptions must always have seemed hopeful to Soviet leaders. With the arrival of cruise and *Pershing II* missiles, the likelihood of Soviet territory being granted sanctuary status declined, and the chance of being able to fight a nuclear war that left Soviet territory unscathed was reduced. Furthermore, to the extent that the conventional phase was devoted to preparing the ground for the nuclear phase, some favourable opportunities in the conventional area might be lost. There is evidence that Soviet planners now attach more importance to the conventional stage (McConnell 1983) and would hope to achieve their basic objectives without the use of nuclear weapons by either side. Soviet planners have become less sanguine about the possibility of controlling a nuclear war and more confident in the conventional strengths of the Soviet Union.

President Brezhnev announced the Soviet Union's new 'no first use' policy in a message to the UN General Assembly's Special Session on Disarmament in June 1982 (Shenfield 1984). There is a certain convergence here with trends in NATO thinking towards a more substantial conventional phase in future warfare (although NATO has not renounced the option of using nuclear weapons first). There are thus growing grounds for confidence that neither NATO nor the Warsaw Pact would expect a war to start with a nuclear attack, and even that nuclear weapons would not be used early on in hostilities. Nuclear escalation no longer appears inevitable.

A main Soviet priority, if nuclear weapons were not being used, would be to undermine the war-making capability of the UK, and in particular its contribution to any continental land battle. This would involve attacks on barracks, weapons stores, fuel stocks and so on. Special attention would be given to roll-on/roll-off ports and air bases such as Brize Norton which are vital to ferrying reserves to the continent. A secondary objective would be to reduce the ability to use UK or UK-based nuclear weapons (Donnelly 1982). This suggests that West Drayton, the air defence data centre, and Heathrow airport would be the most likely targets in Greater London.

A second possibility for the air offensive would be attacks on the civilian population designed to intimidate and harass, and raise fears of the consequences of eventual nuclear attacks (in fact, any attack by Soviet bombers or missiles is likely to be interpreted as a nuclear attack since neither the government nor the population of London could know what weapons were being carried). The extent to which this sort of attack, in which London would be an obvious target, could be carried out would depend on available resources (which might be sorely pressed in a European conflict). The non-nuclear targets that might be selected in the conventional phase, including the civilian population, would not necessarily be attacked if the conflict moved into a nuclear phase.

The 1985 UK Defence White Paper makes the following statement

> Any Warsaw Pact attack on western Europe would almost certainly include a substantial air offensive against the United Kingdom as well as conventional missile attacks from submarines, extensive mining, and incursions by specialist forces.
>
> (Statement on the Defence Estimates 1985)

The reference to specialist forces raises an issue that has been receiving increasing attention. These forces would undertake what the Soviet military describe as diversionary and reconnaissance missions. Diversion in Soviet terms includes sabotage (possibly of facilities of strategic importance), terror, arson, wrecking, poisoning and propaganda. It is not clear what capabilities the Soviet Union has for these operations (part of which would be an agent network in the UK) and how effectively they would operate in times of tension and war. However, if chemical and biological weapons were to be used against London, this is their least unlikely role.

More detailed scenarios for the use of conventional, chemical and biological weapons against London are considered below.

Scenarios for conventional attacks

The Soviet Union, with its powerful, numerically superior conventional forces, enormous geographical expanse and central strategic position, is nearly invulnerable to conventional attack; NATO cannot seriously contemplate invading and subduing the Soviet Union. Thus, as long as any hostilities that occur remain non-nuclear, the Soviet homeland is fundamentally secure. If the nuclear barrier were breached, however, and escalation occurred to a general nuclear war against cities, industry and the fabric of the country, the Soviet Union and its allies would almost certainly be destroyed as functioning societies. In the literal sense of the word, the Soviet Union's only *vital* interest is the prevention of general nuclear war.

Furthermore, a nuclear war would damage Western European industry and agriculture so extensively that they would be unproductive for many years, and therefore of little use to any 'winning' side. The Soviet Union is also downwind from the UK, and could well be affected by subsequent fall-out and nuclear winter effects. Under these circumstances, the Soviet Union would make every attempt to restrict hostilities to conventional weapons.

Conventional weapons could be delivered by ground attack aircraft, and by medium- and long-range bombers. The first two categories would need refuelling from tankers on bombing trips from the Soviet Union to Western Europe. However, while Warsaw Pact combat aircraft outnumber their NATO counterparts, NATO aircraft and aircrews are believed to be qualitatively superior.

Such a war might start with a central attack on NATO forces in Europe or an attempt to strike from either the south or the north flank. Geographically, the south flank appears difficult, the north more promising. It is possible to envisage a scenario in which Norway, which is vulnerable to attack, was invaded, giving the enemy control of new airfields and the North Sea oil fields. The UK and the Netherlands both have forces trained in mountain and arctic warfare designated to support the Norwegians. The Soviet Union would therefore wish to destroy transport facilities in the UK which could be used to deploy these forces or reinforce NATO's northern flank in other ways. Attacks would be made on roll-on/roll-off ports, and on airfields at Brize Norton, Lyneham, Mildenhall, Heathrow, Prestwick and Manchester, probably using the *TU-26* bomber (see Table 3) which has sufficient range and is capable of penetrating UK defences at low level and high speed.

Attempts would be made to jam and confuse UK radar, and to attack Nimrod Airborne Early Warning aircraft and perhaps the West Drayton air defence data centre.

Apart from attacks on Heathrow and West Drayton, this scenario is of minor consequence to the London area itself. However, GLAWARS also studied the possibility of a conventional attack on London, the aim of which would be to disperse the largest population in the country, induce mass panic, and test the government's will to continue the war.

It can be safely assumed that there will be no large-scale conventional attack on London of the kind that took place in World War 2. Neither the Soviet Union nor its Warsaw Pact allies has sufficient numbers of bombers to risk such an attack, which would involve concentrating almost all their suitable aircraft on London, to the exclusion of other targets in the UK and on the continent. Furthermore, the Soviet Union would not be prepared to risk the destruction of so many of its military aircraft when they could later be required for much more important roles if the war entered a nuclear phase.

However, the increased accuracy of air-to-surface missiles carrying conventional explosives offers an enemy possibilities that did not exist in World War 2. An analysis of possible targets (Kerr 1986) suggests that relatively few weapons might now be used to produce disproportionately large effects on London's services.

The prime targets would be London's energy and water supplies, transport and communications networks, and housing. Kerr identifies 13 electricity targets outside London, and two within it, the destruction of which would so reduce power supplies to London that they would be diverted from domestic users to maintain essential services. Similar effects could be obtained on gas and water supplies by attacking 14 gas storage sites and 8 water pumping stations in or near London. The transport system could be disrupted by attacking London's main line railway stations and London Transport depots, and six of the major road junctions carrying traffic in and out of London. Communications disruption would concentrate on microwave links, particularly structures carrying several antennae such as the British Telecom tower in central London. Finally, housing would be attacked later with air-breathing cruise missiles carrying high explosive and anti-personnel munitions. The attacks would concentrate on densely populated areas and be timed at irregular intervals to keep the population under cover for long periods. The effects of such attacks would be even more pronounced if preceded by the events which could occur during a period of war scare, as described under contingency B above.

The Commission believes that whereas massive attacks on London using conventional weapons can be ruled out, it is definitely possible that London might be subjected to attacks with conventional weapons on a smaller scale – a few tens of plane-loads of bombs or air-to-surface missiles. If such attacks were aimed at disrupting London's infrastructure, the weapons used would have to be extremely accurate; this would not be necessary, however, to have a psychological and political impact on the London population.

The Commission was unable to estimate the probability of such attacks. This would depend on the Soviet views of

1 the value of disrupting London's civilian economy and society in reducing the UK's contribution to NATO in the short run;
2 the operational accuracy of conventional weapons; and
3 the likelihood that the UK government, unable to to mount effective conventional attacks on Moscow, would escalate to the use of nuclear weapons.

Attacks with chemical and biological weapons

Possible attacks against London with either chemical or biological weapons (CBW) were considered by GLAWARS only in a context where these weapons offered a means of achieving objectives that could not be better achieved by other weapons. In fact, unlike all other weapons, CBW damage only living things, or the processes that support life; they cannot damage inanimate targets. In addition, it is easier to protect people against CBW (with gas masks, protective clothing and filtered shelters) than it is to protect them from the effects of other weapons. Because of this, the military uses of CBW are limited.

The use of CBW is proscribed by international law, notably the 1925 Geneva Protocol. Although there have been some violations of its provisions, most recently in the Iran–Iraq war, that treaty has held remarkably well for 60 years. However, common prudence – rather than a belief that an enemy would necessarily flout the law – dictates that any potential threat from CBW be evaluated. If a belligerent were to resort openly to the large-scale use of CBW, he would in effect be signalling his intention to pursue a war through the use of extreme measures. The risk of nuclear retaliation from the UK or NATO forces would be high. This factor alone may be sufficient to restrain the future use of CBW against nuclear states or alliances.

Four possible uses for CBW were identified in the London area in the context of a war between the Soviet Union and NATO:

1 attacks with persistent chemical agents on Heathrow airport (the only large airport in the London area) to limit its utility in providing reinforcements for NATO;

2 the inclusion of persistent chemical agents or, just conceivably, biological munitions within conventional bombloads to discourage re-occupation or repair of attacked areas;
3 CBW attacks on command installations that would impair their efficiencies; and
4 CBW attacks on areas of high population density to degrade public and government morale and, perhaps, impede military movements by mobilizing large numbers of refugees.

Even these four possibilities of CBW attack must be subject to reservation. For example, anti-CBW measures operate in many command installations and hence the third use is plausible only if executed as an act of sabotage that took the installation by surprise. And the fourth possibility, as already mentioned, could provoke a retaliatory nuclear attack. In view of the escalation risk, it is far from clear that the use of CBW weapons in any of these situations is preferable to the use of conventional weapons. It should also be stressed that if the war is already nuclear, none of these possibilities offers any advantage over attacking the same targets with nuclear weapons (Perry Robinson 1986).

GLAWARS also examined a further six, more detailed options:

1 overt chemical attacks on cargo-handling capacity at Heathrow;
2 overt chemical attacks to impede runway repair at Heathrow;
3 the release of airborne CBW agents on populated areas, particularly by covert means;
4 covert CBW operations aimed at the ventilation or drinking water supply systems of large buildings;
5 CBW attacks on water reservoirs; and
6 other forms of CBW attack on water supplies.

The area of Heathrow airport that is potentially vulnerable to attack amounts to about 9 km^2. The Soviet chemical agents that could be used to attack it are limited to three: mustard gas, tabun and thickened soman. If a 10 per cent chance of encountering a contaminated area is considered sufficient to force workers to wear full protective clothing – which is the object of the attack, because it would seriously limit the efficiency of cargo handling or runway repair – then the approximate quantities of agents needed would be:

mustard gas:	18.0 tonnes;
tabun:	12.6 tonnes; or
thickened soman:	1.8 tonnes.

However, if there were even a light breeze, the attack with soman would be expected to affect people living up to 9 km downwind of the airport, over an area of 15–20 km^2. This might be considered sufficient to trigger a retaliatory attack from the UK. Furthermore, although the total payload is well within the capacity of a single *TU-26 Backfire* bomber, several aircraft – perhaps even as many as 20 – would have to be used to ensure that the chemical was evenly dispersed over the target (Perry Robinson 1986). These aircraft would be highly vulnerable to surface-to-air missiles and other defences deployed around Heathrow. This is such an extravagant use of the *TU-26* that it was concluded that munitions other than chemicals would be preferred for degrading Heathrow Airport's reinforcement capacity.

Similar arguments preclude CBW attacks on water reservoirs. For example, two reservoirs at the head of the Lea Valley would make conspicuous targets but their effective contamination would require at least 60 tonnes of nerve gas, or more than 100 tonnes of nerve gas bombs. This would require at least a dozen *TU-26* sorties. Far greater impact could be achieved by conventional bombing of London's water pumping stations.

Acts of sabotage that introduced CBW agents into the air or water supplies of large buildings, or into a water main feeding a reservoir after the water had been treated, seem to be the least unlikely and the most feasible of the CBW scenarios. However, these possible CBW attacks have to be considered in the context of a war which is presumably inflicting considerable damage in other ways. This damage is likely to dwarf the effects of local, covert CBW actions. It therefore does not seem likely that they would involve major consequences for London as a whole. For these reasons, CBW attacks are not considered further in this report.

One further related possibility was examined: what would be the effect of conventional bombing of chemical depots in the London area? The main depots are six sites each holding more than 50 tonnes of chlorine gas, most of which is used for water treatment. There is also a large depot for ammonia.

Estimates revealed that breaching a 50-tonne chlorine store would produce a 50 per cent death rate up to about 1.4 km from the store, if weather conditions were optimum for windborne dispersion. The largest chlorine store in London, 100 tonnes, would produce the same threat up to 2.5 km from the store. The areas in jeopardy would be 25 and 75 hectares respectively.

While these effects are by no means negligible, they do not appear sufficiently serious to merit attention from an attacker. Comparable effects could be achieved by conventional bombing without the need for the very high accuracies required to hit a 50-tonne store.

1.7 The nuclear contingencies: D, E and F

While the probability of nuclear war is small, it is greater than zero. The nuclear arsenals are maintained in a high state of preparedness; military organizations have assigned targets for nuclear weapons and established command structures to ensure that the weapons can be dispatched should national authorities require it. The time between a political decision to strike and the destruction of targets would be measured in minutes; in some cases, not many minutes.

If there were a nuclear attack on the UK, what form would it be likely to take, and how might London be affected? The GLAWARS Commission considered extensive evidence about the nature of Soviet war plans, the changing character of Soviet nuclear weapons, and how a nuclear war would be likely to be conducted in practice. Having done so, it formulated three possible contingencies for a nuclear war affecting the UK:

contingency D: an attack, or series of attacks, designed to reduce the strategic nuclear threat to the Soviet Union from either UK forces or US forces based in the UK;

contingency E: an attack, or series of attacks, to reduce nuclear and non-nuclear UK and US capabilities based in the UK relevant to the conduct of a major war in Europe; and

contingency F: a series of attacks that results either from unplanned escalation (the war gets out of hand) or which is designed to destroy the fabric of the country.

In the first two contingencies, London would be most at risk because of the military facilities within or near its boundaries. However, it is important not to look at London in isolation. Even if the capital escaped unscathed, the effects on London of, for example, a war scare, an influx of refugees or the loss of a harvest would be considerable (see Part 2). Furthermore, attacks on targets well away from London could affect the city severely – fall-out, for example, might create major problems.

Destruction in London could be considerably greater in contingency E than in D, because a large number of missiles would have to be used to attack all major military bases, and the chances of one or more nuclear warheads detonating on or over London in error would be considerably increased. In contingency F, London would be an obvious target should the Soviet Union seek to destroy the UK as a modern industrial state.

As has been made clear, the Commission considers a nuclear attack on London as very unlikely in the near future. Should one occur, however, it believes that attempts would initially be made to limit the damage, and even to limit the damage inflicted on London (contingencies D and E). However, it is an important conclusion of the Commission that it expects such an attempt to fail. In other words, the Commission does not believe that any attempt to sustain distinctions between targets or to limit the conduct of a war that had gone nuclear would be likely to survive the confusion and fear that would arise after the detonation of the first few nuclear weapons. The war would then advance to contingency F, which is judged to be a substantially more likely outcome than either contingencies D or E.

Contingencies D to F differ substantially from the assumptions made in most previous studies of potential nuclear attacks on the UK. Nearly all the latter have been made on the basis of one of the following sets of assumptions.

1 That there is a single token explosion on a well-known landmark – such as Trafalgar Square or St Paul's Cathedral. This approach encourages the false impression that the city centre is the only logical target.
2 That the attack is either extremely limited or amounts to a nuclear holocaust. These scenarios are intended to demonstrate either that nuclear war can be contained, and may not damage cities at all, or that, once started, nuclear exchanges will inevitably escalate to all-out, counter-city attacks.
3 That the attack should be useful for civil defence or crisis management exercises. Many of these exercises assume that 200 Mt or more are targeted on the UK. While such exercises may be useful in their own right, there is a danger that they are subsequently taken to reflect the reality of what might actually happen in a nuclear war.

Two important issues are at stake here. The first is whether London would ever be subjected to the sort of demonstration attack suggested by assumption 1 above. The second is whether any nuclear attack would ever be limited to specific types of targets, to specific geographical areas or to the minimum number of weapons needed to produce a certain level of destruction.

The possibility of a demonstration attack on London is relatively easily dealt with. Such a demonstration attack would presumably be intended to warn the UK or its allies of the foolishness of continued intransigence. This sort of attack gets scant prominence in Soviet strategic literature (Lambeth 1977), largely because such an attack would invite retaliation without achieving anything. It seems barely credible that London could be the subject of a demonstration attack intended to make a point to a government which would probably be destroyed in the process. It is almost equally difficult to conceive of such an attack as a signal to other countries (such as France or the United States) of the fate which might await them if hostilities continued. For these reasons, the Commission concluded that the probability of a demonstration attack on London was too low to merit further discussion.

The possibility that a future nuclear war might be limited in some way deserves far more serious study. The Commission's view – which differs markedly from nearly all previous assumptions made about nuclear attacks on the UK – is that serious attempts would be made to limit a nuclear war but that these attempts would probably fail. This view has important consequences for civil defence planning. If attempts to limit the war failed, there would be little that civil defence could do: the result would be destruction on an unimaginable scale. Should they succeed, however, some forms of civil defence might be useful.

Practically all previous discussions of possible Soviet attacks against the UK assume that such attacks would be very large in scale, and would include an enormous range of possible targets. This assumption is found in both the official and unoffical literature (see, for example, Home Office 1977, Mavor 1977, Goodwin 1981, Butler 1982, Clarke 1982, Greene *et al.* 1982, Home Office 1982, Rogers 1982, Crossley 1983 and Openshaw, Steadman and Greene 1983). Many of the attacks described in this literature assume that about 200 Mt are detonated on the UK in a period of a few hours, and that cities and military targets are attacked simultaneously.

The concept of the 200 Mt attack on the UK dates back to about 1970. Since then, the numbers and yields of the weapons involved have changed dramatically, which implies that war plans have also changed. Many new and more accurate missiles carrying weapons of much smaller explosive power than was formerly the case have been added to the Soviet arsenal. Such weapons are undoubtedly intended for military targets. There are fewer, very large weapons of the type clearly intended to destroy urban and industrial centres.

The consensus view is based partly on Soviet statements rejecting Western concepts of limited nuclear war. These are then interpreted to imply that all weapons would be used in a massive and virtually simultaneous attack. The scale of the attack on the UK is then estimated by dividing up the total Soviet stocks according to the relative importance of the belligerents, each country receiving its appropriate share of warheads. In many of these scenarios, the UK receives between one-sixth and one-third of the weapons which the Soviet Union has available for use in Europe.

This approach does less than justice to Soviet discussions of strategic nuclear targeting. As Meyer (1984) notes

> This has led some Western students of Soviet military affairs to conclude mistakenly that Soviet concepts of combined arms operations require the simultaneous use of every existing weapon in the Soviet arsenal. As a result, the Soviet theatre nuclear offensive has come to be viewed – erroneously – as an orgy of nuclear strikes blanketing Europe.

At issue is whether the Soviet Union, even in the most extreme circumstances, would be prepared to use all its nuclear weapons at once, despite the fact that the military gains from doing so would be minimal. The Soviet Union would probably deem it prudent to reserve at least some weapons for use against further potential adversaries, particularly China. Furthermore, the only hope of deterring a retaliation (a second strike) to a Soviet first strike would be the ability to threaten a third strike. Certain Soviet forces seem to be intended to serve as a strategic reserve for a third strike (Freedman 1986).

The concept of economy of force must also be considered. In any attempt to use nuclear weapons in Europe, this concept would need to be applied. As a Soviet author, A. A. Sidorenko, wrote as long ago as 1970: "Use of nuclear weapons against insignificant, secondary objectives contradicts the very nature of this weapon. The selection of targets should be approached with special care and nuclear weapons should not be thrown around like hand grenades" (quoted in Meyer 1984).

The second question is whether Soviet planners have any concept of limitations other than those imposed by possible shortages of weapons and the need to reserve a third strike. Several Soviet statements exist which suggest – at least superficially – that they do not. For example, since Robert McNamara proposed a cities-avoidance strategy in 1962, Soviet leaders have made clear their distaste for US attempts to establish 'Marquess of Queensberry' rules for nuclear war, rules which they suspect would be carefully framed to put the West at an advantage.

However, it would certainly be naive to interpet such evidence without considering its linguistic implications and the motivations that may have produced it. Western notions of limitation may be rejected by the Soviet Union for a number of reasons, and not simply because Soviet planners believe that the only logical course would be to unleash an unrestrained attack. In nuclear strategy, as in many other fields of activity, there may also be a sharp distinction between declaratory policy and actual policy.

The Soviet Union has an undoubted antipathy towards the use of the word limited as applied to nuclear war. For example, a substantial counter-force exchange between the superpowers directed against missile silos, command and control centres and submarine pens might be characterized by the United States as limited (in the sense of focussing on one set of targets to the exclusion of others). Yet to the Soviet Union this would appear as the most logical form of attack – the essence of strategic warfare (for an elaboration of this point, see Meyer 1985). Given the proximity of some key military targets to civilian areas, the Soviet Union (in company with many others) might well object to an adjective such as limited to describe the results of such an attack. Soviet planners, understandably enough, seem to find the word 'limited' an inappropriate description of any form of nuclear war.

Soviet planners might also be anxious to disabuse their US counterparts that other types of attack should be considered limited. They would certainly not designate nuclear attacks on Soviet territory as limited simply because they were launched from European bases and were related to the course of a land war in Europe. There is evidence that the Soviet Union interprets current US strategy as an attempt to wage war against the Soviet Union and the Warsaw Pact without involving the United States (Garner 1983). It need surprise no one if the Soviet Union rejects the idea of calling such a war 'limited'.

None of this necessarily means, therefore, that the Soviet Union has no concept of limiting a nuclear war. On the contrary, the existence of such a concept has been articulated in a number of ways. Apart from the limitations that stem from the need to maintain a strategic reserve, two others can be clearly identified.

The first concerns regional limitations. There has been a number of indications of a Soviet view that attacks on the territory of the superpowers are considered to be of a quite different order to attacks on allies. Soviet leaders recognize a concept of homeland sanctuaries in which the major nuclear powers inflict damage on each others' allies but not each other. In 1972, the Soviet Union even proposed to the United States a treaty in which the two sides would pledge not to use nuclear weapons against each other's homelands, even if they were being used against the territory of their Warsaw Pact and NATO allies (Kissinger 1979 and Meyer 1985). In this sense, the transformation from limited to total war takes place when the first weapons explode on Soviet territory.

Secondly, the Soviet Union clearly distinguishes between different types of targets. As Table 2 shows, there are clear priorities, starting with Western nuclear forces, moving on to conventional forces, and concluding with economic and political targets. This reveals a great deal about Soviet intentions. To debate whether or not it also reveals the existence of the US concept of 'limitation' involves little more than word play.

Finally, an important point concerning international law must also be considered. The Soviet Union is a party to numerous laws of war agreements which, while they do not explicitly regulate the use of nuclear weapons, do establish general principles about proportionality, discrimination, and prohibition of attacks on purely civilian targets – principles which would be applicable to the use of nuclear as well as other weapons. While it is difficult to decide how much weight should be attached to such statutes, it would be disingenuous to ignore them completely (Roberts 1986).

Table 2 Target categories for Soviet strikes

Target categories
Group I: Strategic nuclear targets
Medium and intermediate range missiles, and submarine bases
Long-range strike aircraft and bases
Nuclear storage sites
Strategic command, control and communications centres
Group II: Tactical and operational nuclear targets
Tactical aviation, and aircraft carriers and bases
Short-range cruise and ballistic missiles
Nuclear storage depots
Command and control centres
Group III
Ground forces
Strategic and operational reserves
Stores of non-nuclear ammunition, weapons
Petrol, oil and lubricants
Naval bases
Group IV
Air defence airfields
Air defence missile complexes
Group V
Military/industrial centres
Political/administrative centres
Transport nodes

Source: Meyer 1984.

Having considered these issues, the Commission's views are that the Soviet Union's approach would be to use nuclear weapons in the most decisive manner possible. In the course of attacking the critical targets, which would be almost wholly military, enormous damage would be done to civilian life and property. However, the Soviet Union has good reasons for not attacking civilian life and property in general. These include:

1 fear of a counter-city retaliation from UK nuclear forces;
2 fear of the effects of such an attack affecting the Soviet Union – particularly from fall-out or the onset of a nuclear winter caused by smoke particles generated by the destruction of a large city;
3 the need to maintain central government in London★, perhaps because termination of the war is expected to be negotiated with the government (military command and control could be disrupted without destroying London itself);
4 the irrelevance of destroying urban-based centres of defence production (if nuclear weapons were already being used, a surge in UK defence production would be unlikely to affect the outcome of hostilities);
5 the possible need for the Soviet Union to preserve Western economic assets for its own use;
6 the need to ignore lower priority targets if the supply of weapons were limited; and
7 issues related to ideology and international law which militate against the targeting of civilian populations *per se*.

These factors would help to restrain the intensity of the initial attack on the UK. However, the Commission's view is that that they would be unlikely to do so for long. Once the nuclear barrier were broken, virtually complete national destruction would appear imminent to both sides. The planning considerations listed above would lose influence; the over-riding objective – the only true significant objective – would be national survival. Furthermore, effective central control of the nuclear forces would probably be lost to a greater or lesser degree. In this situation, attacks on one or several cities might well seem – to either the authorities of the central governments or their unauthorized subordinates – the best means of destroying their enemies as functioning nations

★Plans exist to evacuate the Prime Minister and senior cabinet ministers to regional centres in the event of hostile attack. However, most government offices would have to stay in London and it is unclear to what extent – or when – evacuation would occur in the event of limited attacks. Clearly, from the UK viewpoint, the destruction of London is synonymous with total war. On the other hand, while London survives there could still be a basis for negotiated settlement.

or of shocking them into leaving the war. As Jervis (1984) points out, manipulating this threat of national survival – essentially by manipulating the threat to destroy cities – would be the essence of nuclear strategy in actual nuclear operations, to the extent that the operations remained under control after initial nuclear exchanges.

The war would then move to contingency F, in which London could well be a priority target. This contingency is the nearest GLAWARS equivalent of previous views of likely nuclear attacks on the UK. Even so, it still differs from them substantially, in that most previous studies assume some 200 Mt are detonated on the UK; the two largest scenarios considered by GLAWARS assume that about 65 and 90 Mt are used on the UK.

As is made clear in Part 2, the two largest scenarios would be sufficient to destroy London and the United Kingdom. There is therefore no point in considering even heavier levels of attack. It is an important GLAWARS finding that the UK could be destroyed by much lighter nuclear attacks than has previously been assumed.

It remains to assess Soviet capabilities to mount attacks of the type described above, and to provide detailed scenarios of how they might be effected.

1.8 Soviet capabilities

The Soviet Union is not short of weapons with which to mount attacks on the UK (see Table 3). The weapons are of three types: older aircraft and missiles, designed for use in Europe, which are now becoming obsolete; older strategic missiles and aircraft which are now deemed less suitable for their original role; and modern missiles and aircraft, especially the *SS-20* missile, and the *TU-26* (code-named the *Backfire* by NATO).

The first two categories include mainly high-yield weapons of limited accuracy; these are the 5–10 megaton weapons, which do not need to land close to their targets to destroy them, so often mentioned in past civil defence exercises. The last category contains weapons with lower yields and higher accuracies. There are now enough of these to attack most of the critical targets. Nuclear explosions in the London area would therefore probably involve kiloton weapons landing within hundreds of metres of their targets. This is one reason for discounting some of the older scenarios for attacks on London and the UK, in which hundreds of megatons are exploded; the rationale for such attacks is based on an earlier generation of weapons.

Individual weapons for particular targets would be chosen for their accuracy, reliability and ability to penetrate the UK's limited air defences. Consideration would also have to be given to other demands on resources. It is likely that in the early stages of a war the most urgent targets would be close to the central front.

In the conventional stage, the most likely aircraft to be used against the UK would be the *TU-16* (the *Badger*) and the *Backfire*, the latter for high priority targets. The conventional phase could last for some time.

These aircraft might also be used in the nuclear phase. Their air-to-surface missiles would probably be used against point targets. Missiles – essentially the *SS-20* – would be used against the larger fixed targets. If devastation of urban-industrial areas were contemplated, the *SS-N-6* would probably be employed.

The number of Soviet weapons available could be affected by future arms control agreements. It is highly unlikely that the key weapons – the *Backfire* and the *SS-20* – would be eliminated but their numbers could be reduced to levels where targeting priorities become more critical. However, some weapons of strategic designation, such as the *SS-19*, could well be used against European targets. Furthermore, new generations of weapons, such as a reported successor to the *SS-20* and a variety of cruise missiles, could become available in the near future. One of the older Soviet weapons – the *Bear* bomber – is now being produced again in a new variant designed to carry the *AS-15* long-range cruise missile. It can therefore be assumed that there are no serious hardware constraints to mounting nuclear attacks, and that most of the weapons would have yields of a few hundred kilotons (though low megaton weapons might be used in attacks on cities).

The only serious constraint would be UK air defences. After the 1957 defence review in the UK, air defences were allowed to run down and have only recently received serious attention again. Meanwhile, the Soviet air force has expanded dramatically. Because of their extended range, Soviet aircraft could fly around and under the British radar system which can effectively cover only the northerly and easterly approaches. It is hoped that new radars and computers, and the delayed *Nimrod* advanced early-warning aircraft, will provide improved cover within a few years.

The major interceptors available in the UK are the *Tornado* and *Phantom* defence aircraft, backed up possibly by *Hawk* trainers fitted with *Sidewinder* missiles. Point defence is provided by *Bloodhound* and *Rapier* surface-to-air missiles and some anti-aircraft guns. These defences might be inadequate to counter a major Soviet air offensive. (Some estimates suggest that about 120 UK aircraft would be pitted against 500 Warsaw Pact bombers with fighter escorts.) However, conventional air attacks on key bases might prove difficult for the

Warsaw Pact; the main USAF bases in the UK, for example, have begun to improve their defences with *Rapier* missiles. This means that should hostilities move into a nuclear phase, some key bases might well remain operational and thus be targeted. By this time, however, the UK's defence would have been seriously impaired (Freedman 1986).

Recent discussions of new strategic defences against ballistic missiles, bound up with President Reagan's Strategic Defence Initiative, are of little relevance to this report. The systems envisaged are unlikely to be available until the next century. In any case, the preponderance of scientific opinion currently suggests that defences are unlikely ever to provide more than partial coverage and will be vulnerable to new developments in offensive systems.

Table 3 Soviet weapons available for attacks on the UK

AIRCRAFT

Type	Service	Combat radius (km)	Weapons	Numbers[a]
TU-16	1955	2500	1 bomb	Air force 220
			1–2 AS-2/-3/-6	Navy 190
			6 AS-5	
TU-22	1962	1500	1 bomb	Air force 125
			1 AS-4	Navy 35
TU-26	1974	4000	2 bombs	Air force 130
			1–2 AS-4	Navy 105
SU-24[b]	1974	1600	2 bombs	630
TU-95[c]	1956	6500	2–3 bombs	100
			1–2 AS-3/-4	
MYA-4[c]	1956	5000	4 bombs	43

AIRCRAFT WEAPONS

(i) *bombs*: strategic – 5 megatons; tactical – 250 and 350 kilotons

(ii) *air-to-surface missiles*

Type	Service	Range (km)	Yield	CEP[d] (km)	Number
AS-2	1961	200	200–600 kt	0.5–1.5	90
AS-3	1961	650	800 kt?	0.5–1.5	100
AS-4	1962	500	200 kt	0.5–1.5	830
AS-6	1977	250	350 kt	0.2–0.5	820

Table 3 *Continued*

MISSILES Type	Service	Range (km)	Yield	Number of warheads	CEP[d] (km)	Number
land based						
SS-4[e]	1959	1900	1 Mt	1	2.3	224
SS-20[f]	1977	5000	1.5 Mt	1	0.4	
	1977	5000	150 kt	3	0.4	378
SS-11[g]	1966	10000	1 Mt	1	1.4	
	1967	13000	1 Mt	1	1.4	120
	1982	8800	100–300 kt	3	1.1	
SS-19[h]	1982	10000	550 kt	6	0.3	60
submarine launched						
SS-N-5	1964	1400	1 Mt	1	2.7–4.0	45
SS-N-6	1968	2400	1 Mt	1	2.8	
	1973	3000	1 Mt	1	0.9	368
	1974	3000	500 kt	2	0.9	

Notes
[a] Relevant weapons likely to be those used by Soviet Air Force.
[b] SU-24 assigned to Frontal Aviation. Unlikely for use against UK.
[c] Numbers likely to be reduced – new long-range bomber soon.
[d] CEP (circular error probable) = the radius of a circle round a target within which there is a 50% probability that a weapon aimed at that target will fall.
[e] SS-4s are now being steadily withdrawn.
[f] It is assumed that most SS-20s now carry three smaller warheads rather than one large one.
[g] These are variable-range ICBMs, of which some 120 were deployed for medium and intermediate ranges. Most probably still carry a single large warhead.
[h] These are variable-range ICBMs of which at least 60 have been deployed for medium and intermediate ranges, apparently only in the multiple warhead version.
Source: Freedman 1986.

1.9 The five nuclear scenarios

GLAWARS considered five possible scenarios of nuclear attacks that would affect the Greater London area (see Table 4). They relate to the nuclear contingencies as follows:

Contingency D: nuclear attacks on nuclear weapons targets

scenario 1: attaçks on UK or UK-based nuclear capabilities
(8 Mt on the UK, none on London)

scenario 2: attacks on UK or UK-based nuclear capabilities, and on command and control centres
(13 Mt on the UK, including 2 Mt on London)

Contingency E: attacks on nuclear and non-nuclear military targets

scenario 3: air force and naval bases targeted
(31 Mt on the UK, including 1.35 Mt on London)

Contingency F: attacks also involving urban and industrial targets

scenario 4: a 65 Mt attack on the UK, including 5.35 Mt on London
scenario 5: a 90 Mt attack on the UK, including 10.35 Mt on London

It is not difficult to identify either the likely targets or the sort of weapons that would be used to implement these scenarios, and this has been done with some precision. To maintain as much realism as possible, specific assumptions are made in each scenario about the numbers and locations of weapons which would fail to detonate or miss their targets. In the first two scenarios, in which the nuclear weapons would be delivered by bomber, assumptions are also made about which aircraft would be shot down by UK defences, and whether they were shot down before they reached their first, second or third targets.

Because of the dangers of fall-out to the Soviet Union, it is assumed that air bursts would be used wherever this was consistent with destruction of the target. The proportion of ground bursts would therefore be low compared to other, similar studies, and the effects of fall-out would be considerably reduced. Details of these and the other assumptions made in constructing the scenarios can be found in Appendix 4.

The attacks range in intensity from an attack on the UK involving a total of 8.05 Mt, all targeted on nuclear capabilities outside the London area, to a 90 Mt attack, of which 10.35 Mt fall on London.

Scenario 1 is the smallest nuclear attack that could achieve a military purpose (destruction of UK or UK-based US nuclear forces). The weapons would be delivered by 20 bombers which would carry 56 air-to-ground missiles with 200 kt warheads, of which 21 either failed to detonate or were shot down with their aircraft before delivery. The remaining 35 weapons would be successfully detonated as ground bursts. The bombers would also carry four 350 kt bombs intended to destroy the cruise missile bases at Greenham Common and Moles-

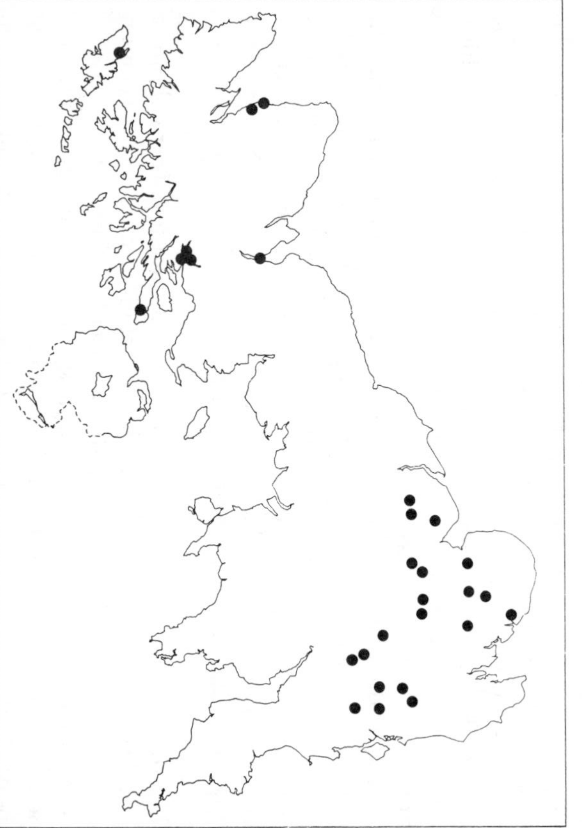

Figure 2 Scenario 1: pattern of attack on the UK

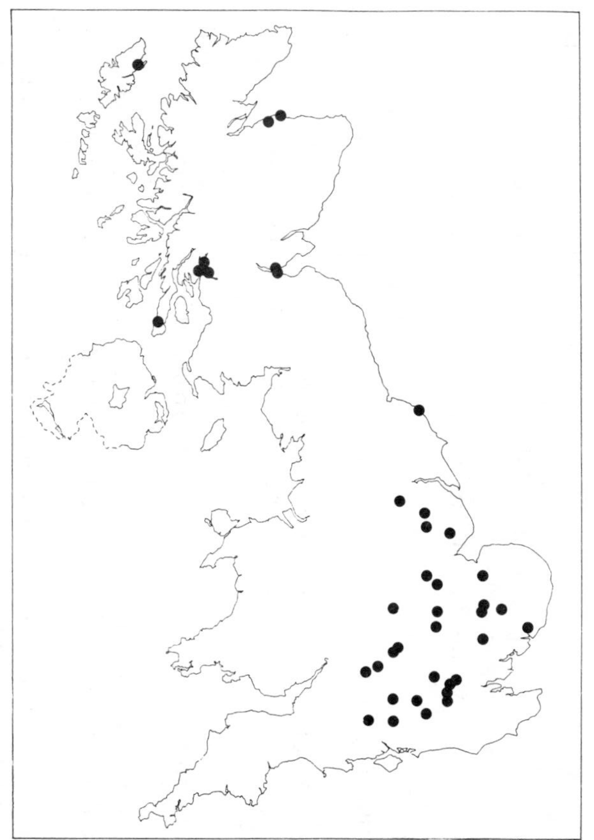

Figure 3 Scenario 2: pattern of attack on the UK

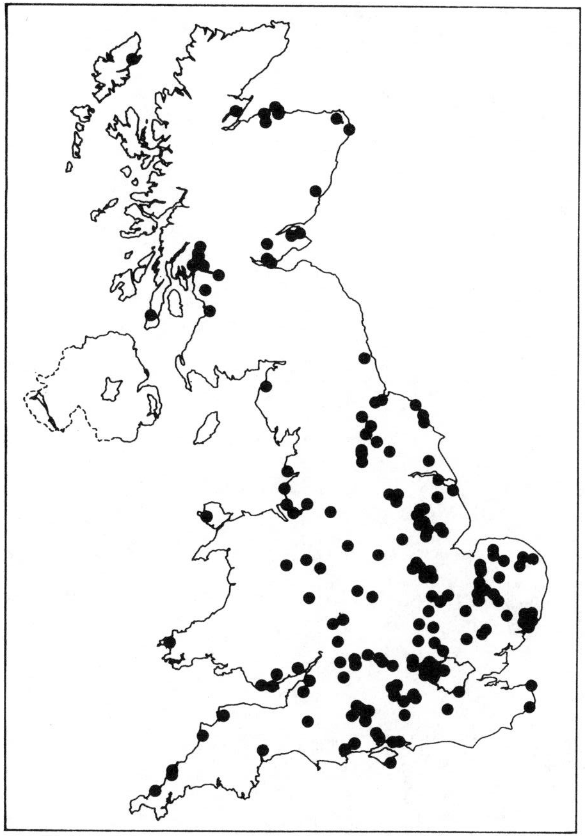

Figure 4 Scenario 3: pattern of attack on the UK

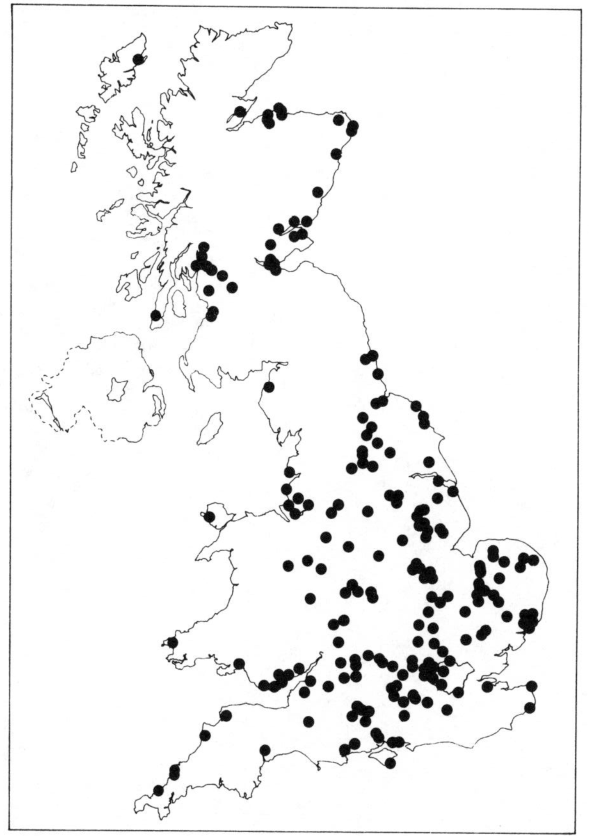

Figure 5 Scenario 4: pattern of attack on the UK

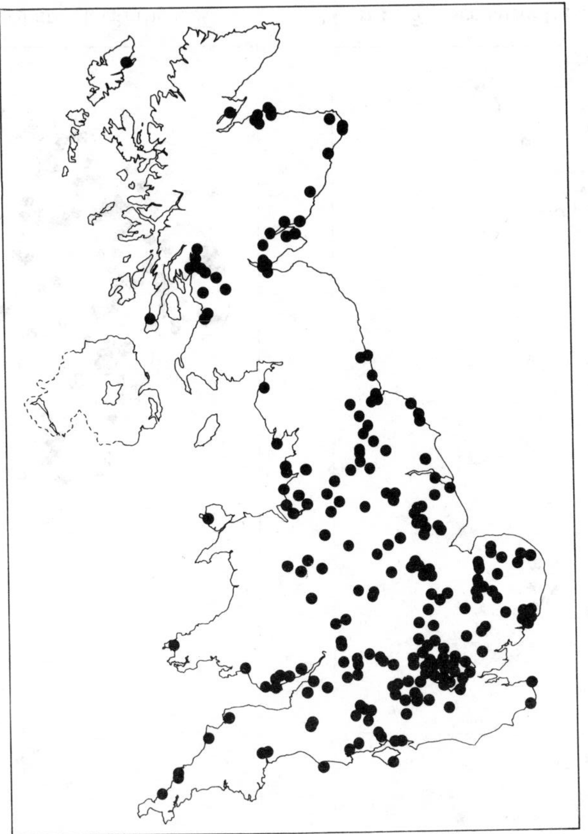

Figure 6 Scenario 5: pattern of attack on the UK

worth. Three of these would be detonated as air bursts at 2000 metres, and one would fail to detonate. No weapons would be exploded on the London area.

Scenario 2 is an expanded version of scenario 1, in which command and control centres would also be targeted. An additional eight bombers would be used in this attack, carrying a further twelve 200 kt missiles and twelve 350 kt bombs. Four targets would be hit in the London area: Heathrow airport (with one bomb and one missile), the West Drayton air defence data centre (one bomb and one missile), the RN and NATO headquarters at Northwood (one bomb and one missile) and the No 11 Air Defence Group at Stanmore (one bomb). In all, London would be hit by 2 Mt of nuclear weapons, all to the west and north-west of the city.

Scenario 3 is a much more substantial attack, involving nuclear and non-nuclear military targets. Attention would be concentrated on sea and air power, rather than land power, which is considered sufficient to put the UK at the mercy of the Soviet Union. Some 31 Mt would be involved, and there would now be seven targets in the London area. All the weapons would be *SS-20* missiles carrying 150 kt warheads. Hampstead would be hit in error by a nuclear weapon intended for Heathrow. This would make a critical difference to the outcome (see Part 2) but is a realistic reflection of the scale of attack being mounted. Although the total explosive power detonated on London (1.35 Mt) would be smaller than in scenario 2, there would be nine detonations rather than seven, and the targets would be more widely dispersed. As a result, damage to London would be very much greater.

Scenarios 4 and 5 are much more severe. They would involve a total of roughly 65 and 90 Mt respectively. By this stage, the war would have escalated to a degree where targeting assumptions are more difficult to assess, and are less relevant. The war would be essentially out of hand, and the result would be chaos. Scenario 4 includes industrial targets in the London area, and the number of targets in the London area would rise to 12 (of which four would be hit with 1 Mt weapons). In scenario 5, nine 1 Mt weapons would fall on the city in addition to nine smaller weapons. Both scenarios would be equivalent to an attempt to destroy London. As Part 2 shows, they would unquestionably succeed.

Scenarios 4 and 5 were identified by the GLAWARS Commission as the most likely outcome of a nuclear war involving the UK.

The Commission is well aware that even larger attacks on the UK are possible. No specific scenario for such an attack has been considered, however, for the good reason that the damage created – certainly in the London area – would be only marginally different. The destruction

Table 4 Five attack scenarios

Type of target	Weapons used	Number failing to detonate or aircraft shot down	Number of detonating weapons	Total yield	Targets in London area	Total yield on London area
Contingency D: *Scenario 1*						
UK nuclear capabilities	20 Backfire bombers:					
	56 AS-4 missiles (200 kt)	21	35	8.05 Mt	none	none
	4 × 350 kt bombs	1	3			
Contingency D: *Scenario 2*						
UK nuclear capabilities, command and control centres	28 Backfire bombers:					
	68 AS-4 missiles (200 kt)	24	44	13.0 Mt	Stanmore Northwood (2) Heathrow (2) West Drayton (2)	2 Mt
	16 × 350 kt bombs	4	12			
Contingency E: *Scenario 3*						
UK naval and air power	81 × SS-20s carrying 243 × 150 kt warheads	36	207	31.05 Mt	Stanmore Northwood (2) West Drayton (2) Biggin Hill Heathrow Northolt (fail) Hillingdon Hampstead (in error)	1.35 Mt

Contingency F: *Scenario 4*						
UK military and industrial centres	81 × SS-20s carrying 243 × 150 kt warheads	36	207	65.05 Mt	as for 3 above, plus 1 Mt on each of: Enfield Whitehall Croydon (fail) Clapham Kingston	5.35 Mt
	48 × SS-N-6 carrying 48 × 1 Mt warheads (launched from 3 Y-class submarines)	14	34			
Contingency F: *Scenario 5*						
enhanced version of 4, above	81 × SS-20s carrying 243 × 150 kt warheads	36	207	90.05 Mt	as for 4 above, plus 1 Mt on each of: City of London Euston Victoria and Albert Docks Hackney (in error) Sutton (in error)	10.35 Mt
	80 × SS-N-6 carrying 80 × 1 Mt warheads (launched from 5 Y-class submarines)	21	59			

created by scenarios 4 and 5 is more or less total, and any analysis of even more severe scenarios is pointless.

Table 5 lists the targets in London which feature in the scenarios, and gives a brief indication of their importance. Figures 2–6 show the patterns of attack on the UK as a whole, and the complete list of UK targets, with their grid references, is included in Appendix 4.

None of these scenarios would be likely to occur without parallel attacks on Europe, the United States and the Soviet Union. The extent of the latter would be important in determining whether or not nuclear winter effects would occur. For this purpose, it is assumed that scenarios 1, 2 and 3 would be part of a global nuclear exchange amounting to about 3000 Mt. Scenarios 4 and 5 would be part of a 6500 Mt nuclear exchange (Kelly, Karas and Wigzell 1986).

No high-altitude nuclear explosions designed specifically to generate EMP and damage communications facilities are included in the scenarios. However, one or more of these explosions would be likely from scenario 2 on, and their EMP effects are considered in Part 2.

Table 5 London targets

Military targets	
Stanmore	RAF base, No 11 Group Air Defence
Northwood	Naval headquarters for NATO and RN
Heathrow	Major airport
West Drayton	Air defence data centre (command centre)
Biggin Hill	RAF base and airfield
Northolt	USAF and RAF communications centre, military airfield
Hillingdon	USAF communications (AUTOVON, automatic phone network for US military)
Industrial and political targets	
Enfield	Royal Ordnance Factory
Whitehall	Normal seat of government, Ministry of Defence
Croydon	Railway junction
Clapham	Railway junction
Kingston-upon-Thames	Defence industry centre
City of London	Financial centre
Euston station	Railway station
Victoria and Albert Docks	Power stations
Hackney	In error, from the Whitehall target

References

Blechman, Barry, and Kaplan, Stephen, *Force without War*. Washington DC, Brookings Institution, 1978.

Bracken, Paul, *The Command and Control of Nuclear Forces*. London, Yale University Press, 1983.

Butler, S. F. J., 'Scientific Advice in Home Defence'. In Barnaby, F., and Thomas, D. (eds.), *The Nuclear Arms Race*. London, Francis Pinter, 1982.

Campbell, Duncan, *War Plan UK: The Truth about Civil Defence in Britain*. London, Burnett Books, 1982.

Campbell, Duncan, 'War Laws 1, 2 and 3'. In *New Statesman*, 6, 13 and 20 September, 1985.

Clarke, Magnus, *The Nuclear Destruction of Britain*. London, Croom Helm, 1982.

Crossley, George, *British Civil Defence and Nuclear War: A Critical Assessment with Reference to Economic Considerations*. Bradford, University of Bradford, February 1983, Peace Research Reports No. 1.

de Kadt, E. J., *British Defence Policy and Nuclear War*. London, Cass, 1964.

Donnelly, C. N., 'The Soviet Operational Manoeuvre Group: A New Challenge for NATO'. In *International Defense Review* XV:9, 1982.

Freedman, Lawrence, *GLAWARS Task 1: The Military Threat*. London, South Bank Polytechnic, 1986, mimeo.

Fritz, C. E., 'Disasters'. In Sills, D. L. (ed.), *The International Encyclopaedia of the Social Sciences*, Vol. 4. New York, Macmillan and the Free Press, 1968.

Garner, William, *Soviet Threat Perceptions of NATO's Eurostrategic Missiles*. Paris, The Atlantic Institute for International Affairs, 1983, Atlantic Papers No. 52–53.

Goodwin, Peter, *Nuclear War: the Facts on our Survival*. London, Ash and Grant, 1981.

Greene, Owen, Rubin, Barry, Turok, Neil, Webber, Philip, and Wilkinson, Graeme, *London after the Bomb: What a Nuclear Attack Really Means*. Oxford, Oxford University Press, 1982.

Home Office, *Training Manual for Scientific Advisers*. London, Home Office, 1977.

Home Office, *Domestic Nuclear Shelters*. London, HMSO, 1982.

Home Office, *The Government's Planning Assumptions for Civil Defence*. London, Home Office, 1984, Home Office Circular No. ES1/1984.

Home Office, *Guidance on Planning Assumptions – Commentary*. Letter sent to the GLC, the Nuclear Free Zone Steering Committee, and other local authorities, 30 July 1985.

International Institute of Strategic Studies, *The Military Balance, 1984–85*. London, International Institute of Strategic Studies, 1985.

Jervis, R., *The Illogic of American Nuclear Strategy*. Cornell, Cornell University Press, 1984.

Kelly, P. M., Karas, J. H. W., and Wigzell, M., *GLAWARS Task 7: Potential effects of a nuclear war on the atmosphere, weather and climate in the Greater London Area*. London, South Bank Polytechnic, 1986, mimeo.

Kerr, D. B., *GLAWARS Task 3: Conventional Attack*. London, South Bank Polytechnic, 1986, mimeo.

Kissinger, Henry, *The White House Years*. Boston, Little Brown & Co., 1979.

Lambeth, Benjamin, 'Selective Nuclear Operations and Soviet Strategy'. In Holst, Johan, and Nerlich, Uwe (eds.), *Beyond Nuclear Deterrence: New Aims, New Arms*. London, Macdonald and Jane's, 1977.

Loizos, Peter, and Marsh, Alan, *GLAWARS Task 4: Concern with the Unthinkable*. London, South Bank Polytechnic, 1986, mimeo.

Mavor, Leslie, 'The Post-Strike Scene: UK'. Address to the NATO Civil Defence Training Seminar, 1977, mimeo.

McConnell, James, *The Soviet Shift In Emphasis from Nuclear to Conventional: the long-term perspective*. Alexandria, Virginia, Center for Naval Analyses, 1983.

Meyer, Stephen M., *Soviet Theatre Nuclear Forces. Part I: Development of Doctrine and Objectives*. London, International Institute of Strategic Studies, 1984, Adelphi Paper 187.

Meyer, Stephen M., 'Soviet Perspectives on the Paths to Nuclear War'. In Allison, Graham T., Carnesale, Albert, and Nye, Joseph S. (eds.), *Hawks, Doves and Owls: An Agenda for Avoiding Nuclear War*. New York, W. W. Norton, 1985.

Ministry of Defence, *Government Response to the Report of the Study Group on Censorship*. London, HMSO, Cmnd 9499, 1985.

Openshaw, Stan, Steadman, Philip, and Greene, Owen, *Doomsday: Britain After Nuclear Attack*. Oxford, Basil Blackwell, 1983.

Perry Robinson, Julian, *GLAWARS Task 1: An Assessment of the Chemical and Biological Warfare Threat to London*. London, South Bank Polytechnic, 1986, mimeo.

Roberts, A., *GLAWARS Memorandum: Civil defence and international law*. London, South Bank Polytechnic, 1986, mimeo.

Rogers, P., 'Possible Nuclear Attack Scenarios on Britain'. In Dando, M. R., and Newman, B. R., *Nuclear Deterrence: Implications and Policy Options for the 1980s*. Tunbridge Wells, Castle House Press, 1982.

Shenfield, Stephen, 'The Soviet Undertaking not to use Nuclear Weapons First and its Significance'. In *Detente*, October 1984.

Statement on the Defence Estimates 1985. London, HMSO, 1985, Cmnd 9430–1.

Williams, Phil, *GLAWARS Task 1: Crisis Management and Civil Defence*. London, South Bank Polytechnic, 1986, mimeo.

2

Effects on London

GLAWARS was required to assess the effects of attack on London, with particular reference to deaths and injuries, buildings and roads, essential services such as energy, water, transport and communications, health care, food and agriculture, the nuclear winter, and economic activity.

The research commissioned on these topics involved several person-years of work. In all, 32 individual researchers were involved in studying the effects of attack on London, contributing more than 20 original publications (see Appendix 3). In addition, a workshop was held in London on the effects of nuclear attack on the biosphere. The end result is a body of knowledge that describes, in more detail than has ever been achieved before, the effects of varying levels of attack on a large city.

Because the principal danger is from nuclear weapons, most of this research was concentrated on the effects of nuclear attack (contingencies D, E and F). Where appropriate, however, the effects on London of contingencies B (war scare) and C (non-nuclear attacks) are also described.

Any analysis of the effects of attack on a large city must break the subject down into its constituent parts. This provides only a partial picture of what the final results of attack might be, for two reasons. First, the end result is the cumulative effect of all the damage inflicted, from deaths and injuries to the population to the social, economic and political consequences. A true impression of the results of attack can therefore be gathered only by superimposing all the individual effects. Secondly, the end result also depends critically on the interdependency of many individual effects. For example, the psychological effects of attack would be likely to prevent many Londoners from going to work; many would also try to leave London. One result is that all the essential services, such as the supply of water and energy, would be seriously understaffed, further amplifying the direct effects of attack on these services. Section 2.10 provides an overall view of the cumulative effects of each contingency, as far as they can be assessed.

A further complication is that some effects can be described in much more detail than others. The damage to buildings, and the numbers of deaths and injuries, can be estimated quantitatively, and the figures produced provide a vivid illustration of the effects of attack. Although the psychological, social, economic and political damage cannot be so estimated, it would be equally important in the long run.

Many of the studies on which Part 2 is based involve computer modelling, and the results are presented in some detail. However, GLAWARS wishes to stress that this level of detail does not imply a corresponding level of precision. Computer models of the effects of nuclear war involve making estimates of variables that are often difficult to quantify with accuracy. While this does not invalidate them, it does mean that they should be interpreted indicatively rather than exactly. In some cases, the calculated margins of error are 20 per cent or more. While it would have been possible to present the results in ways that indicate this, valuable information would have been lost in the process. For example, there is clearly a case for rounding off estimates of total casualties to the nearest 5000 or even 10,000. If that had been done, however, it would have appeared that there were no radiation casualties in London after certain levels of attack and under certain wind directions. Such a result would be incorrect.

This proviso about the precision of results applies to all the computer models described in Part 2. It is not repeated in every instance because this would have encumbered the text with needless repetition.

2.1 Deaths and injuries

Estimates of the immediate numbers of deaths and injuries caused by the five GLAWARS scenarios were made using a computer model (Steadman, Greene and Openshaw 1986). The principal results of this model are presented first, followed by a discussion of the model itself (section 2.1.1) and a detailed analysis of the results and their sensitivity to assumptions made in constructing the model (section 2.1.2).

Under standard assumptions about factors such as wind speed and direction, the percentages of deaths and total casualties (deaths plus serious injuries) that would result from the five nuclear scenarios are summarized in Table 6. This table, and the computer model used to provide the figures for it, include casualties caused only by the three direct effects of nuclear explosions: thermal radiation (causing flash burns), blast and local fall-out (Appendix 6 provides details of the physical effects of nuclear explosions).

Table 6 Percentage of deaths and casualties from flash burns, blast and radiation, by scenario

Scenario	United Kingdom		London	
	Deaths	Casualties	Deaths	Casualties
1	1.1	1.6	0.0	0.0
2	3.4	5.2	9.9	15.5
3	9.1	15.6	11.5	23.0
4	26.4	39.5	67.6	84.9
5	36.8	50.1	90.4	97.0

In all but the first scenario, in which there are no casualties in London, London fares considerably worse than the UK as a whole. In scenario 2, the casualty rate is three times higher in London than it is in the country as a whole. In scenarios 4 and 5, nearly all Londoners are either killed or injured, and London is in effect wiped out. Even in scenario 3, nearly a quarter of Londoners are killed or injured.

These figures are based on very conservative assumptions, and do not include the huge numbers of people who would be killed or injured in fires, or who would die after an attack from starvation, disease or nuclear winter effects.

In spite of this, the casualty figures are very high. As stated in Part 1, it is a significant finding of GLAWARS that even very low levels of nuclear attack on the UK and on London would produce huge numbers of casualties. An attack only half as large as most previous exercises have assumed would kill or injure at least half the UK population, including 97 per cent of Londoners.

2.1.1 The computer model

The computer model used to estimate these results makes calculations for the whole of England, Scotland and Wales although estimates for local areas, such as Greater London and the London boroughs (see Appendix 7), can be selectively presented.

The model uses census data to represent the distribution of population. The effects of weapons are calculated in relation to a 1-km square grid, based on the Ordnance Survey.

The use of the census in the casualty calculations implies a night-time, 'at home' distribution of the population. The differences between the day-time and night-time populations of central London, under normal circumstances, are large: for example, more than 1 million people commute through central London alone each day (GLC 1985). A surprise day-time attack would therefore lead to much larger casualties in the GLC area than the model predicts because there would be more people in London and they would be more vulnerable. However, an attack without warning is considered very unlikely by the GLAWARS Commission.

In the likely event of a warning, the GLAWARS survey revealed that large numbers of people would try to leave London, even if officially instructed not to do so. The effect on casualty levels of a spontaneous evacuation of this kind, under present civil defence policies, is not clear. People living near targets would certainly have a better chance of surviving the immediate effects of the attack if they moved to shelter in an untargeted area. However, if they were caught in the open by the attack (perhaps due to congestion caused by the movement of large numbers of people trying to leave via a restricted number of routes), then they would be more vulnerable to heat and blast from nearby explosions, and have less protection from fall-out.

In the case of a smaller nuclear attack (GLAWARS scenario 2), however, casualties would be likely to be reduced either if the London population were previously given information about local targets or if specific plans had been made for evacuation from the areas likely to be worst affected. Since no such plans exist, they could not be evaluated on the computer model. This could be done fairly simply, however, should the GLC or its successor decide to implement plans for internal evacuation within the London area in the future.

Figure 7 is a simplified flow chart of the computer model*. The basic inputs consist of the population data and a list of targets, with weapon yields and height of detonation. The three effects – thermal radiation, blast and fall-out – are then considered in that sequence, which is the order in which they would actually occur after a single nuclear explosion.

The first part of the model takes each weapon in the attack in turn, and calculates the intensity of thermal radiation produced at the ground at various distances from that explosion. It then calculates the resulting

*This model was based on the best methodology available in spring 1985. Since then, Daugherty, Levi and von Hippel (in press) have argued that such models double count some people as being killed by both thermal radiation (flash burns) and by blast. These authors also advance a method of calculating deaths from fires, which cannot be done with the model used by GLAWARS. This methodology would, if adopted, lead to estimates in which there were more deaths, fewer injuries and slightly more casualties overall. The GLAWARS Commission believes that if the computer model were revised to incorporate this 'conflagration model', the results would not differ substantially except in scenarios 2 and 3, where many of the injured would become fatalities.

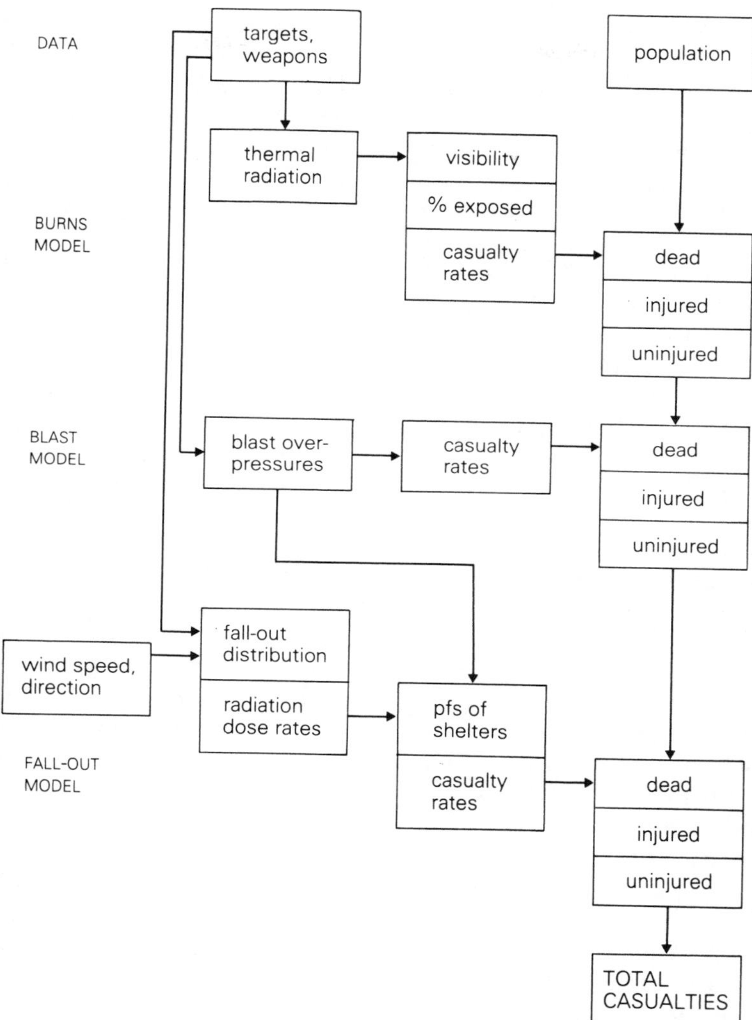

Figure 7 Flow chart of computer model for estimating casualties

numbers of deaths and injuries from direct burns among the population in range. The population data are modified after each bomb is considered: those counted as dead are removed, and those injured are recorded separately.

The next part of the model calculates the levels of blast pressure produced at the ground at different distances from each explosion, and hence calculates the numbers of deaths and injuries from blast among the population in range. Again those counted as dead are removed from the population data, and those injured are recorded separately; those injured by both thermal radiation and blast are assumed to die.

Finally, the model predicts the pattern of fall-out resulting from each ground burst, making assumptions about wind speed and wind direction. This produces an estimate, for each affected grid square, of the radiation dose that would be accumulated by any people present over a two-week period following the explosion. These doses apply to people in the open. They are modified for people in shelters or buildings of any kind, by making allowance for the degree of protection that those buildings offer against radiation from fall-out.

The model then estimates numbers killed and injured by fall-out (again, those previously injured people who are now injured by radiation as well are assumed to die). The end product is a set of totals of deaths and injuries from all causes, and a number of uninjured survivors after all three effects. The totals are initially recorded for each 1-km square, but can then be aggregated to larger units such as districts or counties, if required.

In attacks with multiple weapons, the effects of two or more bombs often overlap. Inevitably, people may then be counted as being injured twice (or more). The somewhat arbitrary assumption is made in the estimates that anyone injured by more than one bomb will die. This assumption is crude but seems reasonable (the model records only 'serious' injuries and ignores the far more numerous minor injuries).

One consequence is that it is not easy to distinguish the precise causes of death in the final totals (since some deaths will be from multiple injuries), nor to keep track of the numbers injured from each cause (since some of these may subsequently be killed by other causes). What can be tabulated are the numbers killed and injured after thermal radiation alone, after heat and blast together, and after all three effects.

The problem of overlapping fall-out plumes from different weapons – which are extensive – is treated differently from overlapping blast and heat effects. A cumulative total is kept, for every grid square, of the radiation doses received from all weapons affecting that square. This total accumulated dose from all bombs is then used in estimating casualties. No possibility therefore arises of people being counted as receiving multiple but separate radiation injuries from different bombs, as with the other two effects.

Several simplifying assumptions are involved in these calculations. First, it is in effect assumed that all weapons are detonated more or less simultaneously. If the explosions were spread out over many hours or days, then the radiation dose rates from overlapping fall-out plumes would be different. It is not obvious what the consequences would be for calculated numbers of radiation casualties. The dose accumulated in the first few hours would be reduced, but radioactivity levels would remain high for longer. People initially without good shelter but who found it some hours later and remained in it would receive a reduced dose. On the other hand, people who took refuge initially but left the shelter after a day or two would be at greater risk. If the explosions were spread over a few hours, the calculations of total casualties would probably remain fairly accurate. If they were spread over several days, uncertainties would mount.

With blast and heat effects, it is arguable that this assumption of simultaneity results in casualties being underestimated. In assessing thermal radiation injuries, it is assumed that a constant proportion of the population (say 5 per cent) is outdoors or otherwise exposed to the fireball. This proportion would in reality be likely to increase as successive weapons in the same area caused increasing blast damage to buildings and the resulting fires forced people to flee outside.

Similarly, in assessing blast damage, it is assumed that the pressure needed to demolish a typical house remains constant; whereas, typically, a lower level of pressure would be needed to destroy an already damaged house (this effect is allowed for in the model of damage to the built environment, see section 2.2).

In calculating heat and blast effects, it is assumed that the weapons are exploded over flat ground. As a result, the contours showing the distances to which given levels of thermal radiation or blast pressure extend are represented as perfect circles. In reality, hills and valleys would reflect and channel the blast wave, and some zones in the 'shadow' of the hills could be protected from both heat and blast. Since the topography of London is relatively flat, this is perhaps not so serious an approximation as it might be for other cities. (In any case, large air bursts, such as those employed in scenarios 4 and 5, would occur at relatively high altitudes.)

The problem of calculating fall-out distribution patterns is simplified radically by assuming that the direction and speed of the wind are constant for the whole time that the cloud is moving. The 'effective' speed of the wind is taken as the average of speeds at different altitudes. Allowance is made for a 15° 'wind shear' in widening the cloud as it drifts away from ground zero. The result is for the predicted pattern to approximate to an ellipse or cigar shape, whose long axis lies in the direction of the wind (Glasstone and Dolan 1977). The idealized elliptical plume may not give an accurate prediction of the resulting levels of radioactivity at particular points on the ground but it will give a tolerably good estimate of the total quantity of fall-out, and of the total area affected.

Several short-term effects of nuclear explosions which could cause injury and death are omitted from the estimates altogether. The first is initial nuclear radiation (INR). For high-yield strategic weapons, the range to which dangerous INR extends is less than that at which practically the entire population present would be killed by blast and burns. Nevertheless, it is possible that some cases of radiation sickness could be caused by INR from weapons with yields of the order of 100–200 kt (such as *SS-20* warheads). Those affected would be relatively close to ground zero, either out of doors but shielded from the fireball, or else in buildings or shelter offering rather little protection against radiation but who somehow managed to escape death from blast effects.

A second, much more serious omission is the possibility of casualties from fires (the burns injuries which are included are flash burns caused by direct exposure to the fireball). These could be very numerous. They are omitted only because of the difficulty of making casualty estimates but fires are included among the effects of attack on buildings – see section 2.2.

The fall-out calculations do not allow for the possibility that, in a general European war, fall-out from targets attacked on the continent could, under suitable wind conditions, drift over southern England, including London. Additional radioactive fall-out from debris from attacked nuclear reactors or nuclear weapon stores is also neglected. This omission is unlikely to lead to serious underestimates in the two-week accumulated radiation doses. However, since the radioactive decay rates of this debris would be much slower than for fall-out from nuclear explosions, it would pose severe long-term hazards. All longer-term effects of radiation, and the additional effects of radiation from fall-out arriving more than two weeks after the attacks, are also omitted. Deaths in the aftermath of attack from other possible causes such as starvation, epidemic diseases, exposure due to lack of shelter, or cold due to climatic changes are not estimated.

The computer model is based on widely accepted and published data, much of it from the US Departments of Defense and Energy, and from the Office of Technology Assessment of the US Congress. A similar model has been developed by the Scientific Research and Development Branch of the Home Office. The Home Office model is used for making casualty and damage estimates in connection with civil defence plans and exercises.

The contrasting assumptions embodied in these two models and their differing results have been the focus of some controversy in the UK. Many of these were brought to public attention in the British Medical Association's report *The Medical Effects of Nuclear War* (BMA 1983). At that time, the details of the Home Office model were publicly available in the form of papers by Bentley (1981) and Butler (1982). In their report, the BMA concluded that the model developed by Steadman, Greene and Openshaw, which is the basis of the model used in the GLAWARS study, and the assumptions embodied in it, was more reliable than that of the Home Office.

Since then, the situation has changed. Successive ministers have announced that the Home Office is in the process of changing its methods of calculation and some indication has been given as to what the nature of these changes might be (*Journal of the Institute of Civil Defence* 1984). But no specific details or new publications have been released. It is thus difficult to identify what exact differences remain between official government assumptions, and those made here.

Flash burns. The amount of thermal radiation to which people or buildings are exposed – the 'radiant exposure' – is usually measured in calories per square centimetre (cal/cm^2). The range at which a certain level of thermal radiant exposure will be produced varies with the yield of the bomb, the height of detonation, and the conditions of the atmosphere. If the air is clear, the effects will extend further. If it is misty or smoggy, the range will be reduced. There are other ways in which the weather can have an influence. If the bomb explodes below a layer of cloud, the heat flash will be reflected from the underside of the clouds, and this will increase the range for a given level of radiant exposure.

The first step in the calculations is therefore to determine the amounts of heat falling on surfaces at different distances from each explosion. This is done following methods set out in Glasstone and Dolan (1977). The GLAWARS calculations assume clear visibility (20 km) and no cloud cover.

It is then possible to estimate the resulting burns casualties, making assumptions about the proportion of the population exposed to the fireball and the levels of heat that cause death and injury.

The proportion exposed (those either outside and unshielded, or inside a building but with a window or opening in line of sight of the fireball) is obviously difficult to predict. It is affected by the time of day or night, the time of year (and hence the weather), what warning time was given, and the possibility that earlier bomb damage might leave more people exposed to weapons following later. The standard assumption is that 5 per cent of the population is exposed.

Glasstone and Dolan (1977) give estimates of 'skin burn probabilities' for given levels of radiant exposure and different weapon yields. The seriousness of the burns is expressed in terms of the accepted medical classification into first, second and third degree. These are largely distinguished by the depth to which the skin is burned in each case. Another important factor is the percentage of the body surface affected. It is assumed that all those with third degree burns are killed; and that half those with second degree burns die and half are 'seriously injured'. In the aftermath of attack, few if any burns victims will receive more than the most rudimentary medical treatment.

In Home Office casualty calculations up until 1983, no account was taken of flash burns. This was justified on the grounds that the civil defence warning system would be fully effective and that the entire population would be under cover. However, Bentley (1981) has said that "Later, it is intended to establish whether the effects of thermal . . . radiation make any significant difference to total casualty figures."

The 5 per cent figure used here is conservative. The OTA (1980) study looked at the consequences for burns injuries of a range from 1 to 25 per cent exposed. The assumption of clear visibility is, on the other hand, rather unrealistic for London at many times of the year and would lead to over-estimation of casualties. For weapons exploded later in an attack, atmospheric visibility could be reduced by the smoke and dust raised by earlier bombs.

Differing assumptions about the percentage of the population directly exposed to the flash produces wide variations in the number of predicted burns. However, the effect on total casualties is not large (Openshaw, Steadman and Greene 1983). One reason is that blast and fall-out are likely to kill and injure many more people than burns. A second and more important reason is that the area in which burns will be caused overlaps extensively with the area in which people will be killed or injured by blast.

Blast. The first step in the blast calculations is to determine the maximum overpressures produced at different distances from each explosion. These relationships are given in Glasstone and Dolan (1977). In the computer model, distances are calculated for a series of specific overpressure values: 12, 5, 2 and 1 pounds per square inch (psi). In this way, a number of concentric rings are defined for each weapon. These particular overpressure ranges relate both to the effects on buildings and to the assumptions then made about the relationship of building damage to resulting blast casualties.

Above 12 psi, practically all buildings will be destroyed including those with concrete or steel-frame structures. At about 5 psi, brick houses will be totally destroyed. In the range 2 to 5 psi, houses will suffer serious damage, with roofs blown off and walls cracked. And between 1 and 2 psi, houses will be slightly damaged, with roof-tiles removed, windows smashed and external doors blown out. But 1 psi is not the limit of damage; it is simply taken as the limit of the zone where a significant proportion of the population would be seriously injured by the effects of blast.

The distances at which given overpressures will be produced by air bursts vary with the height of detonation. An attacker would want to adjust the height of the explosion deliberately, in such a way as to subject the largest possible area to blast damage at some chosen overpressure level. The height is then said to be 'optimized' for the given overpressures. In the GLAWARS calculations, the heights of detonation of air bursts are optimized for the 10 psi level. This is a middle-range value. Attacks on cities might be optimized for lower levels of blast damage, those on 'harder' industrial or military targets perhaps for higher levels. Particularly in the case of GLAWARS scenarios 4 and 5, where the 1 Mt air bursts are all aimed at soft targets, this assumption could tend to lead to underestimates of casualty levels and building damage.

Given the predicted maximum overpressures at different points on the ground, the next step is to relate these values to percentages of the population killed or seriously injured as a result. The assumptions here are those made in the OTA (1980) study, which the OTA in turn obtained from the US Department of Defense. These give percentages killed and injured in the four overpressure ranges; for example, at 5 psi slightly more than 30 per cent of the population is assumed killed and about a further 40 per cent is assumed to receive serious injuries – the total casualty rate is therefore somewhat more than 70 per cent.

Before 1983, the Home Office Scientific Research and Development Branch made assumptions in their model about blast casualty rates which differed markedly from the OTA rates adopted here. The differences were such that for an identical weapon, assumed to be detonated over an area of uniform population density, the OTA rates would predict about twice as many deaths as would the Home Office. For serious injuries, the discrepancy was greater still.

The explanation was that the Home Office did not derive their blast casualty rates from studies of nuclear weapons but from information collected about the effects of conventional explosions in World War 2. But these are not comparable with the effects of nuclear explosions. Many more blast casualties would occur from a nuclear weapon, at the same level of overpressure, because that overpressure and its associated winds last for much longer than after a chemical explosion.

Fall-out. The method for calculating fall-out rates follows Glasstone and Dolan (1977). The standard 'effective' wind speed is taken to be 24 km/h. Corrections can be made to allow for different wind speeds.

It is also necessary to make corrections for two other factors. The first is the fraction of the explosive yield which is obtained from fission reactions. This is usually taken for high-yield thermonuclear weapons to be 0.5. This reduces all the reference dose-rates values by one half.

The second factor is what is called a 'ground roughness' or 'terrain shielding' factor. A person standing in the open will receive radiation from fall-out deposited over the surrounding land. The theoretical dose rates are calculated on the assumption that this ground surface is perfectly flat. But if the ground is rough, as it usually would be, the radiation will need to pass through the ground or other obstacles to reach the person and will be attenuated in the process. The GLAWARS calculations assume a value for this factor of 0.7, which implies 'moderately rough terrain'.

In the model, each ground burst weapon is considered in turn. A wind speed and direction are chosen, which in the standard GLAWARS assumptions are 24 km/h and south-south-westerly. The idealized dose-rate ellipses (corrected for fission fraction and ground roughness) are positioned in relation to ground zero, with their long axes oriented correctly to the chosen wind direction, in relation to the National Grid. Then for every grid square affected, the one-hour reference dose rate can be found.

For each grid square, the time at which the radioactive cloud arrives and fall-out begins to be deposited is determined, taking into account the wind speed and allowing for the size of the cloud itself. The dose rate at this time can then be found. Fall-out accumulates on the ground until the cloud has passed overhead. All the while, the level of radioactivity of the fall-out is decaying, at a rate which can be expressed as $(\text{time})^{-1.2}$. These processes of build-up and decay were modelled after an approximate method developed by the Home Office (Bentley 1981). The radiation dose accumulated over 14 days is then calculated (more than three quarters of the two week dose would usually be received within the first two days). Since the fall-out from different bombs will overlap in many places, this accumulated dose has to be calculated in turn for each weapon affecting the grid square in question. All the doses are then added together.

The next step is to derive, from the doses that people would receive in the open air, the doses that they would receive should they be sheltering in buildings. It is often assumed that all people still alive after an attack will remain indoors rather than outdoors. This is doubtful. The effects of blast and fire will be to destroy or seriously damage buildings over large areas, and in these zones the protection available against the effects of radiation will be minimal.

Away from the main blast-affected areas, however, there will be buildings only partly damaged or completely unscathed. People sheltering inside them would certainly obtain substantial protection from radiation. In areas that are some distance down wind of the nearest ground bursts, people may have an hour or two to take shelter before the fall-out arrives.

The level of protection against radiation offered by a building is expressed as a 'protection factor' (PF). This is the ratio of the radiation dose which would be received in the open to the dose received inside the building. A PF of 5 would mean that people inside would receive one-fifth of the dose they would receive outdoors. Some unmodified (but undamaged) buildings have PF values of 10 or more, and special purpose fall-out shelters have PF values of hundreds or even thousands. The values assumed for PFs are thus very significant.

The PFs of buildings or shelters depend on the thickness and density of the materials of which they are made. The denser the material, and the greater its thickness, the higher the PF. For example, a 60 cm thickness of water increases the PF ten times. To estimate the PF for a complete building, it is necessary to allow for the relative areas, and thickness, of solid walls, windows, doors and roof. One building can also gain protection from other adjoining structures. Thus a terrace house is shielded by its neighbours, and offers better protection than does a semi-detached house, which in its turn is better than a detached house or bungalow. Fall-out particles will accumulate on any flat surface – on the ground but also on flat or gently sloping roofs. In multi-storey buildings, the best above-ground protection would be in the centre of the middle storeys, away from both roof and ground. Some studies fix a single average PF value to cover all conditions. Others take a range of values to allow for different types of house and flat.

The PF value which is applied in calculations of casualties must also take account of the time people spend in and out of buildings and shelters. This is difficult to predict. After an attack, people may go outdoors, although aware of the hazards, to seek food, water or fuel; or they may be driven out by intolerable conditions inside the shelter. Others might be ignorant or heedless of the dangers.

Under normal conditions, the effective PF offered by unmodified buildings, allowing for the average amounts of time people spend in and out of doors, might be around 3. On this basis, some US studies have taken values of 3–6 for houses and flats. Katz (1982), in a massive study of life after nuclear war in the US, takes an average value for the basements of US houses of 10. However, only a small proportion of the UK population has access to basements: around 3.5 per cent in London, for example. Rotblat (1981) suggests a value of 5 for the effects of radiation immediately following an attack, and 3 in the longer term.

The GLAWARS calculations use a single average PF value of 8 for buildings in areas suffering less than 1 psi of blast overpressure. Some buildings in these zones will be completely undamaged, but many will have windows broken and other light damage. In areas suffering more severe blast damage, the average PF is reduced in proportion to the seriousness of the damage. A PF of 1 is used for the two highest overpressure ranges, in excess of 12 psi and from 5 to 12 psi, since most buildings and practically all houses will have been demolished here. A value of 2 is taken where overpressures are between 2 and 5 psi, since here roofs would probably be missing and walls cracked or severely damaged. A value of 5 is taken for areas suffering overpressures between 1 and 2 psi, where doors would be blown out and roofs damaged. These assumptions rest on calculations made by Greene *et al.* (1982). The effects on casualties of assuming different PF values are examined later.

In Home Office calculations, at least up until 1983, the assumption was made that people will block the more vulnerable door and window openings with bricks, concrete blocks or furniture, as recommended in *Protect and Survive* (Home Office 1980), so as to raise the PF. The Home Office also assumes that people will build 'internal refuges' with doors, sandbags and furniture, in order to increase radiation protection still further.

In the Home Office model, the protection factors of buildings were not measured by a single national average, but were expressed as a spectrum of values to represent different building types. The range of this spectrum was from 2 to 70, with most dwellings assigned values between 9 and 26. These values are open to serious criticism (Greene *et al.* 1982, and Steadman, Greene and Openshaw 1986). Recently, Webber (in press) has calculated that a PF of 5 is most appropriate for an undamaged two-storey brick house.

The final stage in estimating casualties from fall-out is to calculate the deaths and injuries resulting from radiation exposure, having taken PF values into account. This is a topic on which much controversy has recently centred.

The effects of radiation on the human body vary considerably between individuals. For this reason, the effects are usually expressed statistically, in terms of the percentage of people, out of a large number exposed to a given dose, that would be likely to die or fall ill as a result. A figure often referred to is the LD_{50} (lethal dose 50 per cent), which is the dose that results in half the population dying. The effects also vary according to the period over which the total dose is received. The body has a certain capacity for repairing the harmful effects of radiation, and so a given dose spread over weeks or months will not be as serious as the same dose received in days or hours. It is on these questions, the human

LD_{50} value, and the effects of protraction of dose, that the controversy centres (Adams 1984, Rotblat in press, and Steadman, Greene and Openshaw 1986).

In the GLAWARS calculations, the assumed relationship of dose to percentage killed and injured is as shown in Figure 8. The doses refer to doses measured in gray (to the surface of the body) received over the two-week period following the attack. It is assumed that some deaths will occur at doses above 3 gray; that the LD_{50} is 4.5 gray; and that deaths reach 100 per cent at 6 gray. These values are taken to allow for the protraction of dose over 14 days and for the fact that most of the dose will be received within 48 hours. It is assumed that little or no medical treatment is likely to be available. These values are supported by evidence from, among others, the British Institute of Radiology (1982) and the US National Council on Radiation Protection and Measurements (NCRP 1974).

The Home Office computer model embodies assumptions about the relationship of radiation dose to resulting injury and deaths which are based on advice from the Protection against Ionising Radiation Committee (PIRC) of the Medical Research Council. The PIRC advised the use of an LD_{50} value for casualty calculations of 6 gray (to the surface of the body) for doses received within a few minutes. When doses are received over a period of hours or more, the actual doses are modified in Home Office calculations (BMA 1983, Adams 1984 and Martin 1984). This has the effect that the LD_{50} for a dose received in one week, for example, would be taken as 9 gray (to the body surface). Recent

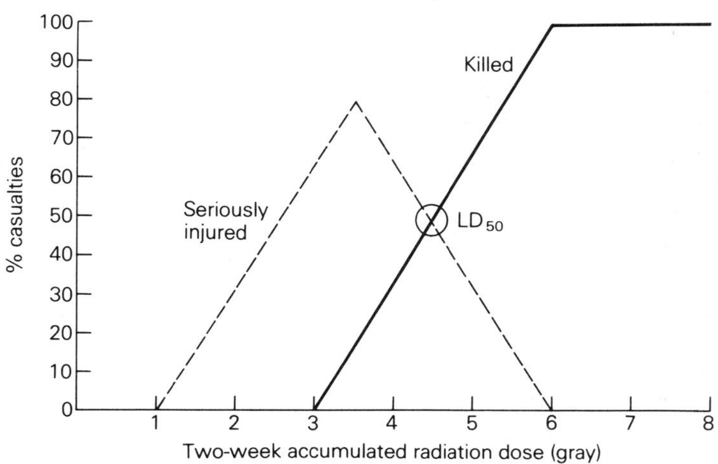

Figure 8 Percentage deaths and injuries by radiation dose

evidence indicates that such values are far too high, especially for war-time conditions. Rotblat (in press) argues that the appropriate LD_{50} may be as low as 2.2 gray.

The controversy about the lethal level of radiation dose is of considerable scientific interest. Nevertheless, its consequences for casualty calculations are not large, in percentage terms. In previous national studies, variations in PF factors have proved to produce the largest variations in total casualties. In the GLAWARS scenarios, and for London, the largest variations are produced by altering assumptions about wind speeds and directions, as is made clear in what follows.

2.1.2 The results

The scenarios: a recapitulation. Before discussing the casualty figures that result from the model just described, the principal characteristics of the five nuclear attack scenarios are presented again in Table 7.

Table 7 Principal characteristics of the scenarios

Scenario	Number of warheads	Yield in air bursts (Mt)	Yield in ground bursts (Mt)	Yield on London (Mt)	Total (Mt)
1	38	1.05	7	–	8.05
2	56	4.20	8.8	2	13.00
3	207	11.55	19.5	1.35	31.05
4	241	45.55	19.5	5.35	65.05
5	266	70.55	19.5	10.35	90.05

It is important to note that the proportion of ground bursts, with their accompanying local fall-out, decreases dramatically as the attacks become more severe. This is to be expected because the smaller attacks are concentrated on military targets, which are assumed to be hardened and therefore require ground bursts if they are to be destroyed. As the intensity of the attacks increases, however, more and more weapons are targeted on industrial and urban centres, and the proportion of ground bursts decreases. In these scenarios, therefore, the casualties produced from fall-out, though still very severe, are somewhat lower than those reported in other studies.

Appendix 4 lists all the targets attacked, with their grid references, weapon yields and altitudes of detonation.

National casualty levels. Estimates of casualties on the national level are presented first. Table 8 shows the total casualties for each scenario for the standard assumptions: 24 km/h SSW wind; protection factors of 1, 1, 2, 5, 8 for blast zones A (> 12 psi), B (5–12 psi), C (2–5 psi), D (1–2 psi), and less than 1 psi respectively; and an LD_{50} for radiation dose of 4.5 gray. The effects of varying some of these assumptions are examined later.

Scenario 1 is estimated to result in about 860,000 casualties. In scenarios 2 and 3, the casualties would increase to about 2.76 and 8.32 million respectively. The relatively large increase in casualties between scenarios 1 and 2 is due less to the increased weight of the attack than to the fact that in scenario 1 the attack is confined to relatively isolated military bases, whereas in scenario 2 command and communications centres are also included. These tend to be closer to population centres. In scenario 4, this effect is seen again as industrial targets are added to the list. In scenario 5, the casualty levels would increase by another 5.64 million to include about half the population of the UK.

The casualties for each scenario, under standard assumptions, were also calculated by county, for both a SSW and a WSW wind. The results can be found in Steadman, Greene and Openshaw (1986).

Table 9 shows the effects on casualty levels of varying wind direction and speed. This affects the number of radiation casualties. On the national scale, the effects of wind direction are noticeable but relatively small. In scenario 1, the changes result in a variation of total casualties of less than 50,000 (a variation of about 6 per cent). In scenarios 4 and 5, the variation is only about 2 per cent. This reflects the fact that a larger proportion of the casualties in scenario 1 is caused by fall-out than in the two largest scenarios. In scenarios 2 and 3, the effects of wind direction are more marked, causing variations in total casualties of about 23 and 7 per cent respectively. These variations are probably caused by specific geographical relationships between a few large conurbations and the ground bursts, exaggerated by the greater vulnerability of people to fall-out due to more extensive blast effects than in scenario 1.

As for changes in wind speed, only the effects of an increase (to 40 km/h) are considered. This is because the 'standard' wind speed of 24 km/h may be too slow to give an accurate picture of the likely effects of fall-out. Although Meteorological Office records show that the wind speed at ground level in south-east England is usually in the range 12–22 km/h in summer, and 15–28 km/h in winter, the speed increases rapidly with altitude. For example, at 400–1200 m altitude average wind speeds are about 2.5 times those at ground level, and they increase still further at higher altitudes (Meteorological Office 1966). Nuclear explosions would loft much of the radioactive dust to altitudes of several kilometres, so the effective wind speeds would be relatively high.

Table 8 Flash burns, blast and fall-out casualties in the UK from the five GLAWARS scenarios

Scenario	Flash burns		Blast		Fall-out		Total dead	Total casualties	
	Dead	Injured	Additional deaths	Injured after blast and burns	Additional deaths	Injured after all 3 effects		Number	% of initial population
1	20,000	7000	237,000	359,500	320,000	281,000	577,000	858,000	1.6
2	50,500	18,000	1,168,500	1,117,500	578,500	959,500	1,797,500	2,757,000	5.2
3	340,500	142,000	2,104,500	3,525,500	2,438,500	3,437,000	4,884,000	8,321,000	15.6
4	1,542,000	487,500	9,465,000	7,953,500	3,078,000	7,022,500	14,085,500	21,108,000	39.5
5	2,461,000	735,000	13,861,000	8,508,500	3,334,500	7,093,500	19,656,500	26,750,000	50.1

Initial UK population: 53,435,000.
Assumptions: steady 24 km/h SSW wind, standard protection factors, LD_{50} 4.5 gray.
Source: Steadman, Greene and Openshaw 1986.

The effect of increasing wind speed is generally to spread the hazard from fall-out over wider areas, thus exposing more people to radiation.

Table 9 Effects of changes in wind speed and direction on total casualties

	Total casualties (millions) (rounded to nearest thousand)				
			Scenario		
Wind	1	2	3	4	5
24 km/h					
SSW	0.858	2.757	8.321	21.108	26.750
WSW	0.905	3.406	8.486	21.142	26.723
NNW	0.901	2.760	7.891	20.684	26.426
ENE	0.884	2.814	8.065	21.067	26.914
40 km/h					
SSW	0.910	2.909	8.820	21.562	27.151
NNW	0.961	2.871	8.800	21.478	27.199
ENE	1.021	3.049	6.165	21.680	27.480

Source: Steadman, Greene and Openshaw 1986.

GLAWARS researchers also investigated the effect on radiation casualties of varying the assumed protection factors (PFs). If the PFs are reduced to 1, 1, 2, 3.5 and 5 for the appropriate blast zones for a SSW wind, the effect is to increase the number of casualties, but not by a large amount. In scenario 1, the increase is about 110,000 (12.8 per cent), in scenario 2 it is 265,000 (9.6 per cent), and in scenarios 3, 4 and 5, it is about 1,035,000 (12.4 per cent), 770,000 (3.6 per cent), and 550,000 (2.0 per cent) respectively. Reductions in total casualties by similar amounts are found if the standard protection factors are doubled in blast zones other than zone A (where it remains the same). The main reason why the effects are not greater is that most of the casualties are caused by blast.

Casualties in the GLC area. The locations of the targets attacked in or near the GLC area, and the yields and altitudes of the detonations, are listed in Appendix 4. Total casualties in the GLC area for each scenario are summarized in Table 10.

Table 10 Flash burns, blast and fall-out casualties in the GLC area from the five GLAWARS scenarios

Scenario	Flash burns		Blast		Fall-out			Total casualties	
	Dead	Injured	Additional deaths	Injured after blast and burns	Additional deaths	Injured after all 3 effects	Total dead	Number	% of initial population
1	0	0	0	0	0	0	0	0	0
2	14,000	6500	529,000	437,000	94,500	357,000	638,000	995,000	15.5
3	75,000	32,000	496,000	732,500	166,000	739,000	737,000	1,476,000	23.0
4	606,500	186,000	3,335,500	1,273,500	399,500	1,109,500	4,341,000	5,450,500	84.9
5	1,092,500	310,000	4,370,000	650,000	338,000	423,500	5,801,000	6,224,500	97.0

Initial GLC population: 6,417,500.
Assumptions: steady 24 km/h SSW wind, standard protection factors, LD_{50} 4.5 gray.
Source: Steadman, Greene and Openshaw 1986.

1. Thermal radiation. Figures 9–12 show the extent of various levels of thermal radiation intensity over the GLC area for scenarios 2–5, on the assumption of 20 km visibility. The radii of the thermal radiation rings would be reduced by about 20 per cent for 10 km visibility, and by some 50 per cent for 4 km visibility (estimated from Kerr *et al.* 1971). However, cloud cover above the explosions could increase the thermal radiation intensity at any given point by as much as 50 per cent (Glasstone and Dolan 1977).

Below about 3.5 cal/cm^2, few serious (second degree) burns would be expected. Though many people would suffer first degree burns and thus experience real discomfort, only a small proportion would receive 'serious injuries'. People with exposed skin subjected to between 3.5 and 7.0 cal/cm^2 will mostly suffer second degree burns. The proportion of people affected by first or second degree burns depends on the heat intensity and the yield of the explosion, and is calculated from data found in Glasstone and Dolan (1977). Above 7.0 cal/cm^2, most people exposed to the direct heat from the fireball can be expected to receive third degree burns. In scenario 1, none of the warheads would detonate sufficiently close to London to lead to burns casualties within the GLC area. However, in some circumstances, Londoners looking towards distant explosions, over Farnborough for example, might be temporarily blinded.

Materials such as paper and dry leaves can be ignited if exposed to thermal intensities of 4–6 cal/cm^2 or more, and the 7.6 cal/cm^2 contour roughly corresponds to blast levels at which secondary fires might be ignited, due to damage to domestic or industrial gas supplies or fuel stores, for example. Fabrics begin to be ignited at thermal intensities of 9 cal/cm^2 so the 12 cal/cm^2 contours can be taken to show the zones within which a high density of fires could be expected.

Fires and the possibility of fire spread are important effects. However, there are many complexities and uncertainties. Researchers at Earth Resources Research Limited collaborated with others at the Open University to develop new models of possible fire effects, including the effects of combined blast and fire. To avoid repetition, these are not discussed here (see 2.2, *Damage to the built environment* and Hodgkinson *et al.* 1986). Estimates of total casualties from fires were also produced by Rotblat, Haines and Lindop (1986) in a separate exercise, and included in their calculations of casualties from all effects.

The effects of thermal radiation would be serious in the west of the GLC area in every scenario except the first. By scenario 4, most of the GLC area would be expected to be affected by intense thermal radiation and fires. Rotblat, Haines and Lindop (1986) estimate that the chance of a fire starting anywhere in the GLC area in scenarios 4 and 5 is about 50 per cent.

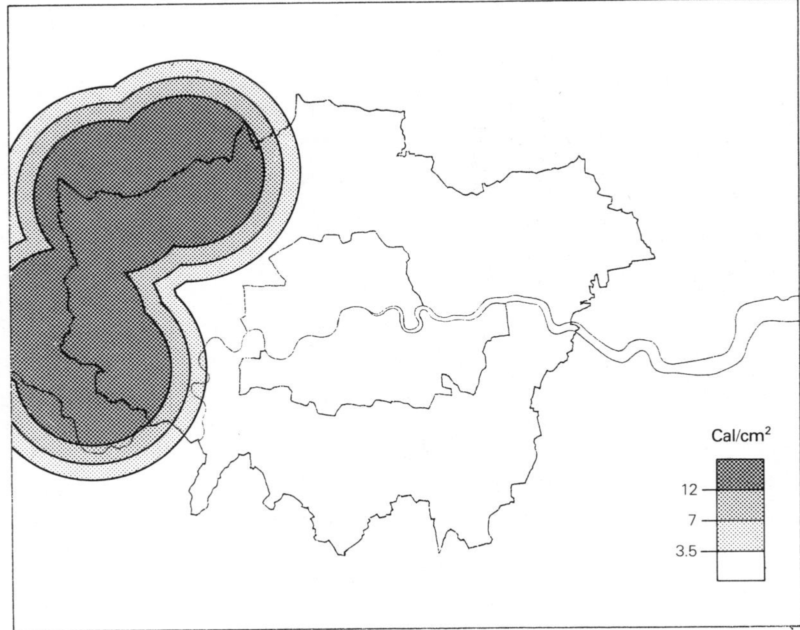

Figure 9 Thermal radiation levels in Greater London: scenario 2

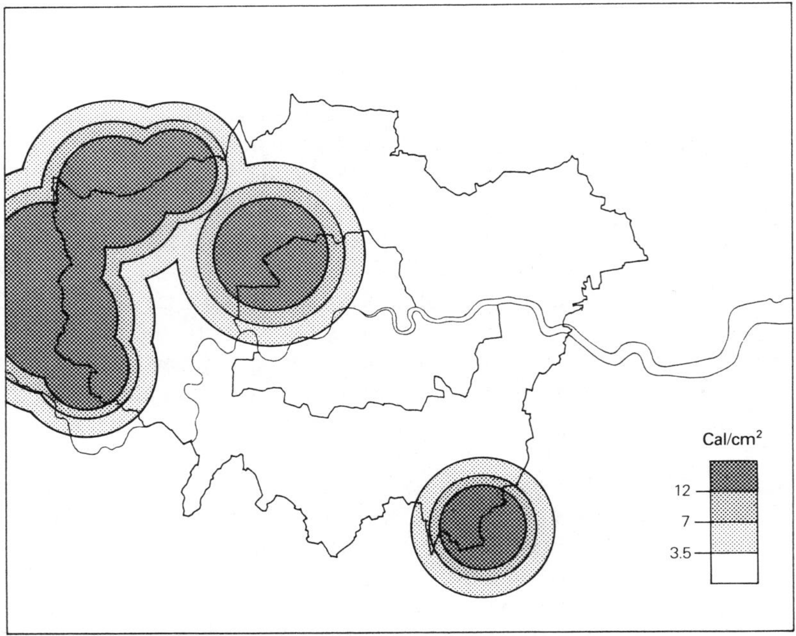

Figure 10 Thermal radiation levels in Greater London: scenario 3

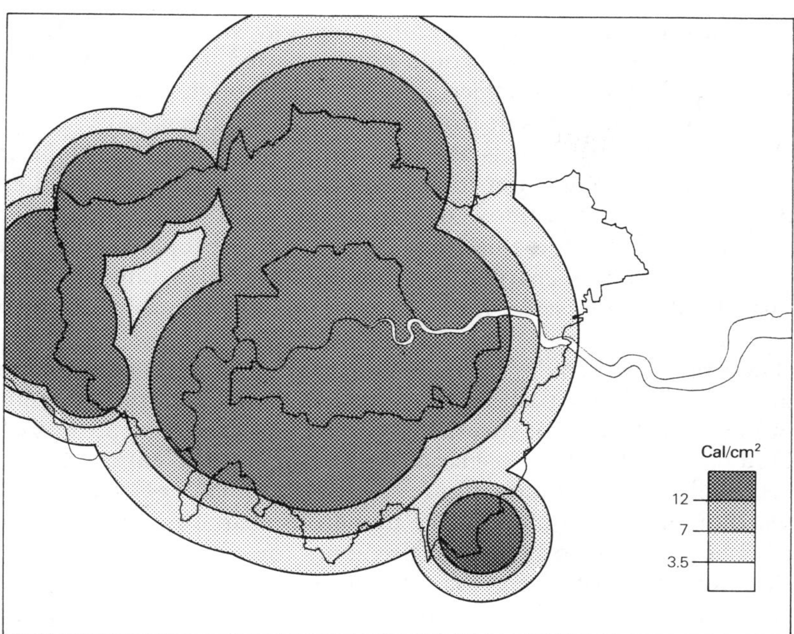

Figure 11 Thermal radiation levels in Greater London: scenario 4

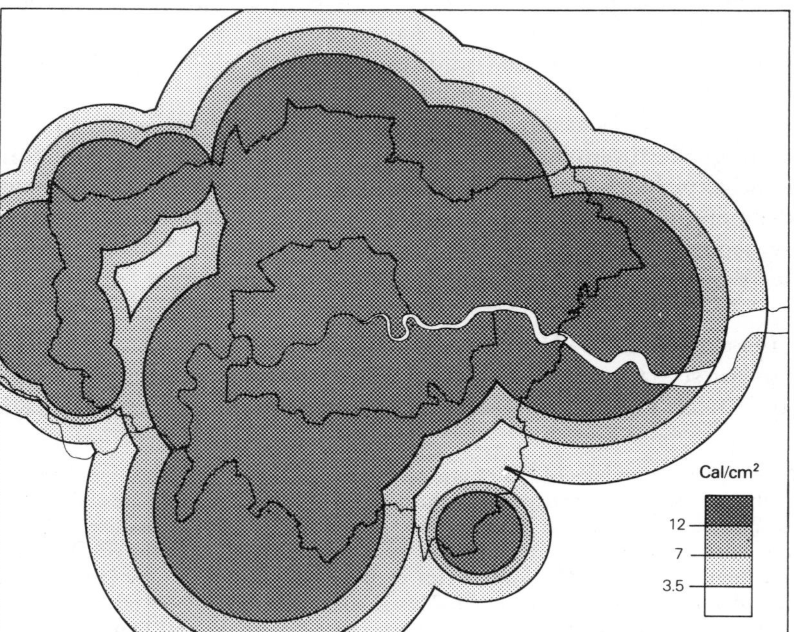

Figure 12 Thermal radiation levels in Greater London: scenario 5

No burns casualties due to thermal radiation would result in the GLC area from scenario 1. Fires would not be started in London as a direct result of the heat or blast effects of the attack, though it is possible that a few casualties would result from fires started by other causes.

As explained earlier, it is assumed that 5 per cent of the population would either be caught outside by the attack or be exposed to thermal radiation through a window or gap in the walls of the building they were sheltering in. On this basis, some 14,000 people would receive lethal flash burns in scenario 2. A further 6500 people would be seriously injured by flash burns. All these casualties would be located in the west of the GLC area.

These numbers would be much higher for scenario 3, for which more than 100,000 serious flash burns casualties (lethal plus serious injuries) would be expected. Not surprisingly, the number of flash burns victims would be enormous* for scenarios 4 and 5; about 800,000 and 1,400,000 respectively. None of these figures includes estimates of casualties from fires, though these could be very numerous. Large numbers of people would be expected to be within fire zones for scenarios 2–5.

An indication of the effect of varying the percentage of people assumed to be exposed to thermal radiation can be obtained by simple multiplication or division (although this is not precise). Thus, if only 1 per cent of the population were exposed in scenario 2, roughly 3000 lethal flash burns and 1300 serious injuries would be expected, whereas a 25 per cent exposure rate would result in some 70,000 lethal flash burns and 33,000 serious flash burn injuries.

These estimates assume that casualties from thermal radiation can be meaningfully disentangled from blast casualties. This is possible only if all the explosions occur simultaneously. In fact, exact simultaneity is extremely unlikely, and in any case the blast wave would arrive only a few seconds after the heat from the nuclear fireball. The additional effects of blast on casualty levels are considered next.

2. Blast. Figures 13–16 show the extent of the 12, 5, 2, and 1 psi blast rings for scenarios 2–5. The warheads detonated in scenario 1 would be too far from London to cause much damage in the GLC area. However,

*Note that the numbers of flash burn casualties can exceed the 5 per cent of the initial population assumed to be exposed to the flash. This is because many areas would receive damaging levels of thermal radiation from more than one bomb. As explained earlier, those killed by flash burns are removed from the population before the effects of the next detonation are calculated. However, for each new detonation, a new 5 per cent of the population is assumed to be exposed. This seems reasonable in view of the fact that each detonation would cause blast damage or otherwise expose previously unexposed people to the flash from the next detonation.

the 200 kt ground burst on Farnborough could result in many windows being smashed in Walton-on-Thames, Esher, Staines and other parts of the south-west edge of the London conurbation.

Scenario 2 would result in severe blast damage over large parts of west London. Even at this stage, light damage to roofs would be expected over much of the GLC area, and windows would be smashed over most of London. By scenario 4, it is clear that nearly all of London would be subjected to levels of blast sufficient to damage most buildings severely. Indeed, the greater part of the GLC area would be seriously affected by blast from more than one bomb.

No blast casualties are predicted in the GLC area for scenario 1. For every other attack, however, blast is easily the most important cause of casualties. In scenario 2, more than 500,000 people would be killed by blast, and more than 400,000 would be injured.

In scenario 3, an additional 1,200,000 casualties are added by blast. In scenarios 4 and 5, this number increases further to 4,420,000 and 4,700,000 people respectively. The fact that the additional 5 Mt used in scenario 5 results in 'only' an additional 280,000 blast casualties shows that, after scenario 4, there are relatively few people left to injure or kill.

3. Radioactive fall-out. Figures 17 and 18 show the accumulated radiation dose which someone in the open would receive in two weeks (surface tissue dose) for each scenario. A steady 24 km/h SSW wind is assumed, and the plots are built up by summing the effects of the idealized fall-out plumes from relevant ground bursts.

A SSW wind direction was chosen as standard because it is the prevailing wind direction in south-east England. As will become clear, a steady SSW wind results in intermediate levels of radiation in the GLC area: other wind directions would result in significantly greater or lesser radiation hazards for Londoners. Figures 19 and 20 show the effects of a different wind direction. The greatest radiation hazard to the GLC would come from a WSW wind – also quite a common wind direction in the south-east of England. In fact, the WSW wind may be a very common wind direction as far as fall-out distribution is concerned. As already mentioned, winds above a few hundred metres are more relevant to fall-out plumes than those at ground level. Winds tend to veer in a clockwise direction with increasing altitude (Meteorological Office 1966).

Scenario 1 would result in little or no short-term radiation hazard in the GLC area for most wind directions, though the radiation levels could well be far higher than would be acceptable in peace time. A WSW wind would be most dangerous; fall-out from the ground burst on Farnborough (together with fall-out from the more distant explo-

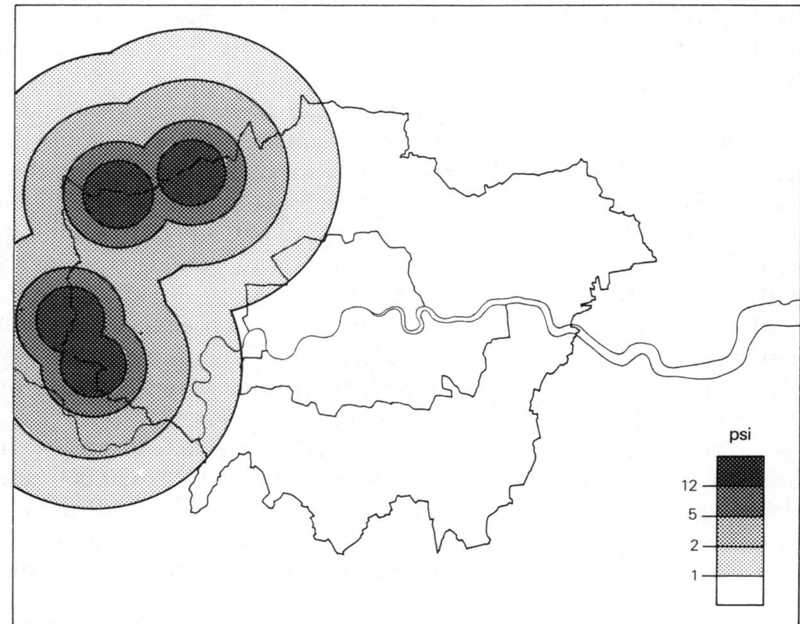

Figure 13 Blast overpressure levels in Greater London: scenario 2

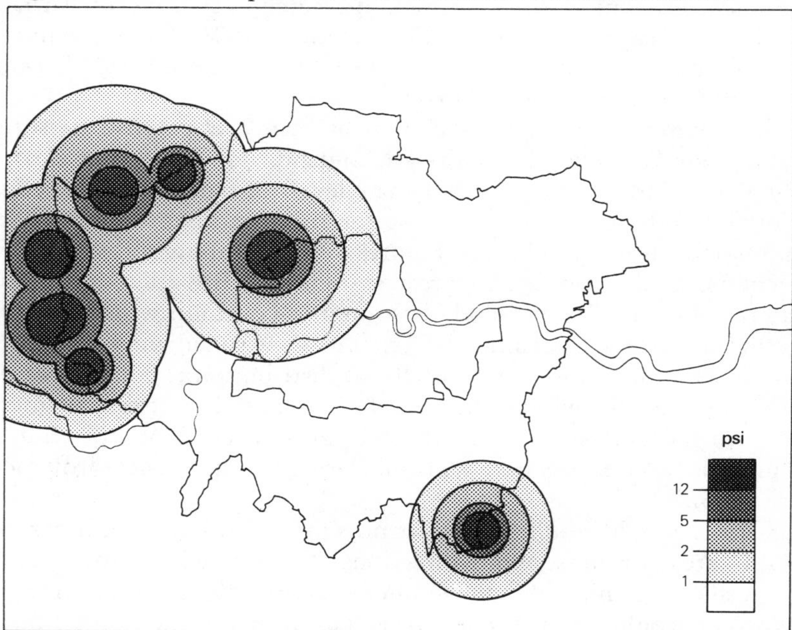

Figure 14 Blast overpressure levels in Greater London: scenario 3

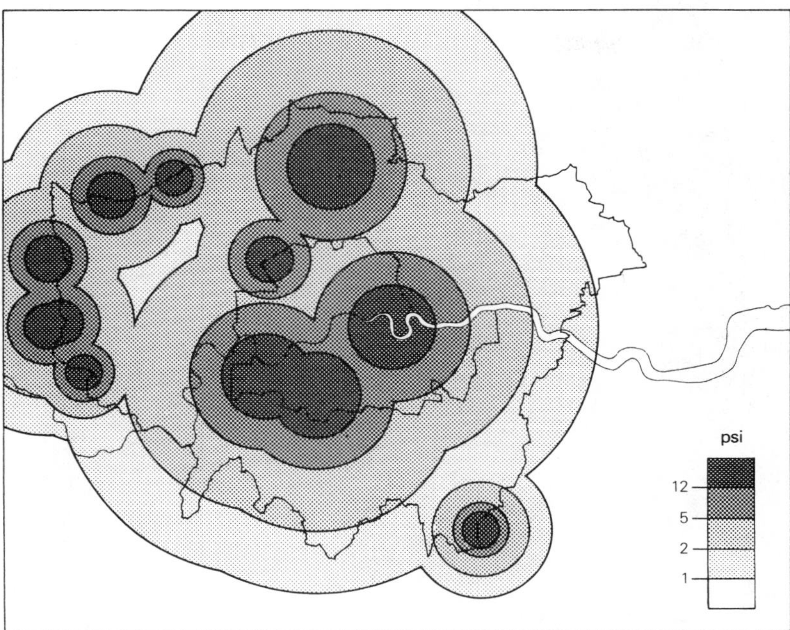

Figure 15 Blast overpressure levels in Greater London: scenario 4

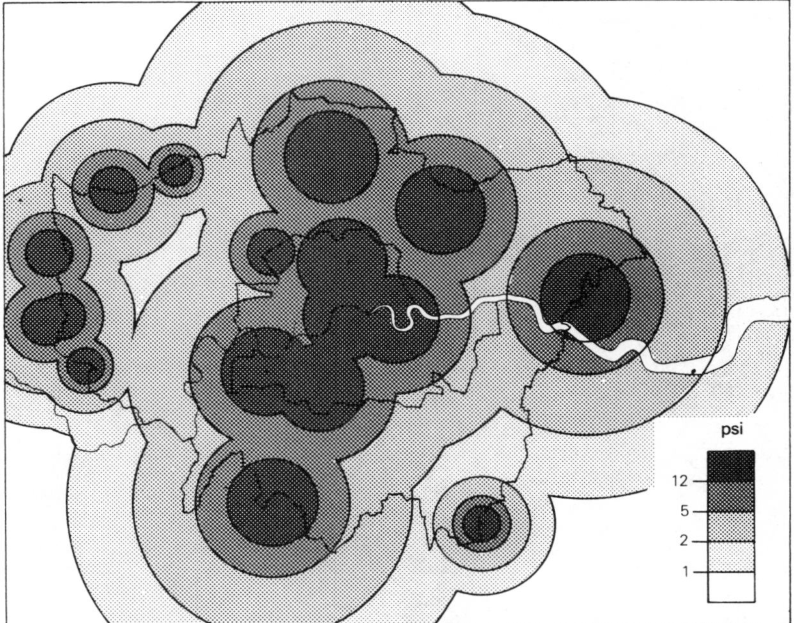

Figure 16 Blast overpressure levels in Greater London: scenario 5

Figure 17 Radiation doses accumulated in the open in Greater London: scenario 2, SSW wind

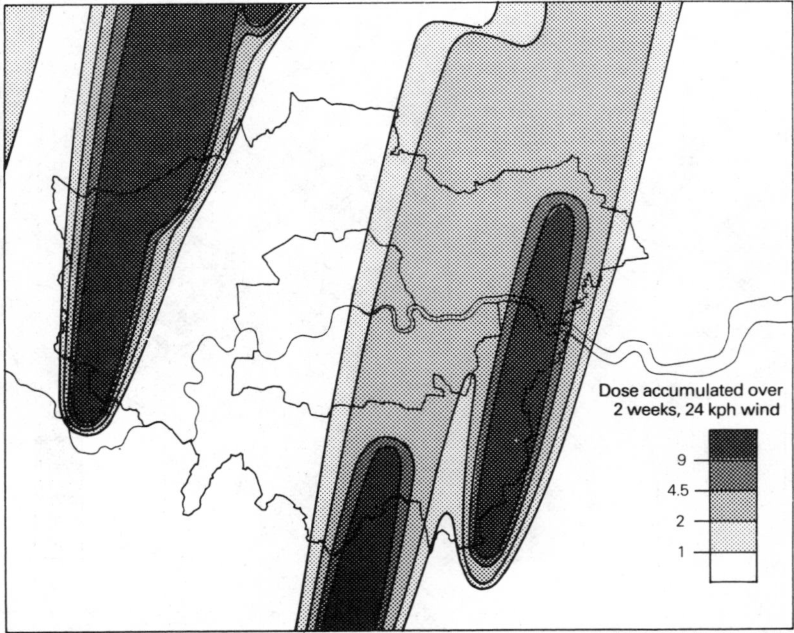

Figure 18 Radiation doses accumulated in the open in Greater London: scenarios 3, 4 and 5, SSW wind

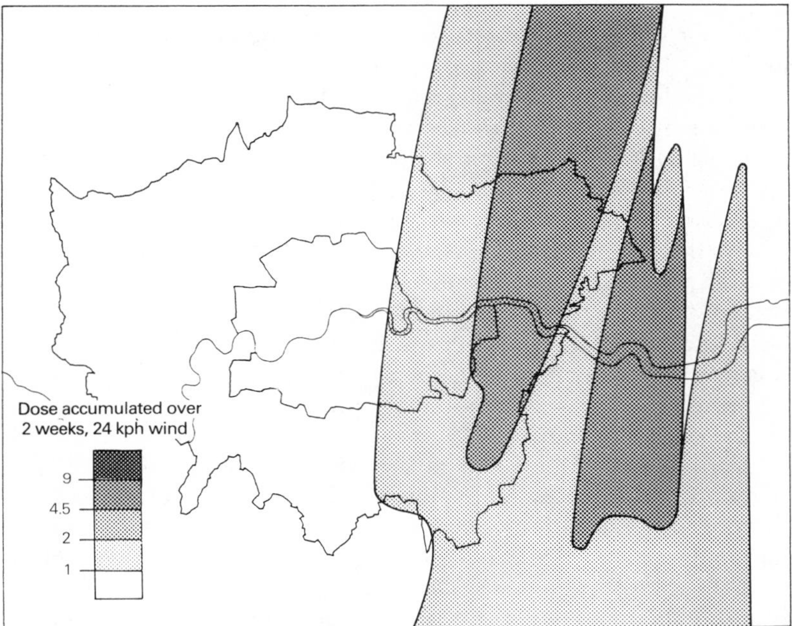

Figure 19 Radiation doses accumulated in the open in Greater London: scenario 2, NNE wind

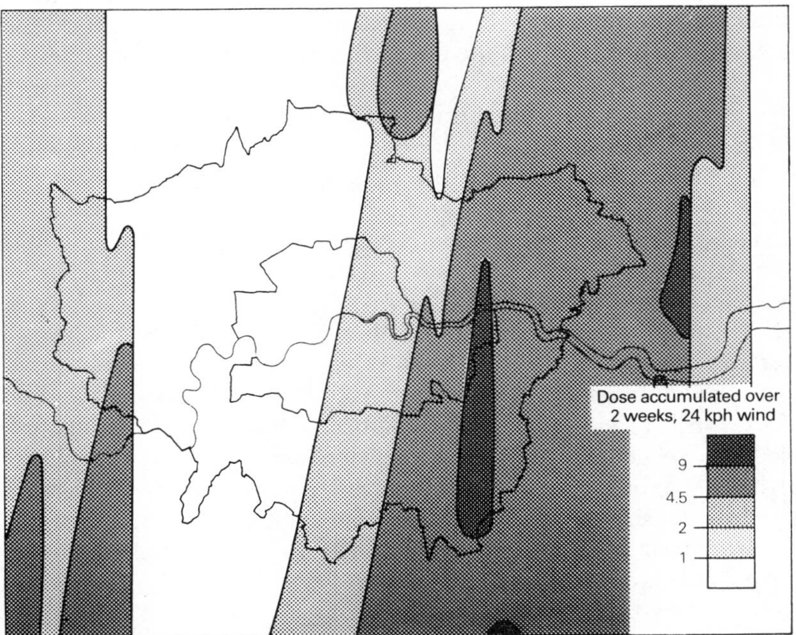

Figure 20 Radiation doses accumulated in the open in Greater London: scenarios 3, 4 and 5, NNE wind

sions on Greenham Common) could result in radiation levels of more than 6 gray over large parts of south-west London, and even higher levels if the wind speed was greater than 24 km/h. A dose of 6 gray would be sufficient to kill nearly everyone subjected to it, according to most experts. People without shelter in such regions would be in great danger.

In scenario 2, London would be subjected to fall-out from ground bursts within the GLC area as well as from more distant explosions. Specifically, the 200 kt ground bursts targeted on West Drayton, Heathrow and Northwood would be sources of intensely radioactive fall-out lined along the west of the GLC area. In scenario 2, it is westerly winds that are, unsurprisingly, the most dangerous to Londoners. SSW winds result in relatively low radiation levels in most of London apart from the west (see Figure 17).

In scenario 3, ground bursts are assumed to occur at Stanmore, Northwood, Heathrow and Biggin Hill in the GLC area, and at numerous other locations close enough to London to pose a severe radiation hazard (particularly from High Wycombe, Chatham, Gatwick airport, Hatfield, Luton, Stansted and Aldermaston). The effects of the ground bursts on Gatwick and Biggin Hill, and the three ground bursts in the west of the GLC area, can be clearly seen in Figure 18. Fall-out from targets north of London, such as Hatfield, can be seen in Figures 19 and 20. No additional ground bursts are included in scenarios 4 and 5 and so the fall-out levels in the GLC area remain the same as for scenario 3.

As explained earlier, the number of fall-out casualties depends on the protection factor of the buildings in which people shelter (and the amount of time they spend in these shelters) as well as on the radiation dose that would be received without any protection. Blast (and fire) damage would reduce the amount of protection given by a building.

The baseline assumption in the GLAWARS study is that people would have effective protection factors of 1, 1, 2, and 5 in blast zones A, B, C and D respectively, and an average PF of 8 in areas subjected to less than 1 psi overpressure. This may well over-estimate the effective PFs for most people: many would not stay inside their shelters for the full two weeks, and recent calculations indicate that even an undamaged dwelling would typically offer a PF of only 5 (Webber in press). Furthermore, buildings would suffer light damage and windows would be smashed a significant distance beyond the 1 psi blast ring. However, the estimation of appropriate PF values in blast-damaged (and even undamaged) areas is uncertain, and arguments could be made that the 'baseline' PFs underestimate the protection people could obtain with adequate warning and instruction. To examine the sensitivity of the casualty estimates to changes in assumptions about PFs, fall-out casualties were also estimated for lower and higher sets of PF values.

An indication of the zones within which survivors of blast and burns would be expected to be killed or injured by radiation can be obtained by superimposing the blast rings on the fall-out maps. In an area within blast zone C, for example, the standard PF is taken to be 2. At a point in this zone where the outside radiation dose would be less than 2 gray, people would not be expected to suffer from short-term radiation injury. Where the outside radiation dose is estimated to be 4.5–9.0 gray, most people would be expected to be injured by radiation, and some would receive a lethal dose. Similar calculations can be made for other zones.

In the standard case – SSW, 24 km/h wind – no fall-out casualties are predicted for scenario 1. For the other scenarios, however, there are large numbers of radiation casualties. In scenario 2, almost 100,000 people are estimated to die from radiation, mostly because they were already injured by blast or burns. This number rises to well over 300,000 for attacks 4 and 5. The additional number of casualties caused by radiation in scenario 5 is less than half the number in scenario 4, and the number of people killed by radiation is also smaller in the larger attack. This is because radiation levels would not increase in scenario 5, but the total number of burns and blast casualties would. There are simply not that many people left to be killed or injured by radiation.

4. Total casualties. Total casualties in the GLC area (Table 10) jump from about 15 per cent and 23 per cent for scenarios 2 and 3 to about 85 per cent and 97 per cent in scenarios 4 and 5. This is not surprising. A single one megaton explosion in the centre of London could produce more than 1 million casualties from blast alone. In scenario 4 there are four such explosions, and in scenario 5 there are nine.

Sensitivity of results to variations in assumptions. Some of the effects of varying assumptions about wind direction, wind speed and PF values have already been examined on the national scale. Tables 11 and 12 summarize similar results for the GLC area (see also Steadman, Greene and Openshaw 1986). These variations affect only the numbers of radiation casualties.

For most wind directions, there would be no fall-out casualties in the GLC area in scenario 1. Although radiation levels in London might be high (several gray in some cases), the lack of blast damage means that everybody is assumed to be in a shelter with a relatively high PF. It is only for WSW winds that radiation casualties result in spite of the PF of 8 – implying that radiation dose levels in some areas are more than 8 gray. Even in this case, however, only about 1300 people suffer from serious radiation sickness, or about 0.02 per cent of the GLC population. In reality, people in a given area would have a range of PFs, instead of the uniform value assumed in the model. Even in areas with little blast damage, some people would be outside or in very flimsy shelters. Hence a few radiation casualties could be expected in scenario 1 for a wider range of wind directions than the results indicate.

In scenarios 2 and 3, the casualty levels are rather sensitive to some changes in wind direction. A shift from SSW to WSW results in a 60 and a 25 per cent increase in total casualties respectively. This change in wind direction makes the difference between the fall-out from ground bursts in the west of London falling on areas in the GLC where blast and burns casualties are relatively low, and falling only on heavily damaged areas where casualty rates from burns and blast are already high. Other changes in wind direction result in only relatively small changes in casualty rates.

Changes of wind direction in scenarios 4 and 5 give similar effects to those in the two smaller scenarios. In scenario 4, the change from SSW to WSW results in about 450,000 additional deaths, though because of reductions in the number of people surviving with serious injuries, 'only' about 100,000 are added to the total number of casualties. In scenario 5, an additional 46,000 people would be killed in a WSW wind, but the total casualties increase by only about 7000. As explained earlier, at this scale of attack so many people are killed or injured by burns and blast that variations in wind direction could have only a relatively small effect.

For the standard SSW wind direction, increases in wind speed are predicted to make very little difference to the total casualties in scenario 2, though radiation doses in some areas are sufficiently increased to kill some 9000 people who would only have been injured at the slower wind speed. This is because all the areas subjected to heavy radioactive fall-out are so close to the relevant ground bursts that increased wind speed would not result in new areas within Greater London having high radiation levels. In scenario 3, where the radioactivity levels from the ground bursts on Biggin Hill and Gatwick are spread over wide areas by faster wind speeds, the total casualties are increased by about 62,000, though this still represents an increase of only about 4 per cent. The casualty increase is about the same for scenario 4, and is only about 12,500 in scenario 5.

For other wind directions, the effects of increases in wind speed from 24 km/h to 40 km/h are greater. For WSW winds, where the fall-out from the bombs in the west of London would be carried right across the city, the effects of increases in wind speed are more marked: in scenario

2, total casualties increase by about 310,000; by about 260,000 in scenario 3; by about 95,000 in scenario 4; and by roughly 32,000 in scenario 5. In scenario 2, this represents a 20 per cent increase but in scenario 4 the increase is only about 1.7 per cent. In scenario 1, the increase in wind speed for a WSW direction increases the radiation levels from the Farnborough bomb greatly, though the casualties remain below 1 per cent of the initial population. It is, however, important to note that the combined effects of a shift in wind direction to WSW and an increase in wind speed have a marked effect on the casualty rates in London, particularly in scenarios 2 and 3. In view of the arguments made earlier about the likelihood of relatively fast WSW winds in south-east England, this case should perhaps be given more weight than some of the other sensitivity studies.

As can be seen from Table 11, the situation for the other wind directions examined is that increases in wind speed have significant but relatively small effects on the total number of casualties.

To test the sensitivity of the results to assumptions about protection factors, the casualties for each scenario were also calculated using relatively low and relatively high PFs. The low values were taken to be 1, 1, 2, 3.5 and 5 in blast zones A, B, C, D and outside, and the high

Table 11 Effects of changes in wind speed and direction on casualties in the GLC area

Scenario	Wind speed (km/h)	Wind direction	Casualty rate in GLC area (%) (rounded to 0.5%)	Total casualties in GLC area (rounded to 500)
1	24	SSW	0	0
		WSW	0	1500
		ENE	0	0
		NNW	0	0
	40	SSW	0	0
		ENE	0	0
		NNW	0	0
2	24	SSW	15.5	995,500
		WSW	25.5	1,621,500
		ENE	15.5	991,000
		NNW	15.5	984,000
	40	SSW	15.5	995,500
		WSW	30	1,931,50[illegible]
		ENE	15.5	995,0[illegible]
		NNW	15.5	991[illegible]

Table 11 *Continued*

Scenario	Wind speed (km/h)	Wind direction	Casualty rate in GLC area (%) (rounded to 0.5%)	Total casualties in GLC area (rounded to 500)
3	24	SSW	23	1,476,000
		WSW	29	1,863,000
		NNW	23.5	1,517,000
		ENE	21	1,355,000
		SSE	23	1,469,500
	40	SSW	24	1,538,000
		WSW	33	2,124,000
		NNW	26	1,665,000
		ENE	20.5	1,314,500
4	24	SSW	85	5,451,000
		WSW	86.5	5,551,000
		NNW	82.5	5,299,000
		ENE	82	5,258,500
		SSE	82.5	5,307,000
	40	SSW	86	5,508,000
		WSW	88	5,647,000
		NNW	83	5,326,500
		ENE	82	5,264,000
		SSE	83	5,339,000
5	24	SSW	97	6,224,000
		WSW	97	6,231,000
		NNW	95.5	6,140,000
		ENE	96	6,149,000
		SSE	95.5	6,135,000
	40	SSW	97	6,236,500
		WSW	97.5	6,263,500
		NNW	96	6,156,000
		ENE	96	6,151,500
		SSE	96	6,151,000

Source: Steadman, Green and Openshaw 1986.

values were 1, 2, 4, 10 and 16 respectively. The results of changing these assumptions are shown in Table 12.

In scenario 2, the effect of reducing the PFs is to leave the number of fall-out casualties exactly the same as for the standard assumptions. This is not an error: other counties do show increases in the number of casualties. The reason for this result, in this scenario, is that all the relevant GLC areas with high radiation levels are in A, B or C blast zones. However, the PF is not lowered from the standard assumptions in these zones, and so the number of fall-out casualties would be expected to be the same. In scenarios 3 and 4, the casualties due to

Table 12 Effects of changing protection factors on casualties in the GLC area

Scenario		Casualty rate in GLC area (%) (rounded to 0.5%)	Total casualties in GLC area (rounded to 500)
1	standard	0	0
	low PF	0	0
	high PF	0	0
2	standard	15.5	995,500
	low PF	15.5	995,500
	high PF	15.5	990,000
3	standard	23	1,476,000
	low PF	25	1,604,000
	high PF	21.5	1,373,500
4	standard	85	5,451,000
	low PF	86.5	5,536,500
	high PF	82.5	5,305,500
5	standard	97	6,224,000
	low PF	97	6,321,500
	high PF	96.5	6,178,000

Note:

Blast zone	A	B	C	D	less than 1 psi
standard PF	1	1	2	5	8
low PF	1	1	2	3.5	5
high PF	1	2	4	10	16

Source: Steadman, Green and Openshaw 1986.

radiation increase significantly, leading to an additional 2 per cent and 1.3 per cent of the initial population being killed or injured by the attacks. In scenario 5, the effects are smaller.

The effect of increasing the PFs is to reduce the casualties by similar amounts, though in this case some reduction is also seen in scenario 2, because the PF values in blast zones B and C are changed.

References

Adams, G. E., 'Lethality from acute and protracted radiation exposure in man'. In *International Journal of Radiation Biology* 46, 209–217, 1984.

Bentley, P. R., *Blast overpressure and fall-out radiation dose models for casualty assessment and other purposes*. London, Home Office Scientific Research and Development Branch, 1981.

British Institute of Radiology, *The Radiological Effects of Nuclear War*. London, BIR, 1982.

British Medical Association, *The Medical Effects of Nuclear War*. Chichester, John Wiley, 1983.

Butler, S. F. J., 'Scientific advice in home defence'. In Barnaby, F., and Thomas, G. (eds.), *The Nuclear Arms Race – Control or Catastrophe?* London, Frances Pinter, 1982.

Daugherty, W., Levi, B., and von Hippel, Frank, 'The consequences of "limited" nuclear attacks on the US'. In *International Security*, in press.

Glasstone, S., and Dolan, P., *The effects of nuclear weapons*. Washington DC, US Government Printing Office, 1977.

Greater London Council, *London Industrial Strategy*. London, GLC, 1985.

Greene, O., Rubin, B., Turok, N., Webber, P., and Wilkinson, G., *London After the Bomb*. Oxford, Oxford University Press, 1982.

Hodgkinson, S., Fergusson, M., Nectoux, F., with Barrett, M., and Greene, O., co-ordinator Howes, R., *GLAWARS Task 5: The impact of a nuclear attack on London's built environment*. London, South Bank Polytechnic, 1986, mimeo.

Home Office, *Protect and Survive*. London, HMSO, 1980.

Journal of the Institute of Civil Defence, Editorial. Oct–Dec 1984.

Katz, A. M., *Life After Nuclear War: The Economic and Social Impacts of Nuclear Attacks on the United States*. Cambridge, Mass., Ballinger, 1982.

Kerr, J., Buck, C., Cline, W., Martin, S., and Nelson, W., *Nuclear weapons effects in a forest environment – thermal and fire*. Washington DC, Defence Nuclear Agency, 1971, Report N2:TR2 – 70.

Martin, J. H., 'Radiation exposure and civil defence'. In *Journal of the Institute of Civil Defence*, Oct–Dec, 6–21, 1984.

Meteorological Office, *Surface and 90 mb wind relationships*. London, HMSO, 1966, Scientific paper No. 23.

National Council on Radiation Protection and Measurements, *Radiological Factors affecting Decision-making in a Nuclear Attack*. Washington DC, NCRP, 1974, NCRP Report No. 42.

Office of Technology Assessment, *The Effects of Nuclear War*. London, Croom Helm, 1980.

Openshaw, S., Steadman, P., and Greene, O., *Doomsday: Britain After Nuclear Attack*. Oxford, Blackwell, 1983.

Rotblat, J., *Nuclear Radiation in Warfare*. London, Taylor and Francis, 1981.

Rotblat, J., 'Acute radiation mortality in a nuclear war'. In *The Medical Implications of Nuclear War: Proceedings of the Institute of Medicine Symposium, September 1985*. Washington DC., National Academy Press, in press.

Rotblat, J., Haines, A., and Lindop, P., *GLAWARS Task 6: The health impact of nuclear attack*. London, South Bank Polytechnic, 1986, mimeo.

Steadman, P., Greene, O., and Openshaw, S., *GLAWARS Task 3: Computer predictions of damage and casualties in London*. London, South Bank Polytechnic, 1986, mimeo.

Webber, P. R., *Residential Shielding Factors in Nuclear Attack*. In press.

2.2 Damage to the built environment

The second major task in assessing the effects of nuclear attack on London is to estimate the damage caused to buildings in the city. This part of the exercise is critically important, for two reasons. First, it determines how much shelter remains for the survivors after an attack. Secondly, the degree of damage to London's buildings determines the protection from fall-out that these buildings could subsequently provide. Current civil defence plans rest primarily on the somewhat dubious assumption that those surviving heat and blast will be able to protect themselves from fall-out in their own homes.

GLAWARS therefore commissioned a wide-ranging study of the issues. This resulted in the most detailed assessment of the effects of nuclear war on a city's buildings (Hodgkinson *et al.* 1986) ever undertaken. Using a computer model, researchers were able to build up, in impressive detail, a picture of the kinds of damage inflicted on 12 different building types in the London area under each scenario. The model studied the effects of both blast and fire. From this, estimates were made of the levels of protection these buildings would subsequently provide from fall-out. Finally, calculations were made of the time and cost of clearing rubble and improvising repairs on damaged property. The results suggest that, in the worst scenarios, these jobs would be so daunting that they would never be undertaken; even in the lighter scenarios, the process would take many years. Reconstruction itself, if it occurred, would take much longer.

London's buildings. London comprises more than 3 million buildings, of which some 2.6 million are houses and the rest are non-residential buildings, spread over an area of about 1500 km^2. The latter include about 33 million m^2 of office space, of which 55 per cent is in the central districts of the City, Westminster, and the southern parts of Camden and Islington. In the central areas of London, population densities are extremely high, reaching 100 people/hectare. In the suburbs, this figure falls to 30–50 people/hectare. However, in the central areas workers outnumber residents by about 5 to 1 as a result of the scale of commuting through central areas – more than a million people move in and out of central London on every working day.

The first job was to collect information about the number and location of London's various buildings. Twelve categories were included: houses, builders' yards, storage sites, chemical stores, schools, universities and polytechnics, hospitals and nursing homes, government offices, commercial offices, industrial sites, public buildings and shops.

London includes many Victorian and pre-Victorian brick-built terraces of three to four storeys. Contrary to popular supposition, this stock has major weaknesses associated with its age and method of construction: brickwork is poor in many of the later terraces; the slate roofs are fragile; and window frames and structural woodwork are often in poor repair.

The constructional characteristics of the offices vary. In Westminster and the City, around 80 per cent of offices were built before 1915. Many governmental offices and major institutional buildings are of monumental masonry construction, and would be very resilient to blast damage. The more modern developments use reinforced concrete construction with infill panels. While their structural frames are strong, overall resistance to damage would depend on the panelling construction – glazed panels tend to render the interiors of these buildings highly susceptible to both blast and fire damage. In the new outer London office centres, many developments are of this nature. In central London, however, perhaps a third of London's total office floor space is of traditional unreinforced brick construction (City of Westminster 1978). The likely resistance of these structures to blast is similar to that of London's Victorian housing.

The initial survey of London's built environment immediately revealed a finding of direct relevance to civil defence: only 3.5 per cent of Londoners have access to any kind of basement or cellar. This is significant since cellars are often cited as providing the best protection from fall-out. In fact, the few cellars that exist in London are often unsuitable as shelters. Many are open to gardens and only partially below ground level; and nearly all are covered with ceilings of light timber construction that are likely to collapse as a result of falling masonry after an attack.

Furthermore, relatively few Londoners have access to gardens. Even fewer have access to gardens long enough to provide a place for a shelter that would be safe from falling masonry. In any case, in most areas of London the water table is so near ground level that holes dug in gardens for shelters would fill with water in a few hours. After a nuclear attack, furthermore, the water table would be expected to rise and even those shelters that were initially dry might be flooded (Lippold 1986 and section 2.3.2).

The computer model. The data base for the computer model was information on the location, on a 1-km square grid, of the different types of buildings in London. This was compiled from three principal sources: the 1981 Population Census (OPCS 1985), the 1978 Greater London Housing Condition Survey (GLC 1978), and the 1971 Greater London Land Use Survey (GLC 1971). The information was collected on a computerized map of London's built environment. Each building type, and its various components, such as windows, doors and roofs, was then assigned a set of criteria defining its likely resistance to the blast and fire effects of nuclear weapons. Finally, by establishing the weapons effects that would be experienced within each grid square under each attack scenario, it was possible to calculate the overall damage that would be caused to London's built stock. This model is, so far as is known, the only one to allow an analysis of both blast and fire damage to the built stock from a nuclear attack.

Past attempts at modelling the fire damage from nuclear attacks have generally drawn on empirical data from a variety of sources, including conflagrations triggered by natural disasters, incendiary bombs, nuclear devices and forest fires. This model, however, included an assessment of the probability that the initial thermal flash produces ignition and assumes that 5 per cent of structures that are destroyed or structurally damaged by blast are ignited due to other causes, such as the rupturing of gas supplies or damage to electrical wiring. The model does not include the effects of fire spreading outside the initial fire zone nor of possible conflagrations and firestorms. Fire damage is therefore likely to be underestimated. Details can be found in Hodgkinson *et al.* 1986.

The methodology used to calculate blast effects was based on a study undertaken by the Stanford Research Institute (Stanford Research Institute 1971). This established a set of blast resistance criteria for those structural types which typically make up the built stock of US cities. These were compared and matched with London's stock which was then accorded a detailed set of blast damage criteria. The details can be found in Hodgkinson *et al.* 1986.

An additional factor that generates uncertainties is that of multiple bursts. While many buildings may escape collapse from a relatively weak shock wave, they may be structurally weakened and hence collapse from a second shock wave of similar strength. The GLAWARS model calculates the numbers of buildings that are structurally weakened but not demolished by each weapon; where blast from more than one weapon affects any structure, the probability of it collapsing, and hence the total damage caused, is increased.

The model thus provides estimates, for each of the GLAWARS attack scenarios and by kilometre grid square, of the numbers of each building type that are:

1 destroyed by the collapse of one or more major structural elements (the repair of such buildings would not be considered worthwhile under normal circumstances);
2 structurally weakened and so would not offer useful shelter without major repairs;
3 damaged non-structurally; these buildings – with damaged roofs, doors and windows, for example – are considered potentially usable for fall-out shelters and for other non-domestic purposes, and are repairable under normal circumstances.

Levels of damage. The major findings of the study are summarized in Tables 13–15. The original findings are itemized in considerably more detail and include estimates of damage to individual London boroughs. This detail can be found in Hodgkinson *et al.* 1986. Comments on the effects of individual scenarios follow the tables.

Scenario 1. Damage is marginal, and confined mainly to broken windows, dislodged slates and broken guttering in parts of south-west outer London that are affected by blast from explosions on Farnborough and Greenham Common. Even so, several tens of thousands of houses are affected.

Damage to the non-housing stock would be somewhat more severe. In Hillingdon and Hounslow, an estimated 30,000 m^2 of industrial and commercial building, 166,000 m^2 of schools and more than 600,000 m^2 of shops and public buildings would be affected by light damage.

Scenario 2. Some 347,000 dwellings, 13 per cent of the total, would be demolished in this attack, with Hillingdon and Harrow totally devastated. More than two thirds of all homes in Hounslow, and about a third of those in Barnet, Brent, Ealing and Richmond, would also be destroyed by blast. Severe structural damage – such as the collapse of the roof or at least one external wall – would occur in a further 134,000 homes. None of these half million odd homes would be habitable, and they would provide little protection against fall-out.

Table 13 Destruction (des) and structural damage (dam) to the built environment by scenario (percentage of totals)

	Scenario									
	1		2		3		4		5	
	des	dam	des	dam	des	dam	des	dam	des	dam
Housing	0	0	13	5	18	12	81	11	95	4
Storage sites	0	0	14	8	18	16	90	6	97	3
Builders' yards	0	0	10	2	13	4	80	7	93	4
Chemical stores	0	0	7	0	4	1	68	6	92	3
Schools	0	0	19	5	18	9	76	13	92	7
Universities, polytechnics	0	0	23	3	19	3	77	4	88	2
Hospitals, nursing homes	0	0	13	4	13	5	68	9	88	5
Industrial sites	0	0	13	4	16	8	81	6	94	2
Government offices	0	0	6	2	9	6	94	2	98	1
Commercial offices	0	0	7	3	12	15	93	3	98	1
Public buildings	0	0	21	2	21	5	70	8	87	6
Shops	1	1	17	8	25	19	91	5	99	1

Note: percentages are of numbers of houses; of floor space for storage sites, builders' yards, chemical stores, industrial sites, government and commercial offices, and shops; and of site area for schools, universities and polytechnics, hospitals and nursing homes, and public buildings.
Source: Hodgkinson *et al.* 1986.

Table 14 Non-structural damage to housing stock by scenario

	Scenario									
	1		2		3		4		5	
	No	%	No	%	No	%	No	%	No	%
Windows	47	2	1880	83	1747	82	482	100	133	100
Doors	24	1	636	28	787	37	440	91	133	100
Partitions	0	0	185	8	351	16	312	65	125	94
Roofs	9	0	280	12	398	19	309	64	120	90
Floors	0	0	155	7	300	14	278	58	116	87
Walls	0	0	155	7	303	14	280	58	117	88

Note: numbers are in thousands of houses affected, percentages are of houses left standing. London's total housing stock is 2,602,000.
Source: Hodgkinson *et al.* 1986.

Table 15 Destruction of housing stock by borough

Percentage of housing destroyed	Scenario 1	Scenario 2	Scenario 3	Scenario 4	Scenario 5
Over 75%	None	Harrow Hillingdon	Brent Harrow Hillingdon	City Barnet Brent Camden Enfield Hackney Hammersmith Haringey Harrow Hillingdon Hounslow Islington Kensington Kingston Lambeth Lewisham	City Barking Barnet Bexley Brent Camden Croydon Ealing Enfield Greenwich Hackney Hammersmith Haringey Harrow Havering Hillingdon
50% – 75%	None	Hounslow	Camden Westminster		
25% – 50%	None	Barnet Brent Ealing Richmond	Barnet Hammersmith Hounslow Kensington		
Under 25%	City Barking Barnet Bexley Brent Bromley Camden Croydon Ealing Enfield Greenwich Hackney Hammersmith	City Barking Bexley Bromley Camden Croydon Enfield Greenwich Hackney	City Barking Bexley Bromley Croydon Ealing Enfield		

Haringey	Hammersmith	Greenwich	Merton	Hounslow
Harrow	Haringey	Hackney	Newham	Islington
Havering	Havering	Haringey	Richmond	Kensington
Hillingdon	Islington	Havering	Southwark	Kingston
Hounslow	Kensington	Islington	Sutton	Lambeth
Islington	Kingston	Kingston	Tower Hamlets	Lewisham
Kensington	Lambeth	Lambeth	Waltham	Merton
Kingston	Lewisham	Lewisham	Wandsworth	Newham
Lambeth	Merton	Merton	Westminster	Redbridge
Lewisham	Newham	Newham	Croydon	Richmond
Merton	Redbridge	Redbridge	Ealing	Southwark
Newham	Southwark	Richmond	Greenwich	Sutton
Redbridge	Sutton	Southwark	Bromley	Tower Hamlets
Richmond	Tower Hamlets	Sutton	Barking	Waltham
Southwark	Waltham	Tower Hamlets	Bexley	Wandsworth
Sutton	Wandsworth	Waltham	Havering	Westminster
Tower Hamlets	Westminster	Wandsworth	Redbridge	None
Waltham				Bromley
Wandsworth				None
Westminster				

Source: Hodgkinson *et al*. 1986.

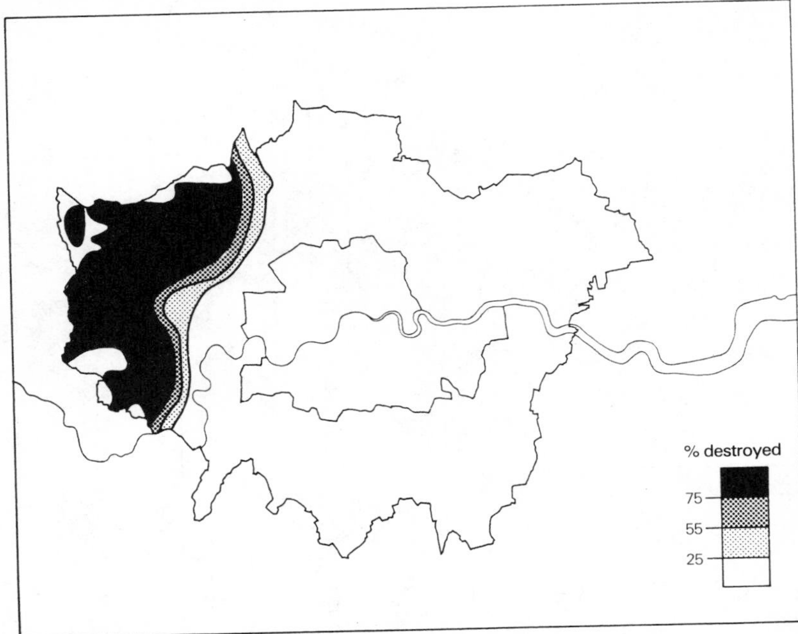

Figure 21 Destruction of housing stock: scenario 2

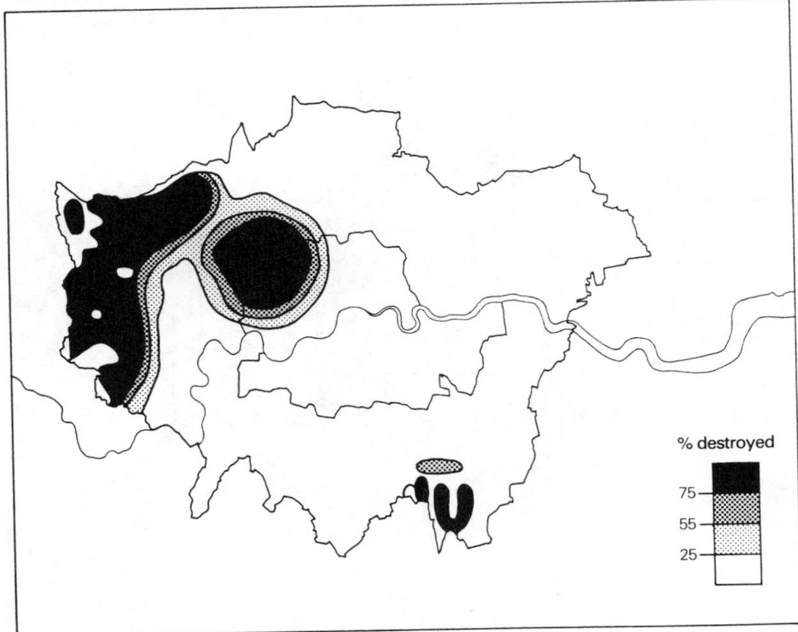

Figure 22 Destruction of housing stock: scenario 3

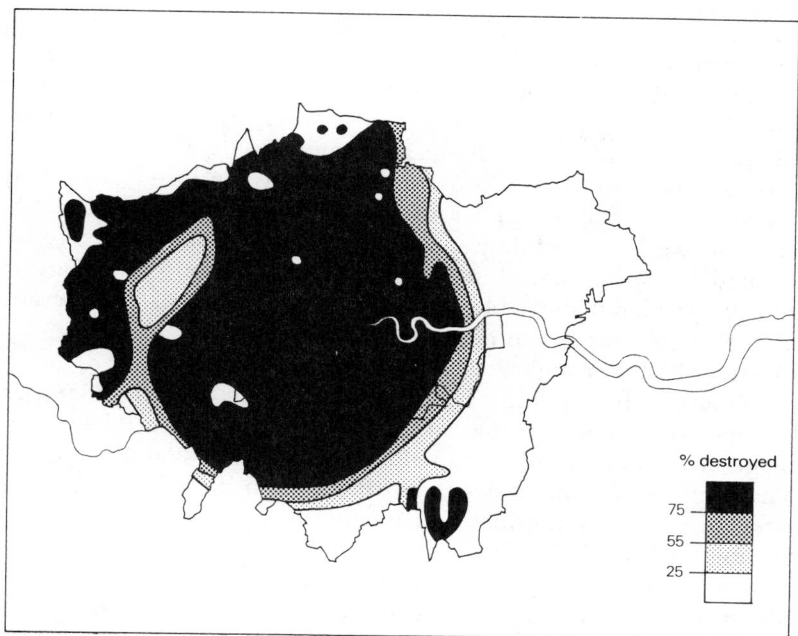

Figure 23 Destruction of housing stock: scenario 4

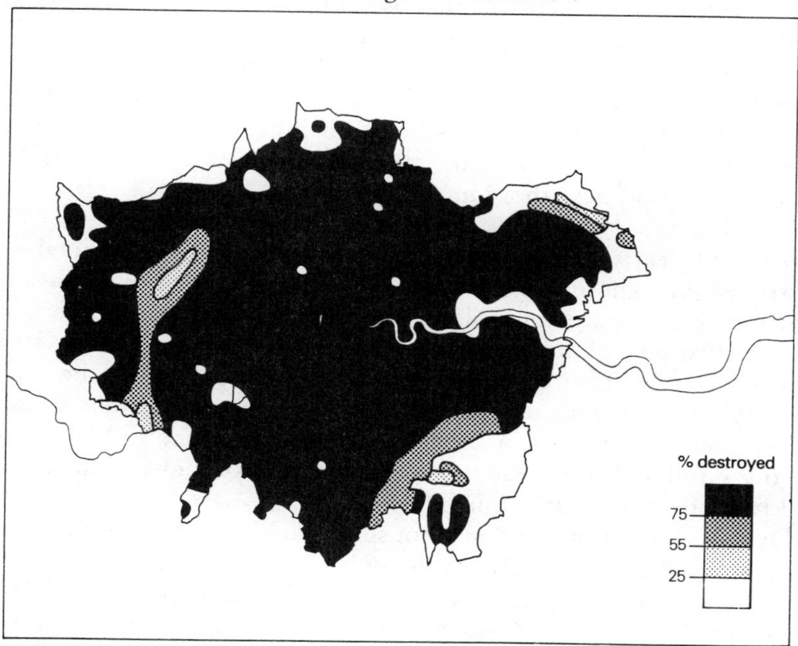

Figure 24 Destruction of housing stock: scenario 5

Fire would create many additional problems. In Ealing, for example, it was calculated that 15,000 to 20,000 homes would be ignited. Fires on this scale could well lead to conflagrations, spreading the fire zone eastwards, even into the city centre. It is estimated that at least three-quarters of all the dwellings in Barnet, Brent, Ealing, Hounslow and Richmond would, as a consequence of blast and fire, be destroyed or made uninhabitable. Under such circumstances, these boroughs – plus what was left of Hillingdon and Harrow – would be likely to be evacuated by survivors. If so, a quarter of London's housing stock would be rendered unusable by what is a very small nuclear attack confined to four targets in north-west London.

Outside these boroughs, windows would be damaged in 83 per cent of the houses left standing. There would also be extensive damage to doors and roofs. For example, at least 10,000 homes would suffer roof damage in each of Camden, Enfield, Haringey and Wandsworth.

The number of houses destroyed in London would be 50 per cent greater than the total number destroyed in the whole of the UK during the whole of World War 2.

Damage to other property might be even more severe. According to Hodgkinson *et al.* (1986), as much as 30 per cent of all goods in storage would be lost in the London area, partly because warehousing is heavily concentrated in west London. Because of the high inflammability of the contents of builders' yards, 27 per cent of their supplies would be lost. Some 20 per cent, on average, of most of the other types of property would be destroyed. In fact, in the seven most badly hit boroughs, damage to buildings such as schools, halls and community centres would be so severe as to make them useless as foci for attempts to restore order and help those in need.

Scenario 3. Nearly half a million homes – 18 per cent of the total – are destroyed outright in this scenario. The numbers of houses with severe structural damage are doubled, to more than 300,000. The bomb falling on Hampstead would destroy or seriously damage some 70,000 dwellings in Camden alone (more than 90 per cent of that borough's housing). In Westminster, 80 per cent of houses would be unusable. Only about 3000 homes in Brent would survive without damage. Just the one bomb in Hampstead would make three boroughs uninhabitable, and two others largely uninhabitable.

Overall, a third of London's housing would be rendered uninhabitable, with roughly ten times as many homes destroyed in London in a few minutes as were destroyed in six years during World War 2. London's shops are also devastated, with 25 per cent destroyed outright and a further 19 per cent seriously damaged. Offices suffer a great deal more damage than in scenario 2: more than 3 million m^2 are destroyed outright and nearly a further 4 million m^2 suffer severe structural damage. In addition, 92 per cent of those surviving have broken windows, 81 per cent damaged doors and 20 per cent ruptured partitions. This would add up to a level of damage and disruption which is considerably larger than the 12 per cent figure for destroyed offices immediately suggests.

Scenario 4 and 5. Damage is so extensive in these scenarios that there is little point in considering them separately. In both cases, more than 90 per cent of homes are rendered uninhabitable; this, in effect, also makes London uninhabitable. Even of the homes remaining, all would have broken windows, and more than half would also have damaged floors, roofs, partitions, doors or walls. In 25 of London's 33 boroughs, more than 75 per cent of dwellings are destroyed in scenario 4; in scenario 5, only one borough, Bromley, escapes with less than 75 per cent damage. Here some 50,000 homes might be left standing but only 8000 of these would be likely to have their walls and roofs intact; none would have doors or windows, and so even these might not be habitable without major repairs. This is essentially all that is left of London's housing.

Even in the few less damaged boroughs, fires would rage so fiercely that any survivors there would be forced to leave, if they could. There is little point in cataloguing the destruction in further detail. In scenario 5, as Hodgkinson *et al.* (1986) put it, the addition of a further 5 Mt of explosive yield 'would reduce virtually the whole of London to rubble'.

Protection from fall-out. The Home Office (1985) states that:

> Most houses in this country offer worthwhile protection against radioactive fallout. That protection can be potentially improved by quite straightforward do it yourself measures concentrating on the provision of fallout rooms in the most suitable part of the building. There would be an intensive campaign, on television, radio, and in the press informing people of what they could do quickly in their homes and what other steps they could take to increase their prospects of survival.

A number of questions must be raised about the realism of these planning assumptions. These questions relate not only to the effectiveness of the protection that would be offered by London's homes against radiation, but also to whether, and how many, survivors could or would seek shelter from radiation in the aftermath of the attack.

The best protection that any 'staying put' household could obtain against fall-out is generally to be found in basements or subterranean shelters. However, as already mentioned, only 3.5 per cent of dwellings in London have basements which are suitable for the construction of simple shelters. For most households in London, the best protection would be, as the Home Office states, through the construction of a 'refuge room' within their own homes.

The basic aim would be to block external windows and door ways and to line the room with dense materials such as heavy furniture, books, bags of earth and sand. What protection factors (PFs) would be offered by such shelters? The Home Office has produced an illustrated document giving guidance as to the protective qualities of 18 basic housing types typically found in the UK (Home Office 1981a). The current edition of the Home Office's publication *Domestic Nuclear Shelters: Technical Guidance* gives details of the method used by the Home Office for calculating PFs (Home Office 1981b).

This method contains a number of errors and oversights:

1 As Webber (in press) has pointed out, the Home Office calculations use average wall thicknesses including apertures such as windows and doors. This is incorrect because radiation is not attenuated linearly by wall density but by a logarithmic variation. Webber's corrected calculations for a typical two-storey, end-of-terrace house in the most protected ground floor position give a PF value of 5.25, or around half of that calculated by the Home Office.

   Webber goes on to show that the Home Office calculations arrive at the correct PF value for a house with the doors and windows blocked up with material of the same density as the solid parts of the walls. The Home Office advises households to block up the apertures to their inner refuge in this way, advice which for most people would be entirely unrealistic. At a rough estimate, it would take 364 million bricks and a lot of sand and cement to fill in one aperture for each dwelling in London. Most people either could not or would not do so.

2 Government assumes in calculating its PFs that no fall-out enters the building or is deposited on walls, window sills, or other projections. This assumption is incorrect for damaged houses, into which fall-out might well penetrate through opened roofs, broken windows and doors, and removed walls. Under scenarios 2 and 3, about four-fifths of the houses that were not totally destroyed by fire or blast would have broken windows. In scenarios 4 and 5, all the remaining houses would have broken windows. The PF values for the inner refuges of these houses could be even lower than those calculated by Webber, probably in the range of 2 to 5 depending on the level of damage.

3 Inner refuges would be vulnerable to blast damage. Given their flimsy construction, they would probably collapse at around 1.5 psi. Where they had collapsed and not been re-erected, the protection

offered by the damaged house itself against radiation would in many cases not be worthwhile.

Allowing for these considerations, Hodgkinson *et al.* (1986) were able to estimate the numbers of houses for each scenario that might be fitted with an inner refuge, and the PFs such structures would provide (see Table 16).

Table 16 Fall-out protection offered by remaining housing stock

Scenario	Surviving population[a] A	B	% of London's pre-attack homes offering different protection factors after attack PF<2	PF 2–5	PF 5–10
1	100	–	–	2	98
2	92	6	13	72	14
3	92	12	18	67	15
4	42	54	81	19	–
5	18	83	95	5	–

[a] A = % of population not killed by blast or fire
B = % of population A who are seriously injured

PF<2: all dwellings suffering structural failure
PF 2–5: all dwellings suffering structural weakening
PF 5–10: all other dwellings
Source: Hodgkinson *et al.* 1986.

The table shows that in scenario 1, with the existing dwelling stock undamaged, all households remaining at home would receive reasonable protection against the relatively low levels of fall-out that would affect London. Under scenarios 2 and 3, the percentage of survivors would grossly exceed, by a factor of more than six, the number of dwellings that had the potential to offer a PF of more than 5. Under these scenarios, most of the surviving population would probably, if they chose to remain at home, have to content themselves with PFs of 2–5. This would not be adequate to protect them against high levels of radiation. In scenarios 4 and 5, the problem of shelter would be much more acute: most of the survivors sheltered at home would probably not receive worthwhile protection against fall-out from the remaining dwellings, given the very high levels of radioactivity that would occur throughout London, and given the high levels of damage that would result to the building stock.

These PF figures are significantly lower than those used in section 2.1 to calculate fall-out casualties. It is therefore highly likely that the figures for total deaths and injuries given in that section underestimate fall-out casualties.

Several other factors must also be taken into account. Previous calculations of casualties assume that everyone in London follows government advice and stays put. In practice, many would not do so; and unless they moved well before the attack, they could be caught on the move without shelter of any kind. Furthermore, of those that did stay put, not all would build internal refuges. Many would feel that attempts at protection were virtually impossible. Others would be rendered incapable of effective action by their anxiety. Yet others would not have the physical or material resources to construct an effective shelter.

Even assuming that a substantial portion of London's population did actually construct rough and ready shelters in their homes, there is no guarantee that these people would be near their shelters at the time of attack, or that they would remain in them after the attack.

Radiation casualties, in short, would be far higher than previous estimates suggest. And London's housing would not offer the kind of protection from radiation that the government currently envisages.

The reconstruction of London. Finally, attempts were made to calculate the cost and time required to rebuild London after each scenario. As already mentioned, scenarios 4 and certainly 5 reduce London to little more than rubble. In these circumstances, the city would not be rebuilt within any meaningful time span. The process would take several decades, if not more than a century, even assuming that London's entire construction industry and supplies were completely undamaged. Under the kind of post-war conditions that might be expected, the obvious conclusion is that London is permanently destroyed and is never rebuilt.

Hodgkinson *et al.* (1986) did, however, estimate the cost of rebuilding London for scenarios 2 and 3 and, for comparison, for scenario 4. The results are shown in Table 17.

Two major conclusions can be drawn from this table:

1 the value of housing destroyed under scenarios 2, 3 and 4 is about 30, 43 and 185 times the current annual output of London's house-building industry:
2 the total cost (excluding infrastructure) of damage and destruction under scenarios 2, 3 and 4 would be equivalent to 8, 11 and 42 years of the current annual output of London's building industry.

Table 17 Values of new construction orders in Greater London (1983 prices) compared to cost of repair and reconstruction by scenario (£million)

Sector	Greater London orders (1983)	Repair and reconstruction cost for scenario		
		2	3	4
New housing	400	12,000	17,200	74,000
Other new public sector work	400[a]	4,300[b]	4,300[b]	20,600[b]
Private: industrial/commercial	200	1,300	1,700	8,600
Private: shops, offices	1,000	5,300	6,800	31,300
Repair and maintenance:				
Housing	600	1,400[c]	2,300[c]	n/a
Public, non-housing	300[a]	500[b]	600[b]	n/a
Private, non-housing	300	800[c]	1,800[c]	n/a
Totals	3,200	25,600	34,700	134,500

[a] including infrastructure costs
[b] excluding infrastructure costs
[c] excluding costs of maintaining undamaged stock
Source: Hodgkinson *et al*. 1986.

A realistic assessment would also have to allow for the massive organizational problems that would be encountered, the shortage of construction materials, the diminishing supply of operational plant and casualties among the construction force. Hodgkinson *et al.* (1986) estimate that even under scenario 1 output levels of the construction industry would be reduced to 60–80 per cent of their previous values. In scenario 2, they would further reduce to around 40 per cent. Initial rubble clearance of road and rail networks would then take a year or two, and the improvised repair of moderately damaged buildings and infrastructure another 6–10 years. Reconstruction would take far longer.

Under scenario 3, construction materials would be very scarce, with timber and glass totally unavailable for many years. Production might be reduced to 25 per cent of its former level, and essential rubble clearing and basic repairs to surviving buildings and infrastructure could take 15–20 years. Reconstruction itself would again take far longer, if indeed it were attempted. The question of London's survival after scenario 3 is dealt with more fully in section 2.10.

References

City of Westminster, *Employment Offices and Industry*. London, Westminster Borough Council, 1978, Topic Paper T7.

GLC, *Greater London Land Use Survey*. London, GLC, 1971.

GLC, *Greater London Housing Condition Survey*. London, GLC, 1978.

Hodgkinson, S., Fergusson, M., Nectoux, F., with Barrett, M., and Greene, O., co-ordinator Howes, R., *GLAWARS Task 5: The impact of a nuclear attack on London's built environment*. London, South Bank Polytechnic, 1986, mimeo.

Home Office, *Protective Qualities of Buildings*. London, HMSO, 1981a.

Home Office, *Domestic Nuclear Shelters: Technical Guidance*. London, HMSO, 1981b.

Home Office, *Emergency Planning Guidance to Local Authorities*. London, Home Office, 1985.

Lippold, C., *GLAWARS Task 3: London's water system and the effects of a nuclear attack*. London, South Bank Polytechnic, 1986, mimeo.

OPCS, *Census 1981*. London, HMSO, 1985.

Stanford Research Institute, *Probabilistic Air Blast Failure Criteria for Urban Structures*. Stanford, California, Stanford Research Institute, 1971.

Webber, P. R., *Residential Shielding Factors in Nuclear Attack*. In press.

2.3 Damage to essential services

A nuclear attack would damage much more than the population and buildings that comprise London. Survivors would, to some extent at least, be deprived of many services that they normally take for granted: heat, light, water, sewage disposal, the phone, radio and television, cars, taxis, trains, tubes and buses, and – perhaps most significantly – food. The extent to which these services are damaged or destroyed is examined in the following sections.

The technique used to assess levels of physical damage was a computer model adapted to each particular service (though the model used to study damage to agriculture differed in several respects). This model is described in some detail in the opening section on energy, but this description is not repeated for the other services. The GLAWARS Commission stresses that the results of such computer studies should not be over-interpreted. They provide a highly useful means of assessing approximate levels of damage but they cannot predict the exact nature of that damage because too many variables are involved that cannot be established with precision. That said, much of this study would have been impossible without computer modelling because the computer enables vast amounts of information to be handled with great speed. The energy study alone, for example, analyses the effects of damage on 544 different energy installations.

2.3.1 Energy

Because most of London's energy is imported from elsewhere in the country, an analysis of damage to energy facilities within the London area caused by the five GLAWARS scenarios would not necessarily reveal the extent of energy disruption. GLAWARS therefore undertook an analysis of the likely damage to the UK energy system as a whole (Barrett 1986). This was done using a computer model. Before this is described, however, it is important to establish a number of effects that are either not included in the model or that may occur independently of the level of attack.

The UK's energy system is a complex set of technologies that extracts and transforms primary fuels and, through a system of distribution and storage, delivers fuels to consumers where it is finally converted into useful services. The solid fuel, gas, electricity and oil sub-systems are chains formed of links including primary supply, distribution and final consumption. As with all chains, they are only as good as their weakest link. Thus, even if some electricity generation and distribution were undamaged, this would serve little purpose if items such as pumps, central heating boilers and light bulbs were damaged.

Storage at various points in these chains can delay disruption for varying periods: thus solid fuel stored in domestic bunkers or petrol in vehicle tanks would act as temporary buffers. There is, however, very little storage in the electricity system. Fluctuations in load must be carefully balanced, minute by minute, by altering the output of generating stations. Excessive variations can cause major instabilities in the system, and the unexpected loss of control, generation or load can result in large areas suffering a loss of service. During attack, this effect is likely to be amplified rather than reduced.

No one would be able to predict the extent and nature of an attack before it occurred. The behaviour of Londoners prior to attack is therefore likely to be similar whatever the subsequent scenario. The results of GLAWARS research into behaviour (Loizos and Marsh 1986, MacDougall and Hastings 1986, and Thompson 1986) suggest that few people would go to work if war seemed likely. The disruption of energy supplies (and other services) would therefore be likely because of this factor alone.

It is possible that a nuclear winter would occur in the heavier scenarios, certainly in scenarios 4 and 5, and possibly in scenario 3. Nuclear winter is characterized by abnormally low temperatures, high winds and erratic precipitation (see section 2.7).

Air temperatures might drop 5 to 15°C below normal. Consequently, surface water and the top layer of the earth (1 to 30 cm in thickness) could freeze. This would hinder the operation of energy systems. The movement of fuels (especially oil and coal) might be hindered or stopped by cold ground temperatures because of the freezing of coal stocks and unworkably high viscosities of oil. (Severe weather in the UK causes problems with diesel vehicles, let alone heavier oil such as fuel oil.) The freezing of water would cause difficulties with operations such as coal preparation and power station cooling. Cold weather would also hinder or stop other resources being supplied to the energy sector; these might include essential chemicals and personnel. It is likely that all modes of transport except deep sea shipping would be affected.

Gusts of wind at speeds up to 160 km/h might occur in a nuclear winter. These, in conjunction with unusual precipitation, could damage facilities such as the electricity transmission grid. High winds in normal UK weather can cause transmission failures as a result of trees being blown onto cables. Heavy snow could also bury coal stocks, and flooding could cause widespread damage.

Weather changes would also affect energy demand. Low temperatures would increase the per capita energy demand for space and water heating. Space heating demand increases by about 10 per cent/°C drop in outside temperature. High wind speeds would increase this further still. Water heating would be essential for thawing water to drink. Balanced against this would be the fact that people would perhaps share some heating facilities (for example, by congregating in warm places) and try to use fuels to attain the minimum levels of warmth essential for survival.

Most of the data on energy systems in this report relate to large individual facilities. In addition, energy equipment sited in homes, offices and factories must also be considered. Damage to these devices is assumed to reflect the damage to the building stock. Thus if 30 per cent of houses are destroyed, then 30 per cent of domestic heating systems are also destroyed. The main problem occurs at lower levels of damage. For example, a blast which leaves the main structure of a building intact may render its plumbing and heating systems inoperable. Levels of damage worse than the destruction of partitions can be presumed to destroy most internal energy services.

In scenarios 2 to 5, the whole of the UK might be affected by one or more strong EMPs arising from high-altitude bursts; any EMP from local bombs will be in addition to these. High-altitude bursts, according to Barrett (1986), would

> render the public electricity and gas systems inoperable for several days at least because of damage to communications, control and particular components such as parts of the electricity transmission system. Resumption of normal operation would require skilled personnel and the necessary spare parts and could take several weeks or months, even if these were available. Vital information may have been lost from computer systems and back-up tape dumps may also have been affected; this would take time to replace. In the first 72 hours, it is most unlikely therefore that gas and electricity would be available to domestic consumers.

In the Greater London area, almost all cooking and about 95 per cent of space and water heating is gas or electric. Most dwellings would be deprived of these services because of the effects of EMP alone. The effect on oil and solid fuel systems would be less serious immediately because of larger stocks and less reliance on other fuel supplies and electronic systems. However, refineries and pipelines would probably stop working because of loss of electricity and damage to control systems. It might be difficult to extract oil from stores because there was no electricity to drive pumps. Surface systems at deep and open mines might also be damaged which, in the case of deep mines, could lead to destruction through flooding.

In addition, EMP would damage supporting infrastructure and industries. Damage would be especially severe in those parts of the economy heavily reliant on electronic systems.

Finally, the computer model did not include a study of the effects of conventional attack on London's energy system. However, as pointed out in Part 1, it might not be particularly difficult to destroy or severely damage the London energy system with conventional weapons aimed at specific targets (Kerr 1986).

The computer model. The physical damage to the energy system was calculated (Barrett 1986) from two data bases. The first gives the size, location and altitude of burst for the bombs in the five nuclear attack scenarios. The second is of energy facilities; it details the type, location and size of major energy facilities such as coal depots, gas stores, oil refineries and the 130-odd public generating stations.

The far more numerous minor energy facilities, such as electricity transformers and gas decompression stations, are not included. Nor are energy distribution systems. Data on the location of these systems were too poor to be included in the study. Furthermore, the vulnerability of these systems to blast is highly variable. Pressures of more than 10 psi are needed to damage structures such as underground gas and oil pipes, and even some of the major transmission towers. On the other hand, parts of the transmission system – such as overhead power cables – are highly vulnerable to damage, even from high winds.

An assessment was made of the vulnerability to blast of the major energy facilities on three levels: destroyed, damaged but reparable, and damaged but usable. These assessments do not pretend to be exact estimates of vulnerability and are intended only to indicate the likely vulnerability of the weakest part of any facility – underground coal mines, for example, are not themselves vulnerable to blast but the surface structures associated with them, without which they cannot function, are. Table 18 lists the numbers of each kind of facility, their capacities and their assumed vulnerability to blast.

A computer program was then written to calculate the maximum peak overpressure and thermal radiation to which each facility is subjected in each scenario. Multiple bursts affecting a particular facility were not accounted for, and no attempt was made to account for fire damage, so the resulting estimates are conservative.

These levels of blast and thermal radiation were used in conjunction with the critical damage levels to produce an inventory of damage to energy facilities. Essentially, the program calculates the primary effects of each bomb on each facility within a radius of 15 km. Not all facilities may be damaged by blast at such a range but their functions are likely to be impaired because of damage to local resources such as people, transport or fuel supplies.

The program then prints out a list of all the facilities within 15 km of the nearest bomb. The name, type and size of the facility are given. This is followed by the status of the facility (usable, reparable or destroyed) and the maximum pressure and thermal radiation to which the facility is subjected. The status is calculated by combining the overpressure with the susceptibilities given for each energy facility in Table 18. The strength of the local EMP is categorized as weak, moderate or strong. The final columns give distance from the nearest bomb, and the name and size of the bomb. The program also prints out a summary of the damage to each system for each scenario.

Scenario-related damage. Table 19 shows the percentage damage and destruction to the energy facilities included in the data base for each of the GLAWARS scenarios. The figures for damage include the 'in range' and the 'usable' categories of the computer program. In other words, they include all facilities within 15 km of a detonation. Although some of these facilities might receive only minor physical damage from blast at the outer extremes of this range, they are included as damaged because general disruption in the area would be likely to be sufficient to impair function.

The percentage figures in Table 19 are based on the total number of facilities, not their capacity. They do not therefore necessarily reflect percentage damage to capacity. Some comments on this, and on destruction of energy devices in homes and offices, are included in the individual scenario descriptions that follow.

Scenario 1. In scenario 1, no nuclear weapons would be detonated in the Greater London area. A negligible proportion of coal mines would be affected by overpressures sufficient only to break windows and cause minor damage. However, one of the eight oil terminals would be damaged, as would more than 10 per cent of oil pumps. Two gas compressors would be lightly damaged and one (near Wittering) would be destroyed; this damage might cause some temporary problems in supplying gas to London.

Light damage would be incurred by each of the major national fuel supply systems. However, unless blast and local EMP badly damaged some critical part of the electricity distribution network, which would be a possibility, there should be no severe difficulties in supplying any of the major fuels to the Greater London area.

There would be virtually no damage to energy supply or domestic energy devices in the Greater London area. Londoners would therefore probably not suffer any serious loss of energy supply in scenario 1, apart maybe from some loss of electricity due to EMP effects on the transmission system, and the possibility of a limited interruption of the gas supply in some areas.

Table 18 Data base for energy facilities and susceptibility to blast

Description	Acronym	Number (total)	Number (GLA only)	Capacity	Susceptibility to blast (peak overpressure, psi)		
					Destroyed	Reparable	Usable
Solid fuel							
Merchant yards[a]	Smerc	–	9	314 kt/a	5	2	1
Deep mine	Deepm	166	–	100,482 kt/a	5	2	1
Open mine	Openm	66	–	–	5	2	1
Oil							
Oil terminal	Oterm	8	–	–	5	2	1
Oil refinery	Orefi	20	–	125,225 kt/a	5	2	1
Oil depot	Odepo	78	18	3796 m^3	8	2	1
Oil pump	Opump	23	4	–	12	2	1
Gas							
LPG gas stores[a]	GLPG	–	8	8500 m^3	5	2	1
Gas terminal	Gterm	4	1	–	5	2	1
Gas compressor	Gcomp	19		–	5	2	1
LNG overground	GLNGa	6		–	5	2	1
LNG underground	GLNGb	1		–	10	2	1
Salt cavity store	Gsalt	1		–	10	2	1
SNG production	GSNGp	2		–	5	2	1

Electricity							
Coal pulverized	Cpfco	54	2	37,341 MW	5	2	1
Coal chain grat	Ccgco	1	–	85 MW	5	2	1
Coal slurry	Cslco	1	–	57 MW	5	2	1
Nuclear:							
Magnox	Nmagn	12	–	4367 MW	5	2	1
AGR[b]	Nagr	6	–	6880 MW	5	2	1
Fast breeder	Npfbr	1	–	200 MW	5	2	1
Steam generation	Nsghw	1	–	200 MW	5	2	1
Fuel oil	Ofoil	13	5	14,368 MW	5	2	1
Gas turbine	Ogast	31	6	3056 MW	5	2	1
Diesel[a]	Odies	–	1	–	5	2	1
Gas (int comb)[a]	GasIC	–	2	–	5	2	1
Hydro	Hhydr	14	–	1296 MW	5	2	1
Waste[a]	Waste	–	1	–	5	2	1
Pumped storage	Ppump	4	–	2650 MW	5	2	1
Grid control	Egcon	3	1	–	5	2	1

[a]includes only facilities in the Greater London area
[b]advanced gas-cooled reactor
Source: Barrett 1986.

Table 19 Percentage damage (dam) and destruction (des) to energy facilities for the GLAWARS scenarios

	Scenario 1		Scenario 2		Scenario 3		Scenario 4		Scenario 5	
	dam	des	dam	des	dam	des	dam	des	dam	des
Solid fuel										
Merchant yards[a]			33.3	11.1	44.4	22.2	44.4	44.4	11.1	77.8
Deep mine	1.2		4.2	0.6	21.1	0.5	31.9	2.4	36.1	4.2
Open mine	1.5		3.0		10.6	1.5	22.7	1.5	36.4	1.5
Oil										
Oil terminal	12.5		12.5		25.0		25.0		37.5	
Oil refinery					45.0		50.0	5.0	50.0	10.0
Oil depot	5.1		7.7		59.0	5.1	55.1	17.9	57.7	21.8
Oil pump	13.0		21.7		73.9		73.9		73.9	
Gas										
LPG gas stores[a]			12.5		62.5	12.5	25.0	75.0		100
Gas terminal					50.0		25.0	25.0	25.0	25.0
Gas compressor	10.5	5.3	21.1	5.3	31.6	10.5	36.8	10.5	42.1	10.5
LNG overground					50.0		50.0		50.0	
LNG underground										
Salt cavity store					100		100		100	
SNG production					50.0		50.0		50.0	

Electricity										
Coal pulverized	7.4		7.4		31.5	1.9	35.2	11.1	35.2	14.8
Coal chain grat					100		100		100	
Coal slurry										
Nuclear:										
Magnox					16.7		16.7		16.7	
AGR[b]									16.7	
Fast breeder										
Steam generation										
Fuel oil	7.7		7.7		53.8	15.4	46.2	23.1	46.2	30.8
Gas turbine	9.7		12.9	3.2	51.6		51.6	3.2	54.8	9.7
Diesel[a]					100		100			100
Gas (int comb)[a]					50.0			100		100
Hydro	7.1		7.1		7.1		7.1		7.1	
Waste[a]					100			100		100
Pumped storage										
Grid control							33.3		33.3	

[a]includes only facilities in the Greater London area
[b]advanced gas-cooled reactor
Source: data collated from Barrett (1986).

Scenario 2. In scenario 2, there would be detonations within the Greater London area although most major energy facilities would be unaffected by blast.

Two Greater London area coal merchants' yards would suffer severe damage (2 psi). Machinery might be damaged there, but coal stocks would be substantially unaffected. Less than 1 per cent of national coal production capacity would be lost.

A small proportion of oil storage would be badly damaged in the Greater London area and elsewhere. No other major oil facilities would be affected.

In addition to the compressor near Wittering, four other compressors would be slightly affected. This damage could start to cause problems for the proper operation of the gas grid. The LPG store in West Drayton would be severely damaged but otherwise there would be little damage to gas supplies in the Greater London area.

The Taylor's Lane gas turbine power station in London would be affected by blast, though it might still work.

In scenario 2, blast would not affect a significant part of any of the supply systems, in or outside London. However, approximately 20 per cent of domestic energy devices would be damaged and/or destroyed because of building damage. People previously dependent on these devices would not have any supply. Ruptured pipes and broken wiring in buildings might cause problems to the loads imposed on gas and electricity supply, and some areas would have to be disconnected if possible.

Scenario 3. In this attack, there would be considerable damage to solid fuel systems in London. Out of nine coal merchants' depots, two would be destroyed and a further four damaged. Nationally, however, blast effects on coal production would still be limited.

Many of the Greater London area oil depots would be lightly or moderately damaged. Some 20 per cent of refining capacity would receive heavy and a further 40 per cent light damage, but no plant would be destroyed outright by blast. About 20 per cent of filling stations would receive light damage and about 10 per cent would be severely damaged or destroyed.

Greater London area gas stores would escape with light damage, apart from the one in Uxbridge. Nationally, two of the terminals would suffer light effects. However, of the 14 gas compressors, 6 would be lightly damaged and 2 would be destroyed.

About 30 per cent of power station capacity would suffer light damage, but only 3 per cent would be destroyed. All stations in and near the Greater London area would suffer light damage. About 30 per cent of domestic energy devices would be destroyed or severely damaged.

The increasing likelihood of nuclear winter and the damage sustained by building services would mean that Londoners would be severely affected in this scenario.

Scenario 4. In scenarios 4 and 5, damage would become massive in the Greater London area, and severe to national energy systems.

Of the 9 merchants' yards in the Greater London area, 4 would be destroyed and 4 damaged. About 3 per cent of national mining capacity would be destroyed, 7 per cent heavily damaged and 20 per cent lightly affected.

Of the 18 major oil depots in the Greater London area, 7 would be destroyed and 7 severely damaged. Nationally, about 20 per cent of oil storage would be destroyed, 20 per cent severely and 40 per cent lightly damaged. Two of the 8 oil terminals would be severely damaged. Of refining capacity, 5 per cent would be destroyed, and 20 and 40 per cent damaged severely and lightly respectively.

Gas storage facilities in the Greater London area would be devastated: 75 per cent would be destroyed and the rest would be severely damaged. Nine of the 14 compressors would be affected, with 2 destroyed and 1 severely damaged.

All the major electricity supply facilities in the Greater London area would be destroyed or severely damaged by blast. Nationally, 10 per cent of power capacity would be destroyed and a further 30 per cent would be lightly damaged.

In scenario 4, up to 90 per cent of domestic energy systems would be destroyed or badly damaged. Nuclear winter would be likely, and almost all windows would be broken, leading to intense cold inside buildings. This, coupled with the failure of all the major energy supply systems, would mean that most surviving Londoners would be faced with exposure.

Scenario 5. It is pointless describing the effects of scenario 5 in detail since it simply amounts to increasing the proportion of destruction within the Greater London area from more than 90 per cent to nearly 100 per cent. The London energy system would be completely destroyed.

However, in the UK as a whole, only about 15 per cent of national mining capacity would be destroyed or severely damaged. Of refining capacity, 10 per cent would be destroyed, 25 per cent severely damaged and 35 per cent lightly damaged. Some 75 per cent of oil stores would be damaged, and 15 per cent would be destroyed.

Overview. GLAWARS concluded that the effects of damage on London's energy would be substantially worse than predicted by the computer model, for a number of reasons. First, the model does not account for multiple bursts, EMP, thermal radiation and fall-out. Secondly, many facilities, such as electricity transformer stations and distribution systems, have been excluded from the model. Thirdly, individual facilities have been treated as single components whereas in reality they are in themselves complex systems. Fourthly, the further the analysis goes, the more interdependency is found. Finally, the behaviour of people in times of tension and war has been ignored. As Barrett (1986) concludes, "even if there is no attack of any kind, energy supply may fail because of people abandoning their posts".

Thus in scenario 1, oil and coal supplies would be relatively secure but gas and especially electricity might be adversely affected by local EMP.

In scenarios 2 and 3, gas and electricity supply would fail because of EMP. A large proportion of domestic energy devices in the Greater London area would be damaged. Nuclear winter, if it occurred, would severely affect all energy supplies.

In scenarios 4 and 5, the extent of damage would be so severe in the Greater London area that almost all domestic energy devices would be damaged or destroyed. The state of national systems would therefore not be very important to London. The few surviving Londoners would be without energy of any kind, except for any solid fuel or timber they could find to burn.

It must be emphasized that if energy and other systems remained substantially intact, it would be likely that the authorities, with their emergency plans, would remain in control. In this case, the public would not be likely to receive energy supplies beyond those required to meet essential needs, and even then only after the needs of emergency services, government and security forces had been met.

Thus, regardless of physical damage to energy facilities, it is probable that public energy supplies would be limited or non-existent in time of high tension or war.

2.3.2 Water

London's water and sewerage systems are complicated, antique and decaying. As with many of London's other systems, the job of keeping pace with the destruction wrought simply by the passage of time is large; destruction from attack, by implication, could easily result in disproportionate damage that might be difficult to repair. A complicating factor is that London is prone to flooding.

London's water comes mainly from two rivers – the Thames (73 per cent) and the Lea (14 per cent). The remaining 13 per cent is provided from boreholes and wells. The water is pumped from these sources to 19 storage reservoirs, with a total capacity of about 208,000 m^3, which are designed to provide reserves for periods when demand exceeds available river water supplies. The quantities of water abstracted from the rivers are governed by statute: the Thames Water Authority, for example, is not allowed to abstract from the Thames below Teddington Lock at all, or from above it when river flow is less than 773,000 m^3 per day. Consequently, a number of major reservoirs and intakes are situated to the west of London, in the area where there are prime military targets. There are ten major water intakes from London's rivers.

From the storage reservoirs, water is taken to 15 water treatment works where it is filtered and disinfected with chlorine. It is then pumped to London's consumers, most of whom live and work on higher ground than the water sources. A complete list of all Greater London pumping stations, for both water and sewage, is included in Lippold (1986). These stations are of considerable interest in a war context because they are above ground, susceptible to blast and frost damage, and mostly operated by electric pumps liable to disruption from EMP or as a result of mains failure. Furthermore, the operation of London's water and sewerage systems is dependent on continuous pumping. As the Thames Water Authority points out

> This presents a pumping problem which is probably unique in the world, for whereas certain other undertakings have to pump large quantities and many have to pump against greater heads, none has to pump from such a multiplicity of sources into a complex distribution system which, like so many other things in London, grew from small beginnings with little coordinated planning.
>
> (Thames Water 1980)

The water distribution system in London consists of some 726,000 km of underground pipes of varying sizes, which carry water at an average pressure equivalent to a head of 91 metres. They deliver about 1,789,000 m^3 of water a day to London's users. Because of the age and complexity of the system, Thames Water is planning a major restructuring of the water supply system in London based on a new ring main with far more reliance on gravity feed. The work has not yet started, however, and could not be completed before the late 1990s.

The sewerage system is even more antiquated, and dates from the 1850s. It consists of some 1280 km of main sewers, many of which are constructed of underground brick vaulted arches built in the 19th century and still in use. Sewage effluent is pumped or flows under gravity to 10 major sewage treatment plants.

The risk of tidal floods in London, and the control systems designed to prevent them, are discussed in section 2.4.4. There is, however, another potential cause of flooding in London. The quantities of water used and discharged in London are decreasing due to the decline of industrial activity in Greater London. This drop in water requirements has already led to a significant rise in London's water table: over the past 15 years, it has risen at the rate of one metre a year, creating potential flooding problems in underground tunnels and basements which are alleviated only by continuous pumping. Should industry be devastated by a nuclear attack, all abstractions would be suspended forthwith, causing an immediate rise in the water table and the threat of floods, exacerbated by the lack of available pumping facilities. In low-lying areas in London, cellars may be far from the best places to seek refuge from nuclear attack.

The effects of attack. The possibilities of poisoning London's water supply with chemical or biological weapons (Perry Robinson 1986) have already been mentioned in Part 1. Because some doubts remain about the probability and effectiveness of using a small number of conventional weapons to destroy London services such as the supply of water, this form of attack was not examined in any further detail.

Historical evidence of the effects of a nuclear attack on water systems is available from Hiroshima and Nagasaki, both in terms of the loss of water supply and the spread of fire.

> The public utility system in Nagasaki was similar to that of a somewhat smaller town in the United States, except that open sewers were used. The most significant damage was suffered by the water supply system, so that it became almost impossible to extinguish fires. Except for a special case, described below, loss of water pressure resulted from breakage of pipes inside and at entrances to buildings or on structures, rather than from the disruption of underground mains. The exceptional case was one in which the 12-inch cast iron water pipes were 3 feet below grade in a filled-in area. A number of depressions, up to 1 foot in depth, were produced in the fill, and these caused failure of the underground pipes, presumably due to unequal displacements . . . There was no appreciable damage to reservoirs and water treatment plants in Japan. As is generally the case, these were located outside the cities, and so were at too great a distance from the explosions to be damaged in any way.
>
> Another contributory factor to the destruction by fire was the failure of the water supply in both Hiroshima and Nagasaki. The pumping stations were not largely affected, but serious damage was sustained by distribution pipes and mains, with a resultant leakage and drop in available water pressure. Most of the lines above ground were broken by collapsing buildings and by heat from the fires which melted the pipes.

> Some buried water mains were fractured and others were broken due to the collapse of bridges upon which they were supported.
>
> (Glasstone and Dolan 1977)

The impacts of the attacks postulated in the GLAWARS scenarios on the water system have been calculated with the help of a computer model designed by Barrett (1986) and described in his report on the energy system (see section 2.3.1). The model uses geographical data on the locations of all the major water and sewerage facilities in the London area. These include pumping stations, service reservoirs, storage reservoirs, wells, recharge wells, filtration works, water intakes and sewage works.

As in the energy model, the computer program prints out for each scenario a list of all the facilities within 15 km of a detonation, specifying overpressure, thermal radiation level, EMP level, distance from the bomb, and the target and yield of the bomb. It also classifies the facility as lightly damaged (less than 2 psi), heavily damaged (2–5 psi) or destroyed (more than 5 psi). Table 20 summarizes the percentages of each type of facility that are either damaged or destroyed in each scenario.

The values assumed for vulnerability to blast are only approximations. In reality, there is a wide variety of facilities to be analysed, and their vulnerability to blast would vary substantially. For instance, buried service reservoirs and underground wells would obviously survive an attack better than surface reservoirs and water intakes at the same location. Nevertheless, even though underground assets might remain intact at a certain overpressure, associated plant such as pumps, workshops and stores could still be destroyed; added to this, structures in the surrounding district could be damaged or destroyed, thereby restricting access to the facility.

Damage by scenario

Scenario 1. None of the water or sewerage facilities would be within the range of blast or fire damage from a bomb because all detonations would occur outside the Greater London area. Scenario 1 is therefore not included in Table 20.

Although there would be no exo-atmospheric bomb burst in scenario 1, there is a possibility that there might be some disruption of electricity supplies caused by EMP from bombs landing outside the area. Stand-by plant, where it exists, would be likely to remain operable and could be brought into action fairly quickly to ensure continuing water supplies.

Fall-out originating from bombs exploding to the south-west would

Table 20 Percentage damage (dam) and destruction (des) to water and sewerage facilities by scenario

Facility	Scenario 2 dam	Scenario 2 des	Scenario 3 dam	Scenario 3 des	Scenario 4 dam	Scenario 4 des	Scenario 5 dam	Scenario 5 des
Service reservoirs (78)	22	–	59	6	45	43	38	62
Storage reservoirs (19)	46	15	89	–	89	11	63	36
Wells (65)	8	1	52	1	62	23	51	47
Recharge wells (8)	–	–	37	–	87	13	25	75
Filtration works (15)	39	–	80	–	73	27	53	47
Water pumping stations (115)	19	–	100	–	60	26	50	50
Intakes (10)	50	–	50	–	100	–	80	20
Sewage works (10)	20	–	50	–	80	20	20	80

Source: data abstracted from Lippold (1986).

be carried by prevailing winds to contaminate reservoirs and treatment works in the Thames Valley west of Greater London.

Scenario 2. Bombs targeted on Heathrow, Stanmore and West Drayton would damage many water facilities to the west of the Greater London area.

The Staines, Wraysbury and King George's reservoirs, and the Hanworth Road well, would all lie within 5 km of the Heathrow bomb. The Hanworth Road well would be destroyed. It is uncertain whether the banks of the Thames at Staines would be breached by the overpressure of about 9 psi that would be experienced there, though this must be a possibility. The Wraysbury and King George's reservoirs would probably stay intact after being subjected to about 4 psi and 7 psi respectively. A number of facilities, including the filtration works at Ashford and Kempton, their associated pumping stations and the pumping station at Staines, would be seriously damaged. Since these areas would be hit by more than one bomb, it is likely that the overpressures involved would be higher than those calculated in the program, which could bring these facilities into the destroyed category. Mill Hill would be the only service reservoir to be seriously damaged.

The EMP pulse received at water facilities from local bombs would be small, except in the vicinity of the Staines and King George's reservoirs. Thermal radiation levels would be too low for spontaneous combustion of building materials to take place. Contamination from fall-out, though, would become a serious problem.

Scenario 3. In this attack the bombs in the west would be of a lower yield than in the previous attack, but additional bombs would fall on Hampstead and Biggin Hill.

The water facilities to the west could probably be counted as damaged but reparable in this instance. More serious damage would be suffered by water facilities towards the centre of London as a result of the Hampstead strike. Service reservoirs and pumping stations at Hampstead, Willesden, Shoot-up Hill and Kidderpore would all be totally destroyed, being only 1–2 km from the epicentre of the bomb. The Biggin Hill bomb's epicentre would be only 1.3 km from the well and pumping station at Jewel's Wood, which would be destroyed. West Wickham (North and South) service reservoirs would suffer the same fate. Water treatment works and storage reservoirs in the Lea Valley would be damaged.

Local EMP would be strong in the neighbourhood of the Hampstead and Biggin Hill explosions, where thermal radiation levels would also be very high. High levels of fall-out could be expected to reach the storage reservoirs and treatment works in the north-east, as well as the facilities in the west.

Scenario 4. Further damage would be caused by bombs to the north, north-west and south-west, while more centrally there would be explosions in Enfield, Whitehall, Kingston and Clapham.

Virtually all facilities would be affected by blast and thermal radiation to some degree. About half of all water facilities would either be badly damaged or destroyed. The only facilities that would suffer less than 1 psi overpressure are situated in the Darenth river valley, just outside the eastern boundary of Greater London.

In this attack, facilities just south of the Thames would be damaged or destroyed, including the wells and pumping stations at Streatham and Merton. Those in the north-east would suffer a similar fate. Putney pumping station and service reservoir would be only 0.8 km from the epicentre of the Kingston bomb, and would be completely destroyed by a massive overpressure of more than 33 psi. Hornsey and Goat Bridge water treatment works would be completely destroyed, as would that at Stoke Newington; the Coppermills treatment works would be almost destroyed. Beddington, Kew and Riverside sewage treatment works would be destroyed. The effects of multiple bomb bursts would, in reality, make the situation considerably worse than even Table 20 implies.

EMP would damage installations throughout Greater London. Fall-out would cover the whole area directly.

Scenario 5. More than 75 per cent of water facilities would be seriously damaged or destroyed. There is little point in listing the destruction of individual plants since the water system would be completely devastated.

The general impact. Among the most serious effects on the water system would be the destruction or disruption of electricity and fuel supplies for use at pumping stations and for communications, and the loss of chemicals for purification. The equipment at pumping stations is expected by the water authority to withstand EMP reasonably well because it is old fashioned; it is also believed that the Thames Water communications system is adequately protected against EMP and would survive an attack. However, as these systems become modernized and more sophisticated, they will also become increasingly susceptible to EMP.

Should high altitude exo-atmospheric bomb bursts accompany scenarios 2 to 5, the whole country would be covered by a strong EMP. This would knock out the electricity and gas systems. Thus, even if water works equipment survived, there would be no mains electricity available to operate pumps and communications networks. Since most plants are now run by electricity, they would be put out of action immediately unless non-electrical stand-by machinery could be brought into immediate operation (and much of this would also have been damaged). Flood warning systems would also be knocked out if electricity and communications networks were damaged.

At water works premises, stores of oil, gas and chemicals would provide fuel for fires, especially if containers were ruptured by blast. Leakages of chlorine gas could damage electrical equipment and prevent fire fighters reaching the plant. Pipes might be melted by the spread of fires. Any sudden losses in water pressure could create pressure surges, and some of the more rigid, older pipework might be ruptured and collapse as a consequence. Shallow pipes could be affected by ground movements.

Even where severe structural damage was not experienced, the water system could still suffer destruction. Underground pipework might be left intact but connections into buildings are very vulnerable. The radius of damage in which buildings are damaged beyond repair is taken by Thames Water as the radius of destruction of the water system – this must be regarded as a minimum distance, however. It is calculated that services (including water services) would be destroyed in 20 per cent of houses in scenario 2; in 30 per cent of houses in scenario 3; in 90 per cent of houses in scenario 4; and in 99 per cent of houses in scenario 5 (Hodgkinson *et al.* 1986). This destruction would be caused by internal damage such as ruptured partitions, smashed floors and fallen ceilings rather than by structural failure; it represents an extremely widespread disturbance of the water system. The sewerage system from buildings would not function at all without mains water.

A further possibility that should be considered is the possible breaching of the Thames banks, with consequent flooding. Freedman (1986) mentions the possibility of a nuclear water burst occurring, whether accidentally or intentionally, in the Thames and resulting in devastating effects – including presumably severe flooding. Breaching of the banks of the Thames is certainly a possibility in GLAWARS scenarios 4 and 5. In fact, some work was undertaken in the early 1950s by members of the Department of Public Health Engineering of the London County Council on the likely impact of a nuclear bomb falling in the Thames and its implications for flood control, but the results are now unavailable.

Radiation would contaminate water through fall-out. The radio-isotopes of iodine, tritium and strontium dissolve in water. Iodine isotopes could pose initial problems but have short half lives. (Further information on radiation effects can be found in Moody 1986.) However, the government and Thames Water believe that radiation in water supplies would pose a smaller hazard than those caused by other sources of radiation present after a nuclear attack; epidemics caused by water-borne diseases could prove more dangerous. 'Contamination of water supplies by radioactive fall-out would be a relatively minor hazard for survivors of a nuclear attack compared with the danger from other sources of radiation in the environment . . . Contamination by bacteria would be a greater health hazard than radioactive contamination of water supplies' (Home Office 1984).

High standards of hygiene, nutrition and health provide good protection against the transmission of disease. The provision of potable water and a separate water-borne system of drainage and sewage disposal, both linked with water resource management, has meant that many water-borne diseases associated with overcrowding, lack of proper sanitation and poor health education have been virtually eliminated. After a nuclear attack, however, some of these diseases, such as diarrhoea, food poisoning, poliomyelitis and typhoid, could be spread through faecal contamination as a result of the sewage system breaking down, fractured sewers leaking into water supplies and the use of make-shift latrines.

Lack of natural immunity to such diseases, the loss of acquired immunity to them as a result of exposure to radiation, overcrowding, poor diet and, especially, the loss of water services following a nuclear attack would produce conditions in which infectious diseases could have devastating effects on the initial survivors of a nuclear war.

Water demand after an attack. Survivors need water for drinking, cooking, personal hygiene, washing and scrubbing of radiation-contaminated articles. Small fires in houses could be dealt with from stocks only if a household had a large enough supply. This seems unlikely.

The population would be advised to stay indoors for the first 72 hours after an attack as a protection against fall-out. During this time, water needs would have to be met from stores gathered before the attack or from whatever water might remain in water systems in buildings. Faeces and urine would have to be disposed of at least 15 metres from any source of water to guard against the spread of infectious diseases. If there were no stores of water in the home, people might be able to collect rainwater for drinking but this would expose them to radiation hazards.

Exposure to radiation causes people to drink more and impairs their immune systems. The body loses fluid due to vomiting, diarrhoea or fever, and drinking water requirements may double. Care of sickness and injuries will require water for hygiene purposes.

Conclusion. In scenario 1, the water system would remain essentially intact. However, there could be some shortage of electricity supplies as a result of EMP damage outside the area, and stand-by equipment run on oil or gas would have to be installed. Radiation contamination from fall-out would affect the water works to the west.

In scenarios 2 and 3, the western water facilities would be put out of action by blast and fire, but those in the east would suffer only slight damage. Nevertheless, EMP would cause most of the system to be disrupted because electricity supplies would fail. The system would be further limited by damage to service pipework in many places. High radiation levels would mean that water from exposed sources should not be drunk.

In scenarios 4 and 5, practically all water facilities would be either damaged or destroyed, as would services to buildings. London's water system would be totally devastated.

2.3.3 Telecommunications

Communications immediately before, during and after an attack would be critically important both to Londoners and to those responsible for organizing emergency services in London. GLAWARS research (Thompson 1986) shows that attempts to communicate with family and friends when disaster threatens are very important in determining how people react and behave (see section 2.6). Furthermore, Home Office plans for civil defence depend critically on a system of communications that is assumed to continue to function after attack. The government has a dedicated war-time communications system (the Emergency Communications Network, ECN) that links regional government headquarters to county and London emergency centres, and to the UK Warning and Monitoring Organization. In addition, local authorities are encouraged to develop plans to make the best use of peace time communications networks, including those of voluntary organizations such as the Radio Amateurs' Emergency Network (Home Office 1985).

A nuclear attack would pose two threats to communications networks. The first is from the electromagnetic pulse (EMP); the second is from the effects of blast and fire.

Damage from EMP. All nuclear detonations produce EMP (see Appendix 6). However, the EMP generated by low-level detonations is only local, with a range of a few kilometres. In scenarios 1 and 2, local EMP damage would be slight. However, according to Willan and Dunne (1986), communications equipment would be badly damaged in scenario 3 and almost totally destroyed in scenarios 4 and 5.

As mentioned in Part 1, however, high altitude, exo-atmospheric nuclear explosions designed solely to damage electronic equipment might be included in all nuclear attacks from scenario 2 on. These would generate very powerful EMP effects over large areas – certainly large enough to affect all electronic equipment within the UK, and possibly within most of Europe as well.

Exo-atmospheric explosions would knock out much of the UK communications network. Very few communications systems in the UK, even those of the emergency services, are protected against EMP. This is largely because such protection is expensive. It relies primarily on shielding or screening equipment, and providing radio frequency filters. Replacing copper cable with fibre optics is also effective, but even more expensive. Furthermore, a communications system is effectively protected only if the receiver, the transmitter and the lines linking the two are all protected. Most damage would be likely to occur where communications equipment was left connected to a power source, a land line or an aerial. The Home Office therefore advises that all communications equipment be disconnected should a nuclear attack appear imminent. While such advice is sound enough, its practicality is dubious, bearing in mind the intense need for communications during the period immediately preceding attack, and the fact that attacks could follow one another at irregular intervals.

Some equipment, however, would obviously survive the effects of EMP or be easily reparable. In fact, there is so much redundancy in existing communications that it is likely that some forms of communications could be re-established after a nuclear attack, even if functioning systems were only put together on an *ad hoc* basis from individual pieces of surviving equipment.

Damage from blast. Detailed modelling of the effects of blast on communications proved difficult for GLAWARS researchers for two reasons. First, even in London alone, there are many thousands of different communications systems. Secondly, considerable secrecy surrounds the operation of even civil communications in the UK; many details of the public phone system, for example, are unavailable to the public even though they are not classified.

An attempt was made, however (Barrett, Nectoux *et al.* 1986), to assemble a telecommunications data base on which to assess blast damage in the event that installations survived EMP. For the reasons already mentioned, this data base is not complete, though it does contain a representative sample of telecommunications facilities in London.

The computer model described in section 2.3.1 was then used to assess blast damage to these facilities. All those within 15 km of a detonation and subjected to 0.2 to 5 psi were regarded as damaged but reparable; those subjected to more than 5 psi were regarded as destroyed. The results are shown in Table 21.

Telecommunications would not be damaged in scenario 1. However, in scenario 2 nearly 40 per cent of London's telephone exchanges would be damaged or destroyed by blast. This, coupled with extensive damage to overhead lines, would effectively put the public telephone system out of action. That system, of course, would not be available to the public either before or during an attack; the Telephone Preference Scheme would be used to preserve the system for use only by government organizations during a war, and for use by government and other select categories during a war scare. It is doubtful, however, whether much use could be made of the system from scenario 2 on.

Radio masts are clearly susceptible to blast damage. Even in scenario 2, around one third would be damaged or destroyed. From scenario 3 on, they would be effectively out of action. These masts fulfil a variety of functions, including radio and television relay, and the servicing of radio networks for the military, police, fire and ambulance stations, and hospitals.

Two of the six national security systems would be destroyed, even in scenario 2. These are the air defence data and air traffic control centre at West Drayton, which would be a specific target and would receive a direct hit; and the Home Office Central Communications Establishment at Wealdstone, Harrow, which would be subjected to more than 10 psi.

Table 21 Percentage damage (dam) and destruction (des) to telecommunications facilities by scenario

Facility	Scenario 2 dam	Scenario 2 des	Scenario 3 dam	Scenario 3 des	Scenario 4 dam	Scenario 4 des	Scenario 5 dam	Scenario 5 des
Telephone:								
Headquarters (2)	–	–	100	–	–	100	–	100
Exchanges (113)	35	4	66	6	51	41	44	53
National security communications (6)[a]	–	33	83	17	17	83	17	83
Microwave communications (6)	–	17	33	17	17	33	–	50
Satellite dishes (1)	–	–	–	–	–	100	–	100
Cable TV relay (1)	–	–	–	–	100	–	–	100
Radio masts:								
free standing, high (29)	26	10	51	17	31	58	28	72
free standing, low (46)	21	17	38	26	36	52	26	74
on buildings, high (78)	17	3	78	3	39	57	27	73
on buildings, low (75)	28	6	53	9	34	49	25	73

[a] four of these are protected underground systems, and would be much more resistant to blast than the figures in this table indicate, though still liable to EMP damage (Willan and Dunne 1986).

Source: Barrett, Nectoux *et al.* 1986.

From scenario 3 on, all six national security systems would be classed as damaged or destroyed (the other four are the BBC underground control centre, the Department of the Environment underground phone exchange, the private government phone exchange and the Ministry of Defence exchange). However, as the latter are underground damage would be very slight in scenario 3; in scenario 4, five would experience pressures of nearly 10 psi, creating damage, and in scenario 5 the same five would be subjected to more than 30 psi, probably sufficient to destroy them.

Overall effects. The combined effects of EMP and blast would deprive London (and the UK) of most of its communications systems. Lack of communications would add greatly to the problems of organizing life in a post-attack environment. Communications play a key role in organizing the efficient use of resources; a lack of communications would therefore result in a considerable waste of resources. It would also have damaging psychological effects, increasing the sense of isolation and helplessness that would inevitably follow nuclear attack.

Finally, the political repercussions of a communications shortage might be very severe (see sections 2.6 and 2.9).

2.3.4 Transport

London's transport depends essentially on roads, railways and the underground, although there are also some 70 wharves in London which might provide some basis for an alternative, post-attack transport system.

London contains about 13,000 km of roads. These are basically resilient to blast, and the system contains many redundancies. This means that, assuming there is little need to enter areas subjected to more than about 5 psi, which would be totally destroyed, ways could be found to continue using the road system, once it had been cleared of debris.

Debris in the road would arise approximately as follows:

pressure (psi)	extent of debris
0.15–1.5	glass and roofing materials
1.5–3.5	some building masonry
3.5 or more	building and vehicle debris covering road

This indicates that bicycles and ordinary (as opposed to military) road vehicles would have difficulties in areas subjected to more than 0.5 psi because of punctures and obstruction. At higher levels of blast, roads would have to be cleared to be usable. Clearing of light debris could be done by hand but bulldozers would be required for heavier debris.

The road system in London is highly robust because of the redundancies in its linkage. Assuming that all bar the narrowest streets are large enough for any vehicle, there is generally a large number of separate routes between one point and another. The exception to this is links involving bridges and tunnels across the Thames and the river Lea. Although bridges and tunnels themselves are relatively resistant to weapons effects, blast would create considerable damage to their approaches and to the superstructure of bridges. One consequence is that crossing the Thames after a nuclear attack, except by boat, is likely to be difficult. Tunnels could be flooded if pumps, or their fuel supplies, failed.

Human powered transport would increase in importance in war-time. Such transport does not need fuel (apart from food) and does not require smooth roadways. People would travel either on foot or by bicycle if roads, or other paths, were in a good enough condition. Makeshift carts or barrows, the familiar accompaniments of any major disaster, would be used for carrying goods.

Travel by car anywhere after a nuclear attack appears extremely unlikely. Cars with electronic ignition would have been damaged by EMP, and many more by blast. Petrol rationing would have been introduced before the attack materialized. After the attack, there appear to be two possibilities. If the attack were minor, and some roads usable, then vestiges of organization would be likely to remain and petrol restrictions would apply. If the attack were major, then survivors could doubtless loot petrol remaining in those filling stations which had been subjected to less than about 5 psi and therefore survived. However, after an attack of this kind, roads would be covered with debris and unusable. Clearing of rubble would take many months or years, if it could be organized (see section 2.2).

Public transport. London's public transport system is one of the most extensive in the world. It includes more than 250 overground railway stations and nearly 1000 km of track. The underground operates 3875 cars running between more than 300 stations and over 400 km of track. The bus system operates more than 5500 buses.

Damage to London's public transport system was assessed using the computer model described in section 2.3.1. A grid referenced data base was assembled which included 60 bus depots, 133 railway junctions, 91 stations, 5 crossings (major railway intersections), 9 depots, 303 underground stations, and 25 bridges and 6 tunnels (Barrett, Nectoux *et al.* 1986). These, essentially, are the nodes of London transport and, whether or not the roads and tracks linking them together were destroyed, the system itself would not function if sufficient of these nodes were substantially damaged. These transport nodes were regarded as damaged but reparable if they were within 15 km of an explosion and subjected to between 0.2 and 5 psi; those subjected to more than 5 psi were regarded as destroyed.

Although the underground system is often assumed to be resistant to blast, this may not be the case. Much of the system in outer London is entirely above ground. Furthermore, although underground tracks are unlikely to be damaged by anything other than a direct hit or near miss, an underground system is of limited use if there is limited access to it (though some services might be kept running by simply ignoring stations to which access had been destroyed). The above-ground structures at which there is access, the stations, are as vulnerable to blast as any other building. Furthermore, there is a likelihood of at least the outer parts of the system flooding (see section 2.4.4), either as a direct result of floods or due to the failure of pumps (or their power supplies) used to keep the tunnels dry.

During World War 2, some 600 people drowned in the underground when a water main was fractured by bombing, leading to flooding.

Connections between British Rail and the underground system have not been analysed. The latter uses British Rail lines extensively outside inner London. There are probably ways of connecting the two systems on all lines.

The damage sustained by the London transport system is summarized in Table 22.

Table 22 Percentage damage (dam) and destruction (des) to transport facilities by scenario

Facility	Scenario 2 dam	Scenario 2 des	Scenario 3 dam	Scenario 3 des	Scenario 4 dam	Scenario 4 des	Scenario 5 dam	Scenario 5 des
Bus depots (60)	31	3	73	8	36	58	25	75
Railways:								
Junctions (133)	26	1	71	5	36	56	32	67
Stations (91)	18	1	67	2	36	52	30	68
Depots (9)	22	–	89	–	67	33	22	78
Crossings (5)[a]	20	20	40	20	20	80	20	80
Underground stations (303)	31	9	78	10	29	66	18	82
Bridges (25)	32	–	100	–	–	100	–	100
Tunnels (6)	–	–	17	–	17	50	33	50

Note: several sites fulfil more than one function; Clapham Junction, for example, is a station, a junction and a depot.
[a] crossings are nodes where there is a high density of track.
Source: Barrett, Nectoux *et al.* 1986.

The interpretation of Table 22 is relatively simple, and highlights dramatically the increased levels of damage incurred in scenario 3 over scenario 2 (though the total yield on London would be smaller in scenario 3, there would be more detonations on London). There would be no damage at all in scenario 1, and only minor damage in scenario 2, although eight bridges at Barnes, Chiswick, Kew, Richmond and Kingston would suffer minor damage from blasts of 1–2 psi. However, the electricity system would be likely to fail in scenario 2 (see 2.3.1); this means that the underground, and parts of British Rail that depend entirely on electric trains, could provide no service until power was restored.

By scenario 3, three-quarters of most of London's transport nodes would have been damaged or destroyed. Seventy per cent of London's railway stations would be at least temporarily out of action, as would nearly all the underground stations. Victoria, London Bridge, Liverpool Street, Blackfriars and Waterloo stations would all be subject to minor damage, probably sufficient to put them out of action for some time. Paddington and Marylebone Stations would receive a blast of more than 3 psi from the Hampstead bomb, and would be severely damaged. King's Cross and St Pancras would receive 2 psi, sufficient to cause considerable damage. Furthermore, all London's bridges would be damaged, though not permanently. The Rotherhithe tunnel would also receive minor damage.

London transportation would stop operating after scenario 3. In scenarios 4 and 5, the total numbers of railway nodes affected would increase marginally, but the damage would be very much heavier. All London bridges would be destroyed in both scenarios 4 and 5, most of them receiving blasts of considerably more than 10 psi from bombs falling on Whitehall and Kingston. Three tunnels – Blackwall, Greenwich and Rotherhithe – would be destroyed, the last receiving a blast of more than 20 psi. At this level of damage, as was made clear in section 2.2, it is unlikely that the London transport system would ever be rebuilt.

2.3.5 Food and agriculture

Londoners who survived a nuclear attack would almost immediately face a problem of food shortage. Though they would have been advised to stock up with 14 days' food supplies, it seems unlikely that this would prove possible for many. About 40 per cent of London's food sales are now from supermarkets, which hold only between 1 and 3 days' supplies. Milk and vegetables are brought to the city daily. Furthermore, London's involvement in food processing has been rapidly declining, so there are few large stocks of unprocessed food in the city. Even if there were, attempts to obtain food from them would be an offence under emergency legislation.

Ministry of Agriculture, Fisheries and Food (MAFF) buffer depots are estimated to contain, for the whole of the UK, sufficient to supply basic calorie requirements for 40 million people for 16 days – but there is no government guarantee that such stocks would be available for local use, the stocks do not represent a balanced diet and there are doubts about the usability of their contents (Campbell 1983). There are considerable food stocks within EEC warehouses in the UK, but their location is officially secret (though not classified). They contain several million tonnes of barley and wheat, stored in 330 warehouses in and around 122 towns and cities in the UK (*The Sunday Times* 1985). Although plans exist for the creation of borough emergency feeding centres, mostly in schools and churches, it is hard to imagine how food would be distributed to them after a nuclear attack.

Within perhaps only a few days of a nuclear attack, therefore, surviving Londoners would be dependent on food brought in from outside the city. In peace time, some 65 per cent of UK food is produced within the country, the remainder being imported from abroad. Imports would be expected to cease for a period of at least a year after nuclear war, and the UK population, including Londoners, would then become totally dependent on UK farm produce. GLAWARS therefore investigated the likely direct effects (excluding those of nuclear winter) of the five nuclear scenarios on farm production in England and Wales (Barrett, Fergusson, Greene and Lippold 1986).

The study was carried out using a computer model of similar design to the one used to calculate human casualties (see section 2.1). Two runs were made, one calculating the effects on all farms in England and Wales, the other restricting calculations to those farms within 100 km of Trafalgar Square. The latter is likely to provide the more useful information in view of the considerable difficulties that would be expected in transporting food over long distances after nuclear attack.

The agricultural model. Agricultural data were taken from the Ministry of Agriculture, Fisheries and Food map of agriculture in England and Wales (MAFF 1978). This map shows the position, type and area of each farm in England and Wales. A 10-km square grid was positioned over the map and estimates made for each square of the percentage of land devoted to agriculture (to the nearest 10 per cent) and the proportions of this land used for each of the three main farming activities within the square. This provided a reasonably accurate picture of what type of farming occurs where in the UK. The technique, however, does tend to underestimate the more minor agricultural activities, such as pig and poultry production, which rarely feature as one of the three most important activities in any square. Table 23 shows the total current production figures thus obtained for England and Wales, and for the area within 100 km of Trafalgar Square.

As in the calculation of human casualties, the effects of heat, blast and fall-out were then calculated for each type of farming activity in each square. The technique followed that of Steadman, Greene and Openshaw (1986) closely (see section 2.1), and only the differences from that model are discussed here. The technical details of assumptions made about the sensitivities of livestock and crops to heat, blast and radiation can be found in Barrett, Fergusson, Greene and Lippold (1986). Some of the more interesting aspects of the problem are discussed below.

Table 23 Estimates of current agricultural production[a]

Type of farming	England and Wales	Area within 100 km of Trafalgar Square
Predominantly dairying	944,700	49,100
Mainly dairying	1,800,000	243,400
Cattle	9,409,500	552,500
Sheep	24,557,100	576,300
Pigs	6,991,900	2,096,400
Cereals	18,161,900	6,355,600

[a] figures are in head of stock and, for cereals, in tonnes of annual production
Source: Barrett, Fergusson, Greene and Lippold (1986).

In modelling human casualty rates, it is conventional to consider the effects of gamma radiation alone. This is because it is assumed that people will find some sort of shelter after the attack so that fall-out dust will not actually settle on them. It is also assumed that fall-out dust is not ingested through contaminated air, water or food. In estimating animal casualties, these assumptions would lead to serious errors. Fall-out dust would settle on crops and animals in pasture, and farm animals (particularly ruminants) are likely to ingest substantial quantities of fall-out. The additional dose from beta radiation was therefore included in the agricultural model. Details of how this was done can be found in Barrett, Fergusson, Greene and Lippold (1986).

Secondly, the season of the attack would have a considerable effect on agricultural damage. In the winter, cereals would be little affected and many livestock would be housed, providing them some protection against heat and radiation but exposing them to the dangers of fires, which are notoriously easily started in farm buildings. In the summer, cereals might be severely affected by heat, blast and radiation; livestock would be exposed to all three but would be less likely to be trapped in buildings. To take this into account accurately, it would be necessary to specify the month of the attack and to allow for the different latitudes of each explosion. The GLAWARS model allowed more simply for differing effects during four seasons: winter, spring, early summer and late summer. It also distinguished between animals in the open, those in pens or under light cover, and those housed.

If an animal is seriously injured by two bombs, or by two different effects, then it is assumed to die. This seems reasonable because all injuries counted in the model are severe. Although farmers and vets would be quite unlikely to treat any but a few livestock injuries after a nuclear war, the model assumes that those injured do survive. Tables 24 and 25, which show overall livestock and cereal losses, however, treat both deaths and injuries as constituting a loss.

Cattle. It is assumed that some 25 per cent of animals outside would be shielded from thermal radiation by hedges or trees. Thus a maximum of 75 per cent of the cattle in pasture can be affected by the heat from a given nuclear fireball (though it may be a different 75 per cent for each bomb). This assumption is clearly very conservative for dry weather, though more realistic for wet weather when livestock tend to use any shelter they can.

Cattle in barns are assumed to be affected only by fires ignited by the heat from the fireball. The heat intensity at which these fires begin to be ignited is assumed to be 7 cal/cm^2. Since dry straw can be set on fire at 4–6 cal/cm^2, this effect is unlikely to have been exaggerated.

The indirect effects of blast would be the most significant source of casualties. Roof tiles, glass, timbers or branches could be smashed into the animals by high winds, or the animals could be physically lifted by the winds and then injured. Trees are flattened or stripped of their branches in blast areas of about 2–3 psi, corresponding to winds of 110–160 km/h. At 4 psi, the maximum wind speeds would be about 220 km/h, and at 6 psi they would be 300 km/h. Cattle in pasture are assumed to be at risk of injury for blast levels of more than 3 psi, and deaths start at 5 psi. All animals are assumed killed or injured in winds of greater than 400 km/h (corresponding to 10 psi), and all are killed at more than 20 psi.

Taking account of beta burns and the ingestion of fall-out, the effective LD_{50} for cattle in pasture is 2 gray. Cattle inside buildings are partially protected from the effects of both beta and gamma radiation. For such cattle, the LD_{50} is assumed to be 5 gray. An undamaged barn is assumed to reduce the outside radiation dose by a protection factor (PF) of 3. If the building had been subjected to blast pressures of 1–2 psi, the PF is assumed to be 2, and a PF of 1.5 is assumed where overpressures are greater than 2 psi.

Sheep. The casualty rates for sheep due to thermal radiation and blast are assumed to be the same as for cattle. This can be only approximately true: sheep might be less susceptible to the effects of blast, for example, but their pastures are less likely to afford protection from thermal radiation. Taking account of beta radiation and ingestion, the LD_{50} for pasturing sheep is about 2.5 gray. All are expected to die at doses of more than about 5 gray. Sheep inside buildings are thought to have an effective LD_{50} of about 4 gray, and the same protection factors are assumed as for cattle. All sheep are assumed to be either injured or killed by radiation doses of more than about 3 gray.

Pigs and poultry. If outside, pigs would tend to be burned by lower thermal radiation intensities than cattle or sheep. It is assumed that some 25 per cent of pigs outside would be shielded by buildings or other obstacles from the direct heat from the nuclear fireball. Burn injuries are assumed to begin at more than 4 cal/cm^2 and deaths at 6 cal/cm^2. All exposed animals are assumed to die if subjected to more than 10 cal/cm^2.

Pigs inside sties are assumed to be vulnerable to asphyxiation or burns from fires. Fires are assumed to kill 25 per cent of the sheltered pigs in an area subjected to more than 12 cal/cm^2.

The blast casualty rates for pigs are assumed to be the same as those for cattle. However, pigs inside buildings depend on human care and electricity (for ventilation and heating). All pigs inside and in an area subjected to more than 2 psi are assumed to be killed because of the absence of electrical power.

Pigs tend to be more resistant to radiation than cattle and sheep. The effective LD_{50} for pigs outside is about 5.5 gray. All pigs would die in areas where they would receive more than about 9 gray. Pigs inside or in semi-cover are assumed to have an LD_{50} of 6.4 gray. In semi-cover, the PF is assumed to be 2 where the blast is less than 1 psi, 1.5 for areas subjected to 1–2 psi, and where overpressures would be more than 2 psi the pigs are treated as if they were in the open. Pigs inside more robust buildings are taken to benefit from PFs of 3 in undamaged areas and from PFs of 2 where the blast is between 1 and 2 psi. If the blast were more than 2 psi, such pigs are assumed dead anyway.

The same assumptions have been made for poultry as for pigs because they are farmed in essentially similar ways.

Cereals. For cereals, the model estimates losses in yield. The discussion below assumes that the cereals are spring sown. The model for winter-sown cereals can be deduced by taking the casualty rates for one season in advance.

The heat from the fireball can reduce cereal yield either if it singes and damages the crop or if it starts fires that consume or injure the crop. In winter, it is assumed that there would be no damage because the seed would be protected by the soil. This assumption would be inaccurate if fires were so intense that seed beds were destroyed. Though this is possible, it is rather unlikely. In spring, fires are unlikely to take hold amongst the green shoots, and the crop is likely to recover, at least partially. It is assumed that there would be no yield reductions for thermal intensities of less than 9 cal/cm^2: the maximum loss of yield is assumed to be 40 per cent of normal, and this is reached only in areas subjected to more than 12 cal/cm^2.

In early summer, the plants would still be green, and so fires are likely to die quickly. However, plants that are burned or singed by the heat are less likely to recover than in spring, and the ears of the plants may be injured. Yield losses are therefore likely to be large in areas subjected to high thermal intensities. Where the heat intensity is greater than 15 cal/cm^2, it is assumed that the whole yield is lost.

Crops are most vulnerable to fire in late summer. Once fires are started, they could spread rapidly. Dry grasses can be ignited by thermal radiation intensities of about 6 cal/cm^2 (Glasstone and Dolan 1977). The model assumes that yield reductions begin at that level, and increase to 100 per cent where the heat intensity is greater than 12 cal/cm^2. The model assumes, conservatively, that any fires started would not spread beyond the initial fire zone.

The likely effects of blast on cereal yield can be estimated from data on the usual effects of lodging on yield due to high winds. The data show that winds are unlikely to have any effect in spring (or winter). The more fully grown plants are, however, liable to lodging by winds, either through stem lodging (where the stems are broken) or root lodging (where the roots are dislodged). In damp soil, the root anchorage is much reduced, and root lodging can occur even in winds of less than 50 km/h, which would be generated by about 1 psi. Some lodging is virtually certain at 2–3 psi.

It is unusual for lodging to result in yield losses of more than 30–40 per cent, and so the model assumes a 30 per cent loss of yield in areas subjected to more than 3 psi, going down to no loss below 2 psi for cereals in early or late summer.

Considerable controversy surrounds the sensitivity of cereals to radiation, particularly beta radiation. Technical details can be found in Barrett, Fergusson, Greene and Lippold (1986). The values adopted were chosen to be between the yield reductions in wheat, which is relatively vulnerable to radiation, and oats and rye, which are less vulnerable. Intermediate yield reduction values would apply to barley. Yield is most vulnerable to radiation in early summer, when the ears are forming. In late summer, when growth has effectively stopped, crops are relatively immune to the effects of radiation.

Results of the study. The computer model produced results in three forms: it listed, by type of farming activity and for each scenario, areas affected by different blast levels; the percentage of farm land affected by different blast levels; and numbers of livestock killed or injured (and cereal crop losses in kilotonnes). As already mentioned, the results were calculated for each of four seasons, for all of England and Wales, and for the area within 100 km of Trafalgar Square.

Tables 24 and 25 summarize some of these data, taking all livestock killed or injured as losses. Comments on individual scenarios are included below.

Scenario 1. Although this attack totals only 8 Mt in yield, its effect on certain types of agricultural production would be significant: almost all the detonations would be directed against military targets in non-urban areas; much of the total yield would be in the form of ground bursts; and most of the weapons would fall to the south-east of a line from the Severn to the Humber.

This pattern is reflected in the results. Whereas only a few per cent of grazing land would be subjected to any significant effects – and sheep farming would be virtually untouched – up to 30 per cent of the total area in England and Wales devoted to cereals, cropping, and pig and poultry farming would experience noticeable (though often minor) effects.

Of the area subjected to blast and thermal radiation, a large part would suffer major damage. In some areas, radiation doses would be high enough to kill crops, and over most of the affected areas many animals would die or be injured.

As a result, the computer model predicts a yield loss of around 8 per cent for cereals for an attack during the growing season, representing a loss of about 1.4 million tonnes. For the area within 100 km of London, the percentage figure would be even higher at 10.4 per cent (equivalent to 650,000 tonnes). These figures accurately reflect the fact that damage would be most intense in the southern parts of the cereal growing areas, where the weapons effects would also be at their greatest.

Pigs and poultry, being far more susceptible to radiation than crops, would predictably have very high mortality rates in the areas affected by fall-out. They would also be susceptible to blast and fire damage if housed. Nonetheless, the figure of around 30 per cent losses may be too high for this category because the concentration of production in worst hit areas may have been exaggerated by the mapping technique used. A lower figure may be more reasonable in the light of the distribution of weapons effects.

Scenario 2. In this scenario, the most important differences would be likely to arise from the additional attacks on west London and High Wycombe, on the one hand, and on the Midlands (Rugby and Croughton) on the other. These changes are reflected in the percentages of land that would be affected by the attack which increase by around 4

Table 24 Percentage agricultural losses in England and Wales[a]

	scenario 1				scenario 2				scenario 3				scenario 4				scenario 5			
	W	S	ES	LS	W	S	ES	LS	W	S	ES	LS	W	S	ES	LS	W	S	ES	LS
Predominantly dairying	2.8	1.1	1.1	1.4	3.1	1.2	1.2	1.5	36.9	20.2	20.2	22.6	43.9	25.7	25.7	28.3	48.4	28.7	28.7	31.5
Mainly dairying	6.6	3.9	3.9	4.3	9.2	5.5	5.5	6.1	45.5	24.8	24.8	27.7	50.1	29.2	29.2	32.2	53.9	33.3	33.3	36.3
Cattle	3.0	1.8	1.8	1.9	6.4	3.7	3.7	4.1	26.9	13.3	13.3	15.2	29.2	15.0	15.0	17.0	31.9	17.1	17.1	19.2
Sheep	0.0	0.0	0.0	0.0	0.0	0.0	0.0	0.0	2.6	1.5	1.5	1.5	3.8	2.6	2.6	2.6	5.6	4.1	4.1	4.1
Pigs (and poultry)	31.0	30.0	30.0	30.0	34.9	33.8	33.8	33.8	73.3	71.3	71.3	71.3	77.4	75.4	75.4	75.4	83.0	81.0	81.0	81.0
Cereals	0.0	8.1	7.7	3.8	0.0	9.7	9.3	4.7	0.0	19.7	19.0	10.0	0.0	20.7	21.4	13.4	0.0	21.8	24.3	17.3

[a] losses are percentages of head of stock and annual production of cereals
W = winter (November to February) S = spring (March and April)
ES = early summer (May to July) LS = late summer (August to October)
Source: data from Barrett, Fergusson, Greene and Lippold 1986.

Table 25 Percentage agricultural losses within 100 km of Trafalgar Square[a]

	scenario 1				scenario 2				scenario 3				scenario 4				scenario 5			
	W	S	ES	LS	W	S	ES	LS	W	S	ES	LS	W	S	ES	LS	W	S	ES	LS
Predominantly dairying	21.6	15.8	15.8	16.6	25.2	17.8	17.8	18.9	58.4	44.8	44.8	46.7	62.6	49.7	49.7	51.5	63.0	51.4	51.4	53.1
Mainly dairying	25.5	19.5	19.5	20.3	34.6	27.1	27.1	28.1	63.2	48.1	48.1	50.2	66.9	52.7	52.7	54.7	68.7	55.6	55.6	57.4
Cattle	19.4	16.7	16.7	17.1	31.6	23.8	23.8	24.9	55.9	39.3	39.3	41.6	61.3	44.6	44.6	47.0	62.6	45.9	45.9	48.3
Sheep	0.0	0.0	0.0	0.0	0.0	0.0	0.0	0.0	2.4	0.9	0.9	0.9	2.4	0.9	0.9	0.9	2.4	0.9	0.9	0.9
Pigs (and poultry)	47.1	45.9	45.9	45.9	57.3	55.9	55.9	55.9	91.5	89.3	89.3	89.3	91.6	89.4	89.4	89.4	91.7	89.7	89.7	89.7
Cereals	0.0	10.5	10.2	5.2	0.0	13.7	13.4	7.3	0.0	26.0	24.7	12.2	0.0	26.5	25.9	14.3	0.0	28.5	30.9	21.3

[a] losses are percentages of head of stock and annual production of cereals
W = winter (November to February) S = spring (March and April)
ES = early summer (May to July) LS = late summer (August to October)
Source: data from Barrett, Fergusson, Greene and Lippold 1986.

per cent for all weapons effects for the categories of pigs, poultry and cereals.

Loss in cereal production is predicted to be around 9.5 per cent for an attack during either spring or early summer, declining to half this figure in late summer. Deaths and injuries amongst pigs and poultry would again be high, and it is expected that cropping and horticultural losses would be in line with those for cereals.

Notwithstanding the concentration of the most intensive dairy farming in the west country, the effect on production in this category would also be increased in this attack. This would be especially so for dairy farming in the 'mainly dairying' category, which is more common in the east and south-east. For this reason, losses reach 9.2 per cent in a winter attack, when dairy herds tend to be brought into shelter, and hence are more vulnerable in some respects.

This effect would be seen even more markedly in those areas closest to London, where losses of both dairying and cattle rearing would exceed 30 per cent for an attack in the winter, or around 25 per cent for attacks at other times of the year. This high figure is borne out by the data on the physical effects, which show around 30 per cent of the area of production to be affected by blast and/or thermal radiation, and approaching 25 per cent by significant radiation.

Scenario 3. Scenario 3 represents a dramatic escalation by comparison to scenario 2. Not only would the total yield be increased by nearly 140 per cent, but the number of weapons would be more than trebled. While still concentrated on the south-eastern half of England, a significant number of weapons would also be detonated in the south-west, the west Midlands, the north-west and in Yorkshire. As a result, more than two-thirds of the area devoted to cereals, cropping, and pig and poultry farming would be affected by blast or thermal radiation, with more than 40 per cent suffering significant effects from fall-out. Large areas of livestock production would also be affected by lethal levels of fall-out.

In the area around London, the position would be even worse, with about half of the area devoted to livestock and dairying being affected by some or all of the main weapons effects.

Reduction in cereal yields would approach 20 per cent (or about 3.5 million tonnes) for an attack during the growing season, or half that figure in late summer. Pig and poultry stocks would be reduced by more than 70 per cent, representing approximately 5 million deaths or injuries amongst pigs alone.

Sheep would still be only marginally affected, but losses of cattle and dairy cows would be significant. During the warmer seasons, stock losses in these categories would approach 1.9 million head, or twice that figure for a winter attack. In the latter case, well over half of the total was calculated to be injured rather than killed. However, with veterinary care likely to be wholly inadequate to the scale of injuries, most of the injured animals would have to be destroyed or left to die.

The effects on reduction of stock would be worse for the area near London for all categories except sheep farming. Thus, cereal yield would be reduced by around 25 per cent (1.5 million tonnes) if such an attack were to occur during the growing season, and a similar reduction might be expected for other crops. Total stock losses of dairy cows and cattle would reach about 42 per cent in the same season, or 58 per cent in winter. Barely 10 per cent of pigs or poultry would survive in any season.

Sheep farming presents a notable exception to this pattern in the south-east. Within 100 km of London, sheep farming is concentrated in Kent, which would still be quite lightly affected (especially by fall-out), and stock losses might be only a few per cent. This would leave an estimated population of around half a million head of relatively healthy sheep, which might be a major source of nutrition for the surviving population of London.

Scenario 4. The total yield in scenario 4 would be double that of scenario 3. However, all the extra bombs would be air bursts, and they would be targeted specifically against the larger conurbations. Thus, there would be no increase in the areas affected by fall-out for any category of land use. Similarly, although the additional weapons would all be of 1 Mt yield, and would thus produce high levels of blast and thermal radiation, the most intense effects would be felt in urban rather than agricultural areas. The biggest changes in terms of area affected would be in dairying and cattle rearing, where areas unaffected by blast or thermal radiation would be reduced by between 2.5 and 7.5 per cent. These changes reflect the increased intensity of attack in the Midlands, South Wales and the south-east, along with the air burst at Hawthorn near Bath, one of the few large bombs to be detonated directly over a rural area.

In the dairying and cattle categories, losses in a winter attack would exceed four million head – one third of the original total. Summer losses would be much lower, at 18 per cent. Losses in other categories would be similar to those in scenario 3.

Once again, the position would be rather worse in the immediate vicinity of London. In a winter attack, more than 62 per cent of all cattle and dairy cows would be lost, with a figure of 47 per cent (400,000 head) for a spring or summer war. Losses of pigs or poultry would be about 90 per cent, and cereal yields could be reduced by 25 per cent, in a spring or summer attack.

Scenario 5. Despite the addition of a further 25 Mt of yield, the total of ground bursts would remain unchanged; and so, therefore, would the amount of fall-out and the area affected by fall-out radiation.

In this scenario, though, overpressures of 1–2 psi would be experienced over a much wider area; while this would kill few animals outright, it would cause serious damage to enclosures and shelters, thereby reducing protection factors for livestock under cover. Hence deaths from radiation would be likely to increase, even if fall-out levels did not.

For most categories of land use, more than 50 per cent of the land would suffer some effects. Once again, the main exceptions would be sheep (89 per cent unaffected) and cattle (66 per cent unaffected). The most significant effect from the addition of a number of high-yield air bursts would be on the areas suffering lethal levels of thermal radiation. Some 11 per cent of all dairying land, and 11 to 12 per cent of all crop-growing areas, would experience thermal radiation levels in excess of 12 cal/cm^2 – a level high enough to kill livestock and destroy crops outright.

However, the immediate effects of an attack of this sort would be far less serious for agriculture than for human life itself. Cereal production, for example, is calculated to be cut by only 25 per cent even during a summer attack of this severity, and less at other times. This is not perhaps surprising in view of the high resistance of cereals to radiation, and it seems that a very large number of bombs would be needed to wipe out cereal production by the effects of blast, fall-out and thermal radiation alone. It should also be noted that the ceiling would barely exceed 30 per cent even within 100 km of London, where the intensity of attack would be higher than average.

Pig and poultry farming would be very badly hit, and are calculated to be reduced to 20 per cent of the current stock throughout England and Wales, and as low as 10 per cent in the area around London. For other livestock, however, the situation would be less severe. Fifty per cent of all dairy cows are calculated to be killed or injured in a winter attack, reducing to 30 per cent in summer. The position would be less serious for beef cattle, with losses below 20 per cent for most of the year, and not reaching one third even in the winter months.

Even with an attack of this scale, the stock of sheep would be virtually unaffected. In a winter attack, more than 23 million head of sheep would be uninjured, and up to half a million of these could be within 100 km of London, in east Kent and other areas.

It should be stressed, however, that livestock would be most seriously affected by fall-out, and that all the above figures are based on the assumption of a west-south-west wind.

Other causes of damage. The short-term physical effects of nuclear attack described above would, of course, be supplemented – possibly very substantially – by damage to the country's infrastructure; in addition, long-term radiation damage would cause illness in animals over many months, and toxic radiation products could accumulate in both animals and plants. The possible effects of a nuclear winter are discussed separately in sections 2.7 and 2.8.

Much of the UK's agricultural production relies on inputs from other sectors of the economy. The most important are fuels, agrochemicals, water, veterinary services and engineering maintenance.

The effects of the attacks on fuel supply have already been discussed (section 2.3.1). Gas is not essential for most agricultural processes but electricity is used in milking, drying, cooling, ventilation and milling. Liquid fuels are essential for powering tractors, combine harvesters and other machinery. The absence of electricity and diesel fuel would bring most British farms to a standstill.

Most livestock farms also rely on large quantities of animal feed. After a nuclear attack, these would be unlikely to be available or deliverable. Mixed farms could perhaps rely on barley or oats as a substitute but, unless fuel were available for milling to more digestible forms, their use as animal feed would be very inefficient.

The transport of food from farms to London raises many political and technical problems. The first is whether stocks of food would be released from farming areas for use in London. This would depend on the situation outside London and on how regional authorities saw future supply problems over periods up to several years after attack.

The transport of food to London could be limited by shortage of fuels and electricity, and by damage to road and rail. An alternative is water transport because its routes (sea and canal) are less susceptible to damage and because the use of sail and animal power (on canals) could partly replace motors. Canals and coastal shipping (for example, from the Wash and East Anglia up the Thames) could therefore become important.

The GLAWARS computer model included only the short-term direct effects on agriculture. Damage to the UK economy and infrastructure would not only increase short-term losses but also reduce yield and area farmed for most products. The subsequent losses could be as large or larger than losses due to direct effects. Furthermore, a nuclear winter could reduce production to almost nothing. The losses estimated above should therefore be taken as minima. If there were a long-term shortage of liquid fuels and agrochemicals, UK agriculture would revert to a low productivity system, dependent on animal and human power, similar to that which existed in the 19th century. Few farmers still have the necessary skills to practise this form of agriculture.

References

Barrett, M., *GLAWARS Task 3: Energy Services in London in Wartime*. London, South Bank Polytechnic, 1986, mimeo.

Barrett, M., Fergusson, M., Greene, O., and Lippold, C., *GLAWARS Task 3: The effects of nuclear attack on agriculture in England and Wales*. London, South Bank Polytechnic, 1986, mimeo.

Barrett, M., Nectoux, F., Lippold, C., with Flood, M., and Uden, J., *GLAWARS Technical Supplement: the effect of nuclear attack on certain systems in the Greater London area*. London, South Bank Polytechnic, 1986, mimeo.

Campbell, D., *War Plan UK*. London, Paladin, 1983.

Freedman, L., *GLAWARS Task 1: The Military Threat*. London, South Bank Polytechnic, 1986, mimeo.

Glasstone, S., and Dolan, P., *The effects of nuclear weapons*. Washington DC, US Government Printing Office, Washington, 1977.

Hodgkinson, S., Fergusson, M., Nectoux, F., with Barrett, M., and Greene, O., co-ordinator Howes, R., *GLAWARS Task 5: The impact of a nuclear attack on London's built environment*. London, South Bank Polytechnic, 1986, mimeo.

Home Office, *Consolidated Circular to Local Authorities on Emergency Planning*. London, HMSO, 1984.

Home Office, *Emergency Planning Guidance to Local Authorities*. London, Home Office, 1985.

Kerr, D. B., *GLAWARS Task 3: Conventional attack*. London, South Bank Polytechnic, 1986, mimeo.

Lippold, C., *GLAWARS Task 3: London's Water System and the Effects of a Nuclear Attack*. London, South Bank Polytechnic, 1986, mimeo.

Loizos, Peter, and Marsh, Alan, *GLAWARS Task 4: Concern with the Unthinkable*. London, South Bank Polytechnic, 1986, mimeo.

MAFF, *Types of Farms in England and Wales*. London, MAFF, 1978.

MacDougall, F., and Hastings, S., *GLAWARS Task 10: The economic, social, and political consequences of the scenarios upon the London system*. London, South Bank Polytechnic, 1986, mimeo.

Moody, Richard, *GLAWARS Task 9: The Short and Medium Term Availability of Water as a Factor in Recovery*. London, South Bank Polytechnic, 1986, mimeo.

Perry Robinson, J. P., *GLAWARS Task 3: An assessment of the chemical and biological warfare threat to London*. London, South Bank Polytechnic, 1986, mimeo.

Steadman, P., Greene, O., and Openshaw, S., *GLAWARS Task 3: Computer predictions of damage and casualties in London*. London, South Bank Polytechnic, 1986, mimeo.

Thames Water, Metropolitan Water Division, *A Description of the Undertaking*. London, Thames Water Authority, 1980.

The Sunday Times, 'Grain hoard that costs taxpayers £72 million a year'. London, 17 November 1985.

Thompson, J., *GLAWARS Task 4: The behaviour of Londoners in a future major war:*

estimates from psychological research. London, South Bank Polytechnic, 1986, mimeo.
Water Authorities Association, *The Water Industry in Figures*. London, Water Authorities Association, 1984.
Willan, P., and Dunne, R., *GLAWARS Task 3: Communications and transport*. London, South Bank Polytechnic, 1986, mimeo.

2.4 Damage to emergency services

GLAWARS investigated the effects of nuclear attack on four emergency services; fire, police, ambulances and flood control. A computer model was used to assess levels of damage to the physical infrastructure of the services concerned (Barrett, Nectoux *et al.* 1986). Two provisos should be borne in mind when interpreting these figures. First, their accuracy is intended to be only indicative. Secondly, some organizations proved reluctant to participate in these studies, either because they felt their own plans would not stand up to analysis or because they believed issues of security to stand in the way. For this reason, some of the data bases on which the computer models are based are incomplete. GLAWARS is nevertheless confident that the samples included are sufficiently representative to provide a relatively undistorted picture.

The computer results therefore provide a rough indication of the extent to which the emergency services described below would be disrupted by the direct blast effects of nuclear attacks. They do not, however, tell the whole story.

All emergency services depend critically on good communications. While many communications facilities would be destroyed by blast, it is likely that many more would be destroyed by EMP. In the event of an exo-atmospheric nuclear explosion designed to generate EMP, it is likely that virtually all emergency services communications would be damaged or destroyed, for none of these services has made serious attempts to protect its equipment from EMP. Local EMP could also be expected to cause serious damage. According to Willan and Dunne (1986), local EMP would cause extensive disruption to communications in scenario 3, and knock out virtually all but highly protected communications systems in scenarios 4 and 5 (see section 2.3.3). These effects should be added to those predicted for blast damage. In many ways, they would be more important: police, fire and ambulance staff are virtually helpless if they cannot communicate with their superiors or one another.

The effect of damage on function is also complicated by factors of interdependency. All the services described in this section depend for their success on mutual co-operation, sometimes to a marked degree. Damage to a part of this super-system would therefore have ripple down effects throughout all the other parts. The extent of these effects cannot be predicted but it should be noted.

Finally, damage to any system is in some sense cumulative. As with the human body, localized damage can be absorbed without undue loss of function. But where multiple injuries occur, even small ones, the effects on function begin to mount, resulting in first incapacity and eventually even death. It it not possible to predict the point at which any of the services described here would cease to function completely, though it would be a safe guess that damage levels of somewhere between 30 and 70 per cent would cause any system to be abandoned. As will become apparent, none of the services would continue to function after an attack of the intensity of scenarios 4 and 5. On the other hand, they certainly would function after scenarios 1 and 2. Scenario 3 is the difficult case, and is considered in more detail in section 2.10.

2.4.1 Fire services

The London Fire Brigade reports directly to the GLC. After the latter's abolition in 1986, the Brigade will report to the new London Fire and Civil Defence Authority.

The brigade itself comprises some 7000 officers working at 114 fire stations which house about 350 appliances. In addition, the Home Office has in storage a number of Green Goddess fire appliances reserved exclusively for civil defence work. These would be brought into use with the London Fire Brigade after attack. These are old, petrol engine models without electronic controls and would be likely to survive the effects of EMP.

The brigade is organized into 11 divisions. There are currently three mobilizing control centres – at Croydon, Wembley and Stratford – which receive incoming emergency calls. Information on the location of each individual appliance is stored at these centres, which are thus able to direct the nearest appliances to attend fires. From 1986, these centres will be dismantled in favour of one central computerized control to be located in the Lambeth headquarters. There will be a manual back-up facility in Clapham.

Unlike the police and ambulance services, the brigade does not currently operate a policy of dispersal in the case of nuclear attack. Its 114 stations are, in fact, widely dispersed over the London area. The Home Office has requested that a list of safe havens be compiled within the London area, to which appliances could go for safety if caught in the open during an attack. As of late 1985, however, the location of these havens had not been identified.

The brigade's communications are serviced by a dedicated underground phone system that links all fire stations with one another, and with divisional and brigade headquarters. Radio communications between appliances and control centres can be monitored at the Lambeth headquarters, and a system of walkie-talkies with a range of some 3 km is also in use. The brigade's radio frequencies are to be re-allocated in 1988 and all radio equipment will have to be replaced then, as will hill-top receivers amd transmitters. The new equipment, of which 2000 units have already been ordered nation-wide, will be the same as the police system. This chance to protect fire-fighting communications from the effects of EMP has, however, apparently been ignored. According to Willan and Dunne (1986), 'the London fire brigade is not aware that this has been considered but believes that it would probably have have been ruled out anyway on grounds of cost'.

During a war, the brigade's roles would undergo remarkable change. The brigade would be responsible primarily for rescue work and for the provision of water, both for fire-fighting and drinking. In a nuclear war, it is envisaged that many if not most fires would simply be left unattended. As the Home Office puts it, 'As there might be large areas where fire fighting would be impracticable, perhaps for several days, most fires would probably have to be left to burn themselves out' (Home Office 1985). The reference is to the dangers of radiation, against which the brigade has no special protection. Plans exist to issue instrumentation to determine radiation levels but this has not yet been done. Current plans do not envisage that firemen would be exposed to levels of radiation that would be considered dangerous to other members of the public (Home Office 1984). London, in short, is to be left to burn.

Two other factors suggest that this would be the likely outcome in any case. According to Willan and Dunne (1986), more than half of the brigade's officers live outside the GLC area. The chances of their being able to get to work after a nuclear attack, even should they decide to try, appear slight. The brigade would therefore be likely to be seriously understaffed after attack, even though plans exist to change working hours to a 24-hour shift in the event of attack. In peace time, only one-quarter of the officers work at any one time.

The second major problem is the very high vulnerability of fire stations to blast. Most fire stations have large doors, including a great deal of glass, immediately behind which the appliances are stored. No special measures have been taken to strengthen fire stations, with the exception of the installation of strengthened glass in the Battersea Fire

Station following the Brixton riots. All stations store 14 days' supply of diesel fuel in drums or tanks. How vulnerable these supplies are to damage is not known. There are no stored supplies of petrol for the Green Goddess fire appliances.

Damage to the London fire service would be substantial during a nuclear attack. Although no damage would be incurred in scenario 1, 15 stations would be subjected to more than 2 psi, and 12 to 1–2 psi, in scenario 2. Because of the vulnerability of stations to blast, more would be lightly damaged with appliances possibly put out of action. Probably nearly a third of London's fire stations would be immediately inoperable after even the lightest nuclear attack to affect London directly.

In scenario 3, some 45 stations would be subjected to more than 1 psi, and half of them to at least double that pressure. The Lambeth headquarters would receive more than 1 psi, being 9 km from the Hampstead bomb, and would be damaged. Although the EMP there would be small, the chances of a computerized information system continuing to work after such an attack appear remote. Scenario 3 would probably halve the ability of the fire service to function, excluding any loss of control and communications.

In scenarios 4 and 5, the service would be effectively wiped out. Only four stations in the east of London would remain undamaged in scenario 4, and the Lambeth control centre would be destroyed by a blast of more than 10 psi from the bomb on Whitehall only 4 km away. In scenario 5, all fire stations would be either damaged or destroyed.

2.4.2 Police

The Metropolitan Police, officially because of its duties in protecting Parliament and the monarchy, reports not to the GLC but to the Home Office. It operates over a slightly larger area than that of Greater London and is organized into 75 divisions within 24 districts and 4 areas. There are 191 police stations in the area and 27,000 police officers are employed (plus a further 16,000 civilians). The police undergo regular training for civil defence.

Police communications are the best of all the services. An underground dedicated phone system connects all police units, and might be relatively resistant to EMP. Extensive use is also made of VHF communications from some 3500 sets mounted in vehicles and a further 9000 personal radios. The range of the sets in vehicles is boosted by two transmitters, one in north and one in south London, which enable the system to be used over the whole Metropolitan district. Personal radios are effective over only about 3 km. The Central Command and Control Complex in Whitehall is connected to every divisional transmitter by landline, enabling central control to talk directly to officers on the beat throughout London (Willan and Dunne 1986).

Other communications include 50–60 radio sets with scrambling devices for sensitive communications, system four radiotelephones and the possibility of future installation of the Vodaphone system. There are two mobile command centres, based on articulated lorries, seven radio control vans, and three helicopters with closed circuit television equipment.

Police stations themselves tend to be of better than average construction and, unlike fire and ambulance stations, are probably more resistant to blast than the average building. Police headquarters at New Scotland Yard, which house the Central Command and Control Complex, are, however, located in a tall, glass-fronted building that apparently offers little blast resistance. Its location close to Whitehall means that it would be destroyed in scenarios 4 and 5, and damaged by the Hampstead bomb in scenario 3.

The police are charged with many onerous responsibilities in time of war crisis or war. The first is the maintenance of law and order. In a war scare, if an emergency were declared, the police would be required to arrest and detain all potentially subversive people. Prisons would be essentially vacated for this purpose, and the arrests would be conducted from information supplied by the national police computer in Hendon, which stores 40 million records on vehicles and individuals (Campbell 1983). The police would also be involved with the introduction of petrol rationing, the requisitioning of pre-designated petrol pumps and the control of traffic, with military assistance, along Essential Service Routes.

The Metropolitan Police operates a dispersion policy that falls mid-way between stay put and dispersion. In the event of an emergency, some 124 Police Support Units would be formed, each consisting of 23 officers, one motor bike, one 40-seater coach, one command car and three or four police cars. These units would disperse to outer London boroughs where they would be accommodated in the Community Care Centres that would be created in the event of war.

The police are also responsible for operating London's 501 sirens to give warning of an attack, based on a system linking the UK's 252 Carrier Control Points (CCPs, located in police premises) with the sirens. The same system would be used to issue radiation warnings. Installation of equipment linking the CCPs with the UK Warning and Monitoring Organization is now virtually complete.

The computer model described in section 2.3.1 was used to estimate the damage suffered by police stations according to scenario. No allowance is made for the fact that police stations may be somewhat more resistant to blast than average buildings. There would be no damage in scenario 1. In scenario 2, approximately 25 per cent of stations would be damaged and a further 6 per cent destroyed. In scenario 3, 68 per cent would be damaged and 9 per cent destroyed. By scenario 4, nearly all stations would be damaged or destroyed (35 and 59 per cent respectively). In scenario 5, 24 per cent would be damaged and 76 per cent destroyed. As already mentioned, New Scotland Yard would be damaged in scenario 3, and destroyed in scenarios 4 and 5 (Barrett, Nectoux *et al.* 1986).

The interpretation of these figures is made somewhat more difficult by police plans for limited dispersion. However, the breakpoint clearly comes with scenario 3, at which stage the operation of the Metropolitan Police as a coherent unit would be in serious doubt. By scenarios 4 and 5, it would be virtually destroyed. Furthermore, under such severe assault, it is doubtful that the police would any longer be regarded as a source of legitimate authority (see section 2.9).

2.4.3 The ambulance service

The London Ambulance Service (LAS) is the largest in the world. With a staff of 2760, it operates 1070 vehicles, including 380 emergency ambulances. In peace time, it answers 2000 emergency calls a day and provides transport for a further 10,000 out-patients. The LAS is part of the National Health Service and is administered by the South West Thames Regional Health authority (the effects of attack on other aspects of the health service are examined in section 2.5).

LAS headquarters are in Waterloo Road and four further divisional control centres for non-urgent cases are located in Kenton, Ilford, Bromley and Malden. There are 74 ambulance stations in London, some of them attached to hospitals. Vehicles do not operate from a single station, as do fire appliances, but provide cover where it is needed. During the weekend, for example, it is customary to draw ambulance vehicles towards the centre of London in preparation for incidents on Friday and Saturday nights. During the rest of the week, the LAS is more dispersed.

The LAS works closely with two voluntary organizations, the St John Ambulance Brigade and the British Red Cross Society, which between them operate a further 95 ambulances. During a war, these would come under the control of the LAS.

During an emergency, the LAS would help in dispersing patients from hospitals. Once that was done, the job of dealing with medical emergencies and out-patients would cease, reducing mileages and man-hours by about 80 per cent. Most of the ambulance service would then disperse to sheltered sites, some near hospitals, with no more than two ambulances at any one site. Only a reduced service would be left in operation. The spaces vacated at ambulance stations would be occupied by commercial vehicles, manned by volunteers, to act as auxiliary ambulances. All LAS stations would be designated as First Aid Posts. The ambulance shift would increase from 8 to 12 hours a day during a war, but before an attack ambulance personnel would be given leave to visit their families to help organize their protection. In fact, plans call for all staff not on duty to remain at home until called back for duty. Details of how they might be called back after a nuclear attack are not given (DHSS 1985).

All ambulances are equipped with radios, and the service has five hill-top transmitters used to boost signals so that communications are effective throughout the whole London area. As work with out-patients ceased during an emergency, the radio channels used by the four divisional controls would be freed and held in reserve. Radio equipment not in use would be removed from dispersed ambulances and stored where it could be protected from blast and EMP. After an attack, plans call for a radio communications system to be established between the regional, group and borough health directors, and operational hospitals. LAS communications, in other words, would be borrowed for other purposes.

After a conventional attack, the LAS would be required to assist with military casualties brought back from the continent. After a nuclear attack, according to Willan and Dunne (1986), 'the primary role of the LAS will be to provide radio communication for the surviving branches of government . . . staff will assist at Casualty Collecting Centres . . . The draft War Plan places very little emphasis on a possible first-aid and rescue role for the ambulance service in the event of a nuclear attack.'

To the extent that ambulance stations become First Aid Posts and centres for auxiliary ambulances, the levels of damage incurred in each nuclear scenario are instructive. Barrett, Nectoux *et al.* (1986) used their computer model to predict damage to 66 ambulance stations, four district headquarters and the LAS headquarters itself.

Damage would be negligible in scenario 1 and slight in scenario 2. By scenario 3, however, three of the district headquarters would be damaged, as would the main headquarters in Waterloo Road. About half the LAS stations, now known as First Aid Posts, would still be operational. In scenario 4, the main headquarters would be destroyed by a blast of more than 10 psi, and only two stations would escape completely undamaged, though six others would be only lightly damaged. By scenario 5, all LAS stations/First Aid Posts would be either damaged or destroyed; of these, only three in south-east London

Table 26 Percentage damage (dam) and destruction (des) to the London Ambulance Service by scenario

Facility	Scenario 2 dam	Scenario 2 des	Scenario 3 dam	Scenario 3 des	Scenario 4 dam	Scenario 4 des	Scenario 5 dam	Scenario 5 des
Ambulance stations (66)	27	9	52	12	39	58	29	71
District headquarters (4)	25	25	75	–	50	25	75	25
LAS headquarters (1)	–	–	100	–	–	100	–	100

Source: Barrett, Nectoux *et al.* 1986.

would escape with light damage. As Willan and Dunne (1986) conclude, 'The health services would have been almost totally destroyed in London and would be faced with problems on a scale that would have overwhelmed them even if they had been left intact'.

2.4.4 Flood control

London is susceptible to flooding from tidal surges, the heights of which have been rising steadily over the years. This trend is expected to continue due to the subsidence of the south-east of England and the change in sea level caused by the progressive melting of polar ice.

London's flood defences depend critically on good communications and on electronic controls used to operate the gates and barriers used to prevent flooding. EMP could disrupt both systems. Some of the defences may also be susceptible to blast damage. Furthermore, the risk of flooding in London might be increased by a nuclear winter, especially if the attack occurred before or during a period of high tides. A nuclear winter might give rise to periods of exceptionally heavy precipitation, and a swollen Thames meeting an exceptionally high tide is a classic ingredient for flooding in London. The risk might be increased if, as is possible, the precipitation fell initially as snow and was subsequently suddenly melted by an abrupt change in the weather (see section 2.7). An increased risk of flooding following nuclear attack therefore exists, but the GLAWARS Commission was unable to predict how large the risk is.

Before the Thames Barrier was completed, the chance of a flood occuring in any one year was 1 in 50. An area of Greater London covering about 115 km^2 and lying below the 18 foot (5.5 m) contour was threatened. Some 600,000 people live in this area and a further 700,000 commute to work within it; 250,000 homes, factories and offices were at risk.

Since the new defences were built in the early 1980s, there is little possibility of flooding in Greater London. However, this is a peace time supposition – the situation could be very different in the event of a nuclear war which could make many of the defences inoperable.

The defences. London's main flood defences are summarized in Table 27. The main defence is the Thames Barrier sited in Woolwich Reach. There are also moveable barriers on tributaries of the River Thames, plus about 112 km of raised flood walls and banks. The Thames Barrier and subsidiary defences are designed to provide protection against surge tides that might occur once in a thousand years (Trafford 1981).

Table 27 London's flood defences

Barriers	South bank moveable gates	North bank moveable gates
Thames Barrier	Woolwich Free Ferry	Tate and Lyle (2 gates)
Dartford Creek	Crossness Sewage Works	London Tugs
Barking Creek	Mulberry Wharf	Woolwich Free Ferry
Royal Docks	Erith Deep Wharf	Royal Docks, Gallons Lock
King George V Lock		Royal Docks, Albert Dock

plus 17 moveable gates on the north bank between Barking Creek and The Mardyke (Wennington Marshes).

The Thames Barrier consists of nine concrete river piers between abutments on the north and south banks of the river (Horner 1981). Ten openings – the four main ones are 61 m wide, the others 31 m wide – are fitted with six rising sector and four falling radial steel gates. The gates are operated by hydraulic power supplied by electric pumps. The barrier has its own generating plant to provide electricity, and supplies can also be obtained from the national grid from north and south of the river. A control room on the south bank is permanently staffed by operational teams of GLC engineers and maintenance personnel. Instrumentation monitors estuary tide levels and allows contact with other barriers. Line and radio communications link the control room with the Storm Tide Warning Centre, Port of London Authority (PLA), police and other emergency services.

Moveable barriers are sited downstream of the main barrier, incorporating, where pertinent, duplicate or triplicate power operation and manual back-up systems. They include the Dartford Creek Barrier, the Barking Creek Barrier and the Royal Docks King George V Lock Entrance Flood Gate. Caissons can be positioned beneath the water at dock entrances to reduce flows of flood water into the docks when necessary.

Minor moveable gates give access to wharves and jetties at four sites on the south bank and five sites on the north bank of the Thames. These are statutorily required to remain closed except when access is needed. A further 17 gates are located on the north bank between Barking Creek and Wennington Marshes. Upstream of the Thames Barrier, there are more flood gates and dam boards to protect properties.

The London underground system is protected to some extent by a series of flood gates installed in the tunnels. Their original purpose was to protect the underground against flooding caused by air raid damage. After World War 2, the system was extended to create a ring that would isolate the area of central London that might be devastated by a nuclear attack, outside which the underground could still operate. The secondary gates, as well as some of the primary ones, were installed in special tunnels remote from stations and away from public view. A heavily fortified control centre for the whole system is situated at the Bull and Bush station beneath Hampstead Heath.

The Greater London Council is responsible for sea and flood defences in most of Greater London, and the Thames Water Authority (TWA) is responsible for the remainder (and will take over the GLC's flood responsibilities when the GLC is abolished). The Ministry of Agriculture, Fisheries and Food (MAFF) is responsible for central administration of and financial support for land drainage and flood protection. Contingency plans exist in case defences should fail and floods threaten Greater London. The GLC is responsible for co-ordinating the response of all relevant authorities and organizations which will have drawn up proposals for operation of their services in the aftermath of a serious flood.

Emergency regulations would be brought in at an early stage during a serious flood. Senior officers of the GLC (and subsequently the TWA) and the London boroughs would be authorized to requisition boats, vehicles and food to help the relief effort. The MAFF has standing arrangements to advise the Ministry of Defence on priorities if military help is required to cope with the flooding.

The storm tide warning system was set up after the flooding of 1953 when 300 lives were lost. The development of a surge is monitored as it travels down the east coast and readings are sent to the East Coast Storm Tide Warning Centre at the Meteorological Office in Bracknell. Thus a warning service is provided for the closure of the Thames Barrier and associated defence structures.

The Thames Barrier operators will close the gates against an incoming surge tide about six hours before the predicted time of high water at London Bridge. At this stage the PLA, police and regional water authorities are notified so that shipping can be halted and authorization given for other barriers to be closed. If the flood threat persists, the gates and moveable barriers downstream are all closed four hours before the high tide is due. Closure procedures are routinely implemented when the incoming tide is likely to reach or exceed the 4.87 m contour at London Bridge, which is about 0.4 m below permanent flood defence level.

Faults in the defence system would be known to the operators by the time the barriers should be closed and warnings could be sent out to the population. In this event, the Thames Barrier operators would contact the London boroughs and other bodies with the help of the police. The public would be informed via the radio, television, sirens and other local arrangements.

Risk of flooding. A surge tide could cause severe flooding if the defences were rendered inoperable through bomb damage to the structures, electromagnetic pulse effects, destruction of electricity generation and distribution systems, lack of key staff at flood warning centres and loss of the personnel who could implement manual operations.

Even if defences were operating normally, a very high tide could overtop them if river levels were already exceptionally high as a result of heavy precipitation during a nuclear winter. River embankments and flood walls could also be breached by high water levels. Such breaches could occur as a direct result of a conventional or nuclear bomb (possibly missing the intended target) landing in or near the Thames.

Adverse weather conditions plus high freshwater flows over Teddington Weir could also cause flooding upstream. In this case, river levels would rise still further if heavy rains fell and snow melted after a nuclear strike in the spring which caused a nuclear winter. Effects of flooding would be increased if property owners were unable to operate their local flood defences because they had fled or were killed, injured or sheltering.

The flood threat cannot be assessed exactly because events would depend upon the nature of the incoming surge tide, prevailing weather conditions and the extent and location of bomb damage. Failure of the Thames Barrier could mean that river banks and flood walls were breached or overtopped, and local flooding could occur in all areas lying below the 18 foot (5.5 m) contour. Inundation of the whole area would take several subsequent tides. Flood waters would begin to flow out with the ebb tides but it could take some time for the floods to recede.

Downstream of the main barrier, if a surge tide occurred when the

Dartford Creek Barrier was out of action the River Cray would flood into Bexley and Dartford. A corresponding failure of the Barking Creek Barrier would threaten the populations of Newham, Barking, Dagenham and Redbridge. If defences failed at the Royal Docks, residences and industrial areas of the docklands, part of Newham, could be flooded. Failures of other defences would bring localized flooding in their vicinity.

The effects of flooding. As defences were overcome, water would flood into the streets, tube tunnels, sewers, basements and ground floors of buildings. Buildings would also be damaged by the flotsam carried in the water. Flood water would become contaminated with sewage and other pollutants. The eventual extent of damage is difficult to assess. One estimate puts the cost of a major flood at more than £3500 million.

Sewers might be flooded throughout an area greater than the flood risk area, perhaps as far as the 27 foot (8.2 m) contour, affecting homes in Barking, Newham, Lambeth, Richmond, Hammersmith, Kensington and Chelsea. Toilets would not function if sewers were flooded and mains water pipes broken. Sewage treatment works do not rely on public electricity supplies, but increased flows to plants could result in untreated sewage being discharged to the Thames. Storm water pumping stations do have flood defences and stand-by generators or diesel pumps so they could be kept in operation.

Electricity supplies would be disrupted over much of the flooded area and surrounding areas. About 27 capital and main sub-stations, and 2000 transformer stations, supplying about 400,000 consumers, are sited in the flood risk area. Transformer stations, switch gear and junction boxes are usually brick-built structures at ground level; these are vulnerable to damage as water penetrates windings and insulation materials.

Flood waters would render electrical junctions, outlets and appliances inoperable or dangerous. Premises would become uninhabitable after a few days without electric power. Residents would probably leave their homes if they could no longer cook or had no means of drying out and heating their homes, especially during a winter attack.

Operation of the gas supply system would not be much affected by flooding. However, some equipment could be damaged, and filters and governors could become blocked. Some gas leakages could occur where gas mains had been broken and water entering mains could affect supplies. Dangerous gas and air mixtures could form if leakages caused mains pressure to drop sufficiently.

Thameside oil refining and storage installations, representing a significant proportion of UK capacity, would be affected by flooding.

Major problems would be fracture of pipelines, buoyancy in oil storage tanks and the loss of electricity supplies to facilities. Filling stations would be inoperable without electricity to run the pumps, and equipment might be destroyed by the force of incoming flood waters.

Telephone services would be disrupted throughout the stricken area. Facilities affected would include about 40 local automatic telephone exchanges, one trunk switching centre, four automanual exchanges and some key buildings for international services. All cable distribution networks would be liable to damage, and cable routes traversing London to the south-east would be affected, as would local telephone and telex services in London which cross the Thames. Hence local, south-eastern and international services would all be hit. Telephone service operational buildings in the flood risk area are equipped with emergency generators and flood protection barriers, though it is not certain how effective they would be.

Parts of the Southern and Eastern Regions of British Rail are vulnerable to flooding. Floods could damage viaducts and embankments, as well as some electrical and signalling equipment, but the permanent way lies below flood level only in Thamesmead. Some rolling stock might be lost in the east if it were not moved before the waters arrived.

There are about 16 bus garages sited within the threatened area. The impact of flooding would be determined mainly by whether or not it was possible to evacuate vehicles in time.

The underground is the most vulnerable section of the transport sector with its many inlets such as ventilation shafts, pipe ducts, sub-stations and escalator routes. The tube tunnels would be flooded quickly over a greater area than experienced at ground level and would remain flooded even after surface waters had receded. The District and Circle Lines would be put out of action, as would deep tubes elsewhere. Trains would be affected if not moved to safety in time. Some of the electricity sub-stations supplying the underground would be incapacitated by flood waters. Much of the power for the system comes from London Regional Transport's generating stations at Lots Road and Greenwich, both of which are protected against floods.

The Millwall, Royal and Upper Docks would experience partial flooding, with water accumulating on lower land behind the docks. East coast ports would also be affected by the same tidal surge.

The flood risk area includes several food industries, notably those producing edible oils and fats, refining sugar and milling flour. Some food distribution centres would be flooded but stock losses would be unlikely to be important. Many manufacturing industries are also located in the flood area, including Fords of Dagenham, though none of them is unique in the country.

The aftermath. Most of the organizations responsible for managing essential services in the aftermath of a major flood have adequate plans to deal with the situation in peace time. Priority would be given to helping and evacuating the injured and destitute; restoring electricity supplies, especially to storm water and sewage pumping installations; ensuring potable water supplies were available; clearing roads so that rescue teams and supplies could get through; setting up communications systems for the emergency services, doctors and hospitals; and repairing and replacing vital equipment. Recovery relies on full co-operation from the relevant organizations and from volunteers. Resources and personnel from outside the area, indeed from throughout the country, would be called upon to help. For instance, electricity supplies would be provided via the national grid from other parts of the country; water supplies would be drawn from the west of London; and hospital patients would be evacuated to the suburbs.

Such reliance on mutual aid might well not work after a conventional or nuclear attack. The organizations might not be able to call in outside help because the emergency services would have to be deployed in all areas of the country and not just in the flood risk area. Furthermore, there might be nowhere for the flood victims to be evacuated to if the rest of the nation were devastated by war. Recovery from flooding and warfare would be a long process. Even in peace time recovery of the different services is anticipated to take months or years: 'Mopping up and restoring normal life would be an enormous operation and might well not be completed in under a year' (Department of the Environment 1979).

References

Barrett, M., Nectoux, F., Lippold, C., with Flood, M., and Uden, J., *GLAWARS Technical Supplement: The effect of nuclear attack on certain systems in the Greater London area*. London, South Bank Polytechnic, 1986, mimeo.

Campbell, D., *War Plan UK*. London, Paladin, 1983.

Department of the Environment, *Contingency Planning for Tidal Flooding in London*. London, DOE, 1979.

DHSS, *Civil Defence Planning in the National Health Service*. London, DHSS, 1985, D195/JO7/EM.

GLC, *The Thames Tidal Flood Contingency Plan (Post Barrier)*. London, GLC, 1983.

Home Office, *Fire Service Circular No. 6/1984*. London, Home Office, 1984.

Home Office, *Emergency Planning Guidance to Local Authorities*. London, Home Office, 1985.

Horner, R. W., 'The Thames Barrier'. In *Journal of the Institution of Water Engineers and Scientists*, Vol. 35, No. 5, 1981.

Trafford, B. D., 'The Background to the Flood Defences of London and the

Thames Estuary'. In *Journal of the Institution of Water Engineers and Scientists*, Vol. 35, No. 5., 1981.

Willan, P., and Dunne, R., *GLAWARS Task 3: The services*. London, South Bank Polytechnic, 1986, mimeo.

2.5 Long-term effects on health

The calculations of total numbers of deaths and casualties in the GLC area given in Table 8 are based on the effects of flash burns, blast and radiation occurring over the first few days following an attack. The health of the London population will, however, continue to suffer from the effects of the attacks for years, even decades. The major problems are likely to occur within a two-year period. These problems concern the effects of the attacks on the ability of the health service to provide treatment, and the emergence of long-term medical consequences of the attacks.

Damage to medical resources. Blast will render many hospitals and clinics unusable. Rotblat, Haines and Lindop (1986) classified the damage to hospitals as light, moderate or severe according to the level of overpressure they experienced, having first obtained the addresses of all hospitals in the GLC area. Under the conditions prevailing after a nuclear attack, hospitals in all three damage categories are likely to be put out of action, although after a time limited use could be made of those sustaining only light damage. However, some of these hospitals, as well as hospitals outside the zones of damage, may be gutted by fire.

The hospitals included in this study were Department of Health and Social Security (DHSS) hospitals, post-graduate medical schools, and independent hospitals and clinics. Altogether, there are 270 of these hospitals with 57,620 beds, of which 32 are mental hospitals with 8950 beds. The damage inflicted by scenario is summarized in Table 28.

Even ignoring the hospitals gutted by fire, only about one in seven hospitals would remain in service immediately after the attack, according to scenario 4; in scenario 5, the surviving ratio is one in 14.

The figures for the number of beds available after the attacks are based on the assumption that all peace-time patients would have been evacuated from the hospitals, either being sent home or to hospitals outside London. This is unlikely. The Department of Health and Social Security (DHSS 1985) does not envisage a general evacuation of patients to hospitals outside London. During the period of tension, new admissions may cease, except for emergency cases, and as many patients as possible will be sent home. But the DHSS states that is it impossible

Table 28 Percentage damage to hospitals and hospital beds in the GLC area

Damage	Scenario 2 Hospitals	Scenario 2 Beds	Scenario 3 Hospitals	Scenario 3 Beds	Scenario 4 Hospitals	Scenario 4 Beds	Scenario 5 Hospitals	Scenario 5 Beds
Severe to moderate	3	3	9	9	69	67	79	81
Light	3	3	12	12	16	15	14	13
Undamaged	94	94	79	79	15	18	7	6

Totals: hospitals, 270; hospital beds, 57,620.
Source: Rotblat, Haines and Lindop (1986).

to pre-determine the proportion of beds which could be freed quickly. Amongst geriatric patients, for example, few discharges might be possible. At a rough guess, perhaps three-quarters of the total number of beds would be available for new casualties. This means that in scenario 4 there might be about 7500 beds for a potential demand of 1.1 million, or 150 candidates for each bed (and even this calculation assumes that those injured from more than one effect die instantly and do not require hospital treatment).

To assess damage to medical staff, information was collected on the numbers of medical personnel in the GLC area in peace time. These figures are available for general and dental practitioners, and for ambulance personnel, but not for hospital doctors and nurses. Approximate numbers of the latter had therefore to be deduced from data on the number of hospital doctors and nurses per bed. The calculated numbers of these personnel in the pre-attack period, given in Table 29, are therefore somewhat uncertain.

The numbers of hospital medical personnel uninjured and potentially available for medical services after the war were then calculated, assuming that deaths and injuries occurred in the same proportion as for the general population. The results are given in Table 29.

The situation would be greatly different if extended preparations were made for the war, including evacuation of hospitals and staff to outside London. If the staff could be brought back to London after the attack, then the medical manpower resources would be considerably greater than given in Table 29. However, such a contingency is not envisaged in the DHSS plan. Moreover, casualties would occur among medical personnel even outside London; communication and transport problems would make difficult their return to London after the attack; and some uninjured doctors – even those left in London – might consider it their duty to stay with their families in the immediate aftermath of a nuclear attack.

Table 29 Casualties among medical and auxiliary staff[a]

Type of personnel	Pre-war numbers	Numbers left uninjured in scenario 2	3	4	5
Hospital doctors	9400	7940	7240	1420	280
General practitioners	4054	3430	3120	610	120
Dental practitioners	2790	2360	2150	420	80
Nurses	67330	56900	51800	10200	2000
Ambulance personnel	3525	3000	2710	530	100

[a] calculated from casualty rates to the general population according to Steadman, Greene and Openshaw (1986); similar calculations based on casualty rates provided by Rotblat, Haines and Lindop (1986) indicate even fewer surviving medical personnel.

Table 29 contains information about dental practitioners because their experience in administering anaesthetics might be of value. However, in scenario 4 there might be only 2000 doctors (general practitioners plus hospital doctors) to treat and care for 1.1 million casualties; in scenario 5, there might be 400 doctors available for 200,000 casualties. The doctor/patient ratio works out at 1:550 for scenario 4 and 1:500 for scenario 5. Even if patients could find and reach a doctor it would present enormous logistical problems to arrange for all the injured to be seen by a doctor for just a few minutes. Doctors would need to work round the clock even to examine the patients briefly. Clearly, medical care in the usual meaning would be non-existent. This is indeed admitted in civil defence plans which propose a system of First Aid Posts (FAP) in which non-medical personnel would have to look after the injured in the early stages.

A medical service requires supplies as well as personnel. Hospital pharmacies usually hold only about two months' supplies of drugs and would therefore rapidly run out of stock after a nuclear attack. However, there are nearly 1800 chemists' shops in the GLC area. Their location by postal district and region is given in Rotblat, Haines and Lindop (1986). The great majority of them would be destroyed in the same proportion as other buildings, which means that only between 7 and 15 per cent would remain in scenarios 4 and 5. These would be vulnerable to looting, and in any case would soon be depleted.

There are three regional blood transfusion centres for London, each supplying hospitals only in their own area and receiving blood only from that area. The South London Regional Transfusion Centre is in

SW17 and requires more than 260,000 donations per year to keep up with current demand. It has eight mobile units operating per day and keeps only a small emergency stock which changes according to intake and demand. The North London Centre is situated in Edgware and has 188,000 donations per year, usually around 700–800 per day. It has four or five mobile collection units during weekdays. Its emergency stock and base line is only 100 units of O positive, 20 units of O negative, 100 units of A positive, 20 units of A negative, 20 units of B positive and no B negative. The North East Metropolitan Centre situated in Brentwood, Essex, has 140,000 donations per year and this represents 600 units per day on average. It has six mobile units. The disaster stock of fresh blood is changed every two days.

It is therefore clear that the emergency stock from these three centres would be quite inadequate to deal even with hundreds, never mind hundreds of thousands, of major injuries occurring at the same time. In any case, only the Brentwood Centre would remain undamaged by blast in scenarios 4 and 5 – though it would be likely to be gutted by fire (so would the blood products laboratory in Elstree).

The effectiveness of medical services after the attack would be greatly hampered by loss of communication. Telephone services would be likely to be out of action due either to the destruction of telephone exchange buildings, or to rupture of cables, or to loss of electricity supply. The exchanges that would survive would in any case not be available for private calls, from patients to doctors or hospitals, although doctors might be exempted. Radio communication would be likely to be disrupted by EMP. Only a few radio transmitters, specially hardened, might survive and these would be restricted to use by official authorities. It is not certain how many radio receivers would survive EMP.

Management of casualties during the first few weeks. The management of casualties in the immediate aftermath of the war demands a number of measures: reaching the injured people and bringing them to FAPs or Casualty Collection Centres (CCCs); sorting out the patients according to the principles of triage; taking care of emergency cases; sending suitable patients to hospitals; evacuating others to community care centres; and, finally, disposing of hundreds of thousands of corpses in scenarios 2 and 3, and several million in scenarios 4 and 5.

This work would be hampered by radiation, and rescue personnel would have to limit their time in the open according to the dose they might receive. The only practical way to deal with the situation would be for all rescue workers to be equipped with personal dosemeters – in working order – and take frequent readings to ensure that the total accumulated dose did not exceed acceptable levels. What these levels are is debatable. Rotblat, Haines and Lindop (1986) believe that a total dose greater than 1 gray should be avoided. Even six hours after the attack, this could be accumulated in less than one hour in the most badly affected areas. It follows that a large team of rescue workers would be needed to replace those 'burned out' after spending a certain time in the open. In scenarios 2 and 3, in which the casualty toll among medical personnel would be relatively small, there should be enough people to carry out a satisfactory rescue programme, but in scenarios 4 and 5 areas with a high dose rate would have to be excluded from rescue operations for several days.

When the needs far exceed the resources available – as would be the case in scenarios 2, 3, 4 and 5, particularly the last two – the aim of medical care would be to save the maximum number of lives. This could be done only by refusing medical assistance to those unlikely to recover, and a system of triage would have to be introduced.

The principles of triage evolved mainly from experience of military medical services. People are sorted into three groups: (a) those with a poor chance of survival; (b) those with a reasonable chance of survival if treated; (c) those with a good chance of survival without treatment, or for whom treatment can be postponed. Only those in category (b) are treated.

In the first instance, triage would have to be carried out on the spot, at the disaster area, but usually it would be done at FAPs or CCCs. Quick assessment is essential, since loss of time would result in an increasing shift of the casualties from the category 'survival possible' to the group 'survival improbable'. Simple sorting procedures would therefore be necessary to assess the severity of injuries and the chances of survival. This would have to be accompanied by first aid, in order to maintain vital functions until suitable care could be provided.

According to current civil defence plans (DHSS 1984), Greater London should have 2735 FAPs (one per 2500 residents) which would be activated only after a nuclear attack. They would be manned by members of the St. John Ambulance and the British Red Cross Society, and supported by local volunteers with first aid training. Their function would be to give on-the-spot treatment and to sort casualties into those who could be sent home or to community care centres, and those to be forwarded to the CCCs.

The latter would also be manned only after a nuclear attack. There would be one for every 12,000–15,000 residents, with a total of 530. Their staff would include local GPs, dental practitioners, community health staff including nurses, and other volunteers. 'The essential function of the CCCs is to sort casualties brought from the FAPs, in order to prevent surviving hospitals from being swamped by overwhelming numbers' (DHSS 1984).

Triage would inevitably result in the retention at the CCCs of people so badly injured that treatment with the limited resources would be wasted on them. Surgical cases would be transferred to hospitals, but if patients were unfit to travel, or if the CCC were unable to clear casualties to hospitals, some surgery would have to be undertaken at the Centre. Generally, treatment at the CCCs would be either palliative, until the patients were fit to be transferred to a hospital, or would comprise pain-relieving drugs and nursing care for those so severely injured that they would be unlikely to survive.

All these plans assume that there would be enough GPs and hospital doctors left to man all the CCCs and hospitals, and that medical supplies – even if only simple ones, such as bandages – would be available. This would not be the case with scenarios 4 and 5, and under these conditions triage would be largely symbolic.

For victims of burns, triage requires expert assessment. Under conditions of nuclear warfare, people with burns affecting more than 30 per cent of the body would be unlikely to survive. Mortality rates are much higher among older people; mortality of those in their early sixties is ten times greater than in the younger age groups.

Treatment of patients with severe burns would present an impossible problem. There are only 106 beds in the whole country specifically designated for the care of burn patients. The lack of dressings, and even of drinking water to replace loss of fluid, makes the prognosis for these injuries very poor. Yet, according to Rotblat, Haines and Lindop (1986), there would be an absolute minimum of 1700 burn injuries in the GLC area alone, even in scenario 2; under worst case assumptions, there could be as many as 144,000 in scenario 4. After the 1985 fire at Bradford City Football Ground, medical facilities were overwhelmed by the admission of 83 burns casualties to hospitals in the area, even though there was an established plastic surgery department with a specialist burns centre close by (Sharpe *et al.* 1985).

Radiation exposure presents special problems for triage: it would be difficult and probably not of much value. Anorexia, vomiting and nausea are the most consistent initial symptoms. The time of onset, and the severity and persistence of the symptoms, could provide a rough guide for sorting into lethal, possibly lethal, and non-lethal exposures. Repeated blood analysis, particularly lymphocyte counts, would provide a reliable diagnosis and help to predict the outcome, but this is unlikely to be possible in post-war conditions. The fact that people unexposed to radiation might present similar symptoms caused by stress would make triage even harder. After a few weeks, those exposed to high doses would develop more characteristic signs of bone marrow failure, including skin haemorrhage, bleeding of the gums, gastro-intestinal bleeding, and ulceration of the throat and mouth. In any case, however, the civil defence plan states that 'persons showing symptoms of sickness due to irradiation should not be treated, except for other traumatic injury' (DHSS 1984).

In peace time, the treatment of casualties from major accidents and disasters requires a multidisciplinary medical and nursing approach. Plentiful supplies of blood and intravenous fluids are required but these would not be available after nuclear attack. Ideally, all major casualties should received surgical treatment within six hours of injury. A well organized surgical team might in theory be able to perform up to seven operations in a 12-hour period under ideal conditions but, in the absence of sterilizing facilities, surgical instruments would rapidly become used up. A comparatively small proportion of doctors has any experience in dealing with major disasters. Thus, according to the British Medical Association (BMA 1983), there were only ten disasters involving more than 100 casualties in the UK between 1951 and 1972. Surviving doctors would probably be limited to attending simple fractures and applying make-shift splints, cleaning wounds and stopping haemorrhages. Anaesthetic agents and suturing materials would soon run out. The strong dependence of modern medical practice on high technology would rapidly render medical facilities impotent.

Disposal of the dead. In several major disasters, for instance the 1972 earthquake in Managua, and the earthquake in Guatemala City four years later, the authorities reasoned that large numbers of corpses would lead to epidemics and ordered either evacuation or immediate burials without ceremony in order to avert an epidemic. However, there is evidence that corpses transmit disease much less readily than infected survivors. Whilst human corpses may provide food for rats and other potential vectors of disease, the main health effect of large numbers of corpses may be on the psychological health of the survivors.

In Germany, government authorities estimated that 10,000 bodies remained unrecovered in Hamburg even two years after the Allied bombings during World War 2. In addition, conservative estimates state that 70,000–80,000 bodies were decomposing in the ruins of German cities months after the war ended.

The experience of US troops in Manila, at the end of World War 2, suggested that troops were unable to participate in mass burials for longer than one week at a time, before being overcome by anorexia, nausea, vomiting, depression and insomnia, with nightmares when they did sleep. In the Philippines, trenches 60 metres long and 3 metres deep were used as burial pits; these were created by bulldozers in cemetery areas and public parks. Bodies were dumped into the pits until there were approximately 200 in each. Earth was then piled on top of the pit and compacted by the bulldozer. About 80 men supervised by one officer worked for eight weeks to bury the 39,000 corpses (Orth 1959).

The numbers of people killed in the GLC area would be:

scenario 2:	638,000
scenario 3:	737,000
scenario 4:	4,341,000
scenario 5:	5,801,000

Further comment appears unnecessary (even though the numbers of corpses to be disposed of would be somewhat lower than these figures indicate because those caught close to the fireball would leave no remains).

Infectious diseases. The circumstances prevailing after a nuclear attack are likely to lead to the spread of infectious disease. The reasons include breakdown in sanitation, clustering together of survivors, breakdown of immunization and loss of immunity caused by radiation damage.

Because of the breakdown in water supplies and destruction of sewage treatment plants, it is likely that there would be a shortage of potable water in most of the city. In the months and years following the attack, it is likely that diseases spread by contaminated water would become more common and could form a significant additional cause of death and injury in the already debilitated population of survivors.

Diseases that are likely to occur include shigella dysentery, salmonella infections, infectious hepatitis (particularly type A), and infections from campylobacter and enteropathogenic *E. coli.* It is possible that typhoid fever outbursts would occur but – perhaps more importantly – it is very likely that tuberculosis incidence would start to increase. The GLC area includes some health districts, such as Brent, with a very high incidence of tuberculosis. In 1983, about 2500 cases of tuberculosis were notified in the four Thames Regions, most of them within the Greater London area. The majority of them were pulmonary tuberculosis and must therefore be regarded as potentially infectious. In times of war, the incidence and mortality of tuberculosis frequently rises. In World War 1, for instance, mortality from tuberculosis more than doubled in Warsaw, reaching a peak rate of 974 per 100,000 in 1917. An analysis of 2267 inmates of the Dachau concentration camp at the time of liberation after World War 2 showed that 28 per cent had evidence of tuberculosis, of which nearly 40 per cent were far advanced.

Poor nutrition has traditionally been associated with increased incidence of mortality from tuberculosis, and cramped shelter conditions would facilitate its spread. Even after the shelter period, survivors would have to live in overcrowded conditions in the few houses that still offered adequate shelter. Many of these would lack windows and doors, there would be little or no fuel for heating, and a nuclear winter might cause a sharp drop in temperature. Cramped and insanitary conditions like these could enhance the spread of respiratory diseases (Abrams and von Kaenel 1981) and ailments such as scabies, impetigo and fungal skin infections.

Another infectious disease that may be important is measles, which can cause death in malnourished children. The incidence per 100,000 population was around 1000 per annum in England and Wales between 1940 and 1960, but it dropped steadily following the introduction of measles immunization. It is likely that rates after an attack would increase to near those of the mid-part of this century.

Other diseases whose frequency has been drastically reduced by immunization include diphtheria, poliomyelitis, tetanus and, to a lesser extent, whooping cough. All these diseases would be likely to occur more frequently with the breakdown of immunization, and would become an increasing problem as the general level of immunity declined. No effective treatment would be likely to be available for any of these diseases after an attack.

Other factors that increase the spread of disease include a proliferation of the insect population. Since insects are generally more resistant to radiation than humans and other animals, it is possible that mosquitoes would multiply rapidly after an attack, as would other insects such as flies, cockroaches and lice.

Some estimates suggest that deaths from communicable diseases amongst the survivors may approach 20–25 per cent, with enteric and respiratory diseases representing the major threats.

Exposure to cold. Hypothermia is likely to be a major problem in the months following an attack. Elderly people with a poorer thermoregulatory capacity than young adults would be especially at risk. Infants would also be at risk, particularly in the neo-natal period.

Approximately 14 per cent of the population of the GLC are aged 65 and over, and 6 per cent are 75 and over. The elderly have increased sensitivity to the adverse effects of cold, due to changes in the perception of environmental temperatures. Several studies have suggested that the elderly have a lowered ability to sense the cold. In addition, the elderly may be less able to generate heat on exposure to cold environments. Mortality among elderly patients suffering from accidental hypothermia is high, ranging from 40 per cent to more than 80 per cent in some surveys.

Groups at special risk. Apart from the sensitivity of the elderly to hypothermia, it is obvious that the physically and mentally handicapped would be at grave disadvantage after an attack. Experience from the Third World indicates that children would also be particularly vulnerable. In 1950, for example, the infant mortality rate in the developing world was around 200 per 1000; a similar rate was recorded in Birmingham in 1906. Though few countries have such a high level of infant mortality now, in scenarios in which the restoration of the fabric of society would be likely to be impossible, infant mortality rates might rise to at least 200 per 1000 in the years following the attack. The likely causes of infant death would be diarrhoea, respiratory infections, malnutrition and the common diseases of childhood.

Pregnant women are another vulnerable group. Those irradiated during pregnancy might give birth to deformed children. In the absence of facilities for pre-and post-natal care, and for assistance in childbirth, maternal mortality would be increased dramatically. Iron and folic acid deficiency during pregnancy would become common, and women with toxaemia and other obstetric emergencies would not be cared for. Bottle feeding would become difficult without adequate sterilization facilities.

Insulin-dependent diabetics would probably die in the weeks or months following the attack, once their insulin supplies ran out. There would, of course, be no possibility of any treatment for the complications of diabetes, and therefore poorly controlled non-insulin diabetics who did survive would be likely to be susceptible to diabetic eye damage, with subsequent serious visual impairment and even blindness. Those whose life support depended on high-technology medicine would probably die. Patients with chronic renal failure could not be treated and those receiving dialysis would die rapidly. Other groups at risk would include those suffering from pernicious anaemia, rheumatoid arthritis, hypothyroidism, epilepsy and asthma. Cancer sufferers would not receive treatment and those with high blood pressure would be more likely to suffer strokes and cardiac failure. Iron deficiency is likely to be a particular problem in children and menstruating women, and will also contribute to levels of ill health after an attack.

Radioactive contamination of water and food. Fall-out would contaminate the skin of animals exposed to it; unless the skin were cleansed thoroughly before eating, some fall-out could be ingested by humans. The meat itself would be safe to eat if the animal were slaughtered soon after contamination, before the radioactivity had been absorbed into the body of the animal. Milk would be contaminated by radioactive iodine for some time after the attack, and would therefore be unfit for consumption if it came from cattle which had been grazing on land where fall-out had occurred. Rain or snow occurring up to a few months after the attack could contain appreciable amounts of radioactivity, including the long-lived caesium-137 and strontium-90. In the immediate post-attack period, rainwater could give a high dose of radioactive contamination. Food in cans or plastic containers would be safe, provided that the container itself was wiped clean before opening.

After a nuclear attack it would have to be assumed that all crops had fall-out on them unless it was absolutely certain that farmland had not been contaminated. Crops with smooth surfaces or pods could be wiped clean and peeled, but crops with rough surfaces, such as cabbages, would have to have each leaf separately cleaned. Cereals would have to be winnowed and all husks rejected, but in the process a considerable amount of radioactive dust could be created. In the longer term, crops would become internally contaminated because of uptake of radioactive isotopes through the roots or absorption through the leaves. Radioactivity would also accumulate in the food chains as plants were eaten by animals. This was found to be a problem in the Bikini Atoll used for nuclear weapons tests in the 1950s. By the end of 1980, some islands of the Atoll were declared safe for habitation, but only on the condition that 50 per cent of the food for the inhabitants was imported (Johnson 1980).

The effectiveness of medical services after a nuclear attack. When confronted by many hundreds of casualties, limited stocks of pharmaceuticals and other medical supplies, and in the absence of a functioning medical technology, there is little that a doctor can do to ameliorate the suffering of immediate survivors.

The psychological effects of the attack on medical staff also need to be considered. Many would have divided loyalties to their families and to their patients, and for those who did attend to the casualties their effectiveness after several hours of unrelenting work with inadequate facilities would be open to doubt. For general practitioners and dentists who were staffing CCCs, the situation would be equally desperate, particularly in the case of scenarios 4 and 5.

The medical activities of health professionals would also be hampered by large numbers of patients without major physical injury who clustered round health facilities to obtain reassurance and support, and to search for injured friends and relatives. Even in scenarios 2 and 3, the numbers of casualties would far exceed the capacity of peace-time services to cope with them. Although hospitals have disaster plans, their experience is related to disasters involving tens or hundreds of casualties rather than thousands (or millions). In the longer term, the management and prevention of communicable disease would depend crucially on the provision of clean water and sanitation, and on the restitution of immunization programmes. However, vaccines are rendered useless unless they are kept under constant refrigeration, and it would have to be assumed that nearly all stocks had been spoilt. Use of first aid volunteers might enable more comfort to be provided for those who had been injured but, in strictly medical terms, this would be unlikely to result in any appreciable increase in survival.

The World Health Organization (WHO 1984) found that no health service anywhere in the world could cope with the casualties resulting from nuclear war. They conclude that 'Even the death and disability that could result from an accidental explosion of one bomb from among the enormous stockpile of weapons could overwhelm national medical resources'. GLAWARS concurs with this conclusion.

References

Abrams, H., and von Kaenel, W. E., 'Medical Problems of Survivors of Nuclear War'. In *New England Journal of Medicine*, 305, 1226–1232, 1981.

BMA, *The Medical Effects of Nuclear War*. Chichester, Wiley, 1983.

DHSS, *Health War Plan*, second draft, February 1984.

DHSS, *Civil Defence Planning in the National Health Service*. Draft Document for Consultation, June 1985, HN (85) 16.

Johnson, G., 'Paradise Lost'. In *Bulletin of the Atomic Scientists*, Vol. 36, No. 10, 1980.

Orth, G. L., 'Disaster and Disposal of the Dead'. In *Military Medicine*, 124, 505–510, 1959.

Rotblat, J., Haines, A., and Lindop, P., *GLAWARS Task 6: The health impact*. London, South Bank Polytechnic, 1986, mimeo.

Sharpe, D. T., Roberts, A. H. N., Barclay, T. L., Dickson, W. C., Settle, J. A. D., Crockett, D. J., and Mossad, M. G., 'Treatment of burns casualties after the fire at Bradford City Football Ground'. In *British Medical Journal*, 291, 945–948, 1985.

Steadman, P., Greene, O., and Openshaw, S., *GLAWARS Task 3: Computer predictions of damage and casualties in London*. London, South Bank Polytechnic, 1986, mimeo.

WHO, *Effects of Nuclear War on Health and Health Services*. Geneva, WHO, 1984.

2.6 The psychological issues

Any account of the effects of attack on London must include a description of the likely ways in which Londoners will react to such a disaster. The GLAWARS contingencies provide a convenient framework within which to analyse the three issues that are at stake: the extent to which Londoners feel threatened by attack in peace time (contingency

A); their likely behaviour during a period of war scare (contingency B); and their behaviour after an attack (contingencies C to F).

In assessing these issues, GLAWARS gathered information from studies of the effects of conventional bombing of London during World War 2, the effects of natural disasters such as earthquakes, and the effects of the two nuclear weapons exploded in Japan in 1945. This information was then used as the basis for predictions of likely behaviour during the GLAWARS contingencies and of the likely outcomes of the five GLAWARS scenarios.

Contingency A: the perception of threat. Threat is the condition under which we live at present, which is why the GLAWARS Commission chose to describe contingency A as 'non-belligerence' rather than as 'peace time'. It is evident that a pressing danger exists, but the perception of the threat varies from person to person and from time to time. In the United Kingdom, 52 per cent of teenagers feel that nuclear war will occur in their lifetime, and 70 per cent that it is inevitable one day (*Business Decisions* 1983). Worries appear to be increasing. Bachman (in press) found that the proportion of adolescents often worried about the nuclear threat rose from 7 per cent in 1976 to 31 per cent in 1982. Solantous *et al.* (1984) found that even in non-nuclear and neutral Finland 79 per cent of 12 year olds and 48 per cent of 18 year olds named a probable future war as their major fear.

Adults share this concern. In 1982, a Gallup poll found that 72 per cent of adults were worried about nuclear war and 38 per cent thought that nuclear war would occur. The GLAWARS survey (see Appendix 5) found that over the next 20 years

> only a quarter of all Londoners are prepared to discount entirely the likelihood of a nuclear attack on Britain. A further 30 per cent assign a probability of greater than zero but less than evens, 18 per cent think the chances of such an attack 'about 50/50' while the remaining quarter (24 per cent) feel the threat of attack to be greater than evens. These latter include 6 per cent of Londoners who feel it is 'certain' that such an attack will occur.
>
> (Loizos and Marsh 1986)

Despite evidence of anxiety, the most consistent reaction appears to be some form of denial, which Lifton (1967) describes as 'consistent human adaptation'. Some people avoid the subject totally. Other reactions are resignation, helplessness (Seligman 1975), fatalism and unquestioning trust. The myth of personal invulnerability, that necessary fiction of everyday life, holds strong, and allows people to continue the necessary tasks of living. This fiction also undoubtedly influences the way people behave to warnings of disaster.

Contingency B: war scare. For a warning to be effective, there must be a credible action to take in response to it. However, human beings have considerable shortcomings as estimators of the probabilities of future hazards (Slovic *et al.* 1982, Kahneman, Slovic and Tversky 1982). Even when a hazard is acknowledged, people may perceive it in many different ways, seeing it as improbable or so inevitable as to vitiate human action.

In studies of experimental stress on animals, the least affected groups are those that receive warnings of impending shocks and can reduce the probability of receiving them by avoidance behaviour, however onerous. The groups that suffer most are those that are deprived of warnings and so cannot reduce their impact (Weiss 1971). These animals suffer considerably, and their helpless behaviour has many similarities to human depression (Seligman 1975), characterized by a failure to respond even when doing so might avoid further stress.

This may help explain why conventional bombing attacks on London in World War 2 caused less psychological stress than the V-bombs later in the war. In the first case, air raid warnings and the eventual all clear provided reasonably reliable signals of safety. No warnings or all clear could be sounded against rocket attack.

Some individuals deny warnings until it is too late. During the Hawaiian tidal wave of May 1960, evacuation was minimal (Lachman, Tatsuoka and Bank 1961), and on the banks of the Rio Grande during an earlier flood festive crowds watched and cheered the rising floodwaters (Wolfenstein 1957). These active denials of danger have their place in life, but are dangerous in the face of a real threat. The myth of personal invulnerability still holds. A measure of this delusion is that most people believe they are more likely than average to live past 80 years of age (Britten 1983).

If the danger is admitted, however, those who are trusting may rely too much on official pronouncements and those who lack faith in establishment figures become susceptible to rumour. Precautionary activity depends on the adequacy of information about what needs to be done, and a group effect as people begin to take the warning seriously. Conflicting advice is usual (Churcher *et al.* 1981), and many people may be unable to decide on a consistent response.

Drabek and Stephenson (1971) studied families that had been evacuated from their homes prior to a flood in Denver. At 5.30 pm one cloudy afternoon, after showers throughout much of the day, police cars cruised past suburban houses announcing that 'A 20 foot wall of water is approaching this area. You have 5 to 15 minutes to evacuate. Leave for high ground immediately'.

The events leading to this announcement were as follows. After a tornado earlier in the day, a wall of water was seen sweeping down one of the tributaries of the South Platte River which flows through Denver. The local sheriff raised the alarm at 3 pm. This was received with some incredulity, since a major flood had not occurred for 100 years. By 4 pm, police began evacuating those closest to the river, and by 5 pm broadened the area of evacuation. Throughout the warning period, radio and television responded sporadically. Some stations carried normal programmes, while others gradually shifted to increased flood coverage. This led many people to switch from one station to another in an attempt to confirm conflicting stories which seemed impossible to believe. The wide area of television coverage meant that people in safe areas converged on the danger zone to contact friends and relatives or, in the largest number of cases, simply from curiosity.

The attempts of the families in the danger area to confirm the warnings frequently yielded contradictory information; of those who evacuated immediately, as many as one-third returned home, often infiltrating through police lines set up to prevent looting. At 8.15 pm the floodwaters arrived, causing considerable damage but no loss of life because of the evacuation.

Individual responses to warnings are known to be greatly affected by group memberships, particularly the family. Most people responded to the flood as family members, not individuals, and of those families that were together at the time of warning 92 per cent evacuated together. When family members were separated at the time of the initial warnings, which happened to 41 per cent of the total sample, their immediate concerns were making contact with each other.

Although the mass media often urged evacuation of very specific areas, these warnings tended to be viewed as background information, while a direct request from the authorities was far more likely to get people moving. The mass media seemed to start people looking for further information. Mass media and peers' recommendations to evacuate were received with scepticism by 60 per cent of respondents but, when the authorities were the source, such scepticism occurred in only 22 per cent of cases.

The overwhelming reaction was to interpret the warnings as non-threatening and then search for other cues with which to discount or confirm them. Rather than being sterile receptacles of news, people actively worked on what they had been told; even when they came to accept that a flood was imminent, they still maintained a feeling of personal invulnerability and thought that their own house would not be hit.

Drabek (1969) found that husbands tended to be more sceptical of warnings from peers and from the authorities than were their wives, and made attempts to confirm the warnings which their wives had often been the first to hear. Usually, several different types of confirmation had to be received before people evacuated, although many did so whilst maintaining their scepticism. Drabek and Stephenson draw several conclusions.

1 People acted as family members, not individuals. Telephone conversations with relatives during the warning period were usually a key factor in what people did.
2 The mass media had the least effect. Warning messages from friends and relatives were three times more effective than were those of the mass media.
3 Officials were wrong in expecting a mass panic.
4 Message content should be as specific as possible, including information about both the threat and what to do about it. A general warning is not likely to be effective.
5 Emergency officials ought to plan for more critical needs than the prevention of looting, little of which occurred.

Another study of short warning times, in this case of about one and a half hours, was conducted by Hodler (1982), who surveyed residents in the path of a tornado which had passed through Kalamazoo in Michigan, killing 5 people, injuring 79, and leaving 1200 homeless. Of those interviewed, two-thirds had heard the warning sirens, but 17 per cent of them did not know what they meant. Safety was sought by 48 per cent, the warnings were disregarded by 18 per cent, and 22 per cent tried to confirm the warning by looking outside or turning on their radios and televisions. This means that 40 per cent did nothing or even tried to see the tornado. Michigan had experienced 306 tornadoes between 1953 and 1975, so this lethargic response was not based on ignorance.

Hansson, Noulles and Bellovich (1982) analysed how much residents of a large floodplain in Oklahoma knew about floods and flood warnings. The respondents were people who had lived in their homes for eight years on average, and 40 per cent of them had been flooded before. Only 10 per cent had ever rehearsed a family plan of action, and only a third had tried to protect their homes from flooding. The four hour flood warnings tended to generate anxiety rather than effective defensive action. Those with personal experience of flooding paid greater attention to the threat, and reacted with increased dread. The more often they had been flooded, the higher their scores on measures of depression and family health stress. The more recent the flooding, the stronger was the support for community intervention plans.

Miller (1981) conducted a survey of 248 heads of household living within 15 km of Three Mile Island to find out why people evacuated during the accident at the nuclear plant. Variables such as proximity to the plant, disruption of telephone service and specific directives to evacuate were related to the decision to leave.

Jackson (1981) surveyed 302 residents of earthquake zones on the US west coast and found that there was a preference for crisis response. Even though 80 per cent had experienced an earthquake, and 96 per cent expected earthquakes to occur in the future, few believed that they themselves would sustain damage. Only 7.5 per cent had taken out insurance or made structural improvements to their homes.

It was found that 23.2 per cent denied that they would experience an earthquake, 8.9 per cent expected that they would, and 67.9 per cent were uncertain. Interestingly, those who had previously suffered the most damage showed the least uncertainty, and included a high proportion of people who claimed they would not experience an earthquake. The reasons for this may lie in the notion of a just world, in which those who have been punished will be spared further castigation, a view held by 35 per cent of the sample. In contrast, a mere 15 per cent held the more reasonable view that if you live in an earthquake zone you can expect earthquakes.

A full explanation of people's failure to respond to well-founded threats and warnings is required. Most people do nothing, or very little. People show a preference for crisis response, saying that they will respond when disaster strikes, forgoing precautions in the absence of personal experience, and making changes only in the aftermath of the disaster. People tend to misperceive risks, and deny the uncertainty inherent in nature, or show an unshakeable faith in protective devices such as flood control dams and earthquake building codes. They sometimes flatly deny that a recurrence of a disaster is possible, or misperceive such events as coming in cycles.

These findings do not bode well for the fate of Londoners threatened with possible attack. They suggest that reliance on media such as the BBC to broadcast information may be misplaced, and that the most effective means of persuading people to heed warnings is to issue them with specific advice about what to do. Official plans to provide only high priority telephone services are likely to be counter-productive in that they will prevent family members contacting one another, a frequent preliminary to evasive action. A well conducted public information campaign is clearly a critical component of effective civil defence, though the evidence suggests that even this would not necessarily improve the seriousness with which warnings are likely to be heeded.

Contingency C: conventional attack. Most World War 2 conventional bombing campaigns involved far less explosive power than would be the case in a nuclear war. However, mass raids on some cities caused destruction comparable to that produced by small nuclear weapons. Furthermore, facts and fictions about the Blitz influence both popular and official perceptions of the way Londoners would react to a future bombing campaign.

The raids were preceded by a long period of international tension which gave the public and the authorities time to prepare. Previous data on urban bombing were sparse, and the predictions were that there would be massive casualties, considerable panic, and that deep shelters, if provided, would lead to a 'shelter mentality' in which people would refuse to come out to work. As a projection of the reports from Guernica, this was an understandable view, as was the over-riding fear of a gas attack.

When the bombing began, social cohesion and morale broke down very quickly in the worst affected areas, though censorship ensured that this was not widely known at the time. Badly damaged zones had to be cordoned off by the police, and emergency services were unable to cope. All this occurred despite the fact that there was warning of attack, pauses between attacks, and that one and a half million women and children had been evacuated.

The raid on Coventry on the night of 14–15 November 1940 caused such damage that there was nearly a breakdown of social organization. Food had to be brought in from Birmingham and Stoke-on-Trent, and entry to the damaged areas had to be prevented by armed troops.

In the Southampton raids, large sectors of the population ignored official instruction and began 'trekking', moving out into the country and sleeping in hedges during the night, and then trekking in to work the next day. The stresses of long periods of deprivation and uncertainty caused deep rifts in society which were also noted in Japan and Germany during the air war.

The fact that the bombing could not be maintained without pause, and the fortuitous detonation of a bomb near Buckingham Palace while the East End was receiving the brunt of the attack, defused an explosive social divide. Londoners then began to feel that 'they were all in it together'.

There were fewer casualties than had been expected but the extent of damage and the problems of dealing with the homeless had been severely underestimated. Nearly a quarter of a million homes were damaged beyond repair, while 3.5 million suffered reparable damage, though these losses could not be made good during the war. Emergency services adapted to the new demands, but in many areas of London fires raged uncontrollably.

The authorities had prepared for massive casualties and panic. Instead they got a dazed but functioning population which required food, clean water, shelter and new forms of social organization. Titmus (1950) observed: 'The authorities knew little about the homeless who in turn knew less about the authorities'.

The speed with which dazed and bewildered people could be organized and rehabilitated determined the rate at which the damage could be repaired, production returned to full capacity, and further demoralization avoided. What was needed, the observers of that time agreed, was a 'much more powerful and imaginative organization' to deal with 'the purely psychological and social effects of violent air attack' (Mass Observation 1940, cited in Harrison 1978). This organization was to bring a wave of social help, hot tea and sympathy to snatch people from their introversion and to link them up again with the outside world.

Towards the end of the war, the V-bomb campaign imposed new stresses on London's population. A new evacuation began again. No all clear was ever possible until the launch bases themselves were destroyed. Londoners would face this problem again after any future war on the UK. The absence of an all clear is a factor that must be taken into account in civil defence planning (see section 1.3).

The findings from conventional bombing offer only a very partial view of reactions to nuclear war. The power of nuclear weapons is so great that massive destruction can be caused to a society which is now more interdependent and tightly coupled as an industrial system. It is thus more fragile and will have to absorb more damage without time to recover. However, conventional bombing does provide an analogy. As Thompson (1986) put it, 'The aftermath of a major nuclear war will be like Coventry trying to get help from Hamburg, while Dresden seeks help from both'.

Post-disaster behaviour (contingencies C to F). When disasters are sudden and severe, most people feel that they are at the very centre of the catastrophe. This illusion of centrality, though understandable, may prevent optimum responses since most people will concern themselves with their own local problems. In a tornado, people believe that only their house has been hit. The myth of personal invulnerability, which is so strong in the threat phase, is now called into question. Faced with the reality of death, usual assumptions disintegrate, and mood and beliefs oscillate wildly. As the full extent of the destruction becomes apparent, and help fails to materialize, there is the second shock effect of dismay at abandonment. Intense emotions are felt, and these fluctuate, making later recall of events problematical. Feelings fluctuate between terror and elation, invulnerability and helplessness, catastrophic abandonment and miraculous escape.

All survivors must attempt to make sense of the fact that they could have died, and nearly did, but managed to come through alive. They show the exhilaration of massive anxiety relief, but also the vulnerability to disappointment which is the longer-term effect of the massive fear they have experienced. Joy at having survived may be mixed with colossal optimism that the worst is over. Life itself seems sufficient reward, and in particular joining up with loved ones, who were feared lost, brings intense happiness. The quite random fact of survival may be rationalized by a feeling of personal invulnerability and mission. Those who have had a brush with death are left in a heightened state of emotional turmoil.

This effect is short lived, and soon gives way to the 'disaster syndrome'. Victims appear dazed, stunned and bewildered (Wallace 1956). Contrary to popular belief, their reactions are not the ones associated with panic. Quarantelli (1954) describes panic as an acute fear reaction, developing as a result of a feeling of entrapment, powerlessness and isolation, leading to irrational flight. Such frenzied activity is found only when people are trapped, and when escape is thought possible only for a limited period of time. Then contagious panic can indeed occur, but it is not the norm.

After a disaster, victims are apathetic, docile, indecisive, unemotional, and they behave mechanically. They are still in a state of high autonomic arousal, but appear to be paying for their period of terror by emotional and behavioural exhaustion. Various explanations have been put forward. It may be a protective reaction, cutting people off from further stimuli which would cause them only anxiety and pain. In an account of the Tokyo earthquake of 1894, Balz noted that he observed the terrible event 'with the same cold attention with which one follows an absorbing physical experiment' (cited in Anderson 1942). Again, it could be a form of wishful fantasy – 'if I don't react then nothing has happened'. Or it could be that people feel helpless in the face of the massive damage and the impossibility of repairing their shattered world.

Popovic and Petrovic (1964) arrived on the scene of the Skopje earthquake 22 hours after the event, and in the following five days, together with a team of local psychiatrists, toured the evacuation camps. They found that much of the population was in a mild stupor, depressed, congregating in small unstable groups and prone to rumours of doom. By way of comparison with nuclear war, only 1 in 200 of the people died, and 3 in 200 were injured.

In any disaster, according to Kinston and Rosser's (1974) estimates, roughly three-quarters of the population are likely to show the disaster syndrome. But from 12 to 25 per cent will be tense and excited, able to cope by concentrating on appropriate preparatory activities. They will be capable of making themselves too busy to worry, though their activities may often be of only marginal relevance to the threat they face. Equally, 12 to 25 per cent will fare far worse, and will show grossly inappropriate behaviour, with anxiety symptoms predominating. There will be an immediate increase in psychological distress, as those already vulnerable are triggered into breakdown. Those whose behaviour is contained only by social pressure are likely to behave in psychopathic ways. The crisis will provide an opportunity which some will be willing to exploit.

If the cause of the disaster is seen to pass, and some sort of 'all clear' can be announced, then there will be an opportunity for a return to something approximating a normal psychological state. About 90 per cent of subjects show a return of awareness and recall. They are highly dependent, talkative, childlike, seeking safety and forming unstable social groups. In this state they remain highly vulnerable and emotionally labile. Some respond with totally psychopathic behaviour, and looting, rape, and heavy drinking may occur.

People show a return of energy with a commensurate return of reason. They behave hyper-actively and often irrationally. They become obsessed with communicating their experiences to others, and need to work through the events in order to give them some meaning. The need for explanation is part of dependency, and leads to rumour and absurd gullibility. People will be anxious to obtain reliable news, and will expect their own experiences to be news. Following the murder of President Kennedy, the average US adult spent eight hours per day for the next four days listening to the radio or watching television, behaviour which Janis (1971) interpreted as an attempt to work through the cultural damage.

In this dependent and vulnerable state, chance factors can have a disproportionate effect on the interpretation of the event and the view as to what has to be done in the future. Scapegoats may need to be found, and chance may provide them. Scientists, militarists and politicians may escape initial attention while those involved in bringing relief may be the target of frustration and feelings of betrayal (Lacey 1972).

Once the immediate danger is past, some survivors will begin to take steps to cope with the consequences. Even as the warning of danger is announced people will find themselves in a conflict of roles. They have to decide whether they should continue with their jobs, take up civic and emergency duties or return to look after their families. Killian (1952) found that conflicting group loyalties and contradictory roles were significant factors affecting individual behaviour in critical situations. Typically, it is the person without family ties who leads rescue work, while the others generally return home to discover if their families are in danger. Even so, Killian reported that some who were searching for their families, after a tornado had struck, were capable of helping others they found on the way.

Faced with an overwhelming catastrophe, family bonds are likely to predominate over civic duties, which will be seen as irrelevant and futile by most people. It should be noted that natural disasters generally come without warning, and rarely require emergency workers to leave their families unprotected while moving themselves to places of relative safety, as would apparently be required of them in the event of nuclear war.

Gradually, individual reactions become co-ordinated into an organized social response. Many of the victims will be coping with the consequences of loss and bereavement. This will diminish their capacity to interact socially in a productive manner. Fear and apprehension persist, and many may feel that the catastrophe will recur. Aftershocks of an earthquake commonly cause more fear than the initial shock itself. Disaster persists as a tormenting memory, and is relived again and again.

Prospects for recovery. The study of recovery from massive natural disasters can provide an analogy for the recovery which might be expected after a nuclear war. In all of these studies, however, there has always been an undamaged outside world able and willing to provide assistance. This would not be the case in a major nuclear war, but might conceivably be so in a more limited conflict.

Useful insights can be gained from studying an Italian earthquake in which the initial recovery was good, until a second earthquake halted recovery efforts; contrasting it with a different Italian earthquake in which recovery was very poor (Geipel 1982); and then looking in detail at the post-impact courses of two communities within that earthquake zone (D'Souza 1982).

Geipel (1982) studied the effects of the Friuli earthquake of May 1976, which affected 4800 km^2 of northern Italy. Since the earthquake occurred on a hot summer's evening, most people were out of doors but 939 people perished in the wreckage of the 17,000 collapsing houses; 2400 were injured. After further earthquakes, 189,000 people were left homeless.

The Italian army were conducting manoeuvres in the area at the time, and were able to assist relief organizations. Some 16,000 tents, and railway cars and caravans, were provided for the homeless.

Despite the extent of the damage, there was no means of flight from Friuli, and energetic rebuilding began so that the inhabitants could return home as soon as possible. In mid-September, another earthquake put paid to this reconstruction. Although the second earthquake was a little weaker, the psychological impact was far greater. Landslides blocked escape routes from the mountains, savings invested in reconstruction were lost, and the prospect of a hard winter 'overwhelmed the resistance capacity of a mountain population accustomed to privation' (Geipel 1982).

An earthquake in which the initial response was very different occurred on 23 November 1980 in the hinterland of Naples. An area of

28,000 km^2, including 314 communities, was hit. More than 3500 people died and some 300,000 were made homeless.

The victims showed a far more fatalist and apathetic attitude than those of the other earthquake. Because the area affected was six times as big as Friuli and more remote, communication and administration worked badly. Most of the Italian army was located further north, while the first aid groups to arrive from Rome were delayed by the flood of escaping inhabitants.

Many of the buildings were cheaply constructed blocks of several storeys which collapsed, causing a snowball effect. Mistrust and anger were levelled at the architects responsible, and at the Roman and international aid effort. The disaster response was so poorly administered that some victims were not rescued from the debris until 14 days after the disaster.

In a city characterized by extreme contrasts of rich and poor, the Catholic church was criticized for not opening its many cloisters to the homeless. Both the government and the Camorra (the local Mafia) made political and financial capital out of the catastrophe, and allegations of corruption grew. Little solidarity between victims and helpers arose, the former remaining suspicious, apathetic and demoralized.

D'Souza (1982) has contrasted the post-impact histories of two towns caught in this same earthquake. She points out that the poorest suffer most in catastrophes, since they tend to occupy the most physically vulnerable areas, have the least maintained homes, less resources to cope with disaster and even less political power to influence the fair allocation of aid.

Salvitelle, with a population of 1105, had already experienced emigration of its young people since there were few opportunities in this poor peasant village. It was not at the epicentre of the earthquake, but the lack of younger citizens meant that there was little economic and political clout when it came to requesting assistance. To support exaggerated claims for damages (exaggerated because villagers did not trust the authorities to pay the real amounts without deductions), the town was declared unsafe and essential services cut off. Immediate do-it-yourself repairs were not begun. The mayor was not sufficiently organized to demand help, nor to utilize the few offers he received. Altogether 195 people left the village, 29 of them permanently.

Lioni, with a population of 6277, was severely devastated by the earthquake, with 300 dead, 138 injured and 68 per cent rendered homeless. The centre of the town was virtually destroyed but the mayor, by virtue of contacts established earlier when he was trying to attract new industry to the town, was able to mobilize outside aid. He stressed community participation in reconstruction and used community health centres as a reception centre for the shocked and bereaved. Public debates were held to decide on priorities, outside helpers were organized into a common plan, buildings began to be reconstructed and an ambitious plan made for a new town centre.

As Haas *et al.* (1977) and Kates (1973) have shown, the degree to which local leadership can request and co-ordinate aid helps determine the extent of recovery. Those who own their own homes and who are in work have the greatest will to reconstruct their houses. This highlights the importance, if recovery is to be organized, of providing a social structure in which work can be rewarded and the ownership of property legitimized.

Recovery from threatened radiation effects. Fear of radioactive contamination was the main problem for those who lived near the Three Mile Island nuclear power plant during the March 1979 accident. Goldsteen and Schorr (1982) surveyed 400 long-term local residents who lived within about 6 km of the plant.

About 85 per cent evacuated during the accident, giving as their reasons the need to remove their families from danger, the fear of the unknown and being told to leave by the authorities. A year after the accident, 25 per cent of the sample reported feeling afraid of the nuclear plant very often or fairly often, and 53 per cent felt their chances of getting cancer had increased. On a general measure of demoralization, which had reached a value of 20 three months post-accident, the score of 26 achieved a year later indicated that demoralization was continuing to grow. Periods of extreme worry rose from 5 per cent prior to the accident to 26 per cent eight months later. A majority of 68 per cent felt that federal officials had not told the truth about radiation dangers, 80 per cent did not want the plant to start up again and 56 per cent wanted to move to a house further away from a nuclear plant. The lack of physical damage after the accident contributed to a continued sense of uncertainty about long-term health effects and of vulnerability to unseen and unsensed hazards.

After a nuclear attack, areas of otherwise undamaged territory may have to be abandoned for long periods. The psychological difficulties this might cause can only be guessed at. Loizos (1977) has described the problems encountered by Cypriot refugees whose undamaged houses and orchards remained nearby on the other side of the new frontier. This served as a considerable disincentive to participating fully in the new community, and in some ways made the sense of loss more deep. The refugees had a feeling that everything was provisional, and that until they regained their own land their work had no long-term purpose. Similar problems could well occur near areas which were physically undamaged but contaminated by long-lived radioactive wastes.

The bombs on Hiroshima and Nagasaki. Considering their importance, the bombings of Hiroshima and Nagasaki have been under-reported. Some accounts have been often repeated, but much of the film material collected at the time has only recently been released, and the work done with the survivors was incomplete and often exaggeratedly technical, avoiding personal accounts and by-passing a mass readership. As Thompson (1986) puts it, 'The absence of proper follow-up studies is itself a psychological phenomenon worthy of note, since it suggests that the scientific community itself averted its eyes from the long-term consequences of the disaster'.

The experiences of Hiroshima and Nagasaki provide only limited insights of what a future nuclear war might be like because the bombs exploded were far smaller than those now likely to be used and society itself has changed substantially over the past 40 years. The account that follows is based largely on Thompson (1985), and should be interpreted as providing insights only into contingency D; the results of heavier nuclear attacks would be far worse.

Lifton (1967) picked 33 survivors at random from lists kept by local Hiroshima research institutes, plus 42 who were particularly articulate or prominent in the A-bomb problem. A structured interview explored the individual's recollection of the original experience.

No account can hope to capture what the survivors experienced. They were submitted without warning to an explosion so vast that it seemed that the world itself was coming to an end. At 8.15 am on 6 August 1945 most people in Hiroshima were in a relaxed state, since the all clear had just sounded. Few could recall their initial perceptions, some seeing the 'pika', a flash of light, or feeling a wave of heat, and some hearing the 'don', the thunder of the explosion, depending on where they were at the moment of impact. Everyone assumed that a bomb had fallen out of a clear sky directly on them, and they were suddenly and absolutely shifted from normal existence to an overwhelming encounter with death, a theme which stayed with each survivor indefinitely (Lifton 1963). A young university professor, 2500 metres from the epicentre, summed up those feelings of weird, awesome unreality in a frequently expressed image of hell

> Everything I saw made a deep impression – a park nearby covered with dead bodies waiting to be cremated . . . very badly injured people evacuated in my direction . . . Perhaps the most impressive thing I saw were girls, very young girls, not only with their clothes torn off but their

> skin peeled off as well . . . My immediate thought was that this was like the hell I had always read about . . . I had never seen anything which resembled it before, but I thought that should there be a hell, this was it.

In Nagasaki a young doctor Akizuki (1981) was preparing to treat a patient when the bomb exploded. After pulling himself from the debris of his consulting room, he was eventually able to look out of the window.

> The sky was dark as pitch, covered with dense clouds of smoke; under that blackness, over the earth, hung a yellow-brown fog. Gradually the veiled ground became visible, and the view beyond rooted me to the spot with horror. All the buildings I could see were on fire . . . Electricity poles were wrapped in flame like so many pieces of kindling. Trees on the near-by hills were smoking, as were the leaves of sweet potatoes in the fields. To say that everything burned is not enough. The sky was dark, the ground was scarlet, and in between hung clouds of yellowish smoke. Three kinds of colour – black, yellow and scarlet – loomed ominously over the people, who ran about like so many ants seeking to escape.
> (Akizuki 1981)

After encountering so much horror, survivors found that they were incapable of emotion. They behaved mechanically, felt emotionally numb, and at the same time knew they were partly trying to pretend to be unaffected in a vain attempt to protect themselves from the trauma of what they were witnessing. Most survivors focussed on one ultimate horror which had left them with a profound sense of pity, guilt or shame. A baby still half-alive on his dead mother's breast, loved ones abandoned in the fire, pathetic requests for help which had to be ignored – each survivor carried a burning memory.

Survivors were so profoundly affected by what they had experienced that all aspects of their subsequent lives were marked by it, and they felt that they had come into contact with death but remained alive. Survivors attempt to make sense of the fact that they have survived whilst others have perished. Unable to accept this as a chance occurrence, survivors are convinced that their survival was made possible by the deaths of others, and this conviction causes them terrible guilt. Guilt and shame developed very quickly in Hiroshima survivors, as it did in those who escaped concentration camps.

In Lifton's view, Hiroshima and Nagasaki differed from other disasters in that they plunged the survivors into an interminable and unresolvable encounter with death. The immediate horrifying carnage was followed by long-term delayed effects, thus breaking the myth of personal invulnerability in a permanent way. In experiential terms, every victim saw their secure sunlit world destroyed in an instant. It felt like the end of the world, not just the end of one city.

Applications of disaster research. The evidence summarized above enables some predictions to be made that are of direct relevance to the GLAWARS study. These predictions concern the likely behaviour of Londoners during a war scare (contingency B) and the likely outcomes of the five nuclear scenarios.

Contingency B: war scare. From what has been said, it is clear that many Londoners would ignore initial warning signs, such as troop movements in Europe, bellicose speeches and failed negotiations. Indeed, all these and more have occurred recently without being interpreted as warnings of an impending war. As Freedman (1986) has pointed out, the length of warning time available can be determined only after the event. Had war broken out over Poland, Afghanistan, the Korean airliner incident or the Iran/Iraq war, it would have been easy to see in retrospect that there had been abundant warning.

According to Thompson (1985), the government would have good reasons for not passing on any warning it received to the public. Should it do so, industrial production would be slowed down, roads blocked by evacuees and, as pointed out in Part 1, the London system effectively paralysed. However, a highly visible deterioration of the international scene, with a noticeable upsurge of troop movements, could lead to the public and the press being almost as well informed as the authorities.

Most of the population would then move from the threat to the warning phase of the disaster cycle. The population would become alarmed but not panic stricken. People would be highly dependent on news media, and would monitor these sources obsessively. They would be influenced by the actions of their neighbours, and the media would be used as an information source, but not as a decision source. It is known that between 35 per cent (Loizos and Marsh 1986) and 38 per cent (Gunter and Wober 1982) of Londoners intend to leave the city when a world war seems imminent. Studies of actual evacuation in the environs of Three Mile Island suggest that about 39 per cent of the population evacuated (Cutter and Barnes 1982). This unusual concordance of figures indicates that slightly over a third of Londoners are likely to want to evacuate. Evacuees from London are likely to be families with young children, and younger people in middle class occupations (Loizos and Marsh 1986). The actual evacuees from Three Mile Island were the younger age groups (46.8 per cent of those in their twenties, and only 13.8 per cent of the over sixties) and, above all, families with young children where the parents were well educated and in their thirties. Single people tended to stay put whatever their age. If the neighbours stayed, only 9.7 per cent evacuated, but if the neighbours left then 74 per cent left also (Cutter and Barnes 1982).

Public reactions would be partly influenced by the mass media. If the visible and public signs of international tension were on the increase, then people would be likely to make up their own minds despite official entreaties to stay put. The decision would be made on a family basis, with women more likely to favour leaving if they have children, and men more likely to have a sceptical attitude and want to monitor news bulletins to seek confirmation of the danger (Drabek 1969). If the crisis occurred without many visible signs to the public, then there would be a reaction of incredulity, and most people would monitor the news rather than take any practical steps. Once messages were repeated, and other people showed signs of believing them, the decisions about action would begin to be taken. Many of the choices would be explained away as compromises to keep the peace within the family, and people would move out to family and friends away from London. Cutter and Barnes (1982) found that 74 per cent of evacuated families stayed with friends or relatives, and 20 per cent went to second homes or hotels. Official reception centres would tend to be avoided.

Loizos and Marsh (1986) found that those who intended or had to stay in London wanted to stock up and prepare their homes, but fewer than 1 in 8 were sure they would go to a public shelter. The fact that 38 per cent are certain that they would stock up with food indicates that an upsurge in food purchasing is inevitable. It would be wrong to see this as 'panic' buying, since from the vantage point of the family it makes complete sense. The difficulty lies in the fact that such individual purchases would overtax the distribution system and leave the slowest and least able without provisions, a typical social dilemma of the sort described by Dawes (1980).

For there to be any element of control, food rationing would have to be imposed the instant the crisis was perceived by the population. However, if that were done, it would confirm that war was imminent and lead to more anxiety among those who were still sceptical. The more effective response, in psychological terms, might be to concentrate on food distribution, since nothing reduces preparatory food purchases more effectively than the sight of plenty of food. Whilst any of the national systems remained functional, food distribution would play a pivotal role in determining the perception the public had of the crisis.

London would then become a centre of intense activity, with about one third of the population moving out, and everyone who could stocking up on food, making phone calls to family and friends, listening to the radio, and discussing the crisis avidly. In a bizarre sense, it would be an exciting time. People would begin selectively to disengage from work. Loizos and Marsh (1986) found that only 5 per cent of working Londoners were certain they would go to work. Single people are more likely to continue working than those with family responsibilities. A proportion of the population, possibly as high as 10 per cent, would prefer to deny the crisis and try to maintain their normal rhythm of life. They would ignore the warnings for as long as possible, until other people's absenteeism disrupted their own ability to continue their normal lives.

Scenario 1. London would not be directly targeted. There would be about 850,000 casualties in the UK but none in the GLC area.

People would assume London would be bombed next, and roughly 40 per cent would be expected to evacuate. Levels of fear would be high, particularly about radiation, and there would be an obsessive need for news. Because of EMP, television and radio might not be available in some areas and if newspapers could not fill the gap people would be prone to rumour. Few would continue to work, though a proportion, roughly 5 to 10 per cent, might try to continue their normal life as a denying response.

Although there would be strong fears about radiation, those without food would still be willing to venture out to find some, particularly if smoke were not present and ash were not falling. Panic would be unlikely unless a restriction were placed on leaving the city, or food distributed in a haphazard or apparently unfair manner. Attempts to prevent people from evacuating would be likely to provoke panic, hostility and widespread evasion. Allowing people to leave if they wished would slightly reduce the numbers who would actually do so, and would make those who remained slightly calmer. At the same time, the high levels of arousal would create fluctuating moods, so that a feeling of community spirit at one moment could rapidly give way to feelings of doom and despair.

Scenario 2. Seven nuclear weapons would fall on the north-west of the GLC area. This would be the greatest disaster in London's history and would provoke typical disaster reactions from its population – at least as far out as the 1 psi blast rings. Elsewhere, people would be extremely frightened. Enfield, Haringey, Islington, Kingston, Merton, Wandsworth and Lambeth, all at the outer edges of the explosions, would have survivors moving out through them. Behavioural responses would include tremendous fear of radiation, panic near spreading fires, and bewildered and unco-ordinated attempts to rescue injured relatives. The survivors would be surrounded by what was left of more than half a million corpses, and half as many again who were seriously injured, many of them with radiation sickness.

Many survivors would leave London, on foot if necessary. The route to the west would be cut off, so those who left would do so in other directions, but would be guided by a wish to avoid the smoke, which would serve as the only indicator of fall-out. National casualties of 2.75 million would overwhelm all rescue and health systems. Survivors would be dazed and apathetic, tending to wander aimlessly. They would be highly suggestible, and would be subject to wildly oscillating moods. There would be a short-lived anxiety relief at survival, followed by profound depression because of the losses sustained.

This scenario would effectively create two populations – those with disaster syndrome as a consequence of having been bombed, and those at the peak of the anxiety curve, waiting to see whether it would be their turn next. Since communications throughout the country would be unlikely to survive, there would be an effective news black-out, and no valid all clear could be announced. As survivors moved through relatively undamaged areas, they would give sparse and incoherent accounts of what they had experienced, and a very rough picture of where the bombs had fallen would emerge. The most prominent mood in the uninjured survivors would be indecision. They would wish to flee, but would be afraid of radiation. They would wish to help other victims but would be afraid of the disease, contamination and depletion of their own food resources this would entail.

By the end of the third day, the uninjured population would be waiting, in considerable fear, to be bombed, and the injured population would be waiting, in apathy, bewilderment and misery, to die.

Scenario 3. In addition to the explosions of the previous scenario, Biggin Hill, Hillingdon and Hampstead would be bombed, leading to a casualty rate in the GLC area of between 21 and 33 per cent. Nationally, there would be more than 8 million casualties.

Although the bulk of the attack would fall on the western part of the GLC area, the bomb on Hampstead would cause severe damage and disruption to Islington, Westminster, Chelsea, Fulham and Chiswick where the effects of other bombs would also have made themselves felt. There would be the remains of nearly three-quarters of a million corpses and an equal number of seriously injured survivors. The bomb on Biggin Hill would cut off the apparent escape route to the south. In this scenario, most survivors in the east of the city would have to move further east to avoid fall-out. The level of confusion would be high in the undamaged areas. Communications would be so disrupted that the very best that could be hoped for is that groups would eventually form to look after their own immediate interests.

The behavioural picture would be much as for scenario 2, but the proportion of injured to uninjured would be even higher, and the confusion even greater. The high level of national casualties and damage would place the nation close to breaking point as an entity. The 'command and political centres' would, in theory, be relatively intact, but they would not be connected to a functioning political system, and they would not be able to command and control it. In a functional sense, most of the population would not have a government, and would be concerned only with finding water and food for their families.

Scenario 4. This level of attack would cause 21 million casualties in the UK, and a GLC casualty rate in the range of 82 to 88 per cent. The additional targets in London would be Enfield, Whitehall, Clapham and Kingston, each receiving a 1 Mt air burst. By this stage, it is barely possible to talk about London as an entity, and one can only outline the short-term options for the two not immediately damaged zones. One patch near Ealing and Brent would have been straddled by explosions on all sides, and there would be no clear means of escape. Havering would also escape severe damage, and people might be able to move east to avoid some of the fall-out. Survivors would show the full disaster syndrome and there would be little chance of co-ordinated activity.

With 4.3 million dead and a further 1.1 million seriously injured, the situation in scenario 4 is virtually indescribable. Water and food would be the absolute priority of those few who were able to move, and they would search for them, despite fears of radioactive contamination. In addition to their injuries, most people would also be coping with the first stages of bereavement. Concepts such as rioting and looting would no longer have meaning. Those able to move would use whatever was available to assist them in the struggle for survival.

Scenario 5. This scenario would cause nearly 27 million casualties. London would receive additional air bursts on the City of London, Euston Station, Victoria and Albert docks, Hackney and Sutton, leading to a GLC casualty rate of 95.5 to 97.5 per cent. Apart from Bromley, London would cease to exist for all practical purposes. Nonetheless, there would be some 600,000 survivors, about two-thirds of them seriously injured. The survivors would show the full disaster syndrome, and would not be capable of co-ordinated rehabilitation. After fires had subsided, any survivors capable of moving would make their way out of London in search of water and food.

References

Akizuki, T., *Nagasaki 1945*. London, Quartet, 1981.

Anderson, E. W., 'Psychiatric syndrome following blast'. In *Journal of Mental Science*, 88, 328, 1942.

Bachman, G. G., 'How American high school seniors view the military'. In *Armed Forces and Society*, in press.

Britten, S., *The Invisible Event: An Assessment of the Risk of Accidental or Unauthorized Detonation of Nuclear Weapons and of War by Miscalculation*. London, Meynard Press, 1983.

Business Decisions, *Nuclear Weapons Study – Summary Report*. Survey conducted for the *TV Times*, 1983.

Churcher, J., Gleisner, J., Lieven, E., and Pushkin, R., 'Nuclear war and civil defence: some psychological and social implications'. Paper presented at British Psychological Society Annual Conference, 1981.

Cutter, S., and Barnes, K., 'Evacuation Behaviour and Three-Mile Island'. In *Disasters*, 6(2), 116–124, 1982.

Dawes, R. M., 'Social dilemmas'. In *Annual Review of Psychology*, 31, 169-193, 1980.

D'Souza, F., 'Recovery Following the South Italian Earthquake, November 1980: Two Contrasting Examples'. In *Disasters*, 6(2), 101–109, 1982.

Drabek, T., 'Social Processes in Disaster: Family Evacuation'. In *Social Problems*, 16(3), 336–349, 1969.

Drabek, T., and Stephenson, J., 'Disaster Strikes'. In *Journal of Applied Social Psychology*, 1(2), 187–203, 1971.

Freedman, L., *GLAWARS Task 1: The Military Threat*. London, South Bank Polytechnic, 1986, mimeo.

Geipel, R., *Disaster and Reconstruction*. London, Allen and Unwin, 1982.

Goldsteen, R., and Schorr, J., 'The Long-Term Impact of a Man-Made Disaster: An Examination of a Small Town in the Aftermath of the Three-Mile Island Nuclear Reactor Accident'. In *Disasters*, 6(1), 50–59, 1982.

Gunter, B., and Wober, M., *Television viewing and public perceptions of hazards to life*. Report of the Independent Broadcasting Authority, 1982.

Haas, J. E., Kates, R. W., and Bowden, M., *Reconstruction following Disaster*. Cambridge, Mass., MIT Press, 1977.

Hansson, R. O., Noulles, D., and Bellovich, S. J., 'Knowledge, Warning and Stress: A Study of Comparative Roles in an Urban Floodplain'. In *Environment and Behaviour*, 14(2), 171–185, 1982.

Harrison, T., *Living through the Blitz*. Penguin, London, 1978.

Hodler, T. W., 'Residents' Preparedness and Response to the Kalamazoo Tornado'. In *Disasters*, 6(1), 44–49, 1982.

Jackson, E. L., 'Response to Earthquake Hazard: The West Coast of North America'. In *Environment and Behaviour*, 13(4), 387–416, 1981.

Janis, I. L., *Stress and Frustration*. New York, Harcourt Brace, 1971.

Kahneman, D., Slovic, P., and Tversky, A., *Judgement under Uncertainty: Heuristics and Biases*. Cambridge, Mass., Cambridge University Press, 1982.

Kates, R. W., *Human Impact of the Managua earthquake disaster*. Toronto, University of Toronto, 1973, Natural Hazard Research Working Paper No. 23.

Killian, L. M., 'The significance of multiple group membership in disaster'. In *American Journal of Sociology*, 57 (4), 310, 1952.

Kinston, W., and Rosser, R., 'Disaster: effects on mental and physical state'. In

Journal of Psychosomatic Research, 18, 437–456, 1974.

Lacey, G. N., 'Observations on Abervan'. In *Journal of Psychosomatic Research*, 16, 257, 1972.

Lachman, R., Tatsuoka, M., and Bank, W. J., 'Human behaviour during the tsunami of May 1960'. In *Science*, 133, 1405, 1961.

Lifton, R. J., 'Psychological effects of the Atomic Bomb in Hiroshima: The theme of death'. In *Daedalus, Journal of the American Academy of Arts and Sciences*, 93 (3), 1963.

Lifton, R. J., *Death in Life: Survivors of Hiroshima*. New York, Random House, 1967.

Loizos, P., 'A Struggle for Meaning: Reactions to Disaster Among Cypriot Refugees'. In *Disasters*, 1(3), 231–239, 1977.

Loizos, P., and Marsh, A., *GLAWARS Task 4: Concern with the unthinkable*. London, South Bank Polytechnic, 1986, mimeo.

Miller, I., 'Dispositional and Situational Variables Related to Evacuation at Three Mile Island'. In *Dissertation Abstracts International*, 42(5-B), 2071, 1981.

Popovic, M., and Petrovic, D., 'After the Earthquake'. In *The Lancet*, 2, 1169, 1964.

Quarantelli, E. L., 'The nature and conditions of panic'. In *American Journal of Sociology*, 60, 267, 1954.

Seligman, M. P., *Helplessness: On depression, development and death*. San Francisco, Freeman, 1975.

Slovic, P., Fischoff, B., and Lichtenstein, S., 'Facts versus fears: understanding perceived risk', 1982. In Kahneman, D., Slovic, P., and Tversky, A., (eds.), *Judgement under Uncertainty: Heuristics and Biases*. Cambridge, Mass., Cambridge University Press, 1982.

Solantous, T., Kimpela, M., and Taipale, V., 'The threat of war in the minds of 12–18 year olds in Finland'. In *The Lancet*, 8380, 784–785, 1984.

Thompson, J., *Psychological Aspects of Nuclear War*. Chichester, British Psychological Society/John Wiley and Sons, 1985.

Thompson, J., *GLAWARS Task 4: The behaviour of Londoners in a future major war: estimates from psychological research*. London, South Bank Polytechnic, 1986, mimeo.

Titmus, R. M., *Problems of Social Policy*. London, Longmans Green, 1950.

Wallace, A. F., *Tornado in Worcester*. Washington DC, National Academy of Sciences, 1956, National Academy of Sciences Disaster Study No. 3.

Weiss, J. M., 'Effects of coping behaviour in different warning signal conditions on stress pathology in rats'. In *Journal of Comparative and Physiological Psychology*, 77, 1–13, 1971.

Wolfenstein, M., *Disaster: a psychological essay*. London, Routledge and Kegan Paul, 1957.

2.7 Effects on the atmosphere

A nuclear war is likely to have profound effects on the atmosphere. The consequences for the survivors of nuclear attacks could be as serious as those of the war itself.

Three effects are likely: the onset of a marked change in the weather, characterized by lowered temperatures, darkness, and erratic precipitation; damage to the ozone layer, resulting in increased ultraviolet radiation at the Earth's surface; and chemical pollution of the atmosphere, resulting in acid rain, and contamination of soil and water. These effects have become known as nuclear winter.

The nuclear winter. In a nuclear war, vast quantities of dust and smoke would be injected into the atmosphere and dispersed by the wind. Somewhat surprisingly, the idea that these particles could interfere with the Earth's heat balance sufficiently to produce marked cooling – nuclear winter – has been put forward only recently (Crutzen and Birks 1982, Turco *et al.* 1983, and Ehrlich *et al.* 1983 and 1984). These, and later, studies suggest that, for a period of weeks and possibly months, the amount of solar energy reaching the Earth's surface would be severely reduced. The resulting change in climate could turn summer into winter, dropping temperatures to close to, possibly well below, freezing whatever the season. This would be likely to cause many deaths among poorly fed and sheltered survivors. There would also be severe effects on food production over ensuing growing seasons. Furthermore, buildings and roads might be affected by alternate periods of thawing and freezing, and flooding could be widespread.

The nuclear winter theory, and the risk of serious environmental effects, has now been confirmed by three organizations: the US National Academy of Sciences, the Royal Society of Canada and, most recently, SCOPE (the Scientific Committee on Problems of the Environment of the International Council of Scientific Unions). None has seriously questioned the physical basis of the theory, although all stress the impossibility of making definite predictions.

The US study concluded

> Although there are enormous uncertainties . . . the committee believes that long-term climatic effects with severe implications for the biosphere could occur, and these effects should be included in any analysis of the consequences of nuclear war.
>
> (NAS 1985)

GLAWARS took this advice seriously, and commissioned research on the nuclear winter directed specifically to the UK situation (Kelly, Karas and Wigzell 1986). In addition, GLAWARS organized a workshop on the effects of nuclear war, including the effects of nuclear winter, on the biosphere (Myers and Berry 1986), the results of which are presented in section 2.8.

The SCOPE conclusion, published in late 1985, was even more forthright

> as representatives of the world scientific community drawn together in this study, we conclude that many of the serious global environmental effects are sufficiently probable to require widespread concern. Because of the possibility of a tragedy of an unprecedented dimension, any disposition to minimize or ignore the widespread environmental effects of a nuclear war would be a fundamental disservice to the future of global civilization.
>
> (SCOPE 1985)

No civil defence plan as yet encompasses the effects of nuclear winter. The Home Office made its position clear in summer 1985

> The Report of the National Research Council of the US National Academy of Sciences, while concluding that long term climatic effects with severe implications for the biosphere could occur, and that those effects should be included in any analysis of the consequences of nuclear war, confirmed that more work needs to be done before the theory or the scale of possible effects can be validated. When this work is completed we shall consider the implications for civil defence planning. We await further reports with interest and understand that a report by the Scientific Committee on Problems of the Environment is due later this year. In the meantime however the Government is not prepared to issue revised planning guidance based on an unestablished theory.
>
> (Home Office 1985)

No further Home Office guidance had been issued when this report went to press.

It is true that uncertainties surround determination of the atmospheric consequences of nuclear war. For example, any prediction must be based on a nuclear war scenario, since the effects depend on the number, yields, targets and altitudes of the nuclear detonations involved. Targeting strategy is particularly important because more smoke is produced as a result of attacks on urban and industrial targets than as a result of attacks on military targets; and it is the carbon-based smoke from fires in urban and industrial areas that is largely responsible for the marked cooling. Furthermore, the duration of a nuclear winter depends critically on the height to which the nuclear cloud of dust and smoke is raised. As a result, estimates of duration range from days to months, with weeks being the preferred estimate.

A further complication lies in making predictions for specific areas. Computer model simulations must be used to determine possible effects on climate. Broad-scale estimates, for example on the continental scale, can be considered reasonably reliable but this reliability does not extend to predictions at the level of either the Greater London area or even the United Kingdom as a whole. Indeed, the UK situation on the western maritime edge of a major continent complicates the issues considerably. When the winds are off the ocean, which would take some time to cool down, the UK may be protected to some extent from the severe cooling likely when the winds blow from the much colder continental areas.

Nevertheless, as Kelly, Karas and Wigzell (1986) put it

> It is certain that, in some regions and at some times, the nature of the overlying cloud will be such that marked cooling will occur. The duration may only be hours; it may be weeks. The geographical scale may be localised; it may be continental or even global. There is little doubt that the climate system will be disturbed. It is the extent of the perturbation that is uncertain.

Previous nuclear winter studies. Nuclear winter studies have to do four things:

1 identify plausible nuclear scenarios;
2 assess the quantities of dust, smoke and chemical pollution produced by each scenario;
3 model the behaviour of the cloud of dust and smoke over space and time; and
4 estimate the effects on climate.

Many different nuclear scenarios have now been examined for their possible effects on the atmosphere. One of these, referred to in this report as the baseline scenario, would be expected to produce attacks on the UK of the type described in GLAWARS scenarios 4 and 5. A war of this general nature could produce notable atmospheric effects in the UK. The baseline scenario assumes a global nuclear exchange of 5000 Mt, with around 20 per cent of the yield detonated on urban or industrial targets and close to 60 per cent detonated as ground bursts. There are 10,400 explosions, varying in yield between 0.1 and 10 Mt. Smaller global levels of attack, corresponding to GLAWARS scenarios 1, 2 and 3, were also considered; according to Kelly, Karas and Wigzell (1986), even these scenarios could well have an appreciable atmospheric impact in the UK.

The nature of the war determines the amount of dust and smoke injected into the atmosphere, which depends – among other things – on the extent of the fires created by the nuclear blasts. Greene, Percival and Ridge (1985) have made estimates for a 6000 Mt exchange, comparable to the baseline scenario. They write

> Our 6000 Mt nuclear war scenario would ignite fires over areas bigger than many countries. Making conservative assumptions, the combined

areas of cities and their surrounding conurbations within the ignition zone would be roughly the size of Italy. For smaller towns and villages, the corresponding area could just about cover Switzerland. Fires could be started in forests over an area of more than five times the combined size of the Benelux countries, and the total ignition zones over grass or agricultural land would cover the UK about two times over. Finally, enough dust would be carried high into the atmosphere to dam the English channel with a wall 500 yards high and 30 yards thick.

To make predictions about the effects of this material on the Earth's energy balance requires a knowledge of many other factors, including how much combustible material is contained in the targets, the percentage of material burnt in the fires and the size of the particles produced – particles less than one millionth of a metre in diameter are

Table 30 Smoke production estimates in nuclear winter studies

Parameter	Typical value	Range	Depends on:
Number of explosions/ Combustible targets	6000	Few to several thousand or more	Scenario
Fraction unburned (per cent)	20	Few to 100	Targeting strategy, overlap, likelihood of ignition
Combustible fuel (g/cm^2)	3 in cities 0.5 in forests	0.1 to >10	Target type, for forests, depends on time of year
Area per fire (km^2)	200	10 to 1000	Yield, target, weather, likelihood of spread, burst height, topography
Lofted aerosol fraction with particle size <1 micron	0.03	up to 0.05	Nature of fuel and fire, fraction of fuel burned
Total aerosol mass (million tonnes)	200	10 to 1000	⋆

⋆present US forest fire injection is about 10 million tonnes/year; global atmospheric soot loading is less than 1 million tonnes.
Source: MacCracken, personal communication, 1985.

particularly effective in trapping and scattering radiation from the sun before it can reach, and heat, the ground. Table 30 summarizes the relevant assumptions made in major studies of the nuclear winter.

While the range of these parameters is wide, the uncertainties they produce are less so. To reduce the risk to an insignificant level requires that a number of the parameters fall at the lower end of their range of uncertainty, and this is not likely. The net effect of the uncertainties on the total mass of small smoke particles is a range of 10 to 1000 million tonnes. While injection of 10 million tonnes of smoke is considered unlikely to generate significant large-scale climatic effects, injection of 50 million tonnes or more may produce widespread cooling. Over most of the range of uncertainty, a significant climate impact can be expected. Even at injection levels of 10 million tonnes or so, transient cooling may occur under dense patches of dust and smoke.

The nature of the climatic impact, its strength, geographical extent and duration, will be determined largely by the altitude of the cloud of dust and smoke. Essentially, the higher the cloud, the longer will it persist. Information from atmospheric tests enables fairly accurate predictions to be made about the height which the dust cloud is likely to reach. This is not true for the smoke particles, although it is known that the smoke from rural fires can reach heights of 5 km. Recent model simulations of urban fires suggest that much of the urban smoke could be injected higher, into the upper atmosphere where it may remain for many months. As the cloud top is heated by the sun, it may rise to even greater heights. Within weeks, it is expected to spread out to form a more or less even veil over the northern middle latitudes, with streamers spreading north and south, possibly deep into the southern hemisphere. Modelling of the behaviour of the nuclear cloud is still in its early stages of development. Nevertheless, little doubt remains that the cloud will exist, persist and spread, that it will produce climatic effects, and that these effects, although most severe in northern middle latitudes, will be hemispheric and possibly global in extent.

The next stage is to estimate climatic effects, in the first instance by calculating the ways in which the different sized particles in the cloud affect both incoming solar radiation and the outgoing infrared radiation from the Earth's surface and lower atmosphere. Carbon-based smoke particles tend to absorb energy, while other particles tend to scatter it, altering its original direction. However, in both cases the effect is stronger on incoming than outgoing radiation, producing a reverse greenhouse effect: incoming radiation is attenuated, outgoing radiation is reduced only marginally, and the Earth's surface begins to cool. The effect is then compounded as the normal atmospheric circulation undergoes radical change, due largely to heating of the smoke and dust cloud at height which tends to prevent the convection that normally occurs within the atmosphere. Turco *et al.* (1983) estimate that, in their baseline case, the amount of solar energy reaching ground level could be reduced by more than 95 per cent during the first two to three weeks.

Finally, computer models of the climate system are used to determine the potential effects on weather and climate. Although none of the models can be considered entirely satisfactory, nearly all produce similar sorts of results. An important figure to bear in mind is that a drop in temperature of 5 °C or more over a month or so is beyond the range of natural variability and is climatically, medically and agriculturally very significant. Temperature drops of this order produce appreciable increases in human mortality rates (Macfarlane 1977), and the consequences would be greatly aggravated by the conditions likely to prevail after a nuclear attack. A temperature drop of this magnitude, extended over a whole growing season in the UK, would reduce agricultural production to nearly nothing. Most models of the nuclear winter predict temperature changes over land areas in the northern middle latitudes greatly in excess of 5 °C, for several weeks or longer.

Table 31 summarizes the main results of nuclear winter studies that assume scenarios roughly comparable to those of GLAWARS scenarios 4 and 5.

These models indicate clearly that cooling of tens of degrees might occur in northern middle latitudes. They also reveal a number of other important characteristics of the nuclear winter.

First, the effects are highly dependent on the season of the attack. Greatest effects are felt during the summer, and the smallest during the winter when, of course, the incident solar radiation is at its lowest and the perturbations produced in the climatic system are therefore much smaller.

Secondly, the cooling effects will be greatly reduced over the oceans, which take much longer to cool down, and which will therefore provide some protection to neighbouring land masses.

Thirdly, the duration of the nuclear winter remains the most uncertain factor. Duration depends ultimately on how quickly the nuclear cloud is dissipated. Three stages are currently recognized: an acute stage, lasting for a few days to as long as a few months, during which the impact is most severe; an intermediate stage, with less pronounced effects, lasting from a month to close to a year; and a chronic stage, with small effects, still outside the normal range of temperature variation, lasting from one to five years. The latter may continue long after the nuclear cloud is dissipated because of the lag effects of the cooling of the oceans and the advance of snow and ice during the acute and intermediate stages. However, no detailed calculations have been undertaken for any but the acute stage.

Finally, nuclear winter effects will vary widely over space, being strongest in the middle of continents where the attack took place. The impact may be as great over the northern subtropics, depending on the spread of the cloud. Widespread effects are most likely in the case of a war in northern summer. Smaller changes are expected in tropical regions and in the southern hemisphere but this does not mean that they will be insignificant. It is possible, for example, that an attack in the northern summer would result in the Asian sub-continent not being sufficiently warmed to undergo the annual monsoon. Serious drought would therefore be expected.

Table 31 Results of major nuclear winter models[a]

Group	Scenario	Injection dust	Injection smoke	Length of simulation	Maximum temperature change (continental interior, °C)
TTAPS	Baseline	960 Mt	225 Mt	12 months	−35
CSSAS			600 Mt	1 year	>−30
NCAR 1	NAS	–	180 Mt	20 days	>−30
NCAR 2[b]	NAS	–	180 Mt	30 days	>−25
LLNL 1	Baseline	–	200 Mt	90 days	−30
LLNL 2	Baseline	–	150 Mt	90 days	−8[c]
LLNL 3[b]	Baseline	–	150 Mt	30 days	−35
UM	Baseline			> 4 years	>−20
LA[b]	NAS	–	170 Mt	40 days	>−15

Key:
TTAPS Turco *et al.* 1983 and 1984
CSSAS Alexandrov and Stenchikov 1983, Thompson *et al.* 1984
NCAR 1 Covey *et al.* 1984 and 1985, Thompson *et al.* 1984
NCAR 2 Thompson 1985
LLNL 1 and 2 MacCracken 1983
LLNL 3 MacCracken and Walton 1984
UM Robock 1984
LA Malone *et al.* 1985

[a] only models likely to produce UK attacks comparable to GLAWARS scenarios 4 and 5 are included. Baseline = Turco *et al.* 1983 reference scenario, NAS = National Academy of Sciences (US) 1985 reference scenario. In most cases, the effects of a summer war are simulated.
[b] interactive models, in which cloud behaviour is influenced by nuclear winter effects
[c] northern hemisphere average
1 Mt is 1 million tonnes
Source: Kelly, Karas and Wigzell (1986).

Impact on the UK. To determine the possible impact of a nuclear winter on the UK, GLAWARS researchers studied computer model results for their relevance to the UK situation. Unpublished information specifically concerning effects on the UK was obtained from model simulations undertaken by MacCracken and Walton (1984) at the Lawrence Livermore National Laboratory, and Thompson (1985) at the National Center for Atmospheric Research, both in the United States. On the basis of these and other results, plausible projections were made about the possible course of events in the UK.

MacCracken and Walton modelled the effects of a 150 million tonnes injection of smoke, corresponding to a baseline exchange, occurring on July 1st. Dense concentrations of cloud occur over targeted areas, including the UK, during the first few days. The amount of solar radiation reaching the ground in these regions reduces virtually to zero. Temperatures over the UK drop to close to freezing (even though the month is July) and, though there is then some clearance in the cloud cover, temperatures remain at this level for nearly two weeks. The overlying cloud then clears almost completely and temperatures return to normal. The simulation ends 30 days after the exchange. Longer simulations suggest that severe cooling may recur over following weeks as dense patches of cloud move overhead or as winds blow out of the cold continental interior (Malone *et al.* 1985).

This simulation illustrates just one of a range of possible outcomes. Consideration of a number of model results suggests that, during severe episodes, the UK may well experience an average cooling of some 10 to 15°C in the case of a summer-time baseline exchange (Kelly, Karas and Wigzell 1986). This is less severe than is likely in continental interiors owing to the ameliorating influence of the neighbouring ocean. Cooling of this magnitude is most likely during the first week or so after the attack when the dust and smoke produced locally is most dense. During this period, temperature falls of 20°C or so may occur on shorter time scales of hours to days.

Temperature departures are likely to be less marked in other seasons. Nevertheless, whatever the time of year, average temperatures during the initial phase could well drop to close to freezing, with sub-freezing conditions possible on the day-to-day time scale. Whatever the season of the exchange, during the days and weeks immediately after the attack the survivors could face conditions comparable to those normally experienced in winter.

Another computer model simulation, by Thompson (1985), suggests that the frequency and intensity of depressions in the North Atlantic sector may be enhanced owing to the strong temperature gradients in their spawning ground off the east coast of North America. In the summer simulation, these depressions pass over the UK, and high winds and increased precipitation may result. Enhanced rainfall is likely to increase the rate of wash-out of the dust and smoke, perhaps reducing the cooling experienced locally but increasing fall-out. In winter, the depressions stagnate over the eastern Atlantic, held back by blocking anticyclones over northern Europe – a situation typical of a normal severe winter. Again, these are the results of just one simulation. They cannot be considered a forecast but simply indicate one of a range of possibilities.

As the acute stage continues, temperatures may range from those typical of the present day, when the winds are off the ocean or the cloud overhead is light, to well beyond the range of normal variability – cooling of up to 10°C or so – when the winds are off the land or the cloud overhead is dense. These episodes are likely to last for a couple of days to a week or more. The change from one to the other could occur rapidly, producing dramatic changes in temperature in only 24 hours or so. Within these major episodes, the weather itself will depend on a host of uncertain and, in some cases, unpredictable factors: the rate at which the cloud is removed from the atmosphere, the manner in which it is blown from place to place, the exact direction of the prevailing winds, and so on.

The results of these deliberations are summarized in Table 32. As can be seen, by far the most severe effects occur following a summer attack when average monthly temperatures could fall by 10 to 15°C. During other seasons, the fall is likely to be only a few degrees. Nonetheless, when continental winds are blowing, or when the overlying nuclear cloud is dense, temperatures could fall to freezing point or below, and there could be snow cover, in any season. Daylight intensity will be reduced to less than 10 per cent of normal for periods ranging from days to, perhaps, a couple of weeks (25 per cent of normal light approximates to the onset of twilight, 10 per cent to twilight itself and 1 per cent to a bright moonlit night). When the wind blows off the ocean and the nuclear cloud is light, temperatures may not alter greatly, though there could be torrential rain.

Long-term effects will be crucial in determining chances of survival and recovery. Little attention has been paid to the possibility of prolonged disturbance of the climate system and only one model simulation has been made (Robock 1984). It is difficult to estimate the degree to which the climate system will be altered by the initial rapid cooling, and the rate of removal of the cloud is not well established, but the threat of long-term effects over periods of years is genuine. To provide estimates of the scale of the problem over the first two years, GLAWARS researchers used Robock's results, reducing the temperature departure for northern middle latitudes predicted by his model to take into account the ameliorating influence of the ocean.

Two cases were considered: the first assumed an initial average temperature reduction of 12.5°C in the case of a July attack; the second assumed an initial reduction of half this amount. Values were scaled appropriately for the other seasons. The results, for attacks during each of the four seasons and taking the more severe initial cooling, are summarized below.

January attack Average temperatures fall to close to freezing for about three months. During the following spring and summer, there are temperature drops of about 4°C below normal.

April attack Initially, temperatures fall to about 3°C. Average temperatures never rise above 10°C during the first year.

July attack An initial temperature fall of 12.5°C turns summer into winter. The effect is reduced as winter approaches but not before there is a short period of very intense cold.

October attack Temperatures stay below 5°C for six months, resulting in an extremely long winter.

Whatever the season of the exchange, sub-zero temperatures are possible on any day throughout much of the first year. During the second year, temperatures are still likely to be depressed by a couple of degrees. The effects on agriculture appear likely to be particularly alarming. During the first growing season, there appears little chance of any substantial harvest, regardless of the time of the attack (see Table 32). During the second growing season, average temperatures could still be 1 or 2°C below normal. While this is within the range of natural variability for a particular month, such a period of persistent temperature departures throughout a growing season rarely occurs. The implications of these effects are examined in section 2.8.

These results, it must be stressed, are not predictions: they are attempts to develop a plausible scenario for the UK of what might happen following a major nuclear exchange. It is even more difficult to suggest nuclear winter scenarios following more limited nuclear attacks such as GLAWARS scenarios 1, 2 and 3. Clearly, the effects are likely to be less severe. Nevertheless, even in the case of injections of smoke an order of magnitude less than considered in the baseline case, appreciable cooling may occur, although it is likely to be of limited extent and duration.

During the initial days after an exchange corresponding to GLAWARS scenarios 1, 2 and 3, according to Kelly, Karas and Wigzell (1986), transient temperature drops of 5 to 10 °C could affect the UK in the case of a summer war. As so much depends on the nature of the large-scale exchange accompanying the attack on the UK, even in the case of scenarios 1, 2 and 3 and even if the UK is not targeted, the possibility of more severe effects cannot be excluded.

Table 32 Plausible effects of a nuclear winter on the UK[a]

	Month of attack			
	January	April	July	October
1. Acute stage (lasting weeks to several months)				
Normal mean monthly temperature (°C)	3	8	16	10
severe episodes				
Mean monthly temperature (°C)	0	3	4	5
Mean daily temperature (°C)	0–1	2–4	1–6	4–6
Precipitation (% of normal)	0–50	0–50	0–50	0–50
Light intensity (% of normal)	1–25	1–25	1–25	1–25
mild episodes				
Mean daily temperature (°C)		Normal range		
Precipitation (% of normal)	50–200	50–200	50–200	50–200
Light intensity (% of normal)	25–100	25–100	25–100	25–100
2. Longer-term effects (up to two years)				
Number of months in which mean monthly temperature is:	A B C	A B C	A B C	A B C
<10°C	5 5 4	14 2 1	11 11 0	8 8 7
<5°C	4 3 2	2 0 0	2 0 0	6 0 0

A: severe case, assuming full temperature reduction throughout month (no mild episodes).
B: less severe case, assuming half temperature reduction in severe case (50% mild and 50% severe episodes).
C: normal expectation.

Mean growing season temperatures (°C) – severe case, as A above	January	April	July	October
Normal	13	13	13	13
After attack:				
1st growing season	9	6.5	(4.5)[b]	10.5
2nd growing season	12	11	11	12

[a] due to an assumed 5000 to 6500 Mt nuclear exchange between major powers, equivalent to GLAWARS scenarios 4 and 5.
[b] exchange occurs during the growing season, and the estimate is for the affected fraction of the season only.
Source: adapted from Kelly, Karas and Wigzell 1986

The chemical effects of atmospheric pollution. The nuclear winter is produced primarily by the interaction of smoke and dust particles in the atmosphere with solar radiation. However, many other atmospheric pollutants would be introduced into the atmosphere in vast quantities after a major nuclear exchange.

The nuclear explosions, fires in urban and industrial areas, and blast damage to storage containers would result in the release of large quantities of potentially dangerous chemicals into the atmosphere, both near the surface and at height. Some of these chemicals will be toxic in their own right. Some will undergo chemical reactions and may form photochemical smog, depending on the prevailing atmospheric conditions. Precipitation will wash out the pollutants producing highly acid rain. In the aftermath of a nuclear war, acid rain is not likely to be the principal concern of many of the survivors. However, its effects on agricultural production could be serious. As explained in section 2.8, plants already stressed by extreme cold are rendered more vulnerable to additional insults, of which acid rain would be one of many.

If warheads larger than about 1 Mt are used, nitrogen oxides will be lofted directly into the stratosphere where, at a height of 20 to 25 km, ozone concentrations are at their maximum. This ozone layer plays a key role in biological survival on the Earth. It absorbs most of the sun's damaging ultraviolet radiation before it reaches the Earth's surface. Nitrogen oxides react with ozone in complex ways, and their presence in the stratosphere would reduce ozone concentrations, with the result that more ultraviolet radiation could reach the Earth's surface. As a rule of thumb, a reduction of 1 per cent in the ozone layer increases ultraviolet radiation at the Earth's surface by about 2 per cent.

Several studies have been made of the potential effects of different war scenarios on the ozone layer. The results are summarized in Table 33.

A number of points need to be made about these figures. According to Kelly, Karas and Wigzell (1986), they may underestimate the quantities of nitrogen oxides injected into the stratosphere owing to the lack of consideration of the 'secondary' lofting of nitrogen oxides, with the cloud of dust and smoke, to greater heights in the atmosphere. Thus, although the smaller scenarios are roughly equivalent to GLAWARS scenarios 4 and 5, an improved prediction of likely effects, particularly in the case of a summer war when lofting is most likely, may be gained by considering the larger scenarios in Table 33.

Secondly, there is a considerable delay before the ozone layer drops to its minimum concentration: about one year for the baseline case and nine months for the larger excursion scenario. By this time, the dust and smoke will have cleared sufficiently to allow the ultraviolet radiation through. It may take up to 10 years for the ozone layer to return to normal.

Table 33 Ozone depletion from nuclear exchanges

Scenario	Yield (Mt)	NO (10^{32} molecules) Below 12 km	Above 12 km	Maximum ozone depletion (%)	Note
Baseline	6,500	2,665	3,835	17	a
Excursion	8,500	2,665	5,835	43	b
Chang case A	10,600	560	6,540	51	c
Chang case B	5,300	280	3,270	32	d
Chang case C	5,670	0	3,800	42	e
Chang case D	4,930	560	2,740	16	f
Chang case E	6,720	180	4,340	39	g
Chang case F	3,890	390	2,220	20	h
CB	5,740	4,510	1,230	0	i
CB excursion	10,000	1,375	8,625	65 (45°N)	j
Turco *et al.* (1983)	10,000	1,200	8,400	50	k

[a] No weapons larger than 1.5 Mt.
[b] Baseline scenario plus 100 weapons of 20 Mt yield.
[c] All strategic weapons in the United States and Soviet arsenals successfully detonated. See Chang and Wuebbles (1982) for details of the Chang cases A–F.
[d] Half of the weapons of each type in the strategic arsenals of the United States and the Soviet Union.
[e] All weapons with individual yields greater than 0.8 Mt in the strategic arsenals of the United States and the Soviet Union.
[f] All weapons with individual yields less than or equal to 0.8 Mt in the strategic arsenals of the United States and the Soviet Union.
[g] All weapons in the Soviet strategic arsenal.
[h] All weapons in the US strategic arsenal.
[i] CB = Crutzen and Birks (1982). When the troposphere is included, the CB scenario actually results in a slight ozone increase. The Chang model also gives this result for the CB scenario.
[j] The CB excursion scenario consists of 5000 1-Mt detonations plus 500 10-Mt detonations and is identical to the NAS (1975) scenario.
[k] The blocking of sunlight by nuclear dust and soot was accounted for but the resulting heating of the stratosphere was not.
Source: NAS (1985).

As can be seen, ozone depletion is considerable. According to the NAS (1985), in the first year ozone amounts could drop to 55 per cent of normal, resulting in an increase of ultraviolet radiation of nearly 100 per cent. In the second year, ozone amounts of 65 per cent of normal may occur, and ultraviolet radiation levels could be 70 per cent above normal. According to SCOPE (1985), heavier ozone depletion, and increases in the ultraviolet radiation flux, may occur in certain areas for short periods of time.

What effects this would have on both human survivors and ecology in general is not known. Increased ultraviolet radiation causes certain types of skin cancer and blindness, tends to slow down plant growth, particularly in marine algae, and causes an increased frequency of mutation. The NAS has calculated that each 1 per cent of ozone depletion would increase the incidence of skin cancer by 2 per cent. The implications for agriculture and ecology are examined in the next section.

References

Alexandrov, V. V., and Stenchikov, G. L., 'On the modelling of the climatic consequences of nuclear war'. In *Proceedings on Applied Mathematics*, Moscow, Computing Centre of the USSR Academy of Sciences, 1983.

Chang, J. S., and Wuebbles, D. J., 'The Consequences of Nuclear War on the Global Environment'. In *Hearing before the Sub-Committee on Investigations and Oversight on the Committee on Science and Technology*. Washington DC, US House of Representatives, 1982.

Covey, C., Schneider, S. H., and Thompson, S. L., 'Global atmospheric effects of massive smoke injections from a nuclear war: results from general circulation model simulations'. In *Nature*, 308 (5954), 21–25, 1984.

Crutzen, P. J., and Birks, J. W., 'The atmosphere after a nuclear war: twilight at noon'. In *Ambio*, 11 (2–3), 114–125, 1982.

Ehrlich, P. R., Harte, J., Harwell, M. A., and others, 'Long-term biological consequences of nuclear war'. In *Science*, 222 (4630), 1293–1300, 1983.

Ehrlich, P. R., Sagan C., Kennedy, D., and others, *The cold and the dark: the world after nuclear war*. London, Sidgwick and Jackson, 1984.

Greene, O., Percival, I., and Ridge, I., *Nuclear winter: the evidence and the risks*. Oxford, Polity Press, 1985.

Home Office, *Guidance on planning assumptions – commentary*. Letter sent to local authorities and the Nuclear Free Zone Steering Committee, 30 July 1985.

Kelly, P. M., Karas, J. H. W., and Wigzell, M., *GLAWARS Task 7: Potential effects of a nuclear war on the atmosphere, weather and climate in the Greater London area*. London, South Bank Polytechnic, 1986, mimeo.

MacCracken, M. C., *Nuclear war: preliminary estimates of the climatic effects of a nuclear exchange*. Livermore, California, Lawrence Livermore National Laboratory, 1983, preprint UCRL 89770.

MacCracken, M. C., and Walton, J. J., *The effects of interactive transport and scavenging of smoke on the calculated temperature change from large amounts of smoke*. Livermore, California, Lawrence Livermore National Laboratory, 1984, preprint UCRL 91446.

MacFarlane, A., 'Daily mortality and environment in English conurbations: 1, air pollution, low temperature and influenza in Greater London'. In *British Journal of Preventative and Social Medicine*, Vol. 31, 54–61, March 1977.

Malone, R. C., Auer, L. H., Glatzmaier, G. A., and others, *Nuclear winter: three dimensional simulations including interactive transport, scavenging and solar heating of smoke* (1985, in press).

Myers, Norman, and Berry, Joseph A., *GLAWARS Task 8: Long-term effects of nuclear attack on the biosphere*. London, South Bank Polytechnic, 1986, mimeo.

NAS, *Long-term worldwide effects of multiple nuclear-weapons detonations*. Washington DC, National Academy of Sciences, 1975.

NAS, *The effects on the atmosphere of a nuclear exchange*. Washington DC, National Academy of Sciences, 1985.

Robock, A., 'Snow and ice feedbacks prolong the effects of a nuclear winter'. In *Nature*, 310 (5979), 667–670, 1984.

Royal Society of Canada, *Nuclear winter and associated effects*. Ontario, Royal Society of Canada, 1985, report of the Committee on the Environmental Consequences of Nuclear War.

SCOPE, *The Environmental Consequences of Nuclear War*. London, Wiley, 1985.

Thompson, S. L., 'Global interactive transport simulations of nuclear war smoke'. In *Nature* 317, 35–39, 5 September 1985.

Thompson, S. L., Alexandrov, V. V., Schneider, S. H., and others, 'Global climatic consequences of nuclear war: simulations with three dimensional models'. In *Ambio*, 8 (4), 236–243, 1984.

Turco, R. P., Toon, O. B., Ackerman, T. P., and others, 'Nuclear winter: global consequences of multiple nuclear explosions'. In *Science*, 222 (4630), 1283–1293, 1983.

2.8 Effects on the biosphere

All wars damage the environment. While this is never the first concern of survivors, it becomes critically important after the war when economic and agricultural recovery are delayed by environmental damage. The environmental effects of the Second Indochina War (the Vietnam war) caused by the prolonged heavy use of both chemical defoliants and high explosives have recently been extensively analysed (SIPRI 1980). However, none of the GLAWARS contingencies envisages either as likely in the UK, and conventional attacks on the UK, directed against military targets, are unlikely to produce either profound or lasting effects on the environment. But any nuclear attack on the UK, however small, is likely to cause serious environmental damage.

GLAWARS therefore confined its attention to two problems: the direct effects of nuclear explosions on the biosphere; and their indirect and cumulative effects on agriculture and ecology produced by changes in the weather, the climate and the atmosphere (see section 2.7). GLAWARS held a workshop on 24 March 1985 to investigate these issues (Myers and Berry 1986). The main conclusions of the workshop are outlined below. This is followed by a more detailed discussion of the key effects.

Conclusions of the GLAWARS workshop

1 All the GLAWARS scenarios except the first would result in the

destruction of trees, agricultural crops, and other forms of vegetation, as well as many domestic and wild animals, across hundreds if not thousands of square kilometres in the hinterland of the Greater London area alone.

2 If a nuclear winter ensued, there would be darkness and cold, disrupted rainfall patterns, powerful storms, acid rain and chemical pollution. Much vegetation would be killed or damaged. Many crops would die in the fields or yield only meagre harvests. Under most circumstances, agriculture could provide only marginal quantities of food.

3 The ultimate outcome for ecosystems generally, and for agro-ecosystems in particular, could turn out to feature a 'pest, weed and disease ecology'. This would make the revival of agriculture all the more difficult.

4 Due to the breakdown of farm support, there would be little or no fuel or other forms of power available; nor would there be supplies from off-farm sources. This alone could cause 100 per cent mortality among intensively reared pigs and poultry. Many farmers would be unable to care for their livestock.

5 As land-based supplies of food began to give out, there would be scant prospect of food from the sea. Marine phytoplankton would prove exceptionally sensitive to light depletion, whereupon oceanic food chains would swiftly collapse. Seaboards would be subject to storms of unusual strength, making fishing extremely hazardous.

6 These disasters would occur at a time when the many institutional support systems of the food industry had been largely if not completely eliminated. If available at all, supplies of pesticides, fertilizers and high-yielding seed grain would be in very short supply. Nor would there be any transportation, processing, marketing and distribution systems. This would compound the problems caused by changes in the weather and climate.

7 Such stored food as might be available would remain beyond the reach of most would-be consumers, since they would not know where to find it and would not be able to get to it if they did. Furthermore, there would be an immediate cut-off of the flows of foreign food that make up 35 per cent of UK consumption.

8 These circumstances would not always operate in simple additive fashion. Certain of them would generate a mutually-amplifying impact through synergistic reinforcement.

9 Recovery would probably take the form of successional adaptation of ecosystems to new forms of ecological equilibrium – less productive, less stable and less predictable than before, with impoverished assemblages of fauna and flora. In other words, there would be no true recovery to conditions that obtained before the

nuclear outbreak. Rather there would be an adaptive response, leading to distinctively different types of ecosystems. This would increase the problems of human survival in general, and especially of restoring agriculture, of whatever rudimentary sort.

10 Survivors might well find themselves obliged to practise a hunter-gatherer style of subsistence, supposing there were much to hunt and gather, and supposing they knew how to set about it.

In presenting the results of the workshop, Myers and Berry (1986) drew an even more pessimistic conclusion

> Given what we have learned about nuclear-winter theory during the course of research to resolve many basic matters, it is now realistic to say that as we clear away still more uncertainties, we shall find that our analyses, such as the one presented here, will have proved to be cautious and conservative.

Some of the conclusions reached above are examined in more detail in the sections that follow.

Direct effects of nuclear explosions. Plants and animals, like humans, will all suffer the effects of burns, blast and radiation. Areas within the immediate vicinity of nuclear explosions would, of course, be effectively sterilized. Many years would be needed for biological recovery and, during the period before vegetation becomes re-established, target areas would be subject to erosion.

The effects of blast and burns on plants are summarized in Table 34. Nearly all trees would be blown down by overpressures exceeding 4 psi. Combustible material within an area roughly equivalent to the 2 psi blast ring would receive enough heat radiation to ignite. Given the relative absence of dense forests and the normally moist climate of the UK, the further spread of fires outside urban areas seems unlikely except under rare climatic conditions or during July when the grain crop is mature but not yet harvested. A July attack could, however, result in fires that could consume much of the standing grain crops of the UK.

Animals in the open would be burned if directly exposed to the thermal radiation from the fireball. All humans within the 4 to 5 psi blast ring would receive lethal burns (Harwell 1984). Other animals have similar sensitivity to burns. On a clear day, this threshold is approximately the same as that given in Table 34 for forest blow-down. Climatic conditions and shielding by other materials would play an important role in determining whether injury occurs. Clouds and haze would tend to scatter the thermal radiation, reducing the severity of burns. Any object which could shade the animal from the fireball would offer protection from burns. Topography would be especially important, with the lee side of hills being protected. Grazing animals and birds

Table 34 Damage distances (km) from ground zero for nuclear weapons

Weapon yield (kt)	Forests blown down[a]	Fires ignited[b]	Leaves damaged[c]
Air bursts			
150	4.1	6.5	12
200	4.5	6.8	13.8
350	5.5	8.6	18.3
1000	7.6	12.4	31.0
Ground bursts			
150	2.6	4.1	7.9
200	2.9	4.4	8.4
350	3.5	5.4	11.2
1000	5.2	7.6	18.8

[a] 90 per cent of trees blown down at 4 psi overpressure, according to Harwell (1984). This threshold also corresponds roughly to the limit of fatal burns.
[b] Taken as the 2 psi overpressure range, according to Harwell (1984).
[c] Assumes a threshold of 2 cal/cm^2 for severe burns to leaf tissue.
Source: Myers and Berry 1986.

would be most likely to be exposed. Most other animals would seldom be in exposed open areas, and would be more at risk from damage to their habitat. Most birds and large animals within the 4 psi blast ring would be killed by burns or blast. Their carcasses would present prime breeding conditions for many pandemic diseases, if they were not disposed of rapidly. To bury the carcasses of a 100-cow herd is a major operation, however, even with modern earth-moving equipment.

The leaves and buds of plants could also be burned by thermal radiation with a threshold temperature of about 60°C. The increase in temperature produced by an intense pulse of thermal radiation can be estimated from knowledge of the mass per unit of exposed surface (about 100 mg/cm^2 of leaf area) and its heat capacity (about 1 cal/g). Assuming that the pulse is fully absorbed (leaves typically absorb 80–90 per cent of incident light), and that the pulse of radiation is sufficiently short that re-radiation or convective heat transfer would not cool the leaf significantly, then a pulse of 1 cal/cm^2 would increase the temperature of a leaf perpendicular to the path of the radiation by 100°C. Even if the initial temperature were near 0°C, as might occur on a cool spring or autumn night, the leaf's temperature would exceed lethal values within a second.

The lethal dose would depend upon the cosine of the angle between the leaf and the light path, and upon the initial temperature of the leaf. The lower threshold for burns is about 0.5 cal/cm^2. In a natural canopy, the leaves are at random angles and tend to shade one another. Serious damage to the canopy would, therefore, require more intense radiation. In Table 34, it is assumed that this threshold is about 2 cal/cm^2, which occurs at distances similar to those at which exposed human skin receives a first degree burn. The threshold for damage to individual leaves is much lower. For a 1 Mt air burst fairly complete damage of leaves and exposed buds would occur up to about 30 km, and there would even be some damage 60 km from the explosion. Damage would occur even during autumn or winter when deciduous plants would be without leaves. The bark of young branches and dormant buds would be exposed, and damage would threaten the future viability of the plants.

Cereals would be especially sensitive during the stages from anthesis to crop maturation since the developing seed head is at the top of the canopy. An attack during clear weather in June or early July could destroy much of the developing seed crop. Furthermore, only a few days would be required for the leaves killed by one attack to dry, and these could easily be ignited in a subsequent attack affecting the same area. Fires would spread more readily in already damaged vegetation, creating synergisms between overlapping explosions.

Fall-out from ground bursts would occur over extensive areas downwind of the explosions. In general, the native fauna and flora of the UK would be somewhat more resistant to radiation than humans but, unlike humans, would have no means of avoiding exposure nor of obtaining therapy. According to Longman (1985), radiation would kill between 50 and 100 per cent of exposed farm animals from fall-out downwind from a 1 Mt ground burst, across an area of some 1000 km^2. In adjacent areas, fall-out would cause severe sickness in animals. Many plants would also be affected. Synergisms between radiation exposure and other stresses might further sensitize biotas to radiation effects. These considerations may lead to disproportionately large effects on the native fauna. Long-term contamination of the habitats would certainly occur.

Effects of light depletion. A nuclear winter would cause marked declines in light levels. These could significantly disrupt, if not suspend, the processes of photosynthesis that underlie all food chains. The degree of damage, however, would vary with the degree of light reduction. Light reductions of 10 per cent would lie within the range of natural variation. Some crops can even support reductions of 50 per cent without a large fall in yield. But much depends on factors such as plant architecture and leaf shading (Bjorkman 1981). While individual leaves can be photosynthetically saturated by less than half of ordinary light, entire plants with multiple layers of leaves may remain far from saturated even when ambient light is 90 per cent of normal.

The key factor is the compensation point, the threshold at which photosynthesis fails to keep pace with plant respiration, and so can no longer support growth or reproduction (in the case of crops, this means plants cannot produce grain, fruits or tubers). Below this threshold, a plant will have difficulty even in surviving.

Fortunately, the compensation point is surprisingly low, generally equivalent to about 15 per cent and sometimes as little as 5 per cent of normal noon-time light during the main growing seasons. Not surprisingly, there are few empirical data on major light impairment in spring and summer. But there are some experimental data (Longman 1985): young wheat plants of various ages have been grown at light levels of 1 per cent of normal for periods of 2 to 6 weeks. In every case, the plants either sicken, and produce poor late-harvest grain, or produce no grain at all; or they die.

Being short-lived annuals, major grain species are unusually susceptible to light depletion. Thus severe declines in light would effectively eliminate crop production, and probably kill the plants themselves. Perennial plants, including many grasses, trees and shrubs, maintain greater food reserves, and could survive an extended period of depleted light. But they would be much weakened; and they would probably fail to form seeds or fruits, either because their food reserves would have fallen too low, or because there would be a failure of the triggering mechanisms needed to start the flowering process.

A nuclear winter in the UK could feature repeated phases of several days at least when light values fell to below 25 per cent of normal. So even if reduced light were the only factor at issue, much vegetation would stop growing. Those plants that did not die would be severely injured, which would leave them less capable of resisting reduced temperatures.

Effects of temperature reductions. The British climate, with its relative lack of extremes, deserves to be called temperate. Yet some of the vegetation, in all but the mildest parts of the country, is not far from its climatic limits. Even the hardier trees and shrubs could succumb to a severe winter. For instance, the winter of 1981–1982, by no means the coldest winter of this century, caused exceptional damage to firs, holly and ivy, and killed many pines and cedars.

Plants generally have cold tolerance limits that are related to the low-temperature extremes of their native environments. During a severe nuclear winter, summer-time temperatures could fall below historically recorded seasonal lows in the UK. Moreover, modern agricultural crops – notably wheat, barley, oats, rye, potatoes, beans, peas, rape and sugar-beet – are 'fine tuned' to their environments as a result of lengthy plant breeding. They are therefore closely adapted to particular conditions of temperature, light (including day length), soil fertility and moisture. Marked deviations from normal would result in significant to complete losses of productivity.

If a nuclear exchange were to occur in summer, mean monthly temperatures would fall to freezing point or below. If the exchange were to occur in winter, the subsequent nuclear winter would approximate to a rather harsh winter of the present time. On top of this would be day-to-day temperature variations of up to 15°C below normal, with the most extreme variations in late spring and early summer, when plant life would be at its most vulnerable.

In the most extreme case, following an April or July exchange, it would take much longer for plants to mature than in a normal year. Furthermore, killing frosts would occur in the summer and earlier in the autumn. Under these conditions, it would be difficult for plants to complete their life cycles. Even the perennials might be unable to assume their winter hardened state after such an unusual growing season.

Conditions in the growing season following an October exchange would be less severe. However, light levels would be reduced and temperatures might still vary significantly. It is by no means certain that a wheat crop would mature (assuming that it had been planted prior to the war). Most native plants require longer growing seasons than the crop plants. Production of fruits, seeds and nuts that support the native fauna would probably be more severely affected than the hardy cereals.

In the second growing season, conditions would improve but even one year after a July exchange it would probably be too cold for successful crop production. Perennial plants would be faced with a second severe growing season that would kill many that survived the first season on stored food reserves. The second season following an April exchange would be marginal for wheat production, but would still be too short and cool for normal development of the perennial native plants. The October and January scenarios would approach the normal range of a very cool year. Barring any unusually cold outbreaks, it would be possible for crops to be produced.

The effects of temperature decreases depend on four factors: the amount of the temperature drop; the time of year it occurs; the speed with which it occurs; and its duration.

An average temperature decline of 1 or 2°C lies well within the range of normal climatic variation. A reduction of 3 to 4°C would mean that, in the lowlands, the period of adequately warm temperature would still be long enough to allow virtually all crops to reach maturity. But in upland areas, and in northern parts of the UK, the temperature regime would become limiting, meaning that smaller areas would be capable of producing crops. A reduction of more than 5°C, however, would permit growth only for the shortest-season cereals (and for grasses), and only in low-lying areas. A 5°C drop would cause an immediate retreat southwards of about 750 km (roughly the distance from Inverness to Southampton) for the area suitable for each crop (Clark 1985). A drop of 10 to 12°C would be enough to eliminate all major grain crops.

These reactions would tend to be intensified if the cold arrived suddenly. Plants respond to the steady cooling of autumn by a process of acclimatization or hardening which takes about six weeks. Even one of our most cold-tolerant crops, winter wheat, is killed by a sudden decline of only 10°C during September and October, while an abrupt frost, however mild and brief, during a crop's active growth in spring and early summer is similarly lethal (see Table 35).

Table 35 Threshold temperatures for frost damage

Tissue	Summer	Winter
Leaves	−5°C	−20°C
Buds	−10°C	−40°C
Stems	?	−40°C
Roots[a]	−1°C	−20°C

[a] Temperature of the tissue, which may differ from the meteorological temperature because of microclimatic and inertial effects. Leaves and buds may experience wider variations in temperature than meteorological temperature. Roots and stems tend to reflect the average temperature over the preceding days or weeks.
Source: Myers and Berry 1986.

Spring and early summer would be the critical times. This is the period when many plants feature exceptionally sensitive organs such as germinating seeds, young seedlings, new leaves and shoots, and flowers. Indeed, virtually no temperate-zone plant can harden much once it has started its growing season, even if a temperature decline arrives only gradually. The nuclear winter scenarios postulate a speedy arrival of pronounced cold. It is the shock of ultra-rapid arrival that would probably do most damage, since this would be an experience to which plants would be entirely unadapted – witness the harm done by a single mild frost in late May.

Similarly, brief but large fluctuations in temperatures could prove as significant as continuous cold, or even the absolute minima reached. Each time there was a cold snap, many plants would seek to respond with a measure of immediate hardening (albeit with limited success), using up scarce reserves of stored food to do so. Immediately another warm spell came along, they would lose the benefit. An oscillating sequence of this kind would greatly hamper the hardening process, thus leaving many plants vulnerable to further cold spells.

Provided it has been conditioned slowly during a six-week period of early autumn, winter wheat can endure temperatures as low as −20°C by early winter (some 25°C below typical daytime temperatures in a UK winter). But by late April, it cannot withstand anything colder than 0°C; temperatures in the 5–10°C range during the growing season will prevent development of the grain; and a sharp frost of, say, −5°C during the main growing season is enough to kill the crop (Porter 1983). In southern England, of course, winter wheat virtually completes its development by early July, whereafter any temperature decline would have only a small effect.

In the UK, many trees do not harden to temperatures below −20°C, and they would be severely damaged by the worst nuclear winter conditions (Cannell 1985 and Cannell *et al.* 1985). Furthermore, a sudden drop in temperature during March-May when dehardening is occurring would be almost as damaging as a similar drop in autumn, though there might be a better prospect of eventual recovery. After their spring growth, deciduous trees cannot withstand even slight and transient frosts; conifers, which can withstand air temperatures as low as −90°C in winter, are killed by temperatures only a few degrees below 0°C in summer.

Effects of changes in precipitation. Precipitation levels could double or halve during the two years after a major nuclear attack. This would be significant because it is the amount and timing of precipitation in the UK that enable the present temperature regime to favour arable farming (Clark 1985). A number of moisture-limited crops consume remarkable amounts of moisture: a maize field, for example, producing a typical yield of 5600 kg/ha, needs almost 430 litres/kg of grain. So if nuclear-winter rainfall were substantially reduced, normal crop production would be ruled out through this factor alone. Marked increases in rainfall would also cause many problems – leaching of fertilizers, lodging of crops and sufficient water-logging to prevent operations such as harvesting, ploughing and sowing.

A sharp disruption of rainfall patterns could therefore prove virtually as harmful as a several degrees drop in temperature. Conversely, of course, a decline in temperature would lead to a decrease in evaporation, thus leaving more moisture available for crops.

In addition, many plant pathogens depend critically on moisture. An increase in rainfall, in conjunction with reduced temperature and sunlight, would supply constant films of moisture over crop surfaces for weeks on end, thus promoting population eruptions in pathogens (Heale 1985).

Even without substantial changes in precipitation, there could be substantial changes in the hydrology of landscapes. Most of the water that currently evaporates from the land is from the leaves of living plants. Lower temperatures and widespread damage to plants – especially to forests – could reduce the amount of transpiration causing water to accumulate in soils and aquifers. Lowland areas and stream valleys could become flooded, making this land unusable for agriculture, possibly causing extensive development of bogs and marshes. Re-establishment of forests might be inhibited by water-logged soils, or their development might be slowed because nutrients that previously supported luxuriant vegetation cover were leached from the soil during the nuclear winter.

Effects of radiation and chemical pollution. Ionizing radiation would afflict organisms almost from the outset of hostilities. Trees, particularly evergreens, are highly vulnerable; then, in order of increasing resistance, come shrubs, herbs, grasses, mosses and lichens (Woodwell 1982). So forests, and especially coniferous forests, would suffer the worst damage, and grasslands, including pastures for livestock, much less. Among the most resistant plants are weeds. As for crops, radiation is notably harmful to wheat, barley, rye, oats, maize, beans, potatoes, sugar-beet and tomatoes, especially during their early growth. Radiation would also leave plants diseased and damaged, and thus reduce their capacity to cope with the other stresses of a nuclear winter.

In addition, plants would suffer from air pollutants such as pyrotoxins and acid rain; and later, towards the end of the nuclear winter when the debris cloud started to clear away, from increased ultraviolet radiation, the intensity of which might be as much as twice the normal levels. This not only increases rates of mutation but it also reduces photosynthetic rates (Caldwell 1981 and Teramura *et al.* 1980). As a result, plants would develop abnormally in general, and produce smaller leaves in particular. Increased ultraviolet radiation would also suppress flowering and sterilize pollen, which would make plants incapable of setting seed, and would leave crops unable to produce grain.

Impacts on animals. Declines in light levels would have only marginal impact on animal life, unless they were exceptionally severe (Greene *et al.* 1985, Harwell 1984, Precht *et al.* 1973). But significant declines in temperature would cause major difficulties. A nuclear exchange in spring or summer, with sharp falls in temperature, would catch animals at a time when their cold-resistant stores of fatty tissues, plus other adaptations such as extra wool, fur and feathers, would be much reduced. Migratory birds, which normally avoid winter conditions, would be trapped in conditions they were unable to tolerate. The mammals best equipped to survive would be species such as rats and mice.

Small-bodied insects are capable of withstanding intense cold. The eggs, pupae and larvae of the sawfly, for example, regularly survive winter temperatures of −10°C for 2 to 8 weeks, and −20°C for 1 to 4 weeks. Moreover, small-bodied insects can continue to forage for food in strong winds. Insects are also more resistant to radiation. But larger-bodied insects such as bees would not fare so well – with all that that implies for crop pollination.

The insects that might emerge from a nuclear winter with their populations more or less intact would be 'generalists' in food needs and have high reproduction rates. These species are often viewed as pests. Populations of their natural enemies, especially insectivorous birds, would probably have suffered disproportionate reduction. As a result, there could well be a proliferation of aphids, weevils, wire worms, eel worms, leather jackets and other established pests, together with many pests of novel sorts.

Similarly, it is all too likely that 'opportunistic' plants, those that tolerate both a broad range of environmental conditions and flourish in disrupted environments, would spread. Weeds are more resistant to radiation than most species; and they can swiftly regenerate by virtue of their vast stocks of seeds dormant in the soil. So existing weeds would expand in numbers and range, joined by many new types of weeds. In addition, there could be disproportionate survival on the part of spores that produce fungal pathogens; and radiation-induced mutations could lead to novel forms of pathogens.

In short, the agro-ecosystems of a post-nuclear world would feature a pest, weed and disease ecology.

Implications for livestock. Livestock are poorly adapted to survival without the continuous care of man (Jollans 1985). In particular, dairy cattle, pigs and chickens are unable to survive prolonged cold without feed and shelter, especially when raised in energy-intensive units. Most farms have no back-up power systems to supply heating and ventilation if the main grid system fails; and they usually carry enough feed to last for only a few weeks. Pigs and poultry deprived of these supports would quickly suffer almost 100 per cent mortality (Crossley 1984 and 1985).

Hardier forms of livestock, notably beef cattle and sheep, would enjoy a better chance of survival. But many of their pastures would be contaminated; and grass would all but stop growing for many months (except possibly in the case of a January exchange). Thus many free-ranging animals would sicken from pollutant poisoning, notably radiation; or they would ultimately die through starvation, if not through cold (each factor tending to reinforce the others).

Even this presupposes that farmers would be in a condition to provide some care for their livestock.

Agricultural support. Most crops require large amounts of fertilizers, pesticides, herbicides and fungicides. In the aftermath of a nuclear war plus a nuclear winter, there would be little if any of these available. There would be little fuel for tractors and other machinery, and no new supplies of high-yielding seeds. The supports of agro-technology and social organization that underpin modern agriculture would disappear. So essential are these to modern agriculture, and so widespread would be the breakdown of institutional support systems, that in the wake of a sizeable nuclear war *without* a nuclear winter lack of fuel, fertilizers and other inputs alone would greatly reduce crop production.

Moreover, food supplies are highly dependent on distributive networks, processing inputs, and banking facilities. Each would suffer marked and immediate decline, if not elimination, in the wake of a nuclear exchange. In addition, all supplies of food from outside the UK would be completely cut off – and these supplies now constitute about 35 per cent of all food consumed in the UK.

Effects on the marine ecosystem. The surface waters of the seas surrounding the UK would undergo little cooling, perhaps only two degrees or so, even after a severe nuclear winter. But even moderate light depletion would have severe repercussions. Single-cell algae, the phytoplankton that are the primary producers at the base of marine food chains, are very susceptible to changes in ambient light. They would swiftly start to disappear. This would cause a collapse of populations of planktonic animals dependent on them, and so on up the food chain. This would lead to starvation of the marine carnivores, including many of the fish we eat.

Moreover, most of the commercially valuable fish occur in coastal waters and over continental shelves. These major fishing grounds would become contaminated by chemical pollutants and radionuclides fed in by rivers.

Even if boats and harbour facilities remained available, there might be few fish to catch, and they might prove too contaminated for human consumption. As land-based sources of food declined, there would be little prospect of finding alternatives in the seas, except possibly among deep-sea communities. It is questionable, in any case, whether fishermen would be able to operate for much of the time, since the UK would be periodically swept by strong winds and storms. There could also be persistent fogs, as the warmer oceans pumped moisture into the surface layers of the atmosphere.

Synergisms. Synergism – the process by which two factors jointly produce an effect larger than their sum – is one of the most significant but least understood of ecological phenomena. In view of the multi-dimensional and largely simultaneous impacts of nuclear winter on ecosystems, it is not enough to provide a conventionally linear description of effects, which individually could only hint at the ultimate ecological transformations that would surely result.

There could be cases where synergistic effects would prove beneficial rather than harmful. But judging from what is known about synergisms in the normal world, most of the synergistic effects of a nuclear winter would be harmful. Generally, a biota's tolerance of one stress is lower when other stresses are at work. In some cases, in fact, synergistic responses could produce some entirely unexpected results. For this reason, damage to the ecology of agriculture of the UK is likely to be much more severe than has so far been suggested in this section.

Biological recovery. Some biotic recovery could start within 6 to 12 months after a nuclear attack. Even where vegetation had been killed to the ground, certain forms of plant life could start to regenerate, provided sufficient seed was left in soils that had not been poisoned through chemical pollutants, and had not been too deeply frozen for too long a time or washed away by heavy rain. But recolonization of vegetation-depleted areas generally depends principally upon materials brought in from other communities – and these would be scarce in a post-nuclear UK.

Thus even were a gradual recovery to get under way, it would result in very different ecosystems from those now existing, due primarily to irreversible injury to various ecological elements and processes (Ehrlich 1984). Such ecosystem forms as emerged would remain in a state of flux for lengthy periods, and many years could elapse before stability might be re-established. Eventually, new ecological relationships (predator-prey and host-parasite interactions) would evolve.

In other words, there would not be any real 'recovery' in the sense of the world returning to its former condition. Rather there would be a process of adaptation, leading to new ecological equilibria, with diminished productivity, perhaps for a prolonged period. The short- and medium-term outcome would be an impoverished and unbalanced flora and fauna, with ecological repercussions that cannot be anticipated in detail. In the longer term, and in view of the likely fundamental changes in global terrestrial flora, climate itself might be significantly (and even permanently) altered. This in turn would eventually lead to the evolution of markedly different types of biotic communities that would persist for an indefinite and perhaps permanent period.

Agricultural recovery. The combined consequences of a devastated agricultural system and shattered institutional support are likely to produce the greatest synergism of all – one that leaves little prospect of anything beyond small-scale subsistence farming. Without fuel, agriculture would be set back by more than a century. After a major nuclear attack, according to Myers and Berry (1986), 'food production must revert to something akin to that of medieval Britain – for a period of several years at least, possibly for several decades or even longer'. The prospect for farming in lands that have become ecologically impoverished in ways beyond our worst experience is dismal. Energy would have to be provided by human labour, which means that at least 100 people would be needed to produce the food now produced by one (Pimentel 1985).

In fact, at least some of the survivors would be forced to try and subsist through hunter-gatherer activities. Yet they would turn to natural ecosystems (as distinct from human-directed agro-ecosystems) precisely when wild biotas would have been seriously degraded. It would be a mistake to suppose there would be much for people to hunt and gather – or that survivors, most of them formerly urban people, would know how to set about the task.

One of the most crucial questions is how much food would be available to survivors of a nuclear attack? The answer, of course, depends on the size of the attack. The larger the attack, the easier is the answer. Should the attack produce a nuclear winter (equivalent to GLAWARS scenarios 4 and 5, and possibly even 3), then many field crops and much domestic stock would be destroyed or injured; few crops or livestock could survive the ensuing nuclear winter; and only agriculture of a very rudimentary kind could be re-established during the subsequent growing season (and possibly for several seasons thereafter), because of the breakdown of institutional support.

As a result, according to Myers and Berry (1986)

> for all practical intents and purposes, and whether with respect to the survivor communities of the Greater London area or of Britain as a whole, the amounts of edible and sustaining food available would prove nowhere near sufficient to meet needs during the first year following a nuclear exchange – and the same could well apply for yet another year, possibly for several years. In many areas and for many people, and for extended periods of time, food supplies could essentially prove to be zero.

References

Bjorkman, O., 'Responses to Different Quantum Flux Densities'. In Lange, O. L., Noble, P. S., Osmond, C. B., and Ziegler, H. (eds.), *Encyclopaedia of Plant Physiology*. Berlin, Springer Verlag, 1981.

Caldwell, M. M., 'Plant Responses to Solar Ultraviolet Radiation'. In Lange, O. L., Noble, P. S., Osmond, C. B., and Ziegler, H. (eds.), *Encyclopaedia of Plant Physiology*. Berlin, Springer Verlag, 1981.

Cannell, M. G. R., *Effects of a Nuclear Winter on Temperate Forests*. Penicuik, Scotland, Institute of Terrestrial Ecology, 1985.

Cannell, M. G. R., Sheppard, L. J., Smith, R. I., and Murray, M. B., 'Autumn Frost Damage on Young *Picea sitchensis*: Shoot Frost Hardening, and the Probability of Frost Damage in Scotland'. In *Forestry* (1985, in press).

Clark, J. A., *Agricultural Effects of the Nuclear Winter*. Paper submitted for GLAWARS Task 8 Workshop in London, 24 March 1985.

Crossley, G. J., *The Agricultural Consequences of Nuclear War*. Bradford, Bradford Peace Research Institute, 1984, Peace Research Report No. 5.

Crossley, G. J., 1985. *Nuclear War and Agriculture – Without a Nuclear Winter*. Paper submitted for GLAWARS Task 8 Workshop in London, 24 March 1985.

Ehrlich, P. R., 'When Light is Put Away: Ecological Effects of Nuclear War'. In Leaning, J., and Keyes, L. (eds.), *The Counterfeit Ark: Crisis Relocation for Nuclear War*. Cambridge, Mass., Ballinger Press, 1984.

Greene, O., Percival, I., and Ridge, I., *Nuclear Winter*. Cambridge, Polity Press, 1985.

Harwell, M., *The Human and Environmental Consequences of Nuclear War*. Berlin, Springer Verlag, 1984.

Heale, J., *Agricultural Impacts: Likely Crop Disease Losses*. Paper submitted for GLAWARS Task 8 Workshop in London, 24 March 1985.

Jollans, J. L., *Animal Production*. Paper submitted for GLAWARS Task 8 Workshop in London, 24 March 1985.

Longman, K. A., *Likely Effects of Nuclear War on London's Food and Wood Supplies*. Paper submitted for GLAWARS Task 8 Workshop in London, 24 March 1985.

Myers, N., and Berry, J. A., *GLAWARS Task 8: Long-term effects of nuclear attack on the biosphere*. London, South Bank Polytechnic, 1986, mimeo.

Pimentel, D., *Technological Changes in Agricultural Production After a Nuclear War*. Ithaca, New York, Cornell University, 1985.

Porter, J. R., 'Modelling Stage Development in Winter Wheat'. In *Aspects of Applied Biology* 4: 449–455, 1983.

Precht, H., Christopherson, J., Hensel, H., and Larcher, W. (eds.), *Temperature and Light*. Berlin, Springer Verlag, 1973.

SIPRI, *Warfare in a Fragile World: Military Impact on the Human Environment*. London, Taylor and Francis, 1980.

Teramura, A. H., Biggs, R. H., and Kossuth, S., 'Interaction Between Ultraviolet-B and Photosynthetically Active Radiation on Net Photosynthesis, Dark Respiration, and Transpiration'. In *Plant Physiology* 65: 483–488, 1980.

Woodwell, G. M., 'The Biotic Effects of Ionizing Radiation'. In *Ambio* 11: 142–148, 1982.

2.9 Social, economic and political consequences

An examination of the effects of nuclear war must start with the quantifiable destruction of people and things. But it must also take account of less obvious effects. Some of these, such as the increased demand for medical care and the reduction in medical resources to meet it, are tangible. Others are less easily stated. They include the effects of attack on the complex organization of an advanced urbanized society, and the ability of such a system to survive. If these social, economic and political factors are ignored, the costs of a nuclear attack will be severely underestimated. With one notable exception (Katz 1982), these issues have been largely unexplored in previous studies of nuclear attack. The GLAWARS Commission believes this to be a serious omission.

This is particularly the case if there is a chance that destruction may be limited in some way. In GLAWARS scenarios 1, 2 and 3, there are large numbers of survivors; even in scenario 3, about two-thirds of London's buildings survive. In this situation, it is all the more important to recognize that concentration on physical destruction alone risks overlooking other important effects.

London during a war scare. During their work, GLAWARS researchers found abundant evidence that a war scare could have a paralysing physical effect on the London system. Additional social, economic and political factors are considered below.

The prospects for London's recovery after scenarios 1, 2 and 3 would be affected by what happened during a war scare. The developing chaos of the social and economic environment would probably be exacerbated by the problems of organizations, especially public bodies, and their efforts to cope; decisions taken by them could unwittingly add to the existing difficulties. According to MacDougall and Hastings (1986), there would be 'a crisis of crisis management'.

Any crisis leads to a rush to move money into durable funds such as gold. The subsequent pressure on sterling, and the balance of payments, would become an additional problem for crisis managers. Strains on the domestic banking system would appear as people tried to convert their savings either into cash or into more tangible items such as food. This extra liquidity chasing a fixed amount of goods would – as in the early days of World War 2 – be inflationary, curtailing the purchasing power of the poorer groups.

All financial institutions would be faced with a liquidity crisis; the London-based clearing banks would bear the brunt, but elsewhere businesses dependent on credit, or working on narrow margins, could be forced out. Furthermore, if senior managers decided that there were potentially safer places than London, then a degree of corporate paralysis could ensue. The GLAWARS survey shows that as many as 35 per cent of Londoners might try to leave the city. As in World War 2, these voluntary evacuees would be mostly from the professional, managerial and administrative groups. The consequence of this exodus might be a cumulative immobilization of much of the London economy, including the state support systems on which many Londoners depend.

Unemployment would inevitably rise if the crisis were prolonged. Traditionally under-employed groups – such as black youth, women and the unskilled – would be particularly vulnerable, adding to social and racial tension. If many of the work force evacuated or decided to remain at home with their families, economic activity would decline still further.

It is significant that most military targets in or near London are situated to the west and north-west of the city. These areas contain many of London's minority ethnic communities. Racism could thus increase social tension if these communities tried to move to safer areas. Attempts by the police to prevent this would cause social conflict wherever it happened, but especially where race relations were already strained (Smith and Gray 1985). Where outer suburb houses had been left empty, squatting would lead to further problems.

The pull between family and work is well documented in crises with, historically, the family tending to win. Every Londoner would experience this kind of role conflict as normal social life lost its familiar patterns. The distances involved in travelling to work in the metropolis can be great, and time consuming, and this would increase the likelihood of people, especially commuters, staying with their families – even if there were no official warnings. If military mobilization and a rundown in public transport had occurred, such journeys would be even more unlikely.

Similar arguments would apply to other activities that take people away from home. Children would no longer attend school. Attempts would be made to acquire extra stocks of food, and other essentials. At this point, the vulnerability of the modern food system in London would become apparent, with its reliance on a complex distribution system, limited stocks, and relatively few concentrated retail outlets.

Factors such as increased road accidents, disruption of normal social services and the eviction of hospital patients in anticipation of casualties would increase death and injury rates. Titmuss (1950) estimated that there were 10,000 'excess' deaths from these and related causes during the 'phoney war' from September 1939 to June 1940. This is about a third as many as actually died in the UK from subsequent aerial bombardment.

It is thus clear that a war scare alone, especially if it were prolonged, would be likely to stretch the social fabric to breaking point. The society that was subsequently subjected to attack would not be a normal one.

The government would thus face an increasing range of problems. The worsening domestic situation would require vigorous action. Protests over the prospect of a war would be inevitable, and would be likely to be widespread according to the GLAWARS survey. Challenges to the legitimacy of the government, and its ability to act at home or abroad, or even wage the war in prospect, would ensue.

War impels more authoritarian modes of government. Emergency powers would be taken at some point in the crisis, although 'covert' action to safeguard strategic stockpiles of petrol and food would precede formal legislation. Government would be faced with innumerable dilemmas, becoming more extreme as the crisis lengthened or deepened. Conflicting priorities would abound – and in many instances they would be irreconcilable. For example, fuel and food restrictions could cause adverse public reaction but their absence might run down inventories and reduce post-attack recovery prospects.

Government would be faced with increasing demands for more resources to be transferred to the military. The costs of disruption would be borne by social security and other services. Declining revenue, from loss of taxes on businesses and purchases, would further increase the difficulties, as would the weakening of the financial institutions that would normally receive state support. The British government appears overloaded in peace time; during a war scare, its problems would increase many fold, and there would be little consensus on which it could operate. Even apart from mass demonstrations, there would be protests from within Parliament and from local authorities, many of which have declared themselves nuclear-free zones. The suspension of normal democratic processes would become inevitable.

A society in the grip of circumstances such as these has already been damaged, even before an attack is launched. An attack would therefore hit a society already in deep crisis, and less able to withstand it and recover from it. This would be true even if the attack remained conventional.

Effects on the social system. A nuclear attack on London – even if controlled or limited – would not resemble a modern re-run of the London Blitz. For one thing, the scale and speed of damage would be quite different, far surpassing even the most severe traumas undergone by cities in the past (Iklé 1959). Secondly, the attack could not regenerate the kinds of social solidarity that were a feature of certain periods of the Blitz, particularly in the East End. Although the tightly knit East End communities of 1940 were real and significant, they have long since disappeared.

Where and how people live in London today is influenced not by tradition but by factors such as race, age, size of family and social class. Young people tend to favour the 'bed-sit' territory of inner London, while families with young children prefer the suburbs. Since World War 2, a greater emphasis on the private individualized world of home and material possessions has further eroded older notions of community. London's social organization has changed dramatically over the past 45 years.

Calamities on the scale of a whole society are relatively rare in human experience, but the Black Death of the Middle Ages, which killed around one-third of the populations of Europe, shook the social fabric to its foundations. Basic social institutions, such as the family, were threatened with destruction; many parents simply abandoned their children (Tuchman 1978).

The invisible bonds that link the disparate elements of a society together are essential to its functioning. If there is not a minimal level of co-operation between individuals and groups, some degree of acceptance of social rules, and some minimal satisfaction with the rewards society offers, then the whole basis of that society is threatened. A nuclear attack would change many of the ground rules. For example, the value attached to human life would be one of the main casualties of the post-nuclear world. The presence of death would encourage a more hedonistic, individualized value system – more concerned with the meeting of immediate personal needs – and thereby further weaken the social bonds between people.

Added to this would be the fact that the social map of Londoners' roles in life would be destroyed in a nuclear attack. Many of their community foci – work, homes, schools, friendship networks and so on – would disappear, leaving the individual essentially isolated (Popkess 1980). This effect would be amplified by the disappearance of communications and the mass media, on which all major urban centres depend and on which they feed compulsively.

The most profound effects, both on individuals and on society, would concern the nature of work. Most adults spend the best part of their waking life at work. After a nuclear attack, the concept of work would either disappear or be profoundly modified. As the GLAWARS survey shows, more than 60 per cent of Londoners in work are certain they would not go to work even during a war scare. During and after an attack many more would stay at home, either through choice or necessity. Most Londoners have to commute to work, and transport through a ruined city would be impossible after even a small nuclear attack. Furthermore, the kinds of work many Londoners do – connected as it is with tertiary services – would find no place in a post-attack environment. All offices could be expected to close after an attack, even in undamaged areas. Most Londoners would not go to work, and there would be no work for them to go to if they did.

This situation could prevail for a long time. A return to work presumes two things. First, some economic system would have to be restored through which workers could be compensated for their labour. After minor attacks, the monetary system might still exist. But after major attacks, money would have no value, and compensation would probably have to be in goods. It is not far-fetched to imagine that equivalents of the 'Food for Work' schemes currently in operation in developing countries could become a principal means of providing a reward for workers in a post-attack environment.

Secondly, few Londoners would go to work, even for appropriate rewards, as long as they felt their families were still at risk. That risk might take two forms – the prospect of continued attack from the enemy, or the prospect of attack from within, by deprived members of society, looters, or those who sought short-term gain from the long-term tragedy. After a nuclear attack, conventional ideas of law and order would largely disappear. The concept of property would be greatly loosened, with vast stocks of materials destroyed and others belonging only to the dead. Personal security would be at a premium after nuclear attack, and social systems capable of ensuring even minimum levels of personal protection would emerge only extremely slowly. Nevertheless, until such systems did emerge, few Londoners would be prepared to leave their families for the prospect of uncertain rewards for what would almost certainly be unfamiliar forms of work.

As Thompson (1986) points out, most individuals, as they surveyed the wreckage of their city and their society, would suffer from disaster syndrome, withdrawing into a private world of grief and helplessness. The social institutions that normally support the individual through grief would have largely disappeared. In this sense, it is somewhat academic to distinguish the uninjured from the casualties. After a nuclear attack, all survivors would be casualties.

Death and destruction on a nuclear scale would also have profound effects on demographic structure (Hanunian 1966). In nearly all disasters, and in nearly all records of severe deprivation in World War 2, death rates among the very young and the old increase dramatically, leaving a society dominated by the young and the middle aged. Those who are socially or psychologically vulnerable, people who in peace time depend critically on social support of one kind or another, are also likely to suffer disproportionately. Changes of this kind may not appear to be the most immediate concern of the survivors of a nuclear attack. But any tear in the social fabric of a post-attack world could easily develop into a rip.

For many, all that would be left of the social fabric would be the shattered remains of their family, which would become the shock absorber of the post-nuclear world. Family structures, however, would be under considerable stress. As MacDougall and Hastings (1986) put it

> The bonds that unify the family will be weakened by death and injury. The family's ability to provide a sanctuary for producing and rearing children, and for preparing them for the world in which they are to live, will be greatly reduced. The damage sustained by the wider society will in turn impair its capacity to act as a support for the family. The disarray and damage to the family will increase the sense of social isolation amongst survivors. Families themselves will have to support injured or disabled members. Finally, generalized social disasters may ultimately lead to a breakdown of family loyalties and ties, perhaps with the abandonment of dependent members by the able-bodied. In such cases, the process of social disintegration is well advanced.

The scenario-related analysis that follows pays particular attention to the social damage inflicted by the lighter attacks. In scenarios 4 and 5, for example, physical damage is so great that questions of social structure tend to become academic.

Scenario 1. The threat to London would be invisible – directly in the form of radiation, indirectly in the form of the social paralysis that would result from the war scare, the attack and possibly a shelter period.

The fear of fall-out would be real but would be compounded by the fear of possible direct attack on London itself – especially perhaps in those living close to an identifiable target. Two conflicting forces would then influence mass behaviour – the desire to stay put and the desire to flee. The familiarity of home surroundings, fear of loss of possessions through looting, theft or even requisitioning, plus the high incidence of home ownership in London, would all be restraining factors. The prospect of being caught up in congestion or chaos, and doubts about the availability of food, shelter and other necessities elsewhere, would also act as restraints.

Shelter confinement is itself a period of stress, and the desire to take action would be strong. Flight might seem the most logical course of action and is a frequent reaction to disaster. After the accident at Three Mile Island in the United States, 40 per cent of the population within a 20 km radius evacuated. Within 8 km of the reactor, the proportion rose to 60 per cent. Apart from pregnant women and small children within the 8 km radius, who were recommended to go, the rest were voluntary evacuees (Katz 1982).

London has, in the past, experienced a largely invisible threat resulting in death – the plague. In 1603, London lost about one sixth of its population but nonetheless recovered. However, when an equally high mortality set in in 1665, a mass flight from London occurred.

> The flight was so fast that . . . the houses left empty and foresaken by their owners were far more numerous than those . . . where the plague had entered. For weeks the tide of emigration flowed by every outlet from London towards the country . . . It was checked at last by the refusal of the Lord Mayor to grant further certificates of health and by the effective opposition of the neighbouring townships which, in self defence, set armed guards upon their roads and formed a barrier around the strucken capital.
>
> (Vincent 1667, quoted in Iklé 1959)

Such a flight might ease the problem of supplying the capital with food, but could throw an enormous burden on the feeding and sheltering authorities in host areas. The strains resulting from prolonged evacuation in World War 2 were very serious (Titmuss 1950). Unless the public were much better informed about the location of low-risk areas, they would be likely to see urban areas as dangerous and to try to escape to adjoining rural areas.

'Trekking' was a common feature of bombed cities in World War 2 and could happen under scenario 1. The exodus of the mobile would, however, exacerbate the social situation of the remainder. Those for whom relocation was not possible – the elderly, the disabled, and the poor – could be in a desperate plight as their community and state support systems broke down.

Social tensions, always present within the city, would increase under the strain of vastly different circumstances. Those trekking from inner, west and north-west London would include a large proportion of the ethnic population of London. The racial tensions within London and beyond could become very apparent. Local resistance to the occupation of deserted housing or facilities in the less densely populated outer suburbs would occur as the exclusion processes normally operating in the housing market broke down. Refugees entering London from outside could add to the problem.

The return of evacuees in the longer term would not, of course, be guaranteed. General economic conditions would play an important part in influencing decisions and – as noted earlier – these would be drastically changed. A person's previous role and status in London could not be assured afterwards. In other words, there would be a redefinition of social 'normality' after a nuclear attack, even if London itself were not targeted.

Scenario 2. The metropolis would experience direct nuclear attack under scenario 2. The prospect of outside help – so important at Hiroshima and Nagasaki – would be small, particularly in view of the nature of London's principal economic activities. The social disruption described for scenario 1 would therefore be greatly amplified. In a wider context, the social fabric of the whole of the UK would be very seriously damaged.

Flight from the city would be inevitable, and would be likely to occur under conditions of total chaos. A large proportion of housing and other property would be destroyed, fires would be endemic for several days in the worst affected areas, and the sight of large numbers of people packing a few of their belongings and moving out would be infectious. Flight was one of the first reactions in Hiroshima and Nagasaki, and although the return started soon afterwards, the situation in a devastated London would be very different. The Japanese knew nothing of radiation; Londoners know enough for it to provoke widespread fear. Furthermore, the Japanese had outside help; Londoners would not. It is a sobering thought that, in spite of these differences, it was ten years before the populations of Hiroshima and Nagasaki returned to their pre-attack levels.

The destruction in west and north-west London would cause many survivors to move out of these areas, overwhelming scarce resources in reception areas. Furthermore, some of the worst-affected boroughs – Brent, Hounslow and Ealing, for example – have larger than average ethnic minorities. Their arrival in host areas would increase social tension.

During World War 2, the problems of re-housing the homeless were seriously underestimated, and continued for years after the war ended. After scenario 2, they would be bigger again by orders of magnitude, assuming that even some of those who initially fled decided to return. Even if surviving households in London voluntarily agreed to take in evacuees, and if local authorities took possession of vacant property to help organize re-housing, the scale of the problem would still be overwhelming.

One inevitable result would be an increase in population density in the least damaged areas. The problems this would create would then be compounded by the absence of heat and light. Resumption of energy supplies would be subject to post-war priorities; initially at least, these would be unlikely to include the domestic consumption of scarce energy resources.

The onset of a nuclear winter, with lowered temperatures, chilling winds, and washed out chemicals and other pollutants would, if it occurred, accelerate further the deterioration of the housing stock in general and in damaged areas in particular. Even to maintain its housing stock during World War 2, London needed substantial numbers of outside building workers.

However, urban control and supply networks would also be damaged. Improvements in housing standards and public health in the 19th and 20th centuries led to a dramatic fall in mortality rates in the UK. Diseases that have long been under control in the UK could once again become prevalent as public health broke down. The combination of radiation exposure, poor housing and sanitation, food and fuel shortages, and social and psychological demoralization suggests the prospects of a post-war catastrophe even greater than the original attack (BMA 1983).

Scenario 3. London would be badly damaged in scenario 3, with levels of destruction roughly ten times worse than those that occurred during the whole of World War 2. Furthermore, the destruction would be spread much more widely than in scenarios 1 and 2, with only areas in the east of the city escaping severe damage.

Nearly a quarter of Londoners would become casualties, and there would be 750,000 corpses to dispose of. Even so, there would be huge numbers of initial survivors – more than 5 million – and they would be forced to try to evolve some form of life in which continued survival would be possible. As in scenarios 1 and 2, many would seek improved conditions outside the city. Those that remained would face enormous problems. The pre-war pattern of life would have been totally destroyed. There would be no work, no semblance of law and order, and no social norms with which to conform. In many ways, society would be a *tabula rasa*.

Yet working forms of social organization would be needed perhaps even more badly than they are in peace time. The intensity of the crisis would be such that new forms of social and economic structure would have to be put together if the survivors were to organize for themselves the supply of even minimum levels of water, food, shelter and sanitation. Without these, they would die. Furthermore, the new organizations would have to be established within a matter of days.

Inevitably, many *would* die. It is not possible to predict how quickly new forms of organization could be evolved but, bearing in mind the likely prevalence of disaster syndrome, the prospects would appear bleak. Nor is it possible to predict what would happen in the absence of even rudimentary social and economic systems. All that is clear is that life would carry on, for a limited period only, in conditions that would bear no resemblance to pre-war life in London or anywhere else in the northern hemisphere.

In this situation, it is quite possible that London would have to be evacuated at some point. There is no means of knowing whether such an evacuation could, or would, be effected as a result of outside organization, or whether Londoners themselves would simply opt for that solution in preference to intolerable conditions.

Scenarios 4 and 5. London as a social entity would not exist after scenarios 4 and 5. Survivors, even in family remnants or scavenging groups, would be incapable of any attempt at re-organization or reconstruction, even on the edge of the devastation. Many of the initial survivors – at most 15 per cent of Londoners – would be killed by the secondary effects of attack. The final image of the metropolis would be one of death, compounded by the pollution of fall-out, acid rain and a pall of smoke blotting out the sun.

Prospects for outside help would be zero. Looting of ruined housing for fuel and improvised shelter, and scavenging for food, might sustain individuals or even groups for a period – but the inventories of food would be quickly exhausted, and there would be competition from rats and mice. The abandonment of London for a devastated countryside, perhaps gripped by the frozen hand of nuclear winter, would be inevitable. No protection is possible for London or Londoners from attacks of this magnitude.

Impact on the economy. The destruction of life, property, communications networks and procedures for directing and controlling economic activity would render large parts of the economy inoperative, depending on the severity of the attack. Measuring the effects of this using conventional economic indicators, such as gross domestic product (GDP), are problematic for a number of reasons.

First, it cannot be assumed that what remains of GDP would be available for redistribution to survivors on an equitable basis. Nor is it clear that any authority would attempt such a redistribution in view of the fact that resources would be grossly insufficient to meet the demands of survivors.

Secondly, many markets as we know them would cease to operate after a nuclear attack. Needless to say, 'markets' of some kind would operate for food, clothing, shelter, fuels, personal defence, and so on. But the likelihood that money would exchange hands would be remote in the more serious scenarios since inflation rates in unofficial markets would be very high, and no recipient of cash could be sure that he or she could buy goods or services with it. Thus the very meaning of 'remaining GDP' is open to question.

Thirdly, GDP is a measure of the flow of economic activity and it is typically this that most economists think contributes to human welfare. Some, however, argue that it is the stock of assets, our wealth as opposed to our income, that creates welfare. Given the enormity of wealth destruction that would follow a nuclear attack, any GDP measure could seriously understate the loss of material welfare.

With these reservations in mind, Pearce *et al.* (1986) have analysed what might happen to economic activity, as measured through GDP, over the longer term – that is, after some forms of basic social and economic organization have evolved, and the process of recovery has begun. They comment

> the chances that any government could in fact operate a command structure based on regions and districts with more than a semblance of efficiency in scenarios 4 and 5 seem to us remote. Accordingly, anarchic structures will develop and there will be a general failure of the signals which characterize either planned economies or market systems. In scenarios 1–3 we assume that a large measure of control is exercised by government . . . The recovery process in scenarios 1–3 would come about by an intensification of work activity in an effort to reconstruct: very simply, labour productivity rises. Persons previously unemployed or outside the labour force will enter into productive activity. The 'true' level of economic activity will be higher than might appear to be the case since economic activity will, to some extent, be forced 'underground'.

In scenario 1, there would be no physical damage to London. However, because most of London's economic functions are to provide services for industries and institutions outside London (including, after a nuclear attack, a relocated government), London's economic functions would depend critically on what was occurring outside the capital. Inside the capital, major institutions such the Stock Exchange would unquestionably be closed. Banking would be in chaos. Advertising would be at a standstill. The headquarters offices of the major national and international companies in London would also be closed, unless their business were directly related to the recovery effort.

There would be therefore be a large, redundant labour force. Some of it would be drafted into recovery and special assistance activities. Pearce *et al.* (1986) assume that the effects of increased unemployment would be offset by labour productivity increases elsewhere due to war-time consciousness of the need for increased economic activity.

In scenario 2, there would be a higher loss of GDP. GDP/survivor would decline even more because resources within London would be diverted to emergency services and other activities which would not contribute to gains in net economic activity.

In scenario 3, however, economic outcomes become much more difficult to predict. It would be many years before GDP would have any meaning in the context of a London which might well have been abandoned, at least for a period. Most of London's pre-war economic structure, whether relevant or not to recovery, would have been destroyed. So many of the work force would have been killed that reconstruction of previously existing labour forces would be impossible.

In scenarios 4 and 5, the situation would become so desperate that concepts such as 'income per capita' could have little meaning. Previous forms of the economy would have disappeared, and there would be total economic collapse. Even if food stocks, fuel and shelter were sufficient to permit continued survival, lack of access and 'entitlement' to them in the form of purchasing power would result in many more deaths. This phenomenon is typical of disasters such as famine and would greatly magnify the casualties from direct causes. In scenario 5, there would be only 200,000 initial survivors in London. Most of them would not survive for long.

Even if a 'command' economy functioned efficiently, much of London's surviving population in scenarios 4 and 5 might be deliberately left to starve. Essentially, this is because London's economy is not geared to the production of essential services in the post-attack period. Qualified medical personnel, builders, and a certain number of technicians would be protected. The likely picture, however, is that they would be moved out of London to help essential reconstruction elsewhere.

Agriculture would rely on unskilled workers from any source, as would road building and other civil engineering work, though labour itself could never substitute for the highly productive, energy-intensive technologies in use before the war. Another constraint on this reconstruction activity would be lack of skilled workers, and the ability of government to 'screen out' suitable labour. Rewards would be likely to be proportional to 'socially necessary' skills. Those who were unproductive in this respect and in excess of the manageable unskilled labour force would become a drain on the reconstruction effort.

It is the 'low priority' of London's economy in the reconstruction effort that explains why economic effects have such a profound effect on London, over and above the physical damage. The capacity to organize labour in areas relatively unaffected by bomb damage is critical, and under scenarios 2–5 London would increasingly fail to meet this criterion. Since it would be economically impossible to ensure the continued survival of all the initial survivors, many would be left to eke out what existence they could – or more probably to die – because they failed to constitute a priority concern. While many areas would 'qualify' for this policy of deliberate neglect, London would fare worse than most because of the structure of its economy.

Prospects for recovery. After any form of nuclear attack, recovery to unaltered pre-attack conditions would never be likely to occur. Recovery, in this context, means simply a return to some form of functioning economy, albeit with more modest goals and altered objectives. For this to occur, four important conditions must be met:

1 certain resources, such as labour, energy and property, must be available;
2 output must be geared to something, such as self-sufficiency, a barter system or a continued cash economy;
3 labour must have enough food to be able to work, and be fit enough to do so; and
4 a communications network must exist.

Furthermore, none of these conditions would have any effect on the economy if there were no form of public order. As already mentioned, Londoners would go to work only if they felt their families were likely to be secure during their absence. Table 36 sets out the likely presence of the four conditions listed above under the five scenarios.

Figure 25 shows the probable trends in the London economy, given a number of very optimistic assumptions. It is assumed that the attack occurs in the immediate future with London's GDP at around £40,000 million in terms of constant 1981 prices. In each case, the war scare preceding the attack would have a negative effect on the economy. Scenario 1 would have a small additional impact but this would be immediately offset by increased activity and hence rising labour productivity. Provided the attack was known to be all that would ensue, which is extremely unlikely, most of London's economy might continue to operate, including financial services and overseas trade. In scenario 2, the economy would tend to stagnate for about one year, and then begin a gradual but slow recovery.

Table 36 Presence of recovery conditions for the London economy in scenarios 1–5

	Scenario				
Condition	1	2	3	4	5
1 Resource supply	Largely unaffected	15% labour, capital, energy loss	25% labour, capital, energy loss	Total disruption	Total disruption
2 Exchange system	Continues as cash economy with food rationing	Continues as cash economy with rationing of most consumables	Rationing, efforts to restore money exchange system	Probable anarchy, possible local barter	Anarchy
3 Health of labour	Food supply impact	Food supply impact, disease	Serious impacts via food supply, disease	London uninhabitable	London uninhabitable
4 Communi-cations	Continue to function	Function at limited level	Seriously impaired	Poor to non-existent	Poor to non-existent
Conclusion	Recovery depends on recovery in rest of UK, but would lead it	Eventual recovery depends on recovery in rest of UK, but would lag behind it	Recovery dubious even if London is made habitable	No recovery	No recovery

Source: after Pearce *et al*. 1986.

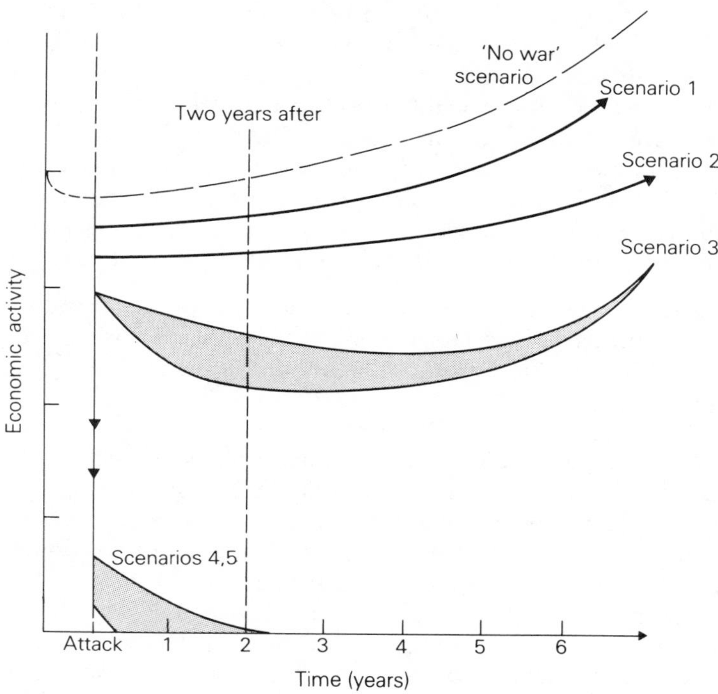

Figure 25 Economic consequences of the five scenarios. Assumptions: rigorous/effective government control; limited psychological trauma; one attack period only – no sustained war; very limited supplies from outside UK.

Scenario 3 defines the dividing point in terms of the economy. The destruction of property and the need to engage in 'unproductive' activities, such as mass burial and road clearance, would lead to a continuing fall in levels of activity contributing to net product. Additionally, many services would be interrupted as labour found itself mismatched to resource availability. An optimistic outcome, if there were sufficient psychological will and adequate control by authorities, would be that activity levels could begin to revive after two years. However, effective 'incomes' would continue to decline for some time after this. The economy could not recover even to the immediate post-attack level for several years. A pessimistic outcome would be that economic activity in London would never revive, and that as surviving portions of the city became less and less habitable, London would eventually be evacuated.

In scenarios 4 and 5, there would be no recovery. London would be either deliberately run down in terms of economic activity because of the impossibility of adequate control, or it would fail to recover because of the lack of a minimum viable resource base from which to operate. Survivors would either die or migrate. These 'no recovery' scenarios would be worsened if a nuclear winter occurred, and recovery in scenarios 1 and 2 would be slower. Recovery in scenario 3 would become even more problematic.

These predictions are based on the following assumptions:

1 that there is a rigorous control over priority areas of the economy by the government – anarchy under the worst scenarios is 'permitted' but contained, with drafting of labour and military/police control of priority regions;
2 that other countries in Europe and North America have been similarly affected so that external relief is available only in the form of limited essential supplies from unaffected countries;
3 that the demoralizing influence of war does not prevent labour responding to government directives – if it did, recovery would not take place and the curves for scenarios 1–3 would all slope downwards; and
4 that, pursuant to 3, the experience of past wars (admittedly conventional ones) is repeated in which a war-time work ethic persists well into the post-attack period.

All these assumptions are optimistic. For example, it is extremely doubtful that 'rigorous control' could be maintained in scenarios 4 and 5; outside assistance after scenarios 4 and 5 would be extremely unlikely from any country; and, in all scenarios, a war-time work ethic is a dubious proposition, about which there is little convincing evidence (MacDougall and Hastings 1986). The latter point is particularly important. Certainly after previous wars civilian populations have often responded to economic loss by rebuilding their economies with speed and vigour. But to extrapolate these situations to the aftermath of nuclear war may be unwarranted. The scale and speed of destruction, the uncertainty about whether more is to come, and doubts about the nature of a society that made destruction on such a scale possible could well make survivors reluctant to commit themselves to such an enormous task as rebuilding their economy and society.

It is also important to consider what might be happening on a smaller scale. For example, if the formal currency system broke down – as is likely at least from scenario 3 on – the trade relationship between urban centres and the surrounding countryside would also suffer (MacDougall and Hastings 1986), leading to de-urbanization and possible economic collapse (Hirschleiffer 1965). The individual entrepreneur would also face impossible problems from scenario 2 on. Many of his former employees would be dead or missing. With banks closed, and their records destroyed by EMP, no one would know how much money they had; if they did, they would not be able to get it; and if they could, no one would work for it. There would be no credit. There would be scant resources for manufacture, no secure market into which to sell, and no way of determining either cost or price if there were. There would, in short, be no incentive or guarantee for the individual producer except on a black market, through a barter system or with the help of some form of central control (Crossley 1983).

In their consideration of the prospects of economic recovery, MacDougall and Hastings (1986) point out that the economic effects of even scenario 1 on London would be considerable because, although demand for essentials would not change, supply would be drastically curtailed and rationing would have to be introduced. Unemployment, already high in peace time and higher after a war scare, would increase dramatically. So would inflation (within four months of the beginning of World War 2, the cost of clothing increased by 25 per cent – Calder 1969). Many of London's one million commuters would fail to get to work. Furthermore, attacks on Greenham Common and Molesworth would have destroyed much of the fastest growing, technology-oriented sector of the region's economy, introducing uncertainties into even those areas of industry normally considered the most secure from unemployment and inflation. These effects would all be much worse in scenarios 2 and 3.

Implications for government and politics. War plays a potent role in shaping politics and political systems. In the UK, World War 2 had profound effects on the British political system, extending the role of the state into many new areas (Marwick 1974). Nuclear war would initiate political changes of even greater magnitude.

The first point to make is that confidence in government, of whatever form, might be seriously eroded by what could be seen as the sharpest political failure in the history of the UK: the breakdown of deterrence theory. For 45 years, the population of the UK has subscribed massive sums of money through taxation to the British nuclear force, on the grounds that this would prevent nuclear war. Once it had failed to do so, that policy would be shown to be sterile. In this sense, the explosion of just a single nuclear weapon on British soil could provoke the most major political upheaval in centuries.

Two views characterize what little discussion there has so far been of the political implications of nuclear war. The first is that the breakdown of social behaviour is such that highly individualistic behaviour becomes the norm. As Hobbes put it, 'There is a war of all against all . . . [and] life is solitary, poor, nasty, brutish and short' (Hobbes 1651). In such a situation, the requirement for government is usually seen as a strong state dedicated to holding individual interests in check in order to secure collective ends.

The alternative view is that a war-time work ethic emerges in which people behave more rationally, suppress their differences, and work harder in view of their recognition of a common enemy (either the enemy itself or the destruction it has caused). Such an ethic did, indeed, manifest itself in the UK at various times during and after World War 2 (though not as continuously or as powerfully as many commentators have claimed). In such a situation, the political system can continue as before; indeed, government can to some extent relax its efforts to establish and maintain its legitimacy because this is more or less taken for granted. To pretend that this is likely to be the political outcome of a nuclear war, however, would be extraordinarily optimistic – though it would be more credible following a limited nuclear attack than a larger one.

Both views, however, appear to ignore the ambivalent attitude of the UK population towards government even in peace time (and the levels of mistrust and hostility to be expected even during a war scare are clearly documented by the GLAWARS survey). Perhaps for this reason, UK government plans lay great stress on the continuity of the machinery of government during a future war – indeed, civil defence plans appear to stress this aspect of survival above all others (Campbell 1983). However, what is proposed is not strictly a continuity of government but the substitution of a new system which does not require the consent of the population to operate and is not subject to the normal democratic process. The legitimacy of the war-time government would rest solely on the principle of a continuity of authority handed down from Parliament (which would be in abeyance). The new style of government would be authoritarian, directive and coercive.

It is not part of GLAWARS' job to provide political criticism of these plans. This has been done extensively elsewhere (see, for example, Campbell 1983 and 1985). However, their implications and their workability must certainly be included in any assessment of the effects of attack on London. They depend primarily on a system of regional government, a form of government which, as MacDougall and Hastings (1986) point out, is not part of the British political experience (London itself has a form of regional government, but even this is shortly to disappear). Government plans would depend for their effectiveness on transferring war-time powers to a number of institutions which, though they exist in peace time, play normally very limited, co-ordinating roles in government. These institutions are essentially untried but they would assume enormous powers during a war. How well they might function can be assessed only in the light of the current problems of government in the UK.

Over the past decade or so, serious doubts have arisen in the UK (and elsewhere) about the ability of government to provide social and economic well-being. Government in the UK has been plagued by conflict with other institutions, notably local authorities and trade unions. Many government departments claim to be victims of overload, and some are clearly unable to cope with the demands made on them. Current attempts to resolve these issues include an increasing centralization of power combined with an attempt to roll back the powers of the state and allow non-government institutions to resolve issues such as wage increases and strikes (McClennan, Held and Hall 1984).

With this as background, it is legitimate to ask whether a war-time government could be expected to discharge its responsibilities efficiently. During a war, the demands placed on government would expand exponentially, government itself would be damaged, making decisions under enormous pressure and within severe time constraints, and would suffer from partial or non-existent information. In addition to all this, the operation of government would depend on an untried machinery of institutions. There is reason enough to doubt that the result would be satisfactory, even given the existence of numerous volunteer services trained and organized by local authorities. The 1983 Civil Defence Regulations place considerable stress on the latter, presumably partly as a response to emerging problems of overload and partly as a possible means of winning increased approval for current civil defence plans. Cynics have also pointed out that voluntary assistance is cheap.

It is important to bear this background in mind while examining the potential political effects of the five GLAWARS scenarios.

Scenario 1. Scenario 1 is likely to pose major problems for political authority, particularly within London. London would not itself be damaged but the effects of a nuclear strike elsewhere would bring the war-time machinery of government into effect and throw social, economic and political life into chaos. The new government machinery would have no time to practise and evolve, as it did in both World Wars 1 and 2. Nor would there be any equivalent of the Marshall Aid that followed World War 2. Furthermore, the government itself could expect considerable internal dissent over major issues such as the allocation of resources between military operations and civil reconstruction. It would also be faced with a fiscal crisis arising from increased demands for government expenditure at a time of declining revenue.

Worsening social and economic conditions, particularly in areas such as London where there is no physical damage, would increase dissent still further. Current plans to involve only the representatives of business and industry – to the exclusion of other groups such as consumer associations and trade unions – in making major decisions in areas such as food and energy would further aggravate the situation.

Government response would be likely to be an increasingly authoritarian stance, with renewed attempts at compulsion and control, and the enlistment of the military in support of civil authority. A downward spiral of mutual mistrust would be the likely end result. Prospects for long-term recovery would be considerably diminished.

The response of the population to increasingly authoritarian styles of government would be likely to be more negative than in peace time. Faced with the horrors of nuclear destruction on their doorsteps – or at least on their neighbours' doorsteps – people would be unlikely to accept further attempts at coercion and compulsion with good grace. As MacDougall and Hastings (1986) conclude, 'considerable civil unrest may ensue'; London as an urban system would not have really 'recovered' within two years – though viable, it would be damaged and unstable.

Scenarios 2 and 3. These scenarios envisage substantial damage to both the UK and London. The initial problem, as described by MacDougall and Hastings (1986), would be the effective isolation of the government from the people:

> A major difficulty will be the basis of political authority. Physically separated in bunkers, and perhaps deprived of effective communications with anyone other than government agencies, the government's ability to evaluate a situation, take an appropriate decision and have it implemented will be in doubt . . . the rules and procedures of the pre-attack society will now be unhelpful, and the severity of the situation will permit no time for adjustment.

The major political problem would be for government to find some way of inducing a change in post-attack behaviour away from actions designed to increase the chances of short-term individual survival towards longer-term requirements for re-organization and recovery. With most communications systems destroyed or damaged, the prospects of being able to do this quickly appear remote. Authorities would have little option but to requisition most remaining stocks of resources as quickly as they could, and probably in the face of considerable public opposition.

Recovery of any form within two years would not be a realistic possibility after either of these scenarios. According to MacDougall and Hastings (1986)

> The basis of pre-attack political authority will cease to have any real significance for not only will that authority itself be fragmented into autonomous regional governments but its relationship with the population will be drastically altered. An unprecedented discontinuity will have occurred in political life . . . For the 4–5 million Londoners remaining alive after these scenarios, survival will have a distinctly new meaning – even its biological continuance will be in question for many, especially the old and young, and those, such as the blind, either disabled before the attack or by it. The outcome for scenarios 2 and 3 therefore lies in the grey area between 'unstable' and 'collapsed', with scenario 3 clearly nearer to the latter.

No organized recovery effort would have begun in London within two years. In scenario 3, there is a possibility that London would be evacuated, and political life in the city would cease.

Scenarios 4 and 5. Those Londoners who escaped death or injury in these scenarios would have no meaningful political life. What capacity the state might have to ease physical survival would enjoy but a short-lived and fortuitous existence on the fringe of the metropolis. After that, the best that could be envisaged would be ill-organized crowds of refugees leading a nomadic life in search of the next meal and the next shelter. The political systems of both London and the UK would have been destroyed. They would not be expected to recover. What forms of political authority might emerge in London or the UK is impossible to predict. However, they would not resemble any of the political institutions operating today.

References

BMA, *Medical Effects of Nuclear War*. London, Wiley, 1983.

Calder, A., *The People's War: Britain 1939–45*. London, Cape, 1969.

Campbell, Duncan, *War Plan UK: the Truth about Civil Defence in Britain*. London, Paladin, 1983.

Campbell, Duncan, 'War Laws 1, 2 and 3'. In *New Statesman*, 6, 13 and 20 September 1985.

Crossley, G., *British Civil Defence and Nuclear War: a Critical Assessment with Reference to Economic Conditions*. Bradford, University of Bradford, 1983.

GLC, *London Industrial Strategies*. London, GLC, 1985.

Hanunian, N., *Dimensions of Survival: Post-attack Survival Disparities and National Viability*. Santa Monica, California, Rand Corporation, 1966.

Hirschleiffer, J., *Economic Recovery*. Santa Monica, California, Rand Corporation, 1965.

Hobbes, T., *Leviathan*. London, Fontana, 1962, first published 1651.
Iklé, F. C., *The Social Impact of Bomb Destruction*. Norman, University of Oklahoma Press, 1959.
Katz, A., *Life after Nuclear War*. New York, Ballinger, 1982.
MacDougall, F., and Hastings, S., *GLAWARS Task 10: The economic, social and political consequences of the scenarios upon the London system*. London, South Bank Polytechnic, 1986, mimeo.
Marwick, A., *War and Social Change in the Twentieth Century*. London, Macmillan, 1974.
McClennan, G., Held, D., and Hall, S., *State and Society in Contemporary Britain*. Cambridge, Polity Press, 1984.
Pearce, D. W., Catephores, G., Markandya, A., and Verry, D., *GLAWARS Task 9: Economic effects of a nuclear attack*. London, South Bank Polytechnic, 1986, mimeo.
Popkess, B., *Nuclear Survivors Handbook: Living Through and After a Nuclear Attack*. London, Arrow Books, 1980.
Smith, D. J., and Gray, J., *Police and People in London*. London, Gower, 1985.
Thompson, James, *GLAWARS Task 4: The behaviour of Londoners in a future major war: estimates from psychological research*. London, South Bank Polytechnic, 1986, mimeo.
Titmuss, R. M., *Problems of Social Policy – History of World War 2*. London, HMSO, 1950.
Tuchman, B. W., *A Distant Mirror: the Calamitous Fourteenth Century*. London, Macmillan, 1978.

2.10 The prospects for London

GLAWARS' assessment of the effects of a war scare and of differing forms of attack on London have important implications for civil defence. These are discussed in Part 3. This section provides a summary of the effects incurred in each of the GLAWARS contingencies, and assesses their long-term consequences for London.

Contingency B: war scare. As stated in Part 1, it is a major finding of this report that a war scare could paralyse London, even before an attack were launched. There would be widespread panic and confusion, a scramble to acquire food, a mass exodus from the capital, and the desertion of most workers from their jobs. Better civil defence planning could do much to improve the efficiency with which London functioned during a war scare.

A war scare would also have a profound effect on London's social and economic fabric, creating severe shortages and increasing unemployment and social tension. Government would be hard put to cope with the demands made of it. For these reasons, London would suffer substantial damage even before any attack was launched. These effects should be considered in assessing the effects of contingencies in which the city would actually be attacked.

Contingency C: non-nuclear attacks. The Commission identified two possibilities: attacks with conventional weapons on military targets and similar attacks on London's services.

There are few military targets in the London area, and nearly all of them are confined to the west and north-west perimeters of the city. Attacks on them with conventional weapons would affect Londoners in those areas, and improvements in existing rescue, fire, ambulance and medical services in the affected areas would help curtail loss of life.

The second possibility is that London might be severely disrupted if a conventional attack were mounted on London's services. The accuracy of modern weapons is such that it might be possible to destroy key facilities connected with London's water, energy and transport systems with only a few tens of aircraft delivering air-to-ground missiles. The Commission was unable to estimate the probability of such an attack, which would depend on the Soviet view of the value of such an attack, the operational accuracy of Soviet weapons, and a Soviet assessment of the chance that the UK might then escalate the war to a nuclear phase. The Commission nevertheless wishes to draw attention to the civil defence implications of this scenario.

Contingency D: nuclear attacks on nuclear targets. Scenario 1 would produce about 860,000 casualties in the UK but none in London. Even so, there would be light damage to buildings in the west of London, and power supplies would be likely to be interrupted in some areas for at least a period. The population would not know whether more attacks were likely, and whether they would include London, so many of those who had not already done so would probably try to leave the city. This would have severe effects on London's services, such as transport and the supply of water and electricity. Commuters would find great difficulty in getting to work, and many of the city's offices would close. Few people would even try to get to work until they could be sure their families were safe from further attacks. Although physically undamaged, the city would thus be severely disrupted. How long it took to recover would depend on the situation elsewhere in the UK and abroad. The fact that nuclear weapons had been exploded on the UK, and the country's expensive posture of nuclear deterrence had failed, would be likely to have severe political repercussions.

Scenario 2 would have much more severe effects. Some 2.76 million people would be killed or injured in the UK, including nearly 1 million in London. This level of casualties would totally overwhelm all rescue and health systems. Many Londoners would try to leave the city, by foot if necessary.

About 350,000 dwellings would be demolished, and a further 134,000 would be structurally damaged. The boroughs of Hillingdon and Harrow would be totally devastated; more than two-thirds of all homes in Hounslow would be destroyed, as would about one-third of the houses in Barnet, Brent, Ealing and Richmond. In addition, fires would rage in all these areas, and might spread inwards towards the city centre.

Overall, the number of houses destroyed in London would be 50 per cent greater than in the whole of the UK during the whole of World War 2. It would take one or two years to clear rubble from London's roads and railway lines, and a further 6–10 years to improvise repairs to the houses left standing. Even if London's house-building industry were completely undamaged, and all materials remained easily available, it would take a further 30 years to rebuild the destroyed housing stock.

If an exo-atmospheric detonation were included in this scenario, EMP would knock out most communications systems, and damage electronic controls and computers. As a result, gas and electricity would be likely to be cut off for at least 72 hours, and probably longer, even in undamaged areas. The water supply system to the west of London would be seriously damaged by blast. The telephone system would be put out of action.

Food stocks would last for only a few days, and there would be a severe shortage of food in London. This would force many more people to try to move out of the capital.

Economic life in London would be totally disrupted for at least two years. Recovery would depend on the speed of recovery elsewhere in the UK but it would lag behind it. In the heavily damaged boroughs, recovery would be very much slower, taking decades. For London as a whole, recovery would be unlikely to mean a return to pre-attack conditions, though London would continue to exist. The impact of scenario 2 on London might be roughly comparable to the Great Fire or the Plague.

Contingency E: nuclear attacks on UK sea and air power. Scenario 3 would produce 8.3 million casualties in the UK, with nearly 1.5 million in London (23 per cent of the population). A third of London's housing would be rendered uninhabitable, with roughly ten times as many houses destroyed in a few minutes as in six years during World War 2. The accidental explosion of a bomb on Hampstead would make three boroughs uninhabitable and two others largely so. Fires would rage throughout much of London. It would take 15–20 years just to clear the rubble from London's roads and railways, and to improvise repairs to those houses left standing. Nearly all London services would be out of action. London transportation would simply stop. There would be no public supplies of gas, electricity or water.

The survivors would be concerned only with finding water, food and shelter for their families. London would cease to function as an economic system, and virtually no one would go to work or have work to go to.

In this situation, the general evacuation of London could be the most likely outcome. Hodgkinson *et al.* (1986) identify four factors that might trigger such an evacuation:

1 the possibility that the government would move out of London to a region where the damage was less severe;
2 the probability that many individual Londoners would evacuate;
3 the possibility that both the government and the regions on which London was dependent for food would see little point in devoting their scarce resources to feeding a population whose principal economic function – the provision of service industries – was of little use to the long-term recovery effort;
4 the possibility that the level of psychological distress amongst London's survivors would be such that morale and social organization would disintegrate even further as more individuals opted to evacuate.

The result would be that London entered a spiral of decline from which it might never recover.

London's ultimate fate would depend on whether outside help were available for reconstruction, as it was, for example, for Hiroshima after World War 2. This seems unlikely. In any event, it would take decades for London to recover as a functioning system. When, and if, it did, it would not resemble the pre-war capital. London might subsequently become a minor city, with the country's capital and the seat of government both located in a less damaged area.

Contingency F: nuclear attacks on military, industrial and urban targets. The outcomes of scenarios 4 and 5 are less ambiguous. In both, more than 85 per cent of Londoners would be killed or injured. More than 90 per cent of homes would be uninhabitable, and there would be no services, and no prospects of services. In 25 of London's 33 boroughs, more than 75 per cent of dwellings would be destroyed in scenario 4. In scenario 5, only Bromley would escape with less than 75 per cent damage, and even there only 8000 homes would still have their walls and roofs intact. Fires would force virtually all survivors to flee, if they could. Those that remained would be unlikely to survive for long. Furthermore, their problems would be greatly compounded by the likelihood that a nuclear winter would follow both scenarios.

In scenarios 4 and 5, London would be reduced to rubble. The city would be abandoned, and would not recover. No set of civil defence measures could alter this outcome.

This does not mean that there would be no survivors. A few Londoners might be able to scavenge a temporary existence from the rubble on the eastern and southern fringes of the capital. But their continued survival would be played out against a backdrop of unmitigated disaster. They would be injured, diseased, cold, hungry, thirsty, isolated and homeless; there would be no one and nowhere to go to for help. These are the people of whom Herman Kahn once asked an extremely pertinent question: 'Would they envy the dead?' (Kahn 1961).

The GLAWARS survey answers this question directly. Asked whether they would hope to survive a nuclear attack, 70 per cent of Londoners replied that they hoped they would not. In fact, their chances of surviving long would be minimal, and their survival misery. Exactly how long and how miserable are questions that GLAWARS cannot answer. Nor does it see a need to do so.

GLAWARS did commission research on these matters (Lewis *et al.* 1986). The results, together with other GLAWARS research, are published separately. However, GLAWARS has not included these findings in its own report because all research on the ultimate fate of bands of post-nuclear refugees stretch the imagination beyond reasonable limits. No one has any experience of a world after a major nuclear attack. The findings of Lewis *et al.* are as likely to be right as any. But speculation about such matters is perhaps better reserved for poets and novelists. As far as GLAWARS' work is concerned, scenarios 4 and 5 raise no implications for civil defence because there is no defence against attacks of this severity.

References

Hodgkinson, S., Fergusson, M., Nectoux, F., with Barrett, M., and Greene, O., co-ordinator Howes, M., *GLAWARS Task 5: The impact of a nuclear attack on London's built environment*. London, South Bank Polytechnic, 1986, mimeo.

Kahn, H., *On Thermonuclear War*. Princeton, Princeton University Press, 1961.

Lewis, J., Jollans, J. L., Moody, R., Nectoux, F., and Pomeroy, J., *GLAWARS Task 9: Recovery after nuclear attack?*. London, South Bank Polytechnic, 1986, mimeo.

3

Civil Defence

Under its terms of reference GLAWARS was required to review civil defence measures in the UK and to compare them with those in other countries. It was asked to consider the cost, suitability and effectiveness of alternative measures, such as mass evacuation and the provision of communal shelter, and to address four specific questions:

1 the effects on death and casualty levels of the 'stay put' strategy;
2 the utility of the domestic self-protection measures recommended by the government;
3 the utility to public survival of local authority control centres; and
4 the utility to public survival of proposed civil defence rescue services and related training schemes.

These four questions are considered in detail in section 3.7, *Civil defence and public survival.*

Early in its deliberations, GLAWARS reached an important conclusion: most civil defence measures can be assessed only in relation to a specific threat. For example, evacuation from areas near military targets may save lives during a limited nuclear attack but would not necessarily do so in a major nuclear war; fall-out shelters may provide protection against radiation but offer little protection from conventional bombardment or nuclear blast. For this reason, nearly all GLAWARS' comments on proposed civil defence arrangements will be restricted to their efficacy against specified forms of attack.

Because most measures would be effective in only some circumstances, GLAWARS is critical of the UK civil defence stance, which plans a flexible response designed to mitigate the effects of all forms of attack. The UK government, in contrast to some others in Europe, consistently refuses to suggest likely patterns of attack or to identify likely military targets. Unless it does so, civil defence in the UK is likely to be of marginal use and its cost effectiveness to remain extremely limited.

The second of GLAWARS' major conclusions about civil defence is that a civil defence programme is of little use unless it receives popular support. Civil defence programmes in both the UK and the United States have run into trouble for precisely this reason. Both countries, unlike others in Europe, have refused to acknowledge that civil defence measures on an affordable scale will be ineffectual against many forms of attack. This has led to widespread public scepticism about civil defence.

This effect has been compounded by attempts to justify civil defence on the grounds that civil defence has value for the UK deterrent posture. When UK civil defence was being reviewed during 1980–81, the Home Secretary, William Whitelaw, described such arrangements as 'an important element of our defence strategy', while his Minister of State, Leon Brittan, told the House of Commons that

> Our central military strategy is to deter attack by an aggressor, and civil defence contributes to deterrence. Indeed, it is essential that our civil preparedness should be adequate if the credibility of our deterrent strategy is to be maintained.
>
> (Hansard 1980)

This position, however, cannot be justified. It would be valid only if it could be shown that UK civil defence was sufficiently developed to prevent an aggressor from inflicting an unacceptable level of damage on the UK or if it could reduce the ability of an aggressor to achieve the objectives of a nuclear attack. Government officials, wisely enough, do not claim that civil defence could do much more than limit damage, and it would be impossible for them to establish otherwise. Should a nuclear attack be limited to military targets, civil defence might provide some protection to nearby populations but it could have no effect on whether the aggressor achieved its objective of destroying those targets. Should a nuclear attack be aimed at cities, no practicable level of civil defence could limit the damage to 'acceptable' levels. The alleged contribution of civil defence to the UK's deterrent posture is therefore unfounded. It is no wonder that such an untenable position has reduced rather than created popular support.

In this context, there is a wider, more philosophical criticism to be made of UK civil defence plans. Current planning guidelines make it clear that civil defence in the UK is primarily geared to the organization, along military lines, of command and control procedures in the event of attack. The emphasis is on maintaining the continuity of government. Only government officials and their staffs will be provided with specially-fitted shelters as a matter of government policy. As Lewis (1986) comments

> The result has been for organization to separate itself off from function; for organization to have an overt concern for itself and its own continuity and protection . . . Civil defence is functionally and institutionally separated from the people it is intended to serve; planning assumptions for survivors refer to "them" and the chances of their continued survival. Civil defence planning is . . . preoccupied with its management system.

This national civil defence stance poses additional problems for local authorities in the UK. However they might wish to plan their own civil defence, they are to some extent constrained to work within a national system that takes a very specific, and somewhat unusual, view of civil defence. This view also militates against both popular support and public participation.

This report concludes with GLAWARS' assessment of civil defence measures (see Table 38). The context of this assessment needs to be clearly set forth because it is not within GLAWARS' terms of reference to formulate a civil defence programme for London. What GLAWARS can do, however, is to identify the key issues that need to be considered by those responsible for planning London's civil defence. Such planning involves a number of steps, and GLAWARS' potential contribution to each of them is spelt out below.

First, a policy for civil defence must be formulated, and a decision made as to the relative weight to be attached to each of several possible goals – for example, protecting as many Londoners as possible from the immediate, short-term effects of attack, increasing the chances of survival after the attack, and ensuring some minimum level of essential services in London before and after the attack. This decision is a political one, and lies outside GLAWARS' terms of reference.

Secondly, a list of all possible civil defence measures must be assembled. Items from this list can then be struck off if, on purely technical grounds, they would be ineffective or counter-productive whatever the goals of the programme. This part of the exercise lies within GLAWARS' terms of reference and GLAWARS therefore makes recommendations as to which measures should be included in the programme and which merit further study. These recommendations are to be found at the end of the report.

Finally, a civil defence budget has to be prepared, and those civil defence measures selected which are likely to be the most cost effective in achieving the goals of the programme. GLAWARS also makes recommendations about how this might best be done. These recommendations are to be found in section 3.6, *The cost effectiveness of civil defence*.

3.1 The basic ingredients

The best known civil defence measures adopted by other countries include the following:

1 fall-out shelters for the population;
2 blast shelters for the population;
3 blast shelters for the leadership;
4 blast shelters for key industrial workers;
5 relocation schemes for the urban population;
6 relocation schemes for the leadership;
7 relocation schemes for key industrial workers;
8 industrial hardening;
9 industrial dispersion;
10 preparations to ensure stable communications systems;
11 preparations of reserves of food, energy, medical supplies, radiological instruments, etc;
12 training for the population in emergency services; and
13 preparations to deal with disasters not related to attack.

Until 1983, UK plans included only an administrative apparatus designed to ensure the continuity of government during and after attack (3 and 6 above), and to ensure that post-attack resources are managed in the best possible manner (11 above). Some attempt has also been made to improve communications (10 above). For the general population, civil defence consisted of plans for the warning of attack, the dissemination of information about the nature of the weapons effects to be expected, and some advice on simple domestic measures to be taken to reduce the dangers of fall-out. The latter consisted basically of instructions on how to construct an expedient home fall-out shelter. The public was told to 'stay at home', build an 'inner refuge' in a 'fall-out room' and remain in place for up to two weeks, awaiting further government advice. On hearing the all-clear, the population was misleadingly told, 'you may resume normal activities' (Home Office 1980).*

The Civil Defence Regulations 1983, however, have now been in force since 1 December 1983. These require local authorities to make more extensive plans for civil defence. The ways in which the new regulations affect London are described in the next section.

* This publication, *Protect and Survive*, has now been officially withdrawn. A new Home Office publication dealing with domestic measures for protection against attack is expected to be published during 1986.

3.2 Civil defence for London

Under the terms of The Civil Defence (General Local Authority Functions) Regulations 1983, the GLC is now required to:

1 make, review and revise civil defence plans for Greater London;
2 provide five emergency centres to control and co-ordinate action in the event of hostile attack or the threat of hostile attack;
3 arrange for civil defence training for GLC and borough staff;
4 take part in civil defence training exercises sponsored by the government; and
5 arrange for the training and exercising of civil defence volunteers to help carry out the plans.

The boroughs themselves are required to help the GLC, if requested, with some of its functions, to provide their own emergency centre and to arrange for civil defence training for their staffs.

The GLC is required to develop 12 types of plans for civil defence. The most important of these are to identify places suitable for shelters, and to plan services for rescue, the accommodation of the homeless, the provision of emergency food supplies, the prevention of the spread of disease, the removal of refuse, the disposal of human remains, and the repair or demolition of damaged property. All plans should be 'capable of being implemented within a period of 7 days and their most vital elements within 48 hours' (Home Office 1984). Additional plans call for the GLC to collect information on the results of attack, to advise the public about its effects, and to co-ordinate action after an attack.

In 1985, the Home Office issued technical guidance on conducting shelter surveys (Home Office 1985a). It suggests that shelters be selected first for their potential protection against radiation and secondly for their blast resistance. Furthermore,

> suitable people, including the authority's own staff and volunteers, should be designated and trained as shelter managers and staff. Detailed consideration will need to be given to ventilation, sanitation, water, light, temperature and food.
>
> (Home Office 1985b)

There is considerable confusion as to what is required by the new legislation in terms of emergency centres. Douglas Hurd, former Minister of State for the Home Office, testified before the Commons in October 1983 that 'We are not requiring local authorities to spend millions or billions of pounds on new resources. We are not asking for new expenditure on infrastructure. We are looking for intelligent and co-ordinated planning for the use of present resources' (Hansard 1983). In Hurd's interpretation, local authorities are required 'simply to designate existing premises which can offer enough protection against the effects of attack to enable essential local civil defence services to be continued'.

The UK is divided into 11 Home Defence Regions, of which Greater London is region number 5. With its headquarters at Kelvedon Hatch, east of London, the London region includes five groups, each containing six or seven London boroughs. In late 1985, only three of the five London groups were equipped with emergency centres; these are in the Northeast (Wanstead), Southeast (West Norwood) and Southwest (Cheam), and are connected with the emergency centres of local borough councils. A fourth group centre (Northwest) is no longer in operation. At the borough level, the degree of preparation varies widely. Only about ten boroughs have an emergency centre for civil defence that could be brought into operation within 48 hours. Most of the centres have old and inadequate communications, and some boroughs have no centre at all. Many of those that do exist would be highly vulnerable to blast damage.

There is great uncertainty over how much money is needed to develop centres which could function in accordance with Hurd's criteria for 'continued services' after attack. Since the 1983 Regulations came into force, the Home Office has approved new emergency centre schemes costing as little as £20,557 (Chichester District Council, West Sussex) and as much as £247,758 (Cambridgeshire County Council). The Hammersmith and Fulham Borough Council costed a centre at about £600,000 (GLC 1985b).

How much progress has been made in recruiting civil defence volunteers is also unclear. According to Home Office Minister of State Giles Shaw, 50 counties (including the GLC) had recruited individual civil defence volunteers as of February 1985. He added that it is 'not yet known' how many London boroughs had recruited civil defence volunteers (Hansard 1985). In the case of the GLC, and probably in the case of many of the counties, these volunteers are scientific advisers rather than volunteers to be trained to carry out plans under the 1983 Regulations.

Financial implications. Local authorities are entitled to a 100 per cent grant from central government for some items, including communications equipment, training programmes, participation in training exercises and courses, and reimbursement of expenses incurred by volunteers. However, grants are not available for administration, building work and office equipment. Some other items, such as adaptation of emergency centres, are eligible for a 75 per cent grant. As Vale (1986a) comments, 'local authorities are still responsible for 25 per cent of the main civil defence administrative costs, including staff salaries, while some other civil defence activities receive no grant aid at all'.

When the new regulations were introduced, the Home Office estimated that the new regulations would add some £1.8 million annually to public expenditure (Home Office 1983). Despite this, the Home Office suggested that the contribution made by local authorities would be unlikely to rise significantly, though it anticipated 'a small increase' in local authority manpower to carry out additional tasks. For 1984/85, Home Office spending on civil defence totalled approximately £77 million, about twice as much in real terms as was spent in 1980. According to the then Home Secretary Leon Brittan, the figure of £77 million is likely to be maintained 'over the next three years' (Brittan 1984).

Calculations made for GLAWARS suggest that, on the contrary, local authority spending on civil defence would have to rise quite considerably if the 1983 Regulations were to be appropriately carried out (Chalmers 1986). Because Home Office guidance on what actually should be done is often vague, amounting to little more than execution of 'reasonable' measures, it is difficult to estimate the costs involved accurately. According to Chalmers (1986), the costs involved are those shown in Table 37. They include annual running costs plus capital costs spread over an initial four-year period.

While these figures should be regarded as no more than rough approximations, it is instructive to compare them with the estimated finance likely to be available from the Home Office for civil defence spending by local authorities. This is due to rise from £11.6 million in 1984/85 to £14.4 million in 1987/88 (both figures at 1985/86 prices). However, if GLC spending were to reach £11 million a year, total local authority spending throughout the UK would probably reach £70 to £110 million a year (extrapolated from Chalmers 1986). Home Office finance could therefore account for only between about 10 and 20 per cent of the total. Even if figures for opportunity costs and minimum shelter improvement were excluded, Home Office finance would provide only 25 to 35 per cent of the total.

It therefore appears that the GLC is required to provide at least a further £3.9 million a year. If opportunity costs and the minimum shelter improvement programme were also included, this figure would rise to some £9 million a year.

Background to the new regulations. The intent of the new regulations can be understood only in relation to other aspects of civil defence in the UK,

Table 37 Estimated annual civil defence costs (£, 1985/86) for London resulting from the Civil Defence Regulations 1983[a]

Measure	Borough costs	GLC costs	Total
Planning		630,000[b]	630,000
Emergency control centres			
Annual capital costs★	1,100,000	200,000	1,300,000
Annual running costs	297,000	53,000	350,000
Staff training			
Training unit		235,000	235,000
Opportunity costs[c]		1,930,000	1,930,000
Volunteer training			
Co-ordination unit		110,000	110,000
Training costs		2,900,000	2,900,000
Public shelter survey		400,000	400,000
Minimum shelter improvement programme[d]			
Annual capital cost★		3,250,000	3,250,000
TOTALS	1,397,000	9,708,000	11,105,000

★ Over four-year period.
[a] Assumptions on which the estimates are based are in Chalmers (1986).
[b] Includes a baseline cost of £310,000 a year, already incurred under regulations introduced in 1981.
[c] Opportunity costs are those necessarily incurred by hiring extra staff to take up the duties of local authority employees when engaged on civil defence exercises, training and preparation.
[d] On the grounds that simply identifying shelters, without making minimum modifications, is not productive. The sum of £1000 is allowed for each of the 13,000 potential shelters estimated to exist by the GLC. This sum would cover no more than the provision of doors, water storage, some ventilation and adequate signposting.
Source: Chalmers 1986.

and the way in which it has evolved since World War 2. As already mentioned, a great deal of attention has been devoted to systems of perpetuating command and control structures during time of war.

In the event of attack, it is planned that central government would remain in control for as long as practical (Home Office 1984). Thereafter, government would devolve into a regional basis, with authority vested in Regional Emergency Committees (RECs). The RECs would have as their chairmen the regional directors of the Department of The Environment/Department of Transport. Representatives of most government departments, local authorities, the police, the military, British Telecom and the Post Office would be included in the RECs (Home Office 1985b).

RECs would be activated in peace time if an emergency threatened. They are intended as a liaison between central government and local authorities. Each committee would ensure that civil resources were deployed in the way most beneficial to national interests. If central government direction became impossible, a War-time Regional Government Commissioner would take over the direction of each of the 11 regions, enabling each region to operate independently.

The Commissioner would be charged with co-ordinating survival and recovery. This would entail allocating resources, providing information to the general public, determining priorities between local authorities and other bodies, allocating assistance from the armed forces, maintaining public order, administering justice, and fixing agricultural and industrial priorities. The Home Office concludes, however, that 'the assessment of local priorities and mutual aid arrangements, operational deployment and the conduct of day-to-day affairs would be left to the local authorities' (Home Office 1984).

Protecting the population. Government advice on population protection is contained in the booklet *Protect and Survive* (Home Office 1980 but unavailable by late 1985). The booklet is intended to be distributed to every household if war threatens. It includes cursory descriptions of nuclear weapons effects, information about attack warning signals and suggestions for the construction of shelters to increase protection against fall-out.

Protect and Survive advocates the designation of a fall-out room, preferably either a basement or a room having the smallest amount of outside wall. It suggests piling up thick dense materials to provide protection against radiation. Within the fall-out room, 'still greater protection is necessary'. This is to be provided by constructing an inner refuge such as a lean-to made with doors, a table covered with furniture, sandbags, earth, books and clothing, or a cupboard under the stairs. Inside the fall-out room should be kept a survival kit consisting of food and water for 14 days, a portable radio, eating utensils, warm clothing and the *Protect and Survive* booklet itself.

For those wishing to construct more robust shelters, the Home Office published *Domestic Nuclear Shelters* (1981) which describes shelters built from manufacturer's kits. Another Home Office volume, *Domestic Nuclear Shelters Technical Guidance* (1981), is directed at trade and professional interests concerned with the design and construction of such shelters. There is little Home Office advocacy for these privately-financed shelters and no government subsidy for them. Moreover, the British Medical Association (BMA 1983) noted that 'none of the designs reported to the Working Party appeared to have satisfactory mechanisms to eliminate dangerous combustion products from the air being drawn into the shelter'.

Evacuation. The advisability of evacuation has been fiercely debated since World War 2. During that war, officially directed evacuation occurred at three different stages, the largest well before any attack on the UK had begun. Between 1 and 3 September 1939, 1.5 million of the 'priority' classes (school children, younger children and their mothers, expectant mothers and the physically disabled) were voluntarily evacuated from London and other cities. A second evacuation took place during the blitz of September-November 1940. The third occurred when, in August 1944, the Germans began a campaign with 'V' weapons – long-range rockets and flying bombs.

These three evacuations were by no means uniformly successful. As the official historian of wartime civil defence concluded, the civil defence evacuations had 'grave strategic implications' (O'Brien 1955). These implications involved the behaviour of the British public rather than that of the German adversary. The first evacuation was followed not by attack but by a full year of further anticipation before the bulk of the air raids began; by Christmas 1939, the ebb tide of evacuation had already brought back half of the 1.5 million mothers and children who had left some 12 weeks earlier. The unofficial private exodus of a further two million during the last half of 1939 provided yet another 'source of much anxiety to the Government'. The result was great disruption

> Evacuation and the general movement of the population had created a degree of interference and inconvenience which seemed only acceptable in conditions of either invasion or massed air attacks. This dislocation of the educational system and other social services added to the general mood of irritation and frustration.
>
> (Titmuss 1950)

It seems likely that this experience provided the historical basis for the government's continued antipathy to evacuation. In the late 1950s, however, Home Office spokesmen were talking of evacuating '45 percent of densely populated areas' (Hansard 1957) and of dispersing '12 million people' (Hansard 1959). Faced with a barrage of criticism, the Home Office spent five years reviewing its evacuation plans. It decided in 1962 to retain an option of evacuating women and children from 19 major cities (Hansard 1963). With the closure of branch railways later in the decade, even these vestigial plans became unworkable, although even in 1982 the Home Office was still 'reviewing' its policy on evacuation (Howard 1982).

Since 1972, all forms of evacuation have been discouraged. *Protect and Survive* stated

> Stay at Home.
> Your own local authority will best be able to help you in war. If you

> move away – unless you have a place of your own to go to or intend to live with relatives – the authority in your new area will not help you with accommodation or food or other essentials. If you leave, your local authority may need to take your empty house for others to use.
> So stay at home.
>
> (Home Office 1980)

More recently, the Home Office has sought to move away from the coercion implied by this passage. The 1983 booklet, *Civil Defence: The Basic Facts*, says that the stay-at-home policy is purely advisory and that 'no attempt would be made to enforce the Government's advice and prevent people moving to other parts of the country' (Home Office and Scottish Home and Health Department 1983).

However, London's network of Essential Service Routes, 16 major radial routes out of the capital and 3 ring roads around it, are to be closed off to the public during a crisis period by the police, possibly with military assistance. The idea is to 'facilitate the free movement of essential traffic of all kinds engaged in the implementation of transition-to-war measures'; and subsequently to meet the likely post-strike requirements 'should the need arise' (Home Office 1971).

This could greatly disrupt the attempts of Londoners to evacuate in defiance of government policy to stay at home (and the GLAWARS survey indicates that millions of Londoners are likely to try to move out of London). The management of refugees trying to head out of London through outlying boroughs would probably be one of the greatest challenges faced by London's civil defence planners, though unclassified Home Office circulars do not discuss this.

However, in response to an October 1984 letter from civil defence officials in the London borough of Camden, the Home Office stated that 'there are no plans to exclude the public from main roads out of London or anywhere else in the country, and there are no plans to hinder self-evacuation' (Sanderson 1984).

It is a central tenet of current UK civil defence policy that there can be no assumptions about 'what targets will be chosen' and that therefore 'no part of the United Kingdom can be considered safe from both the direct effects of the weapons and the resultant fall-out' (Home Office 1980).

The civil defence stay-at-home shelter policy is thus a uniform policy, claimed to be equally applicable anywhere in the country. There is no attempt made to single out some areas as more likely to suffer attack.

Warning and monitoring. Most of the civil defence measures currently proposed for London are only of the expedient and emergency nature of those described in *Protect and Survive*. The vast majority of government spending on civil defence during peace time is devoted instead to readying warning and monitoring systems, and improving the chances that communications networks will remain operable during and after attack.

The United Kingdom Warning and Monitoring Organization (UKWMO) is designed to accomplish several tasks. First, it is intended to provide a communications network for disseminating news about incoming missiles and impending attack. Second, it will report to the government and military leadership about the nature and extent of the strikes. Third, its 870 monitoring posts will report fall-out levels during the first few hours of attack when they are too lethal to be measured by other means. From this information, the UKWMO will help to develop a scientific assessment of the likely path and intensity of fall-out so that informed advice can be transmitted to survivors waiting in shelters. A Home Office booklet describes UKWMO as 'probably our most important life-saving measure' (Home Office and Scottish Home and Health Department 1983).

UKWMO has been substantially improved since 1980 and, according to the former Home Secretary Leon Brittan, 'it is now probably at a better state of readiness than in any other NATO country' (Brittan 1984). Brittan added that 'we are considering how it might be adapted to give warning of conventional and chemical attack'. Those sceptical of the potential of UKWMO to disseminate vital information about fall-out patterns point out that the system is unable to differentiate between bombers carrying conventional and nuclear weapons, and that UKWMO depends on communications links which may be highly vulnerable to EMP.

3.3 Civil defence in other countries

Most countries have no civil defence effort at all or use civil defence primarily to mitigate peacetime natural disasters. Nearly every European state, however, devotes some consideration to civil defence. With a 1984–85 budget of about £77 million, the current UK per capita expenditure for civil defence is similar to that of most other NATO countries, including the United States. It is, however, substantially lower than that of West Germany, Denmark and Norway, and it is an order of magnitude lower than that of Sweden, Switzerland and the Soviet Union.

Civil defence in the United States. United States planners have tried to implement some significant civil defence policies that are not currently in place in the UK. The most important are the shelter identification programme, begun in the early 1960s, and plans for mass evacuation, introduced in the late 1970s and abandoned only in 1985.

Civil defence in the United States has become a matter of major public debate only twice. The first was instigated by President Kennedy during 1961–62 and is the only time when presidential and congressional support merged to approve enough funding for a substantial civil defence commitment. After the Berlin crisis and the Cuban missile crisis were peacefully defused, however, US civil defence receded from public and governmental consciousness; for 15 years, it received only nominal funding. Because the predominant theory of assured destruction implied that mutual vulnerability of civilian populations was both necessary and good, civil defence could be easily ignored or dismissed as destabilizing. Interest in civil defence revived in the mid-1970s, however, beginning in the Carter administration and continuing through President Reagan's first term.

Many factors have influenced post-1945 thinking about US civil defence. The United States has not experienced a 20th century war on or near its own territory. The United States entered both world wars late and never seriously faced the prospect of enemy invasion; war was meant to be fought 'over there'. This attitude contributes to a certain complacency which continues to hinder the development of civil defence. Civil defence was widely implemented in most European states during World War 2, providing precedent and legitimation for its subsequent use in the nuclear age. Americans, never having needed civil defence before, continue to resist it now.

The United States also operates as a relatively open democracy. While policy changes are usually proposed by the President, funding is subject to intense scrutiny in congressional committees whose members are sensitive to public opinion. Thus, civil defence policy, even when not controversial, is very much a matter of public record and is easily intertwined with other provocative nuclear issues.

A final factor is the large land mass of the country. The relatively low population density of many of the non-urban areas has made evacuation schemes potentially viable in the eyes of some planners.

The first major US civil defence programme was the fall-out shelter survey instituted by President Kennedy in 1961. This eventually identified and marked more than a quarter of a million basements, corridors, caves and other areas affording protection from post-attack fall-out. These premises were claimed to provide shelter for 238 million Americans, a figure larger than the total US population of that time (FEMA 1980).

Some of the shelters were stocked with water, food, medical

equipment and other supplies; all could be identified by a yellow and black sign reading 'Fall-out Shelter'. In time, however, the food began to deteriorate and some of the remainder was distributed to drought-stricken Third World countries in the early 1970s. Although further marking and stocking of shelters was reintroduced in the 1980s, most of the existing shelters now seem to be regarded by the general public as little more than curious relics.

Located primarily in the centres of large cities, the shelters do not correspond to the residential distribution of the population. Moreover, at least initially, the proximity of the shelters to likely targets was not considered. Quite apart from their vulnerability to blast, many lack adequate ventilation systems. However, the Federal Emergency Management Agency (FEMA) has indicated a desire to rectify these shortcomings (FEMA 1984). FEMA would like to identify 259 million shelter spaces, only 78 million of which would be in risk areas (those where there are likely to be blast overpressures of 2 psi or more).

The original organizers of the National Fallout Identification programme expected to identify spaces for no more than 50 million Americans, or about one-quarter of the population of that time. Secretary of Defence Robert McNamara claimed that the shelters might reduce fatalities by 10 to 15 million. A statement from a 1961 congressional committee clearly recognized the limited goals of the programme

> While the net contribution of the identification, marking, and improvement program can be better evaluated after the complete survey findings are in, it must be realized that the potentials at best are limited. All deaths from fall-out can be prevented – but not in existing buildings, even when improved. Nationwide, the largest number of structures do not afford even the bare minimum protection factor considered necessary to bring the radiation hazard down to tolerable levels. All that the new program can hope to do is find those corners in the Nation's physical plant, so to speak, which allow a few more millions to survive. We do not mean to deprecate this achievement, only to point out its limited nature.
>
> (US Congress 1961)

More than 20 years later, as British planners attempt their own shelter survey, the limitations revealed by the US effort should not be forgotten.

The second noteworthy US civil defence plan concerns evacuation. Known in the United States as crisis relocation planning, it is based upon an acknowledgement that some places in the United States may be more at risk from nuclear attack than others. FEMA notes that

> While large cities and military installations constitute a small percentage

> of the total US land mass, over two-thirds of this country's population live in and around these possible risk areas, areas that could suffer from nuclear blast and heat in the event of attack. Because a distance of as little as ten miles will remove people from the blast and heat effects of a nuclear explosion, FEMA feels it is prudent to develop plans to relocate high risk area populations.
>
> (FEMA 1980)

FEMA planned to relocate the 145 million Americans resident in 'risk areas' to rural 'host areas', where they would be provided with temporary lodging in schools, churches and other non-residential buildings. The scheme relied greatly on the use of private motor vehicles for transport. According to FEMA

> about 65 percent of the risk population could be evacuated by the end of the first day, about 85 percent by the end of the second day, and over 95 percent by the end of the third day. It would probably take an extra day for the residents of New York City, and up to three or four extra days for all of the people in Los Angeles and San Francisco to relocate.
>
> (FEMA 1980)

People who relocated were expected to bring an initial supply of food and to construct fall-out shelters on arrival in their host areas. FEMA surveys suggested that 80 per cent of the population at risk would take part in the plans.

However, evacuation schemes of this kind must take account of several daunting challenges which critics of the scheme were quick to point out.

Even under FEMA's highly optimistic timetables, evacuation could take several days. More time would be required to construct fall-out protection in the host areas. An attack might not be preceded by a warning period this long. If the attack were to occur during the middle of the evacuation, with millions out on the roads, casualties could be even higher than if the population had remained in place.

There is also some uncertainty as to whether all the host areas would necessarily be safer than the cities left behind. 'Risk area' cities might not be initial targets for direct attack, though areas near military installations probably would be. It was even suggested that weapons might be retargeted upon the 'host areas'.

The relocation of 145 million people at a time of crisis is a mammoth undertaking. The sheer logistics are potentially overwhelming, especially when public transport would be needed to carry those without private vehicles (and there is some doubt that bus drivers would be willing to return to risk areas for second and subsequent loads of evacuees). Many who studied the subject concluded that FEMA's timetable was completely unrealistic. Further delays could be expected in areas of rough terrain or places experiencing bad weather (Leaning and Keyes 1984).

Policing such an enormous dislocation of people and resources would be a tremendous undertaking. Not the least of the problems would be coping with those who chose to evacuate to areas other than those where they were told to go. Feeding and caring for millions of refugees in the host areas would also require enormous resources, not present in the peacetime infrastructure of rural communities.

An evacuation programme must be combined with a system of fall-out shelters for those who have been relocated. Creating the necessary protection in the host areas would be a long and arduous process, especially if there were shortages of supplies such as shovels and sandbags.

FEMA plans provide for 'key workers' and their families to relocate to nearby host areas and continue to commute into the risk areas on a shift basis. It is not known how many key workers would be willing to do this.

FEMA admits that the cost of its evacuation programme would be enormous, possibly exceeding $2000 million a day.

The most difficult challenge is to know when to begin evacuation, and when to cancel it if an attack should not occur. Even if no attack occurred, it would probably be difficult to sustain a population in shelters for more than a couple of weeks. Resources would run short while social tensions would run high. It is also exceedingly difficult to decide when a crisis has passed. The danger of mistiming, especially in the case of massive evacuation, might be so great as to prevent any government leader from ever implementing the programme.

Critics of the programme therefore concluded that the US crisis relocation plan was 'deeply flawed' (Vale 1986b). Recognizing some of these flaws, 120 state and local jurisdictions, representing 90 million people, refused to develop their relocations plans. By March 1985, faced with widespread opposition and inadequate funds, FEMA had quietly abandoned its plans for crisis relocation.

Civil defence in the Soviet Union. Soviet civil defence policies are completely different from those of the United States, for reasons that relate to the nature of the Soviet state and its government's claims to legitimacy. The latter rest partly on the government's proclaimed ability and determination to protect the Soviet people from external attack. Hence the military power of the Soviet Union assumes great importance in internal politics, and the civil defence effort forms part of the military structure. Whether or not civil defence in the Soviet Union would be effective, its existence is of vital importance to central control.

This is in complete contrast to the situation in the United States where the prevention of war, rather than the protection of the population in the event of attack, is the over-riding goal. In fact, the US government tends to lose popular support whenever civil defence becomes a major issue.

One of the more important functions of Soviet civil defence is its ability to support the policies and enhance the popularity of the Communist Party (CPSU). The message the Soviet leadership would like to convey is that the problem of nuclear survival is being brought under control as a direct result of the Communist Party's deeply felt interest in each Soviet citizen. As Vale (1986b) comments, 'In the Soviet Union, where primary attention is given to maintaining the security of the ruling elite, civil defence takes on special significance as an affirmation of CPSU's wisdom and control'.

Civil defence is also integrated with the military to an unparalleled extent. An estimated 100,000 Soviet troops are engaged in civil defence activities full-time; in war-time, the size of the Soviet civil defence force could swell to 16–20 million with the addition of civilian conscripts (Gouré 1983b). As John Erickson puts it, Soviet civil defence is 'designed to protect military effectiveness under conditions of full-scale nuclear attack' (Miles 1983). Finally, the identification of Soviet civil defence with the Soviet Army provides it with a certain added credibility and imbues it with a portion of the same traditional esteem with which the World War 2 Red Army is held.

The Soviet civil defence programme is the world's largest in terms of expenditure, personnel and scope; in its rhetoric, at least, it also makes the largest claims for effectiveness (Vale 1985, and Gouré 1976 and 1983a). It emphasizes both blast shelter construction and evacuation and, while concentrating on the special protection of the upper bureaucracies of government and industry, it also speaks of protection for every worker.

Since 1961, Soviet civil defence has been under the direction of the Ministry of Defence. In the 1960s, the programme took a critical view of the effectiveness of shelters and recognized the advantages of evacuation and dispersal of the population as part of a policy of economic survival. In the years following the appointment of Lt General Aleksandr Altunin as head of civil defence in 1972, the Soviet programme expanded and continued to be orientated towards preserving the economic and political viability of the state. Under Altunin, there was a renewed support for the provision of blast shelters.

While the enormous territory of the Soviet Union has helped to make evacuation a potentially viable option, most of the political success of the programme can be attributed to 'centralized economic control, Communist Party self-interest and military direction' (Vale 1986b).

The crucial function of the centralized command economy for civil defence is the degree of control it provides over war production needs. The desirability, even the necessity, of being prepared to undergo a protracted period of war, even if it is a war fought with nuclear weapons, is a persistent theme in Soviet writings about state survival and civil defence. Central control provides the Soviet Union, at least conceptually, with a much greater ability to adopt a 'war footing' for its economy and to maintain production during and after attack; in turn, preparations for civil defence help to legitimize central control.

Yet, even in peace time, the drawbacks of a centralized economy are apparent. According to Vale (1986b)

> Instructions to incorporate civil defence facilities in new industrial plants are often ignored, based on economic considerations. Centralized planning allows a great deal of local inefficiency to take place unnoticed. More important, the plans for industrial dispersion, touted throughout the post-war period, have not been exercised to a significant degree.

Furthermore, some Soviet industries are more concentrated than their Western counterparts: 25 cities contain almost all of the Soviet chemical plants while only 15 plants comprise 60 per cent of Soviet steel production (Kaplan 1978). This has made the challenge of industrial civil defence protection even more daunting.

The Communist Party is involved in all levels of Soviet civil defence and has directed a propaganda effort of unsurpassed magnitude; with compulsory courses and a multi-media barrage of information, the CPSU has made a concerted effort for more than 25 years to keep the matter before the public. While the effectiveness of this propaganda is uncertain, its size is indicative of the fact that the programme remains of great political importance to the CPSU leadership.

The need to protect the economy in war-time was an important lesson of World War 2; the subsequent development of Soviet evacuation plans is inseparable from the desire to maintain economic production during pre-attack, attack and post-attack periods. In the 1960s and 1970s, the preservation of economic production became a central aim of Soviet war preparation. Soviet military writers have consistently emphasized the importance of protecting the economy, regarding this as a central purpose behind civil defence, equal and inseparable from the task of population protection. In the 1968 edition of *Military Strategy*, V. D. Sokolovskiy maintained that the economic and humanitarian aims of civil defence are intimately connected

> The principal tasks of civil defense are to ensure the required conditions for normal activity of all governmental control agencies during the course of the war and the effective functioning of the national economy. This is

> achieved by maximum defense of the population against weapons of mass destruction, widespread and all-round aid to victims, and the rapid removal of the remains of an enemy nuclear attack.
>
> (Sokolovskiy 1975)

Evacuation is intended for all urban residents and workers at industrial installations thought to be likely targets for enemy nuclear attack. Residents of suburban areas within 8–10 km of high risk cities would also be subject to relocation (Gouré 1983a). Gouré estimates that the Soviet relocation would involve between 100 and 120 million, out of a total population of 272 million.

The Soviet leadership makes a distinction between people designated for 'dispersal' and those who are eligible for 'evacuation'. Dispersal is the organized removal, on foot or by public transport, of those workers of industrial enterprises which are to remain in operation during war-time in high risk areas. These workers will be housed 1–3 hours away from their workplace and organized into two 12-hour work shifts; thus situated, they would ostensibly be able to continue commuting to work. Also designated for dispersal are urban civil defence troops who are assigned the tasks of post-strike rescue, repair and restoration.

Evacuation, by contrast, is for people considered non-essential for war-time economic and civil defence operations. They will be relocated further away from high risk areas, and will not be expected to commute to work. In addition, it is envisaged that in some cases whole enterprises will be evacuated out of high risk areas; in these cases, workers will be relocated along with their workplaces.

Assessments of the probable success of Soviet crisis relocation and sheltering plans vary. Certain shortcomings are, however, uncontested even by those Western observers who are highly impressed by the Soviet civil defence programme.

There are doubts about the adequacy of relocation training and some evidence of public scepticism of the value of the programme. Gouré (1983a) has recently claimed that some aspects of civil defence training have serious problems

> Peace time crisis relocation training has and continues to be plagued by difficulties and shortcomings. In a large part, this appears to be due to the reluctance of some officials and managers to devote in full measure the time and resources required for conducting full-scale, effective exercises. As result, it is not possible to assess the degree of readiness of Soviet civil defence to execute a rapid and effective relocation of the urban population in an actual crisis situation.

Since the 1960s, Western accounts of Soviet civil defence progress have noted the existence of 'widespread apathy or outright mockery' (Vale

1986b). Soviet civil defence authorities themselves express continual dissatisfaction with the state of the programme, seeking to spur it on towards a more complete fulfilment and to reward those regions which proceed more rapidly.

A second group of doubts concerns the inadequacies of Soviet transport. It is estimated that in the whole country there are only about 10 million motor vehicles in working order. Many of the rail lines out of major cities are still single track, and will presumably be commandeered for military purposes. Neither does the Soviet Union have a well-developed highway network. The harsh Soviet climate would compound these problems

> Soviet severe weather conditions hamper what possible road travel exists. During the winter, spring thaw periods, and autumn rainy seasons, Soviet roads are virtually impassable. The Soviets describe their situation as *rasputitsa*, or roadlessness, during those months.
>
> (Weinstein 1982)

Providing for the relocated population is another problem for which Soviet civil defence planning is not yet prepared. Many analysts, both Soviet and Western, point out that food and water may run short. Others note the dependency on power plants that may be destroyed, and the problem of obtaining and distributing the materials needed to build fall-out shelters. The inadequacy of these shelters remains the most compelling drawback of all. It is a declared Soviet goal to have fall-out shelters available in the host areas in advance of the decision to relocate. However, Gouré contends

> At present, hosting areas do not usually have sufficient ready anti-radiation covers to accommodate the urban evacuees. Such shelters could be built over time or during a protracted crisis. Otherwise they will have to be built simultaneously with the crisis relocation by the rural residents as well as the evacuees themselves.
>
> (Gouré 1983a)

Many Western sceptics of the Soviet programme suggest that it is unreasonable to expect reliable shelters to be built, given a shortage of materials and the exhaustion of the evacuees, about 20 per cent of whom may have had to walk from the cities carrying their belongings (Gouré 1976 and Kaplan 1978).

Of the 100–120 million people to be relocated, 50–70 million are destined for dispersal to communities within two or three hours of their workplaces. Sceptics suggest that there is an acute shortage of appropriate host areas and that the desired level of dispersal 'may not be practical in the case of many cities' (Gouré 1976). Gouré also mentions the potential for 'chaotic and dangerously disorganized movement' *within* major cities.

Soviet plans for crisis relocation are impressive but there are serious grounds for scepticism. Public scepticism, climate, transport, lack of fall-out protection and logistics would work against the likelihood of substantial success in implementing the programme. In view of all these issues, 'it remains unclear whether the Soviet leadership would choose to exercise its relocation plans at all' (Vale 1986b).

The existence of super-hardened command centres for the Soviet political leadership has been documented since the 1970s. Some intelligence reports suggest that these bunkers are able to 'withstand direct hits from any nuclear warhead in the American arsenal' (Connell 1984). A study by the Central Intelligence Agency (CIA 1982) concluded that blast shelter protection exists for 110,000 members of the Soviet leadership, including

top national leadership;
5000 party and government officials at national and republic levels;
63,000 local party and government officials;
2000 managers of key installations; and
40,000 members of civil defence staffs.

Since the early 1970s, Soviet officials have stressed the need to 'shelter the entire population in protective structures' (Altunin, cited in Troxell 1983). In practice, what has been constructed are shelters for a portion of the urban industrial workforce; while these may indeed qualify as 'blast shelters', the extent of their effectiveness is unclear. The decision taken in 1974 to proceed with blast shelters is not of course the same thing as actually constructing them.

According to the CIA, the Soviet Union could probably shelter about a quarter of the total workforce at key industrial installations. This means that the Soviet Union could protect 'about 15 million people' in more than '20,000 blast resistant shelters', a figure representing 'slightly over 10 percent' of the total population of cities having populations of more than 25,000. While impressive, such figures fall considerably short of protection for the entire population. Even so, Altunin continues to claim that the 'necessary inventory' of blast shelters 'is being created' (cited in Gouré 1983b). There are wide disagreements regarding the current rate of shelter construction and many doubts remain about the reliability of those that do exist.

Attempts to initiate a programme to protect key aspects of the Soviet industrial economy have also proved less than satisfactory. Altunin describes 'special measures to raise the hardness of each sector and industrial facility' as another one 'of the decisive conditions for ensuring the survivability of the economy in war-time' (cited in Gouré, Kohler and Harvey 1974). Soviet intentions have not been matched by Soviet practice. Still, in 1976 Gouré described the 'required hardening' of 'all service and industrial installations', as well as efforts to protect especially valuable machinery, to shield electric power, steam, water and chemical conduit systems, to establish underground water reservoirs, pumping and power stations, to build duplicate critical bridges and power installations, to develop a redundant communications systems, and to put defence plants and raw materials reserves underground (Gouré 1976). Seven years later, however, Gouré seemed to have more doubts, concluding that 'There is no evidence of a comprehensive industrial hardening program' (Gouré 1983b).

Furthermore, there are no known protective measures for certain categories of installations including

> oil refineries, chemical storage plants, steel-making and petroleum and construction equipment plants, pharmaceuticals, component assembly factories, truck and tractor and rolling stock manufacturies, repair and spare-part facilities, as well as marshalling yards, transport nodes and highway intersections, bridges and tunnels, port facilities and pipelines, airports and shipyards.
>
> (Aspin 1978)

Thus there can be little confidence in the ability of the Soviet industrial infrastructure to withstand a large-scale nuclear attack.

Despite these shortcomings, Soviet civil defence would probably make a significant contribution to the survival of the state in the event of a less than all-out nuclear attack. While there is nothing to suggest that civil defence could make nuclear war any less than an unparalleled catastrophe, it 'could well lead to an increase in the numbers of surviving population and a marginally speedier post-war economic recovery' (Vale 1986b).

Civil defence in Sweden. Sweden's plans for civil defence are among the most highly organized and elaborate in the world. They stem from Sweden's foreign policy of non-involvement in military alliances. In the event of war between other states, Sweden will declare itself neutral. In order to ensure its continued independence, Sweden has made vigorous plans to protect itself from attack with a concept known as 'total defence'.

Total defence includes military defence, civil defence, economic defence and psychological defence. Military defence includes conscription for all men between 18 and 47 years of age, and the total defence force, including the Home Guard, exceeds 850,000 people. All men and women between the ages of 16 and 65 may be called up for civil defence duty. Some 200,000 men and women are currently trained in civil defence, and have specific war-time duties assigned to them.

The form of Swedish civil defence is strictly geared to the perceived threat which is set forth in a long-range assessment made by Parliament every five years. The current threat was last assessed in 1982; its nuclear component differs little from earlier assessments dating from the late 1960s.

The fundamental assumption is that Sweden will not be the sole or prime target for aggression in the case of armed conflict in Europe. However, it is acknowledged that an attempt might be made to gain control of parts of Swedish territory, territorial waters or air space by one of the major power blocs to gain a strategic advantage over its adversary. The basic scenario is that a war in Europe would start with the use of conventional weapons and that Sweden would not necessarily be a target if the war became nuclear.

The principal risk is thus assessed as attack with conventional weapons and the risk of fall-out from nuclear weapons exploding on near-by territory. A secondary risk is from a nuclear attack restricted to Swedish military targets. The Swedish Civil Defence Administration (SCDA) is quite specific about its ability to provide any more general protection for the population

> Nuclear attacks on cities, aimed at the destruction of the civilian population, is acknowledged as a contingency that we are unable to counter effectively (as are all other nations, or so we believe) . . . Complete protection against an extensive, direct attack on our territory with nuclear, chemical or biological weapons is not possible.
>
> (SCDA 1986)

Nevertheless, during the 1950s and 1960s, the Swedes rated a counter-city nuclear attack much more highly, and elaborate plans for urban evacuation were made. Over the decades this has been replaced by a shelter system, complemented by only limited evacuation plans.

The Swedish civil defence system is now based on training for the civil defence organization, a warning and fall-out monitoring system, shelters for most of the population, limited evacuation, and an ability to mount rescue operations. Civil defence command and control centres are protected against blast, fall-out and EMP.

In each municipality, Municipal Boards control civil defence and are required to draw up local protection plans. In contrast to the civil defence plans of most other countries, a specific risk assessment is made for each part of the municipality. Evacuation plans are based on this risk assessment.

The Swedish system is also unusual in that three different levels of civil defence alert can be ordered. The first two involve only partial mobilization; the final one calls for full civil defence mobilization. This progressive system of alert may have important implications for avoiding the sudden switch between GLAWARS contingencies A and B –

continued non-belligerence and war scare. As mentioned in Part 1, a sudden switch of this kind may produce panic and confusion. It seems possible that a more gentle gradation from peace to war would allow a civilian population more time to assimilate the situation and plan accordingly.

The mainstay of the Swedish civil defence system is shelter accommodation financed by the state in localities which it selects (again based on risk assessment). Currently, 342 localities are provided with shelters (SCDA 1986) which include public shelters for 100,000 people in the larger towns and individual shelter places for a further 5 million (Diacon 1984). Sweden's population in 1985 was 8.3 million.

The extent to which these shelters are blast proof varies. The Swedish standard shelter is said to be proof against shockwaves, splinters, chemical weapons and fall-out, and provides protection against blast overpressures of about 7 psi (SCDA 1986), roughly half the minimum value quoted for Swiss shelters. A further 250,000 shelter places are being built annually (Diacon 1984). The long-range goal is to provide shelter for everyone, both at their homes and at work.

Government grants are available for shelter construction. The average grant works out at somewhat more than £250 per person sheltered. However, this is not the real cost of construction. Shelters are widely used in peace time for other purposes – such as gymnasia, public health centres, music rooms in schools, and so on. Furthermore, the grant does not cover the full cost of the building but is intended to reflect the additional cost of making it double as a shelter. The only restriction on the peacetime use of the buildings is that they should be able to be converted to their shelter use within 48 hours.

Evacuation complements the use of shelters but is reserved for special circumstances. The SCDA points out that evacuation results in severe disruption for the individual, the family and work, and may produce greater physical and psychological damage than if people stayed in their home area (SCDA 1986).

However, elaborate plans do exist for evacuation, and four contingencies are catered for: 'air raid evacuation' from around probable targets for people who do not have access to shelter; evacuation of those who live in a shelter locality but do not have access to shelter; 'surface combat evacuation' which may be ordered for any area of the country where there is actual fighting; and 'threat evacuation', for certain urban areas threatened with destruction. The latter is planned to occur in two stages: when the threat becomes apparent, people are evacuated initially to a nearby location, while the threat is further assessed; the second stage involves either returning evacuees to their homes if the threat does not materialize or moving them to a safer and more distant locality if the threat remains.

As part of their research for GLAWARS, the SCDA carried out a study of the potential effectiveness of Swedish standard shelters in London. Casualty calculations were estimated for GLAWARS scenario 2 on the assumption that the attack occurred during the night with a 40 km/h westerly wind. Severe radiation damage was assumed for whole-body radiation doses of 2 gray or more. Some 80 per cent of buildings were assumed to collapse in blast overpressure zones of approximately 4.4 psi or more, resulting in 100 per cent deaths. Between 20 and 80 per cent of buildings were assumed destroyed in the 2.9–4.4 overpressure zones, resulting in 80 per cent deaths and 20 per cent severe injuries. Other assumptions were made to include an assessment of casualties from fires (SCDA 1986).

In the first case, it is assumed that the entire population is indoors above ground level at the time of attack, and that everyone takes cover in some kind of fall-out shelter immediately after the attack, except for those in areas directly affected by blast. They are assumed to leave the area within 30 minutes, and then travel at 1.5 km/h to safer areas.

The scenario results in 1,155,000 dead, 248,000 severely injured and 239,000 lightly injured. These figures compare reasonably well with similar calculations made for scenario 2 by other GLAWARS researchers. The SCDA study concludes that 75.7 per cent of Londoners escape uninjured. Rotblat, Haines and Lindop (1986) conclude that 75 per cent would be left uninjured. Steadman, Greene and Openshaw (1986) conclude that scenario 2 produces 15.5 per cent dead and severely injured while the SCDA's figure is 20.8 per cent.

A further set of calculations was then made, assuming that the entire GLC population takes cover in Swedish standard shelters. The numbers of deaths in the four most seriously affected boroughs are as follows:

	Deaths, without Swedish-type shelters	Deaths, with Swedish-type shelters
Barnet	186,600	16,000
Harrow	195,100	110,000
Hillingdon	221,700	99,000
Hounslow	179,600	48,000
Totals	783,000	273,000

Total fatalities in the most seriously affected boroughs are thus apparently reduced by about two-thirds. However, one serious reservation has to be made about these figures: they do not appear to take into account recent evidence about the possible extent of conflagrations within cities as a result of nuclear attack (see Part 1); this evidence indicates that, in fact, many of those who might otherwise have survived in blast shelters would be likely to be asphyxiated in their shelters or become trapped inside them.

Total Home Office spending on civil defence is currently in the region of £1.40 per head of population (£77 million in total) per year. The equivalent figure for Sweden is £4.72 for general civil defence expenditure, plus a further £7.16 spent on shelters, making a total of £11.88. At the current rate of shelter building in Sweden, it would take about 25 years to provide Swedish-style shelters for the entire population of London. It would cost more than £1700 million at today's prices. This is equivalent to more than £265 per head of the GLC population, or more than £10 per head per year for 25 years.

If shelters were built for the four worst-affected boroughs, which have a population of 928,000, the total cost would be in the order of £245 million, or about £37 per head of the entire GLC population. These figures are not accurate estimates and are intended only as guidelines to thinking about the issues involved in supplying Swedish-style shelters to the London population.

Civil defence in Switzerland. The Swiss civil defence system resembles that of Sweden in that it also forms part of a total defence concept (dating from 1971). Four important factors are responsible for the thoroughness and efficiency of Swiss civil defence.

1 Switzerland has conscripted its population under a 'militia' system for defence for centuries. The system is widely accepted and applied to civil defence. Civil defence service is compulsory for men but not women.
2 Swiss buildings are traditionally constructed with reinforced concrete basements which provide cheap shelters with a high protection factor.
3 The current civil defence programme began in the early 1960s, and coincided with a boom in the building industry.
4 Since the programme began, the national budget has grown rapidly, allowing civil defence costs to be met without cutting other budgets.

Civil defence is based on a number of important assumptions. The official view is that Switzerland is not likely to be the first country attacked in a future war: a surprise attack is therefore ruled out, allowing the Swiss reasonable warning time. On the other hand, the country's geographical position means that it is extremely likely to be affected by any European war. If attacked, it is expected that the targets will be Swiss military installations, rather than the population itself. However, military targets are distributed throughout the civil infrastructure and it has not therefore been possible to declare any part of the country safer than any other. There is no civil defence evacuation plan in Switzerland.

Switzerland believes it is impossible to defend itself against an all-out nuclear attack, and its civil defence plans are restricted to situations in which the use of nuclear and other weapons is limited. The civil defence organizations reject the idea of worst case analysis on the grounds that it undervalues the potential contribution that civil defence can make (Basler 1986). The system is planned to deal with a number of specific scenarios, which would produce the following casualties if there were no civil defence:

1 nuclear attacks on or near Switzerland producing one million deaths, primarily from fall-out;
2 a nuclear war involving Switzerland, comprising roughly 10 attacks on the country, each producing 50,000 deaths;
3 an attack with chemical (and conventional) weapons producing 200,000 deaths;
4 an attack with conventional weapons only, producing 50,000 deaths.

The probabilities of these four scenarios have been assessed, and are taken into account in civil defence planning. The assumptions about fatality levels provide planners with a clear measure of the effectiveness of proposed civil defence measures.

The programme itself was conceived as an optimization process, designed to minimize losses in the civil population from the four scenarios above, given a fixed total budget and time limit (7000 million Swiss francs were to be spent on the programme over 20 years, starting in 1971). The budget has not increased, and is equivalent to an annual expenditure of some 60 Swiss francs (about £20) per person. The time limit has been increased from 20 to 30 years but, because shelter construction actually began some 10 years previously, the programme will really take 40 years to complete. About 500,000 people, roughly 1 for every 12 inhabitants, are trained for civil defence; training averages two days a year.

The programme is based on the idea of providing everyone in Switzerland with a shelter with a high degree of protection and which can be inhabited for relatively long periods. Shelter expenditure accounts for 70 per cent of the civil defence budget and the average total shelter cost per person is 1700 Swiss francs (about £600), 'shelter' in this sense being taken to include all protective structures including private and public shelters, command posts, and shelters for medical and rescue teams. The average shelter can house 30 people and withstand blast overpressures of at least 15 psi (Basler 1986). The goal is to provide good protection for everyone rather than perfect protection for a few.

The programme is organized at three levels – the confederation, the canton and the community. Civil defence in the communities, which typically include at least 5000 people, comprises three basic units: a shelter organization; an industrial civil defence organization; and a local organization for civil defence. Each community has an EMP-hardened, very high frequency radio communication system connected to every shelter in the community. This can also be used to communicate with other communities.

The Swiss system is based on rigorous, quantitative assessment of the risk involved in each scenario. Risk is defined as the product of total casualties multiplied by the relative probability of the scenario. This provides planners with a quantitative means of measuring the effectiveness of the civil defence system, and a basis for drawing up priorities in civil defence spending. The most cost effective measures are then selected, based on calculations which involve summing the expected losses from each scenario, weighted for their relative probabilities. The relevance of this type of risk analysis for the GLC is considered further in section 3.6.

3.4 Implications for the UK

A civil defence measure that is appropriate in one country is not necessarily appropriate in another. The factors that enable a state to choose and implement a civil defence programme are rooted in its own geography, history and politics. Nevertheless, the civil defence experiences of other countries are instructive. The most important lesson is probably that the barriers to success are as much political as technical.

Technical limitations. Analysis of the crisis relocation programmes of the United States and the Soviet Union has already suggested that the policy may be unworkable and unwise, even in countries which have the physical space to make relocation a tempting alternative (which the United Kingdom does not). If the goal is to protect a targeted urban population, only a system of well-engineered blast shelters could begin to suffice. Even these, and even if designed to Swiss standards, would offer no protection within 2 km of a one megaton explosion (Vale 1986c).

The effectiveness of Swedish family shelters against blast is less clearly defined. The Swedish Civil Defence Administration emphasizes protection against conventional weapons, and notes that their shelters give protection against shockwaves, splinters and radiation, but stresses that 'fall-out is the chief concern' (Swedish Civil Defence Administration 1985). The Swedish standard shelter, however, is designed to withstand overpressures of approximately 7 psi.

Swedish civil defence officials clearly state that their programme is not intended to cope with direct nuclear attacks on civilian populations, as envisioned in GLAWARS scenarios 4 and 5. 'Above all,' they insist, 'efforts are made to accomplish protection against the side-effects of such weapons employed beyond our borders.' They view Sweden as too low a priority to be a likely target for direct nuclear attack. If such attack did come, however, they believe it would be directed 'against military targets rather than against cities' and civil defence would need to deal primarily with the collateral effects of these strikes.

The Swiss, by contrast, are less willing to ignore the possibility of direct nuclear attack on their cities. Even so, according to Basler (1986), the Swiss maintain that their programme is 'oriented to cases in which the use of mass destruction weapons is limited' and where military targets would be the main object.

It is highly significant that these two countries, with the most technically advanced civil defence programmes in the world, are also the most willing to specify the limits of their potential for success.

In what follows, only Swiss blast shelters will be considered, as sufficient information about the protection afforded by Swedish and Soviet blast shelters is lacking.

Swiss blast shelters are designed to provide protection up to overpressures of about 15 psi (Swiss Federal Office of Civil Defence 1971) and to protect against fall-out. If similar shelters were used by Londoners, they would greatly reduce immediate casualties, even in GLAWARS scenarios 4 and 5.

Even so, large areas of London are subject to extensive blast damage in scenarios 2–5 (see Figures 13–16). If the 12 psi blast ring on the GLAWARS maps is taken to represent the area where a Swiss-style blast shelter would cease to be effective, then some Londoners would perish in such shelters in each scenario. Even in scenario 2, substantial parts of Harrow, Hounslow and Hillingdon would be subjected to a blast sufficient to destroy Swiss-style shelters. In scenario 3 these boroughs, plus parts of Bromley, Brent, Barnet and Camden, would be unprotected. In scenario 4, damage would also extend to parts of Richmond-upon-Thames, the City of London, Tower Hamlets, Southwark, Lewisham and nearly all of Wandsworth. In scenario 5, Swiss-style shelters would be inadequate in many of the boroughs destroyed in scenario 4, plus parts of Havering, Bexley, Waltham

Forest, Redbridge, Sutton and nearly all of Camden, the City of Westminster, Islington and the City of London. Thus the area of London in which occupants of Swiss-style shelters would not necessarily be protected is substantial. It would be even more substantial if the effects of fires were also taken into account.

While Swiss-style shelters would enable a larger percentage of Londoners to survive, many would still perish. Furthermore, many of the initial survivors would undoubtedly succumb later to the combined effects of nuclear winter, food shortages, and social and economic chaos (see Part 2).

The technical drawbacks of crisis relocation programmes in relation to the Soviet Union and the United States have already been discussed. The Swedish view of evacuation, however, may be of more relevance. According to the Swedish Civil Defence Administration, 'Evacuation is a complement to the use of shelters' and 'shall take place from areas which are assumed to be directly threatened by acts of warfare'. Partial evacuation of people located near likely targets is an important aspect of Swedish policy.

The Swedish evacuation policy assumes that likely military targets can be identified in advance; it advocates evacuation only for those people who would otherwise be inadequately sheltered. In Sweden, given the primacy attached to conventional war scenarios and the assumption that Sweden would suffer only the collateral effects of nuclear attack on others, and given the large inventory of shelters already constructed, evacuation would therefore be on a relatively small scale.

For the UK, however, with its high density of population and military targets, choosing which areas to evacuate would be more problematic. Since many of the likely military targets in the UK are just outside London, rather than within it, evacuation of citizens to less densely populated areas would not necessarily result in greater safety. Moreover, it seems unlikely that London could be singled out for special treatment with regard to evacuation; other areas could make equally valid claims for evacuation.

However, none of this precludes a consideration of smaller scale intra-borough or intra-London relocations, which might involve billeting poorly protected individuals who live near London's military targets in safer areas.

Civil defence planners will need to confront the possibility of mass flight from central London through outer boroughs during crisis periods; if further information were provided about the location of likely targets, it could be that the portion of the public which does not 'stay put' would be more likely to move towards areas of enhanced safety.

In its circulars of the 1970s (now superseded by the 1985 *Emergency Planning Guidance to Local Authorities*), the Home Office suggested that all public movement in a crisis period would be 'random' and that any movement which succeeded in achieving a greater degree of safety would be merely 'fortuitous' (Home Office 1974 and 1977). If likely targets were publicly identified, however, those who were most vulnerable could be relocated and provided with space in communal fall-out shelters several kilometres from the most likely military targets. A broader goal might be to anticipate and encourage public movement towards areas sufficiently distant from military targets to assure that only fall-out protection would be required.

Political limitations. While technical and logistical concerns severely limit the ability of civil defence to cope with heavy nuclear attacks, other issues are also crucial to civil defence policy. The viability and saliency of civil defence depends on six important issues.

1 *Financial resources* While not all states can pay for a large-scale civil defence programme without significant reorientation of priorities, the largest civil defence programmes in the world tend to claim only a tiny fraction of a defence budget. Nonetheless, purpose-built shelters are expensive, and many governments which could afford extensive civil defence prefer to enhance their security by building up offensive strength instead.
2 *Geopolitics* The geographical position of a state in relation to other politically and militarily powerful states affects its perceptions of the need for civil defence; and the ratio of low-density to high-density land areas affects the viability of certain kinds of civil defence measures such as evacuation.
3 *Past experience with natural disasters* Civil defence can contribute to public safety during and after both hostile attack and natural disaster. States that have experienced natural disasters are more likely to perceive the utility of civil defence against hostile attack.
4 *Past experience with wars* Historical experience tends to condition states about the need for vigilance; states which have a long tradition of defending themselves are more likely to concern themselves with civil defence in the nuclear age.
5 *Domestic politics* Civil defence serves many useful domestic purposes, even if it is ostensibly employed to protect against attack. It thrives under centralized political and economic control since it can be used both to affirm the humanitarian intentions of the rulers with regard to their citizens and to provide special protection for the leadership.
6 *Nuclear weapons* States that have nuclear weapons (or are allied with others that do) are less able to develop a strong civil defence

programme. Non-nuclear powers can more easily admit that deterrence may fail; they can therefore take civil defence measures without reference to the complex range of potentially provocative strategic considerations that often preoccupy their nuclear counterparts.

Examination of the civil defence policies of Switzerland, Sweden and the Soviet Union in the light of these six factors reveals illuminating comparisons with the political situation of civil defence in the UK.

1. The Swiss situation. Few would doubt that Londoners would be better off if each family's home were protected not by makeshift 'fall-out rooms' and 'inner refuges' but by purpose-built Swiss-style shelters. Yet Swiss-style civil defence does not come easy; it is the result of a long and expensive process, and one made possible largely by the long tradition of Swiss armed neutrality.

The UK lacks Switzerland's per caput financial resources. Switzerland began constructing its mandatory shelters in the early 1960s, a time which coincided with a building boom. By beginning early and proceeding slowly, the Swiss spread the costs of their programme evenly over a long period. Significantly, though the civil defence programme was instituted as a result of popular initiative, a Swiss civil defence official recently stated that if the shelter laws had been proposed in the current economic climate they might have been rejected.

The UK lacks Switzerland's long experience with natural disasters, and is thus not similarly conditioned to have to cope with catastrophe. It also lacks Switzerland's long experience as an island of peace amid war. It is therefore less attuned to the Swiss notion of constant vigilance. Swiss civil defence is intimately connected with a larger concept of '*défense générale*' and is dependent on conscription of not only the army but the civil defence force itself. Civil defence is viewed as an integral part of Swiss armed neutrality. Similarly, the UK also lacks Switzerland's stable governing coalition in which civil defence is unlikely to become a partisan political issue.

It is impossible for the Swiss to become involved in a war as a result of their own policies. This makes the justification of Swiss civil defence programmes relatively easy. However, the UK – unlike Switzerland – is a nuclear power and is aligned with a major Pact. It therefore cannot easily justify its civil defence as a purely humanitarian concern, divorced from larger political questions of deterrence.

2. The Swedish situation. Many of the factors which contribute to Swiss civil defence have also helped the Swedes develop their programme. Like the Swiss, the Swedes started building shelters early and have spaced out their costs. Swedish prosperity helps per capita expenditure on civil defence to remain approximately ten times as high as that of the UK.

Though Sweden is firmly neutral, Swedish leaders still fear enemy incursion onto Swedish territory, if only for purposes of transit. Yet it is precisely because the leadership regards Sweden as a 'marginal' area of interest to a potential aggressor that it can confidently discount the worst nuclear scenarios. Because the main danger is perceived to come from the indirect effects of fall-out from weapons exploded elsewhere, the Swedes can legitimately promote their fall-out shelters as a prudent form of mitigation.

Like Switzerland, Sweden has developed a long tradition of neutrality which, it believes, must be vigilantly guarded by the presence of conscripted army and civil defence units. As in Switzerland, Swedish civil defence is regarded as one arm of a larger notion of 'total defence'.

Like Switzerland, and unlike the UK, post-war Sweden has retained a stable political leadership. The provision of civil defence came to be seen as one component of a well-established social democratic welfare state; this provides a highly credible context which enables civil defence to be seen as a prudent humanitarian gesture.

Like Switzerland, Sweden has foresworn the acquisition of nuclear weapons. In the absence of such weapons, the Swedish programme can sidestep many of the controversies related to weapons deployment that have distorted the issue of civil defence in the UK.

3. The Soviet situation. The Soviet Union is a nuclear state. Its situation is thus more similar to that of the UK. Yet enormous historical and political differences remain between the two, which go a long way towards explaining the disparity between their civil defence efforts.

While the Soviet Union's per capita GNP is far smaller than that of Switzerland and Sweden, and is also less than that of the UK, the Soviet leadership has an unparalleled ability to marshal resources for civil defence. Soviet spending on civil defence is difficult to calculate since the Soviet Union makes no figures available; furthermore, Soviet civil defence expenditures are integrally related with other expenditures on defence, and defence spending receives top priority in Soviet budget planning.

With nuclear weapons aimed at it from all sides, the Soviet Union's geopolitical position between a hostile West and a hostile China has made military preparedness a prime necessity. The Soviet civil defence system could be of particular value in the event of a nuclear attack by China, which has a limited number of nuclear warheads.

Though the nation has been prone to natural disasters, Soviet planners have considered these an important part of civil defence only since 1972; attack-related civil defence is still the over-riding priority, though civil defence is recognized as useful for peacetime disasters.

Having experienced enormous civilian casualties and vast economic destruction from enemy invasion, the Soviet Union was conditioned to the need for civil defence in the pre-nuclear age. The World War 2 experiences of invasion, siege warfare and aerial bombardment that led to mass evacuation and industrial relocation greatly helped to shape Soviet attitudes towards state survival in the nuclear age.

As a highly centralized and authoritarian state, the Soviet Union is well equipped for imposing measures of civil defence. Extensive civil defence indoctrination, in schools and in the military, provides many real or imagined benefits for the Soviet leadership. Soviet civil defence propaganda is designed to bolster the control of the Communist Party, emphasize the Soviet self-image as an embattled state, provide tangible reminders of the capitalist nuclear threat and underscore ideological belief in the eventual triumph of socialism. Militarized and centralized, Soviet civil defence benefits from the ability of an authoritarian regime to manipulate public opinion.

Finally, though a nuclear power, the Soviet Union has managed to curb nearly all internal criticism of its defence and foreign policies. Moreover, the Soviet regime can take refuge in the undeniable fact that it has done more to provide civil defence protection for its population than any of the Western nuclear powers.

Shortcomings of UK policy. Clearly, the UK possesses few if any of the attributes which seem to be prerequisites for elaborate civil defence development. In the UK, civil defence has neither been nurtured by historically-justified paranoia nor integrated with a tradition of 'total defence'; it has never benefited from consistent governmental support or long-term financial planning and, until the 1983 Regulations, few UK civil defence measures were compulsory.

The failure of the UK (as well as the rest of NATO) to implement a large-scale civil defence programme is rooted, above all, in the uneasiness with which the Western alliance has accepted nuclear deterrence as the basis for its security. With public confidence in the advisability of the UK nuclear deterrent a matter of controversy both in the 1950s, following advances in Soviet missile technology, and again in the 1980s, it became increasingly difficult for UK civil defence authorities to convince the public that its programme was merely prudent and humanitarian. With enormous stakes invested in the preservation of a nuclear balance of terror, any emphasis on civil defence seemed to cast doubt on the government's confidence in this central tenet of its security policy.

The political failure of the UK and the United States to develop civil defence rests on two key shortcomings:

1 the inability of governments to own up to cases where their chosen level of civil defence will be patently inadequate; and
2 the tendency of governments to justify civil defence with the rationales most likely to cause political trouble.

While civil defence programmes in the United States, Soviet Union and Sweden acknowledge that likely target areas are readily identifiable, the UK's Home Office continues to imply that the risk of nuclear blast is evenly distributed. In the absence of Home Office and Ministry of Defence discussion of militarily plausible patterns of attack, it should come as no surprise that the UK public regards the intentions of civil defence planners with suspicion. As long as UK civil defence planners refuse to admit the limits of their programme, the programme will never improve and never gain public acceptance.

UK civil defence advocates have also worked against their cause by justifying it with rationales most likely to create political trouble, in particular the false rationale that civil defence contributes to deterrence (Brittan, in Hansard 1980). Though it has now been five years since the Home Office has publicly reaffirmed this civil defence/deterrence link, civil defence is still associated with provocative issues of nuclear strategy, which distort any humanitarian basis for the programme.

3.5 Issues for London's civil defence planners

Civil defence planning in the nuclear age faces a number of severe constraints. Some are shared by all countries and some are unique to the UK. However, they all pose problems for civil defence planning in London.

1 Civil defence is of little use if a war leads to nuclear attacks on cities. The public, probably rightly, regards this as the most likely outcome of a war.
2 It is particularly difficult for nuclear weapons states to plan credible civil defence programmes. Doing so is interpreted as a tacit admission that the expensive and controversial policy of nuclear deterrence may fail.
3 Ideally, civil defence should provide good protection for everyone. In practice, everyone cannot be protected equally. Even a very ambitious civil defence programme, for example, one that could save the lives of one million Londoners in a nuclear war, can be easily interpreted as a plan that deliberately allowed five million Londoners to die.

4 Potentially effective civil defence programmes can always be undermined by potentially hostile powers. It is much easier to change war plans than it is to change civil defence programmes.
5 Civil defence relies on popular participation and support. Without public acceptance, no civil defence programme can succeed.
6 The prevention of casualties, through evacuation or shelter protection, is much more effective than the organization of efficient rescue services and medical treatment centres. In other words, prevention is better than cure – but it is also more expensive.
7 Effective civil defence programmes are essentially long term. In other countries, they have taken decades to achieve. This means that they must be supported as an essential requirement of the state by whatever political party is in power. The views of the major political parties in the UK on civil defence are neither well developed nor commonly held.
8 Many civil defence measures depend for their effectiveness on the sounding of an all clear at some point after an attack. However, in a war in which long-range missiles were being used, no all clear could be sounded because more missiles could arrive at any time.

To what extent these constraints could be overcome in the UK is problematic. This raises acute problems for those responsible for civil defence planning for London. Civil defence cannot be wholly organized on a local basis without central co-ordination. On the other hand, there are a number of options which could improve London's civil defence and which do not involve national co-ordination. For these to be moulded into an effective and credible civil defence programme for London, however, requires that a number of preconditions be fulfilled. GLAWARS has identified five such preconditions.

1 Planners must stress the humanitarian value of civil defence rather than its role in deterring attack if their plans are to receive popular support. UK civil defence cannot exercise any credible deterrent function, and the tie between civil defence and deterrence is neither convincing nor reassuring to the general public.
2 Planners must concede that if London's civilian population is deliberately targeted, or even if a series of major nuclear attacks is mounted against military installations, civil defence measures will be of little or no relevance. On the other hand, more limited scenarios are possible, if less likely. Civil defence plans should be developed primarily to deal with such limited scenarios.
3 Civil defence in London must begin with a realistic assessment of likely targets, and must view these in the context of militarily plausible attack scenarios such as those proposed by GLAWARS; civil

defence must be based on an honest assessment of risk to each borough of London.

4 Civil defence policy must recognize that some London boroughs are more likely than others to suffer blast and heat effects from nuclear attack. For these boroughs, containing or adjoining targets of nuclear significance, there may be a case for such special measures as the provision of communal shelters, limited evacuation plans and better protected emergency centres.

5 Londoners should be informed about the location of the high risk areas in and around their city. In the likely event that many Londoners would try to leave the city if an attack seemed imminent, this would increase their chances of moving to areas of lower risk. It might also be useful to point out what transport routes would be likely to be taken over by the military and therefore not available for civilian use.

3.6 The cost effectiveness of civil defence

Political issues outside GLAWARS' terms of reference are involved in assessing the key parameter of any civil defence measure: its cost effectiveness. This is because a civil defence programme for London could involve any or all of at least three different goals:

reducing casualties and damage during an attack;
improving the chances of survivors continuing to survive after an attack; and
keeping London's essential services running at some minimum level.

Given that finances for civil defence in London are likely to be limited, it is important that the cost effectiveness of potential measures be determined in relation to these three goals.

In this context, the Swiss method of assessing the cost effectiveness of civil defence measures is of potential interest. Details are to be found in Basler (1986). Although this system is mainly used in relation to the single civil defence goal of reducing casualties, it could be easily adapted to incorporate additional goals. However, the weight to be attached to each of the three goals – or, indeed, to any other goals that London civil defence planners might wish to incorporate – is a matter of political choice which lies outside GLAWARS' terms of reference.

One proviso to the Swiss technique needs to be carefully considered. The technique depends on assessing risk as the product of the relative probability of a specific attack multiplied by the number of potential casualties that it would produce. The latter can be calculated relatively easily, given specific assumptions about factors such as time, location and magnitude of attack, and the speed and direction of the wind. The relative probabilities of different attacks are much more difficult to assess. The GLAWARS Commission was able to make only a qualitative assessment of these probabilities, whereas what is required is quantitative information. The necessary quantitative estimates would have to be based to some degree on arbitrary assumptions.

3.7 Civil defence and public survival

Under its terms of reference, GLAWARS was asked to consider four issues relating to public survival. The Commission wishes to make some general comments about these issues before considering them in the context of specific contingencies.

1 *The effects on death and casualty levels of the 'stay-put' strategy*
These have been calculated in Part 2. By implication, however, what is required is a comparison with the effects of alternative policies such as total or partial evacuation, or a policy of allowing spontaneous evacuation with guidance as to likely high-risk and low-risk areas. GLAWARS reached a number of potentially important conclusions about evacuation. Its studies of evacuation plans in other countries convinced the Commission that total evacuation is an unworkable and potentially dangerous option against any contingency.

Local evacuation, from high-risk to low-risk areas within the London area, appears to have considerable merit against certain contingencies, albeit those with the lowest probabilities. Furthermore, local evacuation is relatively cheap. To the extent that it could be effected using the underground system, one major danger of most evacuation plans – that of being caught in the open when the attack occurs – is considerably reduced. The Commission's reservations about local evacuation, however, centre on its workability. Local evacuation is dependent upon having a specified minimum warning time of the attack. Although a surprise attack is considered extremely unlikely, it is still difficult, if not impossible, to predict exactly when an attack is going to occur. Adoption of a local evacuation policy would therefore place extraordinarily heavy responsibilities on those whose duty it was to decide when to implement such a policy. The temptation to delay, to avoid the ensuing panic, would be great; it might well be so great that the decision was delayed until it was too late. This important reservation should be considered implicit in the Commission's suggestion that this policy be further explored.

Spontaneous evacuation, according to the evidence available to GLAWARS (see Appendix 5), is bound to occur, despite the housing problems that would inevitably follow in its wake. The Commission therefore suggests that a serious effort be made to acquaint Londoners with the high- and low-risk areas within the Greater London area.

2 *The utility of the domestic self-protection measures recommended by the government*
Against certain contingencies, there are domestic self-protection measures that can be taken and that would provide at least a marginal advantage in the short term. However, the Commission wishes specifically to disassociate itself from the government publication *Protect and Survive*, which in places is grossly misleading and could deceive the public about the likely effects of nuclear war. The Commission does, however, suggest that the GLC or its successor produce a publication for Londoners which provides accurate and honest advice about what is to be expected from a nuclear attack, what domestic measures might be taken to reduce risk, and against which contingencies they might have some effect. (The GLC is required to plan to provide information of this kind under the Civil Defence Regulations 1983, Schedule 2, para 3.)

3 *The utility to public survival of local authority control centres*
Although officially designated as 'emergency centres', these have become popularly known (to the limited extent that they are popularly known) as command and control centres as a result of the priority given by government to attempt to perpetuate organizational channels of command in time of war. Their utility to public survival as such is obviously limited.

Their utility is further limited by the fact that the Home Office recommends that such centres need be designed to withstand only 1.5 psi blast overpressures (Home Office 1985b, Section 4 Annex D). This means that in anything but an extremely limited nuclear attack, many if not most of them would be destroyed. To be of even potential use, such centres must be sited outside the 1.5 psi blast ring surrounding likely military targets. Even for scenario 2, this condition cannot be met for some of the boroughs in the west and north-west of London. Such an attack would subject nearly all of the London boroughs of Hillingdon, Hounslow and Harrow, and about half of Richmond-upon-Thames, Ealing, Barnet and Brent, to blast damage of 2 psi or more. In these areas, most residential construction would be destroyed. In addition, blast damage of between 1 and 2 psi would occur in all or part of Enfield, Haringey, Camden, the City of Westminster, Kensington and Chelsea, Hammersmith and Fulham, and Kingston-upon-Thames.

There seems to be little point in equipping poorly-protected structures near military targets with special communications equipment, stand-by generators, and 14 day supplies of food and water if they are likely to be destroyed even by low blast levels.

The Commission recognizes, however, that in the event of some contingencies local authority 'information and co-ordination' centres could have value in promoting public survival. In this context, their utility would depend largely on their ability to communicate. Current plans are for communication to and from higher authorities to be via land lines and radio, and for communication to and from the public to be via community volunteer organizations, with the help of existing radio networks, such as those used by taxi companies and radio amateurs. None of these systems is specifically EMP-hardened. Their ability to withstand EMP damage is dubious.

Swiss co-ordination centres are served by EMP-protected high frequency radio communications which extend even to individual shelters within their areas. Unless similar arrangements are made for UK emergency centres, they could become effectively isolated and ignored after any major attack.

4 *The utility to public survival of proposed civil defence rescue services and related training schemes*

Training in rescue services is an undoubted advantage, if only because the more people know about what to do in an emergency the better. (The extent to which people can assist in rescue work even without training was impressively demonstrated after the Mexican earthquake of September 1985.) To what extent such training is cost effective is another matter. In this context, the Commission wishes to observe that rescue services after an attack contribute far less to public survival than protection or local evacuation before an attack. In civil defence, they must be regarded as a second string (as they are in both Sweden and Switzerland). In the event of nuclear attack, they are likely to play an even more subsidiary role in that high radiation levels may well prevent effective rescue before those trapped have already died.

3.8 Planning for specific contingencies

One of the Commission's main conclusions about civil defence in London is that it must be planned to deal with specific contingencies. It is not possible to meet every contingency, though some measures could reduce casualties in a number of contingencies. GLAWARS was required to consider the cost, suitability and effectiveness of these measures.

GLAWARS identified one major civil defence option – that of an extended concept of land-use planning – with very variable costs. Like all other civil defence measures, its efficacy is related to the contingency against which it is planned. However, because its cost in some cases might be small, little would be lost in using it against contingencies where it might have little effect.

The concept is best explained by example. Given that Heathrow airport is a prime military target, which could be attacked with either conventional or nuclear weapons, it would be foolish to site a future hospital, health centre, emergency food store, civil defence control centre, chemical water treatment store, power station, or water pumping station in its immediate vicinity. Dispersal of such facilities at some distance from prime military targets makes obvious sense in principle; in practice, the peacetime economic, environmental and social costs of implementing this kind of planning could range from negligible to unacceptably high.

This kind of planning, however, is not normally incorporated in the planning procedures of either the GLC or the London boroughs. If it were, it might make a valuable contribution to London's survival in time of war. Virtually the only initial costs would be the preparation of a list of key military targets in and around London, and the drafting of planning regulations to restrict the siting of specified forms of institutions within a certain radius. In the event that this caused new institutions to be sited at less favourable locations, of course, further costs might be incurred. Provision might have to be made to waive planning restrictions should the latter prove exceptionally heavy.

This is the only exception GLAWARS found to the rule that civil defence plans should be directly related to specific contingencies. The Commission's contingency-related analysis follows.

Contingency A: continued non-belligerence. Because of the tensions that exist between the UK and Warsaw Pact countries, GLAWARS believes the current situation is better described as non-belligerence than as peace. This is by far the most likely contingency and obviously requires no civil defence measures. However, the fact that this contingency is termed non-belligerence does imply that other contingencies are possible. An information programme for Londoners aimed at acquainting them with the nature and the probability of the perceived threat, and of the civil defence plans which exist or are planned for London, was considered by the Commission to be cheap and potentially useful, providing it dealt with the issues honestly. Such a programme could incorporate the major findings of GLAWARS and any decisions about civil defence in London that result from it.

One other possibility needs to be examined: the explosion of a nuclear weapon on or over London by accident during a time of non-belligerence. The Commission considers that plans to deal with this contingency would be useful. They would involve co-ordination of fire and rescue services, and the speedy provision of emergency medical treatment, including radiation therapy and plasma transfusion. Londoners should be informed in advance of such an accident what precautions they could take to minimize risk.

Although the accidental explosion of a nuclear device was considered extremely unlikely by GLAWARS, emergency measures to deal with it would be useful in several other eventualities, including an accident at a nuclear power station outside London, an accident involving the transport of nuclear materials (which could occur within the London area), and a major accident involving toxic chemicals. Other countries have already integrated plans for coping with civil emergencies with plans for civil defence, and this is an area in which London might profitably follow suit.

Contingency B: war scare. The GLAWARS Commission considered a war scare to be the most likely of contingencies B to F. Its studies have also shown that the effects of a war scare in London could be extremely damaging. This aspect of civil defence has been relatively neglected in other countries, possibly because war scares in countries with elaborate civil defence programmes are considered less likely to be damaging.

The information programme considered under contingency A would be useful here. But consideration should be given to a wide range of additional measures. The most important would be plans to ensure that essential services are maintained during a war scare. This could play a critical role in keeping the London system going and in lessening general panic. Such a plan would need to identify in advance key workers who would be prepared to continue to go to work during a war scare. GLAWARS' investigations revealed that such people do exist, and that they share two major characteristics: work-oriented lifestyles and lack of strong family ties (Thompson 1986). Identifying such people in key positions in the essential services, and defining their jobs during a war scare, requires delicate negotiation. Whether such plans could be made or executed is, therefore, problematic and needs further investigation.

A run on food stocks is a likely outcome of a war scare. Consideration might therefore be given either to ways of increasing the quantities of London's food supplies during a war scare or to introducing some form of food rationing, or both. The GLC or its successor might wish to consider recommending suitable levels of food stocks to be carried by the average family, as do the Swiss (Basler 1986).

The information and warning given to Londoners during a war scare also merit further investigation. National plans include the declaration of a state of emergency with military mobilization, followed by the mobilization of civil defence plans. The abruptness of these measures seems likely to add to general panic. Consideration might be given to a graduated series of warnings for London, along the lines of the Swedish system (SCDA 1986), in which London's own civil defence plans are brought progressively into operation. Such a system would be especially useful were a decision made to implement any local evacuation plans for the populations of London's high risk boroughs. The key issue is providing Londoners with adequate information about the steps being taken to protect them and keep London running as effectively as possible during a war scare. Panic results from many factors but one of the most important is information deprivation (Thompson 1986).

Contingency C: non-nuclear attacks. Non-nuclear attacks are considered the most likely of the war contingencies, and any possible civil defence measures are therefore of major significance. For reasons outlined in Parts 1 and 2, the Commission concluded that the risk of attack by biological weapons is so small that no specific civil defence measures against biological weapons are warranted beyond the medical facilities in readiness for any major epidemic. With a slightly greater degree of uncertainty, the Commission reached similar conclusions over the use of chemical weapons on a major scale, although conceding the possibility of their small-scale use to induce panic. Civil defence measures against a Blitz-style attack with conventional weapons on London are also considered unnecessary (see Part 1).

Attacks with conventional weapons on military targets to the west and north-west of London are more likely – and are, in fact, considered the most likely event in any of the war contingencies. However, in view of the greatly increased accuracy of such weapons compared to those used in World War 2, the threat to the civilian population near military targets would be somewhat reduced.

Nevertheless, special attention should be directed at those boroughs most likely to be affected. The key issues to be considered are improvement of emergency services, including fire, rescue, ambulance and medical services, arrangements for a limited and local evacuation of the population, the provision of shelters, and the strengthening of local control centres. These measures would also be useful in the event of a limited nuclear attack (contingency D) and are further considered in that context.

The Commission wishes to draw attention to the ease with which the

London system could be totally disrupted by a few, highly accurate conventional weapons directed against any or all of London's essential services, such as the supply of water, gas and electricity, and existing transport facilities (see Part 1). Although the probability of such an attack is rated lower than attacks against military targets, the effects on London would be substantially greater. Civil defence planners may wish to consider the implications of such an attack, and the possibility of avoiding its worst effects through the introduction of redundancies into the system, the provision of standby systems, and improved plans for emergency repair. The range of possible targets in such an attack is identified in some detail in Kerr (1986).

Contingency D: limited nuclear attacks. Limited nuclear attacks were considered by the Commission to be the least likely outcome of any major war in which the UK becomes involved. They are also the only form of nuclear attack against which civil defence can offer any effective measures. This poses an acute dilemma for civil defence planners. While GLAWARS itself is not qualified to resolve all the issues involved, many of which are essentially political, it does wish to point out that if any civil defence against nuclear weapons is considered worthwhile, it is against this contingency that plans should be made.

The cost of doing so could be made more manageable by concentrating on the boroughs to the west and north-west of London, which contain or are near significant military targets. If blast shelters can be shown to be cost-effective, either by the Swiss techniques already mentioned or any other methods, then it is in this region that they should be built. However, London's civil defence planners would need to make a careful assessment of recent evidence about the possible effects of conflagrations on the protection blast shelters might provide before reaching any conclusions.

Under contingency D, measures already proposed for civil defence in London would be effective in these boroughs. Borough emergency centres might have an important role to play, but they must be sited at sufficient distance from military targets within or near the boroughs to have some chance of escaping severe damage and they must be equipped with EMP-hardened communications. If they cannot be so sited, there is no point in locating and equipping them. Improved rescue services and related training measures would also reduce casualties. Even elementary domestic protection measures, of the type cited in *Protect and Survive*, would help under this contingency (though the Commission wishes to point out that they could be made more realistic and effective).

However, in this situation the government 'stay-put' policy seems likely to be counter-productive. While the Commission considers all large-scale evacuation programmes for London to be essentially unworkable, limited evacuation schemes for the worst affected boroughs might save many lives. A population of some one million people is involved, and consideration should be given to evacuating the most threatened to safer areas within London (evacuation to locations outside London would require national co-ordination and involve much greater risks; in particular, the areas outside London to the west and north-west are likely to be severely affected by a limited nuclear attack).

If practical civil defence measures are to be taken to protect special areas within London, the choice lies essentially between blast shelters and local evacuation. Such a choice cannot be taken lightly, and merits more consideration than GLAWARS has been able to provide. Blast shelters would cost a great deal more than evacuation plans but are usable almost regardless of warning time (other civil defence systems plan to house their populations in shelters given only a three minute warning). Local evacuation would require several hours warning, even if detailed plans for executing the evacuation and housing the evacuees had already been prepared. Difficult decisions about when to begin such an evacuation would also have to be faced. However, given the financial restrictions likely to surround civil defence spending in the near future, the Commission considered that local evacuation might prove to be a quicker and cheaper solution than providing blast shelters. It would probably also be equally effective. Shelters which provided protection against only fall-out would be useless within the worst-affected boroughs, as would the domestic self-protection measures recommended by the government.

Consideration might also be given to a combined system of shelters and partial evacuation, along the lines of the Swedish system (SCDA 1986). Prudence would then dictate that those living in the immediate vicinity of military targets be evacuated, while those more distant from them be provided with blast shelters.

Finally, the political problems of providing specific civil defence plans for some parts of London and not others should not be underestimated. Public acceptance of such a plan would depend critically on the elaboration of a credible over-all civil defence plan for London that was clearly justified and widely disseminated.

In this context, there are some measures that might be taken to protect Londoners in the safer areas of their city. One of these – the identification of existing places to act as public fall-out shelters – is now a requirement under the Civil Defence Regulations 1983. The implications of this government requirement appear to have been less than thoroughly explored. Identification in itself is useless, unless plans are also made to equip such shelters with all the facilities needed for their inhabitants to survive for at least 14 days within them: efficient filtered ventilation, sanitation arrangements, two weeks' supplies of food and water, cooking facilities and stand-by power generation equipment, beds and bedding are all essential.

However, no finance is currently available for adapting or equipping these shelters. The Home Office merely states that 'special financial arrangements would apply in a war emergency to expenditure incurred by authorities' (Home Office 1985b). By this time, of course, it would be far too late to make them in the least effective. Such work would probably take months.

The Commission is therefore extremely doubtful that this a workable plan, and does not recommend this measure unless sufficient money is made available to equip the shelters in advance of a war emergency. Were this to be the case, however, and were the GLC to establish that public fall-out shelters were a cost-effective measure against the highly unlikely event of a limited nuclear attack, the Commission considers it essential that all such shelters be equipped with an EMP-hardened communications systems with links to local authority emergency centres. This would not add significantly to the total cost but could be vital. Information deprivation in such a shelter would lead to many occupants leaving during unsafe conditions, and the potential utility of the shelters would be lost.

Contingency E: nuclear attacks on major naval and air force targets. Contingency E is represented by nuclear scenario 3. Nine nuclear weapons are targeted on London, of which one fails and another, intended for Heathrow, hits Hampstead in error. There are very high casualties and widespread damage to London's buildings. Many local authority emergency centres would be destroyed in the attack. Most of Harrow, Hillingdon and Hounslow, plus parts of boroughs as far apart as Bromley, Brent, Barnet and Camden would experience sufficient blast to destroy even Swiss-style shelters. The exact extent of the casualties and damage depends critically on the weapon that misses its intended target. Whether London could recover from such an attack is doubtful. The efficacy of civil defence against such an attack is correspondingly dubious. The Commission therefore had considerable difficulty in reaching any unambiguous conclusions about this contingency.

For example, a local evacuation of some of the worst-affected boroughs in the west and north-west of London would depend for its success on which other areas in London were hit by accident. The type of guided evacuation recommended for contingency D might therefore be useless.

There would be nearly one and a half million casualties under scenario 3, including some 750,000 immediate deaths. Under standard assumptions (see Part 2), the over-all casualty rate in the London area would be 23 per cent. It may be significant that a casualty rate of 30 per cent is regarded by many military authorities as the standard cut-off point for continued action.

Some 473,000 homes, about 18 per cent of London's stock, would be destroyed. A further 300,000 houses would be structurally weakened. Overall, a third of London homes would be rendered uninhabitable. Extensive conflagrations and firestorms would be extremely likely. Both essential and emergency services would be completely disrupted. Lowered temperatures would be likely to result from atmospheric disturbances, and there would be high levels of radiation and pollution.

Two comparisons help provide some insights. During the entire Blitz, spread over a period of six years, damage to housing was only about one-tenth as much – and in scenario 3 the destruction could be virtually instantaneous. The September 1985 earthquake in Mexico City killed an unknown number of people, perhaps as many as 20,000. Scenario 3 is more than 35 times worse, with extensive radiation hazards to follow. It would produce results on London not experienced since the Great Fire of London or the Plague – and it would be worse than both.

Viewed in this light, it is hard to imagine civil defence preparations providing anything other than extremely marginal assistance in some very limited areas. The probability is that London as a city would cease to exist, and that many of those who survived would have little option but to move elsewhere, if they could, in search of less hostile conditions. Under these circumstances, the potential for civil defence is not clearly distinguishable from the situation in contingency F.

Contingency F: major nuclear attacks. No such doubts surround contingency F, which comprises nuclear scenarios 4 and 5. After an attack of this intensity, London would cease to exist. All that would remain would be isolated encampments of people, living as refugee communities in an impossibly malign world.

Only two civil defence measures could be of any use against major nuclear attacks: total evacuation of London's population and the provision of high protection blast shelters for the entire population. Total evacuation has already been shown to be an unworkable plan in the United States and the Soviet Union. Because of the UK's limited land area and high population density, it would be even more unworkable in this country.

The provision of blast shelters for the entire population of London would take at least two decades to build, and probably longer, and cost

Table 38 GLAWARS assessment[a] of civil defence measures for the London area

	Utility against:				
	Contingency A (non-belligerence)	Contingency B (war scare)	Contingency C (non-nuclear attacks)	Contingency D (limited nuclear attacks)	Contingencies E and F (substantial nuclear attacks)
Land-use planning	–	–	Merits study	Merits study	Useless
Realistic public information	Recommended[b]	Recommended[b]	Recommended[b]	Recommended[b]	Useless
Fall-out shelters (light construction)	–	–	Useful but expensive	Useful but expensive	Useless
Blast shelters	–	–	Useful but very expensive	Useful but very expensive	Useless
Evacuation	–	Limited evacuation of boroughs near military targets			
		Merits study	Merits study	Merits study	Useless
Public training in emergency services	–	–	Useful but expensive	Useful but expensive	Short-term benefit
Emergency manning of essential services	–	Recommended[b]	Recommended[b]	Recommended[b]	Useless

Local authority emergency centres	–	Useless as information and co-ordination centres			Useless (mostly destroyed)
Domestic self-protection measures	–	Useful in revised form	Useful in revised form	Useful in revised form	Useless
Food rationing	–	Recommended[b]	Recommended[b]	Recommended[b]	Useless
Food/medical reserves	–	Recommended[b]	Recommended[b]	Recommended[b]	Short-term benefit
Improved communications	–	Recommended[b]	Recommended[b]	Recommended[b]	Useless
Preparations for peace-time disasters	Recommended[b]	Possibly useful	Useful	Useful	Useless

[a] Assessment is of utility of measures planned or executed now against the contingencies as they arise.
[b] Recommended for cost-effectiveness evaluation based on the varying probabilities of the contingencies.

several thousand million pounds. If effected, a shelter programme would reduce the immediate numbers of casualties to a limited extent, even though many if not most of the shelters would be destroyed by blast and might be vulnerable to fire. However, the provision of blast shelters would have little or no effect on the numbers of people surviving over the long term. The effects of disease, lack of food and water, and a nuclear winter, which would probably follow attacks of such a scale, would kill nearly all those who managed to survive initially. The mass provision of blast shelters would therefore be extremely expensive and, in the long run, almost totally ineffective.

In this situation, the provision of local authority control centres – however well protected – is irrelevant. The kinds of protective measures recommended in *Protect and Survive* would be useless, as would civil defence rescue services and related training schemes.

GLAWARS did also consider one further possibility. In this situation, basic survival training might prolong the lives of those few who survived the initial attack without lethal exposures to radiation. However, it is questionable whether such training would enable many to survive in the long term. Furthermore, there is no means of knowing which 2 or 3 per cent of Londoners would survive the initial attack. Any such scheme would therefore have to train 100 people in order that two or three might survive an extra few weeks after an attack. The Commission doubts that any responsible political authority would deem such an exercise a useful way of spending public money.

The Commission therefore concluded that civil defence cannot provide any cost-effective measures against nuclear attacks which are anything other than extremely limited. This is a major finding of the Commission. It results partly from the conclusion reached in Part 2 that London probably would not survive as a city if major naval and air bases were attacked with nuclear weapons, even if the city itself were not specifically targeted.

Attempts to provide civil defence against contingencies E and F, or against even heavier attacks, would therefore be a waste of public money. The Commission suggests that no specific measures be taken to deal with these contingencies and that they be specifically excluded from London's civil defence plans. This conclusion is in keeping with decisions already made by other countries with major civil defence programmes, with the exception of the Soviet Union. The political situation there is so different from that in the UK that the Soviet Union's exceptional stance on this issue has no relevance for the UK.

3.9 Conclusions

GLAWARS principal conclusions on civil defence are summarized in Table 38. It must be stressed that GLAWARS was required not to formulate a civil defence plan for London but to investigate the planning assumptions on which such a plan should be based. Table 38 is therefore designed only to provide background guidance for London's civil defence planners.

GLAWARS conclusions are not optimistic in that, in company with the conclusions reached by most other countries with important civil defence programmes, they do not pretend to offer solutions to major nuclear attacks. Such solutions do not exist.

GLAWARS conclusions, however, are positive in another sense. There are many ways in which London's civil defence could be improved, particularly in relation to a war scare, non-nuclear attacks, and even in the unlikely event of a small nuclear attack. It is, above all, important for Londoners to know where they stand. The information provided for them in this report should enable them to be better informed than the inhabitants of any other city in the world.

We wish to conclude with the words of one of the many researchers who worked for GLAWARS. In the event of a nuclear attack, Lewis (1986) wrote

> Survival will not be St Paul's erect amidst the smoke and flames, nor Buckingham Palace nor the BBC, nor the National Anthem – nor the voice of the Prime Minister. Survival will not be delegated powers, the "all-clear", a working telephone, stirrup pumps and ration books. Survival will not be home and family nor neighbours, lovers, colleagues and friends. Survival is not health, hope nor happiness.
>
> Survival will be fear, exhaustion, disease, pain and long, lonely misery.

Avoiding a nuclear war is still the only way of avoiding such a fate.

References

Aspin, Les, *The 'Mineshaft Gap' Revisited: Soviet Civil Defense and U.S. Deterrence*. December 1978, mimeo, available from Representative Aspin's office, Washington, DC.

Basler, Ernst, and Partners, *GLAWARS Task 12: Alternative Approaches to Civil Defence, Switzerland*. London, South Bank Polytechnic, 1986, mimeo.

Brittan, Leon, *Address by the Home Secretary to the Annual General Meeting of the Society of Industrial Emergency Services Officers*. 28 November 1984, mimeo.

Chalmers, Malcolm, *GLAWARS Task 11: Civil Defence in London: the cost implications*. London, South Bank Polytechnic, 1986, mimeo.

CIA, *Soviet Civil Defense*. Washington DC, CIA, 1982.
Connell, John, 'Russia's Secret Bunkers'. In *The Sunday Times*, 26 February 1984.
Diacon, Diane, *Residential Housing and Nuclear Attack*. London, Croom Helm, 1984.
FEMA, *Questions and Answers on Crisis Relocation Planning*. Washington DC, FEMA, 1980.
FEMA, *Civil Defense Program Overview: FY1983-FY1984*. Washington DC, FEMA, 1984.
GLC, *PSFB 1254*. London, GLC, Public Services and Fire Brigade Committee, 1985a.
GLC, *London and Civil Defence*. London, GLC, 1985b.
Gouré, Leon, *War Survival in Soviet Strategy: USSR Civil Defense*. Miami, Center for Advanced International Studies, University of Miami, 1976.
Gouré, Leon, *The Soviet Crisis Relocation Program*. Mclean, Virginia, Science Applications, Inc., 1983a, prepared for FEMA.
Gouré, Leon, *A Comparison of Soviet and U.S. Civil Defence Programs*. Draft Report for the Federal Emergency Management Agency, May 1983b.
Gouré, Leon, Kohler, F. D., and Harvey, M. L., *The Role of Nuclear Forces in Current Soviet Strategy*. Miami, Center for Advanced International Studies, University of Miami, 1974.
Hansard, 31 October 1957.
Hansard, 18 June 1959.
Hansard, 28 March 1963.
Hansard, 20 February 1980.
Hansard, 26 October 1983.
Hansard, 6 February 1985.
Home Office, *Essential Service Routes*. London, HMSO, 1971, Home Office Circular No. 4/1971.
Home Office, *Public Survival Under Fallout Conditions*. London, HMSO, 1974, Home Office Circular No. ES10/1974.
Home Office, *Advice to the Public on Protection Against Nuclear Attack*. London, HMSO, 1976, Home Office Circular No. ES9/1976.
Home Office, *The Preparation and Organisation of the Health Service for War*. London, HMSO, 1977, Home Office Circular No. ES1/1977.
Home Office, *Protect and Survive*. London, HMSO, 1980.
Home Office, *Civil Defence Act 1948 – Subordinate Legislation*. London, HMSO, 1983, Home Office Circular No. ES1/1983.
Home Office, *The Government's Planning Assumptions for Civil Defence*. London, HMSO, 1984, Home Office Circular No. ES1/1984.
Home Office, *Emergency Planning Guidance Handbook 2: Communal Shelters*. London, HMSO, 1985a.
Home Office, *Emergency Planning Guidance to Local Authorities*. London, HMSO, 1985b.
Home Office and Scottish Home and Health Department, *Civil Defence: The Basic Facts*. London HMSO, 1983.
Howard, J. A., *Response to challenge*. County Emergency Planning Officers' Study Programme, 1982.

Kaplan, Fred, 'Soviet Civil Defence: Some Myths in the Western Debate'. In *Survival*, Vol. 20, May/June 1978.

Kerr, D. B., *GLAWARS Task 3: Conventional Attack*. London, South Bank Polytechnic, 1986, mimeo.

Leaning, Jennifer, and Keyes, Langley (eds.), *The Counterfeit Ark: Crisis Relocation for Nuclear War*. Cambridge, Massachusetts, Ballinger, 1984.

Lewis, James, *GLAWARS Task 9: Recovery after nuclear attack?*. London, South Bank Polytechnic, 1986, mimeo.

Miles, Ray, interview with Professor John Erickson. BBC World Service, 7 June 1983.

O'Brien, T. H., *Civil Defence*. London, HMSO, 1955.

Rotblat, Joseph, Haines, Andrew, and Lindop, Patricia, *GLAWARS Task 6: The Health Impact of Nuclear Attack*. London, South Bank Polytechnic, 1986, mimeo.

Sanderson, N. C., letter to Chief Executive of the London Borough of Camden from Home Office F6 Division, 27 November 1984.

Sokolovskiy, V. D., *Soviet Military Strategy*, 3rd Edition 1968. Washington, DC, Stanford Research Institute, 1975.

Steadman, Phillip, Greene, Owen, and Openshaw, Stan, *GLAWARS Task 3: Computer predictions of damage and casualties in London*. London, South Bank Polytechnic, 1986, mimeo.

Swedish Civil Defence Administration, *The Swedish Civil Defence*. Stockholm, SCDA, 1985.

Swedish Civil Defence Administration, *GLAWARS Task 12: Alternative Approaches to Civil Defence: Sweden*. London, South Bank Polytechnic, 1986, mimeo.

Swiss Federal Office of Civil Defence, *The 1971 Conception*. Berne, FOCD, 1971.

Thompson, James, *GLAWARS Task 4: The Behaviour of Londoners in a Future Major War: estimates from psychological research*. London, South Bank Polytechnic, 1986, mimeo.

Titmuss, Richard M., *Problems of Social Policy*. London, HMSO, 1950.

Troxell, John F., 'Soviet Civil Defense and the American Response'. In *Military Review*, January 1983.

US Congress, House Committee on Government Operations, *New Civil Defence Program*, 21 September 1961.

Vale, Lawrence, *The Limits of Civil Defence*. Unpublished doctoral dissertation, Oxford University, 1985.

Vale, Lawrence, *GLAWARS Task 11: Civil Defence Measures Currently Proposed for London*. London, South Bank Polytechnic, 1986a, mimeo.

Vale, Lawrence, *GLAWARS Task 12: Alternative Possible Approaches to Civil Defence*. London, South Bank Polytechnic, 1986b, mimeo.

Vale, Lawrence, *GLAWARS Task 12: Utility of Soviet, American, Swiss or Swedish Civil Defence for London*. London, South Bank Polytechnic, 1986c, mimeo.

Weinstein, John M., 'Soviet Civil Defense and the U. S. Deterrent'. In *Parameters* (Journal of the US Army War College), Vol. 12, No. 1, March 1982.

Appendix 1

GLAWARS Terms of Reference

The terms of reference of the Greater London Area War Risk Study given by the Greater London Council are to report to the Council on the nature, extent and effects of possible hostile attack on or affecting the Greater London Area, and the efficacy and effectiveness of possible civil defence measures.

The study covers three major topics, described below.

1. The military threat

Reporting on the military situation now and in the near future, the study should examine:

the range of military situations, or scenarios, that would be expected to give rise to an attack affecting the Greater London Area;

the potential form, pattern and weight of attacks, including type of weapons, and the possible duration and extent of their use.

Specific questions to be addressed are:

the length of warning time likely to be available between the time at which the hostilities may be judged by the government to be inevitable (and at which the government has decided to communicate such information to local authorities and/or the general public), and the commencement of an actual attack on the territory of the United Kingdom;

the general likelihood of using high explosive type weapons; chemical or biological weapons; nuclear weapons;

the likely form and nature of such attacks, including weapon types, target types, potential raid strength, duration and intensity;

the minimum likely level of attack once war has commenced;

the likely targets in the Greater London Area, and in other areas outside London where the effects of weapons delivered to such targets (particularly blast, thermal radiation and fall-out) would have a destructive effect within the Greater London Area;

the overall pattern of potential hostile attack against the United Kingdom, insofar as such information may be necessary in order to evaluate aspects of civil defence strategy (such as evacuation, or long-term economic survival prospects);

the overall international pattern of hostilities, in so far as this information may be necessary in order to examine long-term climatic or similar effects of war adversely affecting survival prospects in the United Kingdom;

trends in weaponry and strategy affecting the actual war risk to the Greater London Area; and

the effect on enemy strategy affecting the Greater London Area likely to be caused by the existing United Kingdom defence and civil defence posture, and changes that may be made in that posture (if any).

2. The effects of attack

Reviewing available material on weapons' effects, and in particular on nuclear weapons' effects, the study should report on:

the general effects of attack using high explosive type weapons; chemical or biological weapons; and nuclear weapons:

the combined effects of attack patterns considered likely for military reasons, including long-term effects.

Specific questions to be addressed are:

short-and long-term death and injury levels;

destruction of or damage to buildings and roads;

destruction of or damage to essential services (gas, water, electricity);

destruction of food supplies;

specific and general effects of fall-out;

specific and general effects of the electromagnetic pulse (EMP);

destruction of or damage to health care services, facilities, stocks and production;

destruction of or damage to agricultural production;

effects of the disruption of industrial production and economic functions;

disruption of communications; and

disruption of transport systems.

3. The efficacy of civil defence measures

Reviewing both the civil defence measures proposed by the present government, and considering, for comparative purposes, civil defence strategies adopted in other countries, the study should report on:

the cost, suitability, and potential effectiveness of civil defence measures proposed by the government;

the cost, suitability, and potential effectiveness of putative alternative major civil defence strategies including evacuation, and the provision of mass communal shelter.

Specific questions to be addressed are:

the effects on death and casualty levels of the 'stay put' strategy;

the utility of domestic self-protective measures described in the booklets *Protect and Survive* and *Domestic Nuclear Shelters* and such further Home Office advice as may be issued during the lifetime of the Commission;

the utility to public survival of local authority run control centres; and

the utility to public survival of proposed civil defence rescue service and similar training, when details of such training are announced.

Appendix 2

GLAWARS Commissioners and Rapporteur

The Commissioners

All the Commissioners undertook work for GLAWARS only in their personal capacities and not as members of any institutions with which they were working at the time of the GLAWARS study.

Dr Anne Ehrlich. Since 1959, Anne H. Ehrlich has been actively involved in the biological research programme headed by her husband Professor Paul R. Ehrlich at Stanford Univesity. She has held appointments in the Department of Biological Sciences as research assistant, research associate, and, since 1975, senior research associate. Besides co-authoring technical articles on population biology and teaching a course at Stanford on environmental policy, Anne has co-authored six books and written or co-authored several dozen articles on issues such as human population growth, resources, environmental protection, and the environmental consequences of nuclear war. She has served as a consultant to the US government study *The Global 2000 Report to the President*, as a member of the boards of directors of Friends of the Earth (US, 1976–1985), the Conferences on the Fate of the Earth (1980–1985), and the Center for Innovative Diplomacy (1981–), and is now chair of the Sierra Club's committee on the environmental effects of nuclear war. As an early participant in the review process for research on the nuclear winter, she toured the UK in 1984, together with Paul Ehrlich and two atmospheric scientists from the US and the USSR, to present the nuclear winter findings to local authorities and the British public.

Dr S. William Gunn. William Gunn is a senior international health official with particular involvement in disaster management. He was for many years head of global Emergency Relief Operations of the World Health Organisation and took part in the WHO study on the *Effects of Nuclear War on Health and Health Services*. He has led official emergency missions to many countries in collaboration with the United Nations and the Red Cross and has conducted training courses on disaster preparedness and relief organization. Author of over 100 scientific papers, he is co-editor of the book *Refugee Community Health Care*, compiler of the standard *WHO Emergency Health Kit* and author of the bilingual *Dictionary of Emergency Relief and Disasters*.

A member of the Faculty of Medicine of the University of British Columbia, William Gunn is Fellow of the Royal College of Surgeons of Canada, Fellow of the Royal Anthropological Institute of Great Britain, Honorary President of the WHO Medical Society, and a past founding Fellow of the Cancer Section of the Royal Society of Medicine, UK. A forerunner in establishing disaster medicine as a discipline, he is on the Boards of the World Association for Emergency and Disaster Medicine and the Société Internationale de Médecine de Catastrophe.

Dr J. Stuart Horner. Stuart Horner was a member of the BMA working party which wrote *The Medical Effects of Nuclear War*. He has been a member of the BMA Council for eleven years, and was Chairman of the Central Committee for Community Medicine. He is a member of the Central Ethical Committee. He has worked in the London Borough of Croydon for nearly twenty years, and he is currently District Medical Officer to Croydon Health Authority. In this capacity he is responsible for the organization of health services in time of war. He has taken a particular interest in problems of civil defence planning and speaks on these issues throughout the United Kingdom. His publications include *Planning for Armageddon*.

A graduate of Birmingham University, he undertook post-graduate studies at the London School of Hygiene and Tropical Medicine, and has specialized in public health and community medicine. In recent years, he has developed a particular interest in management issues with special reference to health services. A Fellow of the Faculty of Community Medicine, he is presently a member of the BMA working parties on the involvement of doctors in torture, and on social inequalities in health. He has written extensively on ethical issues applied to medicine.

Vice Admiral John Marshall Lee. Admiral Lee retired in 1973 after forty-two years service in the Navy. In his seventeen years at sea, he served as ship's officer, afloat staff officer, ship's captain (four commands), and task force commander. His World War 2 service was almost exclusively in the Pacific, as navigator of the cruiser *Boise*, as Executive Officer of the destroyer *Wadsworth* in the South Pacific, and as captain of the destroyer *Terry* in the South and Central Pacific. Admiral Lee's last sea assignment was command of the 7th Fleet Amphibious Force in the Western Pacific.

In shore assignments, Admiral Lee concentrated on planning, strategy, and politico-military matters in the Navy, Defense and State Departments, the NATO Military Committee, and the United Nations. His last active duty tour was as an Assistant Director of the US Arms Control and Disarmament Agency.

He now writes and speaks on strategic and arms controls matters throughout the US and in Europe, and has served as Director of a study on the no-first-use of nuclear weapons for the Union of Concerned Scientists. Admiral Lee is a Director of the American Committee on East-West Accord and of the Council on Foreign Relations; and a member of the International Institute for Strategic Studies, the Federation of American Scientists, the Committee for National Security, the Army and Navy Club of Washington, DC, and the St Petersburg Yacht Club.

Dr Peter Sharfman. Peter Sharfman is the Program Manager for International Security and Commerce in the Office of Technology Assessment of the United States Congress. In this capacity he directs all of OTA's efforts relating to military technologies, and to policy issues arising out of military technology. (His work as a member of the GLAWARS Commission, by written agreement with OTA, was carried out while on leave, and OTA has neither reviewed it, edited it, nor accepted any responsibility for it.) He directed OTA's 1979 study of *The Effects of Nuclear War* (reprinted in 1980 in England by Croom, Helm), and has also supervised work on such topics as ballistic missile defence, anti-satellite weapons, countermeasures, and arms control, and new technologies for NATO defence.

He received a BA degree from Harvard College, and MA and PhD degrees (in Political Science) from the University of Chicago. Before joining OTA in 1978, he was an Assistant Professor of Government at Cornell University, a Foreign Affairs Officer at the US Arms Control and Disarmament Agency, a member of the US Delegation to the MBFR negotiations, and an Assistant Director of Net Assessment in the US Department of Defense.

Dr Frank von Hippel. Frank von Hippel, a physicist, is a Professor of Public and International Affairs at Princeton University. His research interests are in the areas of nuclear weapons and energy policy. He is a co-principal investigator of Princeton's Research Program on Nuclear Policy Alternatives.

Von Hippel is an expert on the types of calculations used to calculate the casualties from nuclear attacks and has published two review articles on the subject. Over the past few years, von Hippel and his collaborators have developed at Princeton the capabilities to do computerized calculations of the consequences of large-scale nuclear attacks and to do sensitivity tests on the results of such calculations. Thus far, two sets of results have been obtained using these capabilities: 'The Consequences of a "Limited" Nuclear War in East and West Germany' (published in 1982 in *Ambio*, a journal of the Royal Swedish Academy of Sciences) and 'The Consequences of "Limited" Nuclear Attacks on the US' (in the spring 1985 issue of *International Security*). The latter was originally commissioned by the US Institute of Medicine as a basis for its September 1985 Symposium on the Medical Implications of Nuclear War.

The Rapporteur

Robin Clarke. Robin Clarke is a science writer and consultant, working mainly for the specialized agencies of the United Nations. He was editor of the two semi-popular scientific monthlies *Discovery* and *Science Journal* during the 1960s, and is the author of two books on weapons' effects and military research: *We All Fall Down: the prospect of chemical and biological warfare* (Allen Lane The Penguin Press, 1968) and *The Science of War and Peace* (Cape, 1971). In 1970, he joined the staff of Unesco to help prepare a book on the future of science and society. Since then he has been working on a freelance basis for the UN Food and Agriculture Organization in Rome, the United Nations Environment Programme in Nairobi and Unesco in Paris. His most recent book is *Science and Technology for World Development* (Oxford University Press, 1985).

As Rapporteur of the GLAWARS Commission, Robin Clarke attended all the Commission's meetings and began drafting the report in July 1985, basing the report on the findings of the GLAWARS researchers and the views of the Commissioners. The first draft was presented to the Commissioners in its entirety at their December 1985 meeting, and was re-presented for final approval in early January 1986.

Appendix 3

Research Studies Commissioned for GLAWARS

The Commission identified twelve task areas for investigation, and commissioned research, listed below, under these areas.

GLAWARS task areas

1. The military threat – a range of scenarios where hostile attack affects the Greater London Area.
2. A description of types of weapons and their physical effects.
3. A study of London as a system, describing its organization, networks and infrastructure in peace time; and how it would function if disrupted or partially destroyed by an attack.
4. The behaviour of Londoners when warning of an attack has been received, and also after an attack.
5. An assessment of the long-term impact on buildings and infrastructures.
6. Long-term health effects.
7. Changes in the climate and ozone layer as a result of an attack.
8. Impact on the biosphere for two years after an attack.
9. The availability of food, water, shelter, and clothing after an attack.
10. The problems of social, political and economic organization.
11. A description and review of the cost, suitability and potential effectiveness of civil defence measures currently proposed.
12. An assessment of possible alternative approaches to civil defence.

Research studies

Barrett, Mark, *Energy Services in London in War-time* (Task 3)

Barrett, Mark, Fergusson, Malcolm, Greene, Owen, and Lippold, Catherine, *The Effects of Nuclear Attack on Agriculture in England and Wales* (Task 3)

Barrett, Mark, Nectoux, Francois, Lippold, Catherine, Flood, Mike, and Uden, John, *The Effects of Nuclear Attack on Certain Systems in the*

Greater London Area, technical supplement (Task 3)
Basler, Ernst, and Partners, *Alternative Approaches to Civil Defence: Switzerland* (Task 12)
Chalmers, Malcolm, *Civil Defence in London: The Cost Implications* (Task 11)
Dunne, Roland, and Willan, Phillip, co-ordinator Young, Ken, *London as a system* (Task 3)
Freedman, Lawrence, *The Military Threat* (Task 1)
Hodgkinson, Simon, Fergusson, Malcolm, Nectoux, Francois, with Barrett, Mark, Greene, Owen, co-ordinator Howes, Rod, *The Impact of a Nuclear Attack on London's Built Environment* (Task 5)
Jollans, J. L., *Recovery After Nuclear Attack? Appendix 4: Supplying Food After a Nuclear Attack: The Opportunities and Constraints* (Task 9)
Kelly, P. M., Karas, J. H. W., and Wigzell, M., *Potential Effects of Nuclear War on the Atmosphere, Weather and Climate of the Greater London Area* (Task 7)
Kerr, D. B., *Conventional Attack* (Task 3)
Lewis, James, *Recovery After Nuclear Attack?* (Task 9)
Lewis, James, *Recovery After Nuclear Attack? Appendix 1: Projections from Natural and other Disasters* (Task 9)
Lewis, James, *Recovery After Nuclear Attack? Appendix 6: Alternative Approaches to Civil Defence Planning: A Civil Survival Strategy* (Task 9)
Lippold, Catherine, *London's Water System and the Effects of a Nuclear Attack* (Task 3)
Loizos, Peter, and Marsh, Alan, *Concern with the Unthinkable* (Task 4)
MacDougall, Fiona, and Hastings, Sam, *The Economic, Social and Political Consequences of the Scenarios upon the London System* (Task 10)
Moody, Richard, *Recovery After Nuclear Attack? Appendix 3: The Short and Medium Term Availability of Water as a Factor in Recovery* (Task 9)
Myers, Norman, and Berry, Joe, *Long-Term Effects of Nuclear Attack on the Biosphere* (Task 8)
Nectoux, Francois, *Recovery After Nuclear Attack? Appendix 2: Energy Needs and Resources for Recovery after Nuclear Attack on London* (Task 9)
Pearce, D. W., Catephores, G., Markandya, A., and Verry, D., *Economic Effects of a Nuclear Attack* (Task 10)
Perry Robinson, Julian, *An Assessment of the Chemical and Biological Warfare Threat to London* (Task 3)
Pomeroy, John, *Recovery After Nuclear Attack? Appendix 5: Clothing and Textiles* (Task 9)
Roberts, Adam, *Civil Defence and International Law* (Task 11/12)
Rotblat, Joseph, Haines, Andrew, and Lindop, Patricia, *The Health Impact of Nuclear Attack* (Task 6)
Steadman, Philip, Greene, Owen, and Openshaw, Stan, *Computer Predictions of Damage and Casualties in London* (Task 3)

Steadman, Philip, and Greene, Owen, *Damage to the Physical Infrastructure of Civil Defence in London* (Task 3)
Swedish Civil Defence Administration, *Alternative Approaches to Civil Defence: Sweden* (Task 12)
Thompson, James, *The Behaviour of Londoners in a Future Major War: Estimates from Psychological Research* (Task 4)
Vale, Lawrence, *Civil Defence Measures Currently Proposed for London* (Task 11)
Vale, Lawrence, *Alternative Possible Approaches to Civil Defence* (Task 12)
Vale, Lawrence, *Utility of Soviet, American, Swiss or Swedish Civil Defence for London* (Task 12)
Williams, Phillip, *Crisis Management and Civil Defence* (Task 1)

These studies are published as the GLAWARS Research Reports (1986) by the South Bank Polytechnic, London.

The researchers

Dr Mark Barrett, Research Fellow, Energy Research Group, Open University.
Ernst Basler and Partners, Consulting Engineers and Planners, Switzerland.
Dr Joe Berry, Staff Scientist, Carnegie Institution of Washington, California.
George Catephores, Lecturer in Economics, University College London.
Malcolm Chalmers, Lecturer, School of Peace Studies, University of Bradford.
Roland Dunne, independent policy analyst.
Malcolm Fergusson, researcher, Earth Resources Research Ltd.
Mike Flood, researcher, Earth Resources Research Ltd.
Dr Lawrence Freedman, Professor of War Studies, King's College London.
Owen Greene, Research Fellow, Faculty of Science, Open University.
Dr Andrew P. Haines, Senior Lecturer in Department of General Practice, St. Mary's Hospital Medical School.
Sam Hastings, Senior Lecturer in Government and Politics, South Bank Polytechnic.
Simon Hodgkinson, researcher, Earth Resources Research Ltd.
Dr Rod Howes, Principal Lecturer in Building Administration, South Bank Polytechnic.
J. L. Jollans, Research Fellow, Centre for Agricultural Strategy, University of Reading.
Jaqueline H. W. Karas, Research Associate, Climatic Research Unit, School of Environmental Sciences, University of East Anglia.

Dr P. M. Kelly, Assistant Director (Research), Climatic Research Unit, School of Environmental Sciences, University of East Anglia.

D. B. Kerr, International Institute for Strategic Studies.

James Lewis, Datum International: Hazard Policy Analysis.

Dr Patricia Lindop, Emeritus Professor of Radiation Biology, University of London.

Catherine Lippold, Research Assistant, Energy Research Group, Open University.

Dr Peter Loizos, Senior Lecturer in Social Anthropology, London School of Economics and Political Science.

Fiona MacDougall, Senior Lecturer in Organisational Studies and Management, South Bank Polytechnic.

Dr Anil Markandya, Senior Lecturer in Economics, University College London.

Dr Alan Marsh, independent consultant.

Dr Richard Moody, Senior Lecturer in Nutrition, South Bank Polytechnic.

Dr Norman Myers, consultant in environment and development.

Dr Francois Nectoux, researcher, Earth Resources Research Ltd.

Stan Openshaw, Lecturer in Geography, University of Newcastle Upon Tyne.

Dr David Pearce, Professor of Political Economy, University College London.

Julian Perry Robinson, Senior Fellow, Science Policy Research Unit, University of Sussex.

Dr John Pomeroy, Principal Lecturer in Textiles and Management, South Bank Polytechnic.

Adam Roberts, Alastair Buchan Reader in International Relations, St Antony's College, University of Oxford.

Dr Joseph Rotblat, Emeritus Professor of Physics, University of London.

Philip Steadman, Director of Centre for Configurational Studies, Faculty of Technology, Open University.

Swedish Civil Defence Administration, Director John Tjorneryd.

Dr James Thompson, Senior Lecturer in Psychology, Middlesex Hospital Medical School.

John Uden, researcher, Earth Resources Research Ltd.

Dr Lawrence Vale, independent consultant.

Dr Donald Verry, Lecturer in Economics, University College London.

Mary Wigzell, Research Associate, Climatic Research Unit, School of Environmental Studies, University of East Anglia.

Phillip Williams, Royal Institute of International Affairs.

Dr Ken Young, independent policy consultant.

Phillip Willan, independent researcher.

Appendix 4

The Five Nuclear Attack Scenarios

This appendix provides details of the five nuclear attack scenarios described in Part 1 of the main text and summarized in Table 4.

The background to the construction of the scenarios is discussed in sections 1.7–1.9; they deal with a range of possible forms of nuclear attack on or affecting London that are consistent with current understanding of Soviet strategy and underlying doctrines. The degree of precision involved in those scenarios should not be misunderstood as an attempt at *prediction*; the precision was required to enable subsequent parts of the GLAWAR study to examine the detailed effects and implications of nuclear attack.

A number of simplifying assumptions have been made. Those common to all five scenarios are:

1 uniform and standard yields are assumed for particular weapons (in practice, there would be considerable variations in yield achieved);
2 it is assumed that no key targets have been put out of operation during the conventional air offensive;
3 it is assumed that the variety of weapons used in each attack would be limited; particular missile requirements or task force groups would be used to execute specific tasks (this assumption is intended to reflect the rigidities of Soviet command and control arrangements and the problems of co-ordination).

Scenario 1: the Soviet attack is limited to targets that are directly related to the ability of the UK or the US to attack Soviet forces in Europe or the Soviet homeland with nuclear weapons. None of the targets attacked is within the boundaries of London, so that the direct effects on London are limited to fall-out and EMP.

This scenario represents the most limited nuclear attack against the UK which could achieve a military purpose. The objective is to execute a surprise blow against the UK/US means of attack against the Soviet homeland and vital Warsaw Pact assets. The form of the attack is also based on the principle of economy of force. It is assumed:

1 that Soviet planners are holding all elements of the Strategic Rocket Force in reserve and are reluctant to commit them in order to avoid misapprehensions in Washington;
2 that some of the key targets, especially those relating to military command and control, have been softened by conventional raids; and
3 that bombers would be used for the attack to provide some element of surprise (the nuclear attack might be misinterpreted as another wave in the conventional bomber offensive).

For the Soviet planners there are four issues:

a) The UK *Polaris* and the American *Poseidon/Trident* bases at Faslane and Holy Loch respectively are obvious targets. What efforts should be made to destroy any SSBNs trying to escape into open water? It is assumed that the natural response is water bursts at the openings of Gare Loch and Holy Loch.
b) What action would be taken about the cruise missiles based at Greenham Common and Molesworth (after 1988)? These will total 160 (96 at Greenham and 64 at Molesworth), deployed in ten groups of 16 missiles, each able to move to a great variety of possible launch spots. It has been suggested officially that 'more than 1000 megatons would be needed to destroy the ground launched cruise missiles once they were dispersed'. An alternative view is that the ten convoys could be spotted by satellite or local spies, and that their locations would be known to within about 30 km. In this scenario, it is assumed that the attack on cruise missiles follows that on the submarines. The base is attacked to destroy any missiles that are not on the road, and then two air bursts in the general area, of a higher megatonnage than those employed in the other attacks, are used in an effort to catch scantily protected convoys or at least disrupt their communications.
c) Aircraft can also disperse to bases. It is assumed that all main operating bases are attacked (although this is an area where faulty intelligence could make a difference).
d) It is assumed that command and control centres are not priority targets. This is consistent with the possibility of the relevant centres having been disrupted in conventional raids, and a Soviet assumption that on balance it would make sense to ensure continued central control over whatever nuclear capabilities survived.

The attack is conducted by 20 *Backfire* TU-26 bombers. They are divided into five groups of four. All are armed with *Kipper* AS-4 missiles (200 kt yield; 0.5–1.5 km CEP), except for two in the fourth group, each of which is armed with one AS-4 and two 350 kt bombs. The *Backfires* approach the UK from the north-west. The first group attacks the Stornoway air base en route to England, where it is followed by the next three groups. The fourth group has the cruise missile bases as its primary target. The fifth group veers off to attack the submarine bases at Holy Loch and Faslane. All bombers have been allocated targets on an order of priority and according to their route across the UK. The allocations are set out in Table A4.1. Apart from the water bursts at the mouths of Holy Loch and Gare Loch, and air bursts in the attacks on the cruise missile base surrounds, all the attacks are ground bursts.

Table A4.1 Scenario 1: the planned attack

Aircraft	Targets		
Group A	1	2	3
1	Stornoway	Machrihanish	Scampton
2	Stornoway	Waddington	Coningsby
3	Upper Heyford	Farnborough	Woodbridge
4	Lakenheath	Marham	Coningsby
Group B			
1	Upper Heyford	Brize Norton	Fairford
2	Lakenheath	Honington	Wethersfield
3	Finningley	Waddington	Cottesmore
4	Scampton	Cottesmore	Abingdon
Group C			
1	Upper Heyford	Wethersfield	Finningley
2	Machrihanish	Lakenheath	Abingdon
3	Wittering	Marham	Honington
4	Wittering	Woodbridge	Finningley
Group D			
1	Greenham Common	Fairford	Brize Norton
2	Molesworth	Greenham Common[a]	Boscombe Down
3	Greenham Common	Greenham Common[b]	Molesworth[a]
4	Molesworth	Molesworth[b]	Boscombe Down
Group E			
1	Holy Loch	Faslane	Kinloss
2	Gare Loch[c]	Faslane	Lossiemouth
3	Holy Loch[c]	Rosyth	Kinloss
4	Holy Loch	Coulport	Lossiemouth

[a] air burst 40 km S of target.
[b] air burst 40 km E of target.
[c] water burst at mouth of Loch.

It is assumed that the following aircraft are shot down or suffer accidents during the course of the attack, and that the following weapons fail to detonate.

Aircraft destroyed		Weapons fail to detonate	
Aircraft	Before target	Aircraft	Target
A4	3	A2	1
B4	1	B2	1
C1	1	B3	1
C2	1	B3	2
C4	2	D1	2
E4	1	D1	3
		D4	2

Table A4.2 lists all the targets hit in scenario 1.

Table A4.2 Results of attack in scenario 1: targets hit

Target	Grid reference	Yield (kt)	Altitude (feet)
Stornoway	NB450330	200	0
Kinloss	NJ060610	200	0
Kinloss	NJ060610	200	0
Lossiemouth	NJ230700	200	0
Machrihanish	NR660220	200	0
Holy Loch	NS170800	200	0
Holy Loch	NS190800	200	0
Faslane	NS240890	200	0
Faslane	NS240890	200	0
Gare Loch	NS290810	200	0
Rosyth	NT110830	200	0
Scampton	SK940790	200	0
Waddington	SK970640	200	0
Cottesmore	SK900130	200	0
Upper Heyford	SP490260	200	0
Upper Heyford	SP490260	200	0
Brize Norton	SP290070	200	0
Fairford	SP150010	200	0
Farnborough	SU870530	200	0
Boscombe Down	SU200380	200	0

Table A4.2 (*Continued*)

Target	Grid reference	Yield (kt)	Altitude (feet)
Boscombe Down	SU200380	200	0
Greenham Common	SU480650	200	0
Greenham Common	SU480650	200	0
Greenham Common	SU480420	350	5750
Greenham Common	SU720640	350	5750
Marham	TF710100	200	0
Marham	TF710100	200	0
Coningsby	TF220580	200	0
Wittering	TF050020	200	0
Wittering	TF050020	200	0
Lakenheath	TL710820	200	0
Honington	TL910740	200	0
Honington	TL910740	200	0
Wethersfield	TL730330	200	0
Molesworth	TL070750	200	0
Molesworth	TL070750	200	0
Molesworth	TL070520	350	5750
Woodbridge	TM270490	200	0

Total yield: 8.05 Mt (1.05 Mt air bursts, 7 Mt ground bursts) carried by 38 warheads.

Scenario 2: like scenario 1, the attack is limited to targets related to the capability to attack Soviet forces and territory with nuclear weapons, but includes targets within London.

This attack is similar to scenario 1 except that critical command and control centres are included. It is assumed that the 20 *Backfires* involved in scenario 1 experience a similar fate and success. Two further groups of four *Backfires* are involved in this attack.

The attack takes in the most strategically important command centres (excluding those of the army). It excludes central London targets because, by design, there is no attempt to disrupt central political control; the success of the overall attack is not jeopardized by ignoring possible targets in Central London. The planned attack is outlined in Table A4.3 below.

Table A4.3 Scenario 2: additional attacking force: planned targets

Aircraft		Targets	
Group F	1	2	3
1	Pitreavie Castle	Fylingdales	Bawtry
2[a]	High Wycombe (RAF)	High Wycombe (USAF)[b]	Mildenhall[b]
3[a]	High Wycombe (USAF)	High Wycombe (RAF)[b]	Mildenhall[c]
4[a]	Northwood[b]	Croughton	Bawtry
Group G	1	2	3
1	West Drayton	Northwood	Stanmore
2[a]	Pitreavie Castle[b]	Fylingdales[b]	Rugby
3[a]	West Drayton[b]	Heathrow[b]	Croughton
4[a]	Rugby[b]	Heathrow	Stanmore[b]

[a] *Backfire* carrying one AS-4 (200 kt) and two gravity bombs (350 kt) (other aircraft carry three AS-4s).
[b] 350 kt air bursts.
[c] 350 kt ground burst (all others are 200 kt ground bursts).

It is assumed that the following aircraft fail to reach their targets, and that the following weapons fail.

Aircraft destroyed		Weapons fail to detonate	
Aircraft	Before target	Aircraft	Target
F3	1	G1	3
F4	3	G2	1

Table A4.4 Results of attack in scenario 2: targets hit

Target	Grid reference	Yield (kt)	Altitude (feet)
West Drayton	TQ060783	200	0
West Drayton	TQ060791	350	5750
Northwood	TQ100895	200	0
Northwood	TQ102902	350	5750
Stanmore	TQ163923	350	5750
Heathrow	TQ073743	200	0
Heathrow	TQ081750	350	5750
Stornoway	NB450330	200	0
Kinloss	NJ060610	200	0

Table A4.4 (*Continued*)

Target	Grid reference	Yield (kt)	Altitude (feet)
Kinloss	NJ060610	200	0
Lossiemouth	NJ230700	200	0
Machrihanish	NR660220	200	0
Holy Loch	NS170800	200	0
Holy Loch	NS190800	200	0
Faslane	NS240890	200	0
Faslane	NS240890	200	0
Gare Loch	NS290810	200	0
Rosyth	NT110830	200	0
Scampton	SK940790	200	0
Waddington	SK970640	200	0
Cottesmore	SK900130	200	0
Upper Heyford	SP490260	200	0
Upper Heyford	SO490260	200	0
Brize Norton	SP290070	200	0
Fairford	SP150010	200	0
Farnborough	SU870530	200	0
Boscombe Down	SU200380	200	0
Boscombe Down	SU200380	200	0
Greenham Common	SU480650	200	0
Greenham Common	SU480650	200	0
Greenham Common	SU480420	350	5750
Greenham Common	SU720640	350	5750
Marham	TF710100	200	0
Marham	TF710100	200	0
Coningsby	TF220580	200	0
Wittering	TF050020	200	0
Wittering	TF050020	200	0
Lakenheath	TL710820	200	0
Honington	TL910740	200	0
Honington	TL910740	200	0
Wethersfield	TL730330	200	0
Molesworth	TL070750	200	0
Molesworth	TL070750	200	0
Molesworth	TL070520	350	5750
Woodbridge	TM270490	200	0
Pitrearie Castle	NT090870	200	0
Fylingdales	SE910990	200	0
Fylingdales	SE910990	350	5750
Bawtry	SK650920	200	0
Rugby	SP500750	200	0

Table A4.4 (*Continued*)

Target	Grid reference	Yield (kt)	Altitude (feet)
Rugby	SP500750	350	5750
Croughton	SP540330	200	0
Croughton	SP540330	350	5750
High Wycombe	SU850930	200	0
High Wycombe	SU850930	350	5750
Mildenhall	TL700740	350	5750

There are 18 additional warheads to scenario 1.
Additional yield: 4.95 Mt (1.8 Mt in ground bursts, 3.15 Mt in air bursts).
Total yield: 13 Mt (8.8 Mt ground bursts, 4.2 Mt air bursts) carried by 56 warheads.

Scenario 3: the objective of the Soviet Attack is to reduce the military power (not just nuclear) of the UK.

In this scenario, it is assumed that the basic concern is to attack NATO sea and air power rather than land power. The conditions in which this attack might be implemented could well involve a concentration of retreating NATO air power on UK airfields; these would therefore be high priority targets for Soviet planners. If air and sea power were neutralized, then the UK would effectively be at the mercy of the Soviet Union. There would be no need to attack the UK Army *per se* nor the military-related aspects of the economic infrastructure. If it were felt that an invasion of the UK were necessary, then the relevant troop concentrations could be taken out later. It is also assumed that nuclear power stations would *not* be attacked since their destruction would create an excessive risk of fall-out over the Soviet Union and Warsaw Pact forces on the continent. As with earlier scenarios, it is still assumed that central London would be spared for political reasons.

The attack is conducted with *SS-20*s. As *SS-20*s are launched in groups of nine, it is possible to consider an attack of nine groups of nine *SS-20*s (81 missiles), each with three 150 kt warheads, making a total of 243 warheads in all. If 85 per cent reliability is assumed, then 207 warheads can be expected to detonate as planned, leading to a total yield of 31.05 Mt.

The following targets and accidental detonations are in the Greater London area:

Target	*Description*	*Grid*	*Error* (km)
Stanmore[a]	Air Defence Group	TQ 1692	0.3 NW
Northwood[a]	RN HQ	TQ 1090	0.2 N
Northwood[b]	RN HQ	TQ 1090	0.8 NE
West Drayton[b]	Air Defence Data	TQ 0679	0.1 W
West Drayton[b]	Air Defence Data	TQ 0679	0.5 N
Biggin Hill[a]	RAF airfield	TQ 4160	0.3 SE
Heathrow[a]	Civil airport	TQ 0875	0.1 NE
Northolt[a]	RAF airfield/ communications	TQ 1285	FAIL
Hillingdon[b]	US Communications Centre	TQ 0882	4.2 SE
Hampstead[b]	Residential	TQ 2408	0[c]

[a] Ground burst, 150 kt.
[b] Air burst, 150 kt.
[c] Error: intended for Heathrow.

Table A4.5 Results of attack in scenario 3: targets hit

Target	Grid reference	Yield (kt)	Altitude (feet)
Stanmore	TQ158922	150	0
Northwood	TQ100902	150	0
Northwood	TQ105905	150	4300
Biggin Hill	TQ420610	150	0
Heathrow	TQ081751	150	0
West Drayton	TQ060795	150	4300
West Drayton	TQ050790	150	4300
Hillingdon	TQ050850	150	4300
Hampstead	TQ240850	150	4300
Sumburgh	HU390110	150	0
Saxa Vord	HP630150	150	4300
Stornoway	NB450330	150	4300
Invergordon	NH710680	150	0
Kinloss	NJ060540	150	0
Kinloss	NJ060540	150	4300
Kinloss	NJ060540	150	4300
Milltown	NJ260650	150	4300
Lossiemouth	NJ210690	150	4300
Lossiemouth	NJ230700	150	4300
Mormond Hill	NJ960570	150	4300
Buchan	NK130440	150	0
Edzell	NO630690	150	4300
Leuchars	NO470200	150	4300
Balado Bridge	NO090030	150	4300

Table A4.5 (*Continued*)

Target	Grid reference	Yield (kt)	Altitude (feet)
Hawklaw	NO380160	150	4300
Machrihanish	NR660230	150	4300
Machrihanish	NR660220	150	4300
Glasgow Airport	NS480670	150	0
Beith	NS480670	150	0
Firth of Clyde	NS280800	150	0
Holy Loch	NS170810	150	0
Holy Loch entrance	NS180800	150	0
Faslane	NS250880	150	0
Glen Douglas	NS270990	150	0
Prestwick	NS360270	150	4300
Prestwick	NS360270	150	0
Rosyth	NT100830	150	0
Rosyth	NT110830	150	4300
Pitreavie Castle	NT120850	150	0
Turnhouse	NT160730	150	0
Broughton Moor	NY050330	150	4300
NE Regional Airport	NZ190710	150	0
Eaglescliff	NZ420130	150	4300
Teesside Airport	NZ370130	150	0
Blackpool Airport	SD320310	150	0
Woodvale	SD300100	150	0
Leeming	SE300890	150	0
Fylingdales	SE910990	150	4300
Topcliffe	SE400790	150	0
Dishforth	SE380720	150	0
Linton-on-Ouse	SE490620	150	0
Menwith Hill	SE200570	150	4300
Forest Moor	SE210520	150	4300
Elvington	SE660480	150	0
Leeds/Bradford Airport	SE220410	150	0
Doncaster	SE220410	150	0
Irton Moor	TA010840	150	4300
Staxton Wold	TA020790	150	4300
North Coates	TA370030	150	0
Immingham Dock	TA190160	150	0
Leconfield	TA030430	150	0
Valley	SH300760	150	4300
Valley	SH300760	150	0
Criggion	SH290150	150	4300
Shawbury	SJ550220	150	0

Table A4.5 (*Continued*)

Target	Grid reference	Yield (kt)	Altitude (feet)
Liverpool-Birkenhead	SJ330900	150	0
Speke Airport	SJ410830	150	4300
Burtonwood	SJ570910	150	0
Ringway Airport	SJ820840	150	0
Donnington	SJ710130	150	0
Waddington	SK990640	150	4300
Waddington	SK990640	150	0
Waddington	SK990640	150	4300
Bawtry	SK650930	150	0
Scampton	SK960800	150	0
Scampton	SK960800	150	4300
Scampton	SJ940790	150	4300
Syerston Newton	SK730480	150	0
Cranwell	TF010490	150	0
Cheadle	SK010430	150	4300
Finningley	SK660990	150	4300
Finningley	SK660990	150	0
Cottesmore	SK900130	150	0
Cottesmore	SK900130	150	4300
E. Midlands Airport	SK440270	150	0
Digby	TF040570	150	4300
Binbrook	TF190960	150	0
Coningsby	TF220560	150	4300
Coningsby	TF220560	150	0
Coninsgby	TF220850	150	4300
Wittering	TF030020	150	4300
Wittering	TF030020	150	0
Wittering	TF050020	150	4300
Marham	TF720080	150	4300
Marham	TF720080	150	0
Marham	TF710100	150	4300
West Raynham	TF850240	150	0
Sculthorpe	TF860310	150	0
Watton	TF940000	150	0
Swanton Morely	TG000190	150	0
Coltishall	TG260220	150	0
Neatishead	TG340210	150	4300
Horsham St. Faith	TG220410	150	0
Brawdy	SM850250	150	4300
Brawdy	SM505250	150	0
Cheltenham	SO940220	150	4300

Table A4.5 (*Continued*)

Target	Grid reference	Yield (kt)	Altitude (feet)
Clee Hill	SO590750	150	4300
Defford	SO910430	150	4300
Pershore	SO970490	150	0
Birmingham Airport	SP170840	150	0
Coventry Airport	SP350740	150	0
Croughton	SP560320	150	4300
Croughton	SP560320	150	0
Brize Norton	SP290060	150	0
Brize Norton	SP290060	150	0
Brize Norton	SP290070	150	4300
Upper Heyford	SP510270	150	0
Upper Heyford	SP510270	150	0
Upper Heyford	SP490260	150	4300
Stanbridge	SP960240	150	4300
Cranfield	SP950430	150	0
Thurleigh	TL050600	150	0
Lakenheath	TL740820	150	4300
Lakenheath	TL740820	150	0
Lakenheath	TL710820	150	4300
Mildenhall	TL690770	150	4300
Mildenhall	TL690770	150	0
Feltwell	TL710900	150	0
Hatfield	TL230090	150	0
Molesworth	TL080770	150	0
Molesworth	TL080770	150	0
Cottesmore	SK910160	150	0
Wyton	TL290750	150	0
Teversham	TL490580	150	0
Brompton	TL210700	150	0
Luton Airport	TL120200	150	0
Chicksands	TL110390	150	4300
Stansted	TL540230	150	0
Honington	TL890750	150	0
Honington	TL910740	150	4300
Wethersfield	TL710310	150	4300
Wethersfield	TL710310	150	0
Wethersfield	TL730330	150	4300
Wattisham	TM020520	150	0
Bentwaters	TM350530	150	4300
Bentwaters	TM350530	150	0
Martlesham Heath	TM240540	150	0

Table A4.5 (*Continued*)

Target	Grid reference	Yield (kt)	Altitude (feet)
Woodbridge	TM330490	150	4300
Woodbridge	TM330490	150	0
Woodbridge	TM270490	150	4300
Bawdsey	TM350400	150	4300
Harwich/Felixstowe	TM250320	150	0
Chivenor	SS490340	150	0
Morwenstow	SS210510	150	4300
Barry Island	ST120670	150	0
St Athan	ST006680	150	0
Cardiff	ST160810	150	0
Caerwent	ST460900	150	0
Bristol Airport	ST500650	150	0
Filton	ST600790	150	0
Yeovilton	ST550230	150	0
Kemble	ST960960	150	0
Lyneham	SU000790	150	4300
Lyneham	SU000790	150	0
Middle Wallop	SU300380	150	0
Fairford	SU150890	150	4300
Fairford	SU150980	150	0
Fairford	SP150010	150	4300
Oakhanger	SU770350	150	4300
Odiham	SU740490	150	0
Burghfield	SU650670	150	0
Welford	SU410730	150	0
Welford	SU410730	150	0
High Wycombe, Naphill	SU850970	150	0
High Wycombe, Daws Hill	SU870910	150	0
Greenham Common	SU500650	150	0
Greenham Common	SU500650	150	0
Benson	SU630910	150	0
Abingdon	SU470990	150	4300
Abingdon	SU470990	150	0
Aldermaston	SU590640	150	0
Farnborough	SU860540	150	0
Farnborough	SU870530	150	4300
Bramley	SU630580	150	0
Boscombe Down	SU180400	150	4300
Boscombe Down	SU180400	150	0
Boscombe Down	SU200380	150	4300
Portsmouth/Gosport	SU620000	150	0

Table A4.5 (*Continued*)

Target	Grid reference	Yield (kt)	Altitude (feet)
Lee-on-Solent	SU560000	150	0
Hythe	SU420070	150	0
Marchwood	SU400110	150	0
West Dean	SU260270	150	0
Wilton	SU110320	150	0
Chatham	TQ760670	150	0
Gatwick	TQ270400	150	0
Dover	TR310410	150	0
Manston	TR330660	150	0
St. Mawgan	SW870650	150	4300
St. Mawgan	SW870650	150	0
Portreith	SW650450	150	4300
Plymouth	SX460550	150	0
Devonport	SX440560	150	0
Exeter Airport	SY000940	150	0
Portland	SY680750	150	0
Poole	SZ010910	150	0
Hurn	SZ110980	150	0
Ventnor	SZ560770	150	4300

Total yield: 31.05 Mt (19.5 Mt ground bursts, 11.55 Mt air bursts) carried by 207 warheads.

Scenario 4: the objective is the destruction of the military and industrial potential of the UK; the list of targets in London is determined essentially by the number and types of weapon the Soviet Union might have available for this purpose, and the competing attractions of other targets elsewhere in the UK.

The difficulty in constructing a target set for this attack lies in deciding whether Soviet decision makers would try to achieve specific military, economic or political objectives or whether they would simply acknowledge that an attack of this intensity would destroy the basic politico-socio-economic structure of any society. The latter assumption leads to a somewhat more straightforward if also more brutal pattern of targeting.

It is assumed that there has already been a substantial attrition of Soviet forces in conventional operations, earlier nuclear operations and in the NATO strike that provoked this attack. In these circumstances, the most likely weapons would be the mobile *SS-20*s and submarine-launched ballistic missiles – probably *Yankee* class submarines each with

16 *SS-N-6* missiles. The weapons available for attack are therefore assumed to be the 81 *SS-20*s used in scenario 3 plus 48 *SS-N-6*s (Mods 1 and 2 with 1 Mt yields).

If the *SS-20*s deal with the military targets as in scenario 3, the *SS-N-6*s would need to be allocated to the non-military targets. There would be little interest in sparing central government in these circumstances. Only about 70 per cent reliability is assumed for the 1 Mt weapons, so that only 34 of the 48 weapons detonate. This would result in an extra 34.0 Mt, in addition to the 31.05 Mt produced by the *SS-20*s: a total of 65.05 Mt.

It is assumed that the additional London targets would be:

Target	*Description*	*Grid*	*Error* (km)
Enfield	ROF	TQ 3296	4 SW
Whitehall	Central government	TQ 2979	5.5 E
Croydon	Railway junction	TQ 3365	FAIL
Clapham	Railway junction	TQ 2875	2 S
Kingston	Defence industry	TQ 1869	8 NE

The targets successfully hit in scenario 4 are given in Table A4.6.

Table A4.6 Results of attack in scenario 4: targets hit

Target	Grid reference	Yield (kt)	Altitude (feet)
Stanmore	TQ158922	150	0
Northwood	TQ100902	150	0
Northwood	TQ105905	150	4300
Biggin Hill	TQ420610	150	0
Heathrow	TQ081751	150	0
West Drayton	TQ060795	150	4300
West Drayton	TQ050790	150	4300
Hillingdon	TQ050850	150	4300
Hampstead	TQ240850	150	4300
Enfield	TQ292932	1000	8200
Whitehall	TQ345790	1000	8200
Clapham	TQ280730	1000	8200
Kingston	TQ236746	1000	8200
Sumburgh	HU390110	150	0
Saxa Vord	HP630150	150	4300
Stornoway	NB450330	150	4300
Invergordon	NH710680	150	0
Kinloss	NJ060540	150	0

Table A4.6 (*Continued*)

Target	Grid reference	Yield (kt)	Altitude (feet)
Kinloss	NJ060540	150	4300
Kinloss	NJ060610	150	4300
Milltown	NJ260650	150	4300
Lossiemouth	NJ210690	150	4300
Lossiemouth	NJ230700	150	4300
Mormond Hill	NJ960570	150	4300
Buchan	NK130440	150	0
Edzell	NO630690	150	4300
Leuchars	NO470200	150	4300
Balado Bridge	NO090300	150	4300
Hawklaw	NO380160	150	4300
Machrihanish	NR660230	150	4300
Machrihanish	NR660220	150	4300
Glasgow Airport	NS480670	150	0
Beith	NS340540	150	0
Firth of Clyde	NS280800	150	0
Holy Loch	NS170810	150	0
Holy Loch entrance	NS180800	150	0
Faslane	NS250880	150	0
Glen Douglas	NS270990	150	0
Prestwick	NS360270	150	4300
Prestwick	NS360270	150	0
Rosyth	NT100830	150	0
Rosyth	NT110830	150	4300
Pitreavie Castle	NT120850	150	0
Turnhouse	NT160730	150	0
Broughton Moor	NY050330	150	4300
NE Regional Airport	NZ190710	150	0
Eaglescliff	NZ420130	150	4300
Teesside Airport	NZ370130	150	0
Blackpool Airport	SD320310	150	0
Woodvale	SD300100	150	0
Leeming	SE300890	150	0
Fylingdales	SE910990	150	4300
Topcliffe	SE400790	150	0
Dishforth	SE380720	150	0
Linton-on-Ouse	SE490620	150	0
Menwith Hill	SE200570	150	4300
Forest Moor	SE210520	150	4300
Elvington	SE660480	150	0
Leeds/Bradford Airport	SE220410	150	0

Table A4.6 (*Continued*)

Target	Grid reference	Yield (kt)	Altitude (feet)
Doncaster	SE220410	150	0
Irton Moor	TA010840	150	4300
Staxton Wold	TA020790	150	4300
North Coates	TA370030	150	0
Immingham Dock	TA190160	150	0
Leconfield	TA030430	150	0
Valley	SH300760	150	4300
Valley	SH300760	150	0
Criggion	SH290150	150	4300
Shawbury	SJ550220	150	0
Liverpool-Birkenhead	SJ330900	150	0
Speke Airport	SJ410830	150	4300
Burtonwood	SJ570910	150	0
Ringway Airport	SJ820840	150	0
Donnington	SJ710130	150	0
Waddington	SK990640	150	4300
Waddington	SK990640	150	0
Waddington	SK990640	150	4300
Bawtry	SK650930	150	0
Scampton	SK960800	150	0
Scampton	SK960800	150	4300
Scampton	SJ940790	150	4300
Syerston Newton	SK730480	150	0
Cranwell	TF010490	150	0
Cheadle	SK010430	150	4300
Finningley	SK660990	150	4300
Finningley	SK660990	150	0
Cottesmore	SK900130	150	0
Cottesmore	SK900130	150	4300
E. Midlands Airport	SK440270	150	0
Digby	TF040570	150	4300
Binbrook	TF190960	150	0
Coningsby	TF220560	150	4300
Coningsby	TF220560	150	0
Coninsgby	TF220850	150	4300
Wittering	TF030020	150	4300
Wittering	TF030020	150	0
Wittering	TF050020	150	4300
Marham	TF720080	150	4300
Marham	TF720080	150	0
Marham	TF710100	150	4300

Table A4.6 (*Continued*)

Target	Grid reference	Yield (kt)	Altitude (feet)
West Raynham	TF850240	150	0
Sculthorpe	TF860310	150	0
Watton	TF940000	150	0
Swanton Morely	TG000190	150	0
Coltishall	TG260220	150	0
Neatishead	TG340210	150	4300
Horsham St. Faith	TG220410	150	0
Brawdy	SM850250	150	4300
Brawdy	SM505250	150	0
Cheltenham	SO940220	150	4300
Clee Hill	SO590750	150	4300
Defford	SO910430	150	4300
Pershore	SO970490	150	0
Birmingham Airport	SP170840	150	0
Coventry Airport	SP350740	150	0
Croughton	SP560320	150	4300
Croughton	SP560320	150	0
Brize Norton	SP290060	150	0
Brize Norton	SP290060	150	0
Brize Norton	SP290070	150	4300
Upper Heyford	SP510270	150	0
Upper Heyford	SP510270	150	0
Upper Heyford	SP490260	150	4300
Stanbridge	SP960240	150	4300
Cranfield	SP950430	150	0
Thurleigh	TL050600	150	0
Lakenheath	TL740820	150	4300
Lakenheath	TL740820	150	0
Lakenheath	TL710820	150	4300
Mildenhall	TL690770	150	4300
Mildenhall	TL690770	150	0
Feltwell	TL710900	150	0
Hatfield	TL230090	150	0
Molesworth	TL080770	150	0
Molesworth	TL080770	150	0
Cottesmore	SK910160	150	0
Wyton	TL290750	150	0
Teversham	TL490580	150	0
Brompton	TL210700	150	0
Luton Airport	TL120200	150	0
Chicksands	TL110390	150	4300

Table A4.6 (*Continued*)

Target	Grid reference	Yield (kt)	Altitude (feet)
Stansted	TL540230	150	0
Honington	TL890750	150	0
Honington	TL910740	150	4300
Wethersfield	TL710310	150	4300
Wethersfield	TL710310	150	0
Wethersfield	TL730330	150	4300
Wattisham	TM020520	150	0
Bentwaters	TM350530	150	4300
Bentwaters	TM350530	150	0
Martlesham Heath	TM240540	150	0
Woodbridge	TM330490	150	4300
Woodbridge	TM330490	150	0
Woodbridge	TM270490	150	4300
Bawdsey	TM350400	150	4300
Harwich/Felixstowe	TM250320	150	0
Chivenor	SS490340	150	0
Morwenstow	SS210510	150	4300
Barry Island	ST120670	150	0
St Athan	ST006680	150	0
Cardiff	ST160810	150	0
Caerwent	ST460900	150	0
Bristol Airport	ST500650	150	0
Filton	ST600790	150	0
Yeovilton	ST550230	150	0
Kemble	ST960960	150	0
Lyneham	SU000790	150	4300
Lyneham	SU000790	150	0
Middle Wallop	SU300380	150	0
Fairford	SU150890	150	4300
Fairford	SU150980	150	0
Fairford	SP150010	150	4300
Oakhanger	SU770350	150	4300
Odiham	SU740490	150	0
Burghfield	SU650670	150	0
Welford	SU410730	150	0
Welford	SU410730	150	0
High Wycombe, Naphill	SU850970	150	0
High Wycombe, Daws Hill	SU870910	150	0
Greenham Common	SU500650	150	0
Greenham Common	SU500650	150	0
Benson	SU630910	150	0

Table A4.6 (*Continued*)

Target	Grid reference	Yield (kt)	Altitude (feet)
Abingdon	SU470990	150	4300
Abingdon	SU470990	150	0
Aldermaston	SU590640	150	0
Farnborough	SU860540	150	0
Farnborough	SU870530	150	4300
Bramley	SU630580	150	0
Boscombe Down	SU180400	150	4300
Boscombe Down	SU180400	150	0
Boscombe Down	SU200380	150	4300
Portsmouth/Gosport	SU620000	150	0
Lee-on-Solent	SU560000	150	0
Hythe	SU420070	150	0
Marchwood	SU400110	150	0
West Dean	SU260270	150	0
Wilton	SU110320	150	0
Chatham	TQ760670	150	0
Gatwick	TQ270400	150	0
Dover	TR310410	150	0
Manston	TR330660	150	0
St. Mawgan	SW870650	150	4300
St. Mawgan	SW870650	150	0
Portreith	SW650450	150	4300
Plymouth	SX460550	150	0
Devonport	SX440560	150	0
Exeter Airport	SY000940	150	0
Portland	SY680750	150	0
Poole	SZ010910	150	0
Hurn	SZ110980	150	0
Ventnor	SZ560770	150	4300
Peterhead	NK130460	1000	8200
Aberdeen	NJ900130	1000	8200
Dundee	NO500330	1000	8200
Dundee	NO300300	1000	8200
Glasgow	NS460700	1000	8200
Glasgow	NS600570	1000	8200
Perth	NO110230	1000	8200
Greenock	NS270760	1000	8200
Tyne on Wear	NZ300760	1000	8200
Tyne on Wear	NZ350480	1000	8200
Liverpool	SJ390990	1000	8200
Manchester	SJ890910	1000	8200

Table A4.6 (*Continued*)

Target	Grid reference	Yield (kt)	Altitude (feet)
Bradford	SE160330	1000	8200
Leeds	SE300330	1000	8200
Sheffield	SK320820	1000	8200
Birmingham	SP120880	1000	8200
Birmingham	SP020820	1000	8200
Crewe	SJ700550	1000	8200
Coventry	SP330790	1000	8200
Cheltenham	SO940220	1000	8200
Cardiff	ST240840	1000	8200
Cardiff	ST160760	1000	8200
Swansea	SS660950	1000	8200
Reading	SU720720	1000	8200
Aylesbury	SP820130	1000	8200
Swindon	SU140840	1000	8200
Watford	TQ110960	1000	8200
Guildford	TQ000490	1000	8200
Hawthorn	ST850710	1000	8200
Belfast		1000	8200

Total yield: 65.05 Mt (19.5 Mt ground bursts, 45.55 Mt air bursts) carried by 241 warheads.

Scenario 5: as scenario 4, except even more brutal.

In this scenario, the Soviet attack leaves nothing to chance. Another two *Y-Class* submarines with 32 *SS-N-6* missiles are diverted to attack a further range of targets. As a result, 25 more weapons explode, five of them over the Greater London area (one in error). This results in a total attack of 90.05 Mt.

The five additional weapons that hit London are:

Target	*City*	*Error* (km)
City of London	TQ 3057	2 SW
Euston Station Area	TQ 3008	1 NE
Victoria & Albert Docks	TQ 5108	8 NE
Hackney	TQ 3858	5 NE
Sutton	TQ 2406	0[a]

[a] Error from attack intended against South Coast.

The full list of targets successfully hit is given in Table A4.7.

Table A4.7 Results of attack in scenario 5: targets hit

Target	Grid reference	Yield (kt)	Altitude (feet)
Stanmore	TQ158922	150	0
Northwood	TQ100902	150	0
Northwood	TQ105905	150	4300
Biggin Hill	TQ420610	150	0
Heathrow	TQ081751	150	0
West Drayton	TQ060795	150	4300
West Drayton	TQ050790	150	4300
Hillingdon	TQ050850	150	4300
Hampstead	TQ240850	150	4300
Enfield	TQ292932	1000	8200
Whitehall	TQ345790	1000	8200
Clapham	TQ280730	1000	8200
Kingston	TQ236746	1000	8200
City of London	TQ305795	1000	8200
Euston Station	TQ300840	1000	8200
Victoria & Albert Docks	TQ510810	1000	8200
Hackney	TQ385885	1000	8200
Sutton	TQ240640	1000	8200
Sumburgh	HU390110	150	0
Saxa Vord	HP630150	150	4300
Stornoway	NB450330	150	4300
Invergordon	NH710680	150	0
Kinloss	NJ060540	150	0
Kinloss	NJ060540	150	4300
Kinloss	NJ060610	150	4300
Milltown	NJ260650	150	4300
Lossiemouth	NJ210690	150	4300
Lossiemouth	NJ230700	150	4300
Mormond Hill	NJ960570	150	4300
Buchan	NK130440	150	0
Edzell	NO630690	150	4300
Leuchars	NO470200	150	4300
Balado Bridge	NO090300	150	4300
Hawklaw	NO380160	150	4300
Machrihanish	NR660230	150	4300
Machrihanish	NR660220	150	4300
Glasgow Airport	NS480670	150	0
Beith	NS340540	150	0
Firth of Clyde	NS280800	150	0
Holy Loch	NS170810	150	0
Holy Loch entrance	NS180800	150	0

Table A4.7 (*Continued*)

Target	Grid reference	Yield (kt)	Altitude (feet)
Faslane	NS250880	150	0
Glen Douglas	NS270990	150	0
Prestwick	NS360270	150	4300
Prestwick	NS360270	150	0
Rosyth	NT100830	150	0
Rosyth	NT110830	150	4300
Pitreavie Castle	NT120850	150	0
Turnhouse	NT160730	150	0
Broughton Moor	NY050330	150	4300
NE Regional Airport	NZ190710	150	0
Eaglescliff	NZ420130	150	4300
Teesside Airport	NZ370130	150	0
Blackpool Airport	SD320310	150	0
Woodvale	SD300100	150	0
Leeming	SE300890	150	0
Fylingdales	SE910990	150	4300
Topcliffe	SE400790	150	0
Dishforth	SE380720	150	0
Linton-on-Ouse	SE490620	150	0
Menwith Hill	SE200570	150	4300
Forest Moor	SE210520	150	4300
Elvington	SE660480	150	0
Leeds/Bradford Airport	SE220410	150	0
Doncaster	SE220410	150	0
Irton Moor	TA010840	150	4300
Staxton Wold	TA020790	150	4300
North Coates	TA370030	150	0
Immingham Dock	TA190160	150	0
Leconfield	TA030430	150	0
Valley	SH300760	150	4300
Valley	SH300760	150	0
Criggion	SH290150	150	4300
Shawbury	SJ550220	150	0
Liverpool-Birkenhead	SJ330900	150	0
Speke Airport	SJ410830	150	4300
Burtonwood	SJ570910	150	0
Ringway Airport	SJ820840	150	0
Donnington	SJ710130	150	0
Waddington	SK990640	150	4300
Waddington	SK990640	150	0
Waddington	SK990640	150	4300
Bawtry	SK650930	150	0

Table A4.7 (*Continued*)

Target	Grid reference	Yield (kt)	Altitude (feet)
Scampton	SK960800	150	0
Scampton	SK960800	150	4300
Scampton	SJ940790	150	4300
Syerston Newton	SK730480	150	0
Cranwell	TF010490	150	0
Cheadle	SK010430	150	4300
Finningley	SK660990	150	4300
Finningley	SK660990	150	0
Cottesmore	SK900130	150	0
Cottesmore	SK900130	150	4300
E. Midlands Airport	SK440270	150	0
Digby	TF040570	150	4300
Binbrook	TF190960	150	0
Coningsby	TF220560	150	4300
Coningsby	TF220560	150	0
Coninsgby	TF220850	150	4300
Wittering	TF030020	150	4300
Wittering	TF030020	150	0
Wittering	TF050020	150	4300
Marham	TF720080	150	4300
Marham	TF720080	150	0
Marham	TF710100	150	4300
West Raynham	TF850240	150	0
Sculthorpe	TF860310	150	0
Watton	TF940000	150	0
Swanton Morely	TG000190	150	0
Coltishall	TG260220	150	0
Neatishead	TG340210	150	4300
Horsham St. Faith	TG220410	150	0
Brawdy	SM850250	150	4300
Brawdy	SM505250	150	0
Cheltenham	SO940220	150	4300
Clee Hill	SO590750	150	4300
Defford	SO910430	150	4300
Pershore	SO970490	150	0
Birmingham Airport	SP170840	150	0
Coventry Airport	SP350740	150	0
Croughton	SP560320	150	4300
Croughton	SP560320	150	0
Brize Norton	SP290060	150	0
Brize Norton	SP290060	150	0

Table A4.7 (*Continued*)

Target	Grid reference	Yield (kt)	Altitude (feet)
Brize Norton	SP290070	150	4300
Upper Heyford	SP510270	150	0
Upper Heyford	SP510270	150	0
Upper Heyford	SP490260	150	4300
Stanbridge	SP960240	150	4300
Cranfield	SP950430	150	0
Thurleigh	TL050600	150	0
Lakenheath	TL740820	150	4300
Lakenheath	TL740820	150	0
Lakenheath	TL710820	150	4300
Mildenhall	TL690770	150	4300
Mildenhall	TL690770	150	0
Feltwell	TL710900	150	0
Hatfield	TL230090	150	0
Molesworth	TL080770	150	0
Molesworth	TL080770	150	0
Cottesmore	SK910160	150	0
Wyton	TL290750	150	0
Teversham	TL490580	150	0
Brompton	TL210700	150	0
Luton Airport	TL120200	150	0
Chicksands	TL110390	150	4300
Stansted	TL540230	150	0
Honington	TL890750	150	0
Honington	TL910740	150	4300
Wethersfield	TL710310	150	4300
Wethersfield	TL710310	150	0
Wethersfield	TL730330	150	4300
Wattisham	TM020520	150	0
Bentwaters	TM350530	150	4300
Bentwaters	TM350530	150	0
Martlesham Heath	TM240540	150	0
Woodbridge	TM330490	150	4300
Woodbridge	TM330490	150	0
Woodbridge	TM270490	150	4300
Bawdsey	TM350400	150	4300
Harwich/Felixstowe	TM250320	150	0
Chivenor	SS490340	150	0
Morwenstow	SS210510	150	4300
Barry Island	ST120670	150	0
St Athan	ST006680	150	0

Table A4.7 (*Continued*)

Target	Grid reference	Yield (kt)	Altitude (feet)
Cardiff	ST160810	150	0
Caerwent	ST460900	150	0
Bristol Airport	ST500650	150	0
Filton	ST600790	150	0
Yeovilton	ST550230	150	0
Kemble	ST960960	150	0
Lyneham	SU000790	150	4300
Lyneham	SU000790	150	0
Middle Wallop	SU300380	150	0
Fairford	SU150890	150	4300
Fairford	SU150980	150	0
Fairford	SP150010	150	4300
Oakhanger	SU770350	150	4300
Odiham	SU740490	150	0
Burghfield	SU650670	150	0
Welford	SU410730	150	0
Welford	SU410730	150	0
High Wycombe, Naphill	SU850970	150	0
High Wycombe, Daws Hill	SU870910	150	0
Greenham Common	SU500650	150	0
Greenham Common	SU500650	150	0
Benson	SU630910	150	0
Abingdon	SU470990	150	4300
Abingdon	SU470990	150	0
Aldermaston	SU590640	150	0
Farnborough	SU860540	150	0
Farnborough	SU870530	150	4300
Bramley	SU630580	150	0
Boscombe Down	SU180400	150	4300
Boscombe Down	SU180400	150	0
Boscombe Down	SU200380	150	4300
Portsmouth/Gosport	SU620000	150	0
Lee-on-Solent	SU560000	150	0
Hythe	SU420070	150	0
Marchwood	SU400110	150	0
West Dean	SU260270	150	0
Wilton	SU110320	150	0
Chatham	TQ760670	150	0
Gatwick	TQ270400	150	0
Dover	TR310410	150	0
Manston	TR330660	150	0

Table A4.7 (*Continued*)

Target	Grid reference	Yield (kt)	Altitude (feet)
St. Mawgan	SW870650	150	4300
St. Mawgan	SW870650	150	0
Portreith	SW650450	150	4300
Plymouth	SX460550	150	0
Devonport	SX440560	150	0
Exeter Airport	SY000940	150	0
Portland	SY680750	150	0
Poole	SZ010910	150	0
Hurn	SZ110980	150	0
Ventnor	SZ560770	150	4300
Peterhead	NK130460	1000	8200
Aberdeen	NJ900130	1000	8200
Dundee	NO500330	1000	8200
Dundee	NO300300	1000	8200
Glasgow	NS460700	1000	8200
Glasgow	NS600570	1000	8200
Perth	NO110230	1000	8200
Greenock	NS270760	1000	8200
Tyne on Wear	NZ300760	1000	8200
Tyne on Wear	NZ350480	1000	8200
Liverpool	SJ390990	1000	8200
Manchester	SJ890910	1000	8200
Bradford	SE160330	1000	8200
Leeds	SE300330	1000	8200
Sheffield	SK320820	1000	8200
Birmingham	SP120880	1000	8200
Birmingham	SP020820	1000	8200
Crewe	SJ700550	1000	8200
Coventry	SP330790	1000	8200
Cheltenham	SO940220	1000	8200
Cardiff	ST240840	1000	8200
Cardiff	ST160760	1000	8200
Swansea	SS660950	1000	8200
Reading	SU720720	1000	8200
Aylesbury	SP820130	1000	8200
Swindon	SU140840	1000	8200
Watford	TQ110960	1000	8200
Guildford	TQ000490	1000	8200
Hawthorn	ST850710	1000	8200
Stockton-on-Tees	NZ450200	1000	8200
Preston	SD530290	1000	8200

Table A4.7 (*Continued*)

Target	Grid reference	Yield (kt)	Altitude (feet)
Catterick	SE180970	1000	8200
Barrow	SD200700	1000	8200
Manchester	SD800010	1000	8200
Rochdale	SD890140	1000	8200
Blackpool	SD320350	1000	8200
Birmingham	SO950950	1000	8200
Wolverhampton	SO910980	1000	8200
Shrewsbury	SJ490120	1000	8200
Nottingham	SK550400	1000	8200
Leicester	SK590040	1000	8200
Stevenage	TL230250	1000	8200
Chelmsford	TL700060	1000	8200
Colchester	TL000250	1000	8200
Yeovil	ST550150	1000	8200
Exeter	SX920920	1000	8200
Aldershot	SU860500	1000	8200
Bulford	SU160430	1000	8200
Bracknell	SU870690	1000	8200
Belfast		1000	8200

Total yield: 90.05 Mt (19.5 Mt ground bursts, 70.55 Mt air bursts) carried by 266 warheads.

Appendix 5

GLAWARS Survey of Londoners' Attitudes to Nuclear War and Civil Defence

The questions for the survey were derived from an analysis of 22 depth interviews (Loizos and Marsh 1986). A pilot version of the questionnaire was tested with a further 25 respondents. The final version of the questionnaire fell into four sections.

1 What do Londoners feel will happen? How likely is such an attack, what would be its effects, how likely is survival?
2 What do Londoners know? What advice have they encountered about what to do in such an emergency, where did they obtain this advice, does their work give them a role to play and, if so, could they carry out such duties?
3 What would Londoners do? Would they stay in London or try to leave? Would those staying try to take protective measures? If so, what would they do? Would those trying to leave head for a prepared destination, do they feel they would succeed in leaving and, if not, what would bar their flight? Would they take political actions to try to oppose the war and, if so, how far are they prepared to go in their protests?
4 What do Londoners think the authorities could or should do? How much help might emergency services be able to provide? Do they feel the authorities are well prepared for such an emergency and, if not, what ought they to do now to be better prepared?

The questions were framed with particular care to avoid the kind of bias that hypothetical questions can attract. Respondents were not asked somehow to become experts on the risks of nuclear war or on civil defence matters. They were asked to say what they thought and felt about these problems. When they say, for example, that there is a finite probability of such an attack, or that the local authorities should be better prepared, that is what they believe as individuals.

Interviewing was carried out by professional interviewers trained and employed by Market and Opinion Research International in 69 sampling points randomly selected throughout the Greater London area. A quota controlled sampling procedure was used, yielding a total sample of 1005 Londoners aged 18 upwards. An analysis of the personal and social characteristics of those selected for interview – by age, sex, social class, employment, housing tenure and so on – suggests that the sample was closely representative of the population of Greater London.

The following tables have been selected from the analysis of the survey data (Loizos and Marsh 1986).

Table A5.1 The likelihood of nuclear attack

Respondents were asked what they thought was the likelihood of a nuclear attack, replying with a number on a scale of 0 (absolutely certain it will not happen) to 10 (absolutely certain it will happen).

	Q.1 An attack on Britain in next 20 years (%)	Q.2 An attack on Britain in next 5 years (%)	Q.3 That London would be attacked (%)	Q.4 That one's own neighbourhood would suffer damage (%)
10 Certain it will happen	6	3	57	53
9	2	1	10	10
8	6	2	9	10
7	6	1	3	5
6	4	2	2	2
5 '50/50'	18	7	6	6
4	5	3	1	2
3	8	6	2	2
2	9	9	2	2
1	8	13	2	1
0 Certain it will *not* happen	25	50	5	3
'Don't know'	4	5	3	3
Base for percentages	(1005)	(1005)	(1005)	(971)[a]

[a] This question was not asked of those scoring zero on Q.3

Table A5.2 The extent of belief in limited nuclear war

	'All-out war' asked first (%)	'All-out war' asked second (%)	Combined responses (%)
'Do you agree that . . .'			
'. . . once the first few nuclear weapons are exploded, nothing can stop all-out war following?'	61	73	67
'. . . the destruction will force both sides to stop the war?'	39	27	33
	100	100	100
Base for percentages	(434)	(422)	(856)
'Don't know' = 14% overall			

Table A5.3 The likelihood that essential services would be available following a nuclear attack on London

	Very likely (%)	Fairly likely (%)	Fairly unlikely (%)	Very unlikely (%)	Don't know (%)
'How likely or unlikely is it that . . .'					
1. Food would be available in the shops?	2	6	15	74	3
2. Drinking water would be available?	2	8	17	70	3
3. Heating and lighting would be available?	2	6	16	74	3
4. There would be radio or TV broadcasts?	5	17	17	56	3
Base for percentages = 1005					

Table A5.4 The likelihood of survival

	All (%)	Most (%)	Half (%)	Few (%)	None (%)	Don't know (%)
'What proportion of the population of London would you expect to live through a nuclear attack?'	*	3	12	67	12	6

'How likely or unlikely is it . . .'	Very likely (%)	Fairly likely (%)	Fairly unlikely (%)	Very unlikely (%)	Don't know (%)
'. . . that you yourself would live through the attack?'	2	8	18	67	6
'. . . that you would survive for 2 weeks afterwards?'	4	20	18	47	10
'. . . that you would survive for 6 months afterwards?'	3	11	14	60	12

	Hope to survive (%)	Hope not to survive (%)	Don't know (%)
'. . . do you hope that you would survive such an attack or do you hope you would be among those who do not survive?'	23	70	7

Base for percentages = 1005

* Less than 0.5 per cent.

Table A5.5 Thinking, talking and worrying about a nuclear attack

	Almost all the time (%)	Once or twice a week (%)	Once or twice a month (%)	Once or twice a year (%)	Almost never or never (%)	Don't know (%)
Think about it	4	6	17	24	47	1
Talk about it	2	4	15	26	52	1

When you do think about it, how anxious do you feel about the possibility that London may be attacked with nuclear weapons?

	Very anxious (%)	Fairly anxious (%)	Not very anxious (%)	Not at all anxious (%)	Don't know (%)
	21	21	24	30	4

Base for percentages = 1005

Table A5.6 Respondents' anxiety about the possibility of a nuclear attack on London by their estimates of the likelihood of such an attack

'When you think about it, how anxious do you feel about the possibility that London might be attacked with nuclear weapons? Do you feel . . .?'

	Likelihood estimated on a 0–10 scale:				
	0 (%)	1–4 (%)	5 (%)	6–10 (%)	All (%)
Very anxious	11	16	26	38	22
Fairly anxious	12	23	27	25	21
Not very anxious	24	33	27	17	26
Not at all anxious	53	28	20	20	31
	100	100	100	100	100
Base for percentages	(242)	(294)	(175)	(220)	(931)

Table A5.7 The advice that respondents can recall seeing or hearing, by age

	18–24 (%)	25–34 (%)	35–44 (%)	45–54 (%)	55–64 (%)	65+ (%)	All (%)
1. Build shelters	14	10	12	13	16	11	12
2. How to build shelters	6	9	8	5	9	7	7
3. Take down doors for shelters	5	3	8	3	1	2	4
4. Barricade doors, seal house, etc.	10	13	15	19	4	2	11
5. Board up windows	8	8	13	6	0	6	8
6. Paint windows white	10	6	3	0	0	3	4
7. Build deep shelters underground	10	6	11	13	9	7	9
8. Store water	10	15	12	5	4	2	10
9. Store food	20	19	18	9	7	5	15
10. Keep useful supplies (blankets, torches etc)	2	3	2	2	0	0	2
11. Stay indoors	11	15	14	8	7	13	12
12. Listen to radio	2	6	3	2	0	0	3
13. Protect, cover oneself and family	3	2	4	6	2	0	3
14. Where to go	10	16	14	5	10	5	11
15. 'Protect and Survive'	6	6	3	2	1	0	4
16. How to dispose of dead	4	1	3	0	0	0	2
17. Saw official source	10	6	6	2	3	5	6
18. Saw advice in media	9	8	7	5	6	5	7
19. Saw official film	6	4	1	3	3	2	3
20. Showed effects (general)	3	3	5	5	4	2	4
21. Showed what to do (general)	2	2	3	3	4	3	3
22. Only elites will get shelters	1	1	3	2	1	5	2
23. Don't panic	0	1	1	2	0	2	1
24. Derogatory comments	4	3	2	3	3	5	3
25. Other answers	9	8	5	5	3	5	6
26. Cannot remember	14	15	19	23	21	27	19

Base for percentages = 565 (all those recalling any advice). Percentages will total more than 100% because many respondents gave more than one reply.

Table A5.8 Likely destinations for those who might leave London, by intentions to leave

		Would stay in London (%)	Would try to leave (%)	All (%)
'Is there anywhere in particular you would want to try to get to?'				
	Yes	39	70	49
	No	61	30	51
		100	100	100
	Base	(589)	(300)	(889)
'Do you have friends or relatives there, or not?'		%	%	%
	Yes	71	71	71
	No	29	29	29
		100	100	100
	Base	(228)	(210)	(438)
'Have you ever discussed with friends or relatives outside London whether you might go there in such an emergency?'		%	%	%
	Yes	2	7	4
	No	98	93	96
		100	100	100
	Base	(589)	(300)	(889)

Table A5.9 The likelihood of success in leaving London by initial intentions to leave or stay

	Stay in London (%)	Try to leave (%)	All (%)
'Do you think you would succeed in leaving London if you tried to leave?'			
Yes	19	41	26
No	71	44	62
Don't know	10	15	12
	100	100	100
Base	(586)	(300)	(886)
'Why do you feel you would not be able to leave?'	(%)	(%)	(%)
1. The authorities would stop us	26	27	27
2. Too much panic, blocked roads, etc	83	82	83
3. Too many people trying to leave at once	3	2	3
4. Not enough time, too late	3	2	3
5. Other answers	6	6	6
Base	(362)	(175)	(557)

Table A5.10 The protective measures Londoners might take in an emergency

	Certain I would do this (%)	I would probably do this (%)	I might do this (%)	Certain I would not do this (%)	(Base)
Keep the family at home					
Stayers	65	14	7	14	(520)
Leavers	54	21	7	19	(263)
Stock up with food					
Stayers	39	23	15	24	(578)
Leavers	53	21	12	14	(288)
Fill water containers					
Stayers	54	20	9	17	(577)
Leavers	64	17	8	11	(288)
Build a shelter					
Stayers	11	9	12	68	(572)
Leavers	21	19	16	44	(287)
Make some sanitation arrangement					
Stayers	33	20	13	35	(555)
Leavers	43	22	12	23	(284)
Find public shelter in London					
Stayers	9	12	17	62	(560)
Leavers	23	14	19	44	(279)
Go to work					
Stayers	16	7	5	72	(229)
Leavers	5	5	7	83	(157)

Table A5.11 Whether those in work would go to work during the emergency by the choice to leave or stay, by sector

	Would you go to work? Yes	No	
Public sector			
Stay in London	27	41	= 100%
Try to leave	8	28	Base = 157
Private sector			
Stay in London	12	40	= 100%
Try to leave	6	42	Base = 199

Table A5.12 Londoners' potential for protest against a nuclear war that threatened in two weeks

(MC = Middle Class WC = Working Class)	Under 35				35–54				Over 54				
	MC		WC		MC		WC		MC		WC		
	Men (%)	Women (%)	Men (%)	Women (%)	Men (%)	Women (%)	Men (%)	Women (%)	Men (%)	Women (%)	Men (%)	Women (%)	All (%)
Join in mass demonstrations													
Certainly	17	20	12	8	11	14	10	16	12	12	10	7	13
Probably	8	12	11	9	6	7	10	5	3	7	7	1	8
Might	17	18	22	15	26	14	9	14	10	6	8	7	14
Would not	60	51	54	67	57	65	71	65	75	75	74	86	66
Use direct methods of protest													
Certainly	9	10	9	5	6	6	9	11	6	6	4	3	7
Probably	5	10	10	9	4	10	9	7	2	4	6	2	7
Might	11	15	17	9	9	8	6	7	5	6	2	2	9
Would not	75	65	64	77	72	76	77	76	88	85	88	92	77
Use violent means of protest													
Certainly	6	3	7	1	4	3	8	3	3	3	1	2	4
Probably	3	5	8	4	0	1	2	3	0	3	3	1	3
Might	11	5	16	4	4	4	6	7	3	1	3	0	5
Would not	80	87	80	92	93	92	85	88	94	93	93	97	88
Base for percentages	(79)	(118)	(90)	(85)	(53)	(80)	(68)	(74)	(67)	(72)	(97)	(90)	(976)

3% 'Don't knows' have been excluded from this table

Table A5.13 Anti-nuclear activity by partisan choice

	Conservative (%)	Alliance (%)	Labour (%)
(a) To oppose nuclear weapons respondents have . . .			
Signed petitions	6	14	27
Given money to CND etc	4	11	19
Contacted elected representatives	2	2	5
Gone on demonstrations	3	4	15
Done something else	1	4	7
Done nothing	92	82	61
	★	★	★
(b) If war in two weeks, respondents would	(%)	(%)	(%)
(i) Demonstrate against the war			
'yes'	17	43	51
'no'	83	57	49
(ii) Use direct action methods to oppose the war			
'yes'	9	29	37
'no'	91	71	63
(iii) Use violent means of protest against the war			
'yes'	3	12	20
'no'	97	88	80
Base for percentages	(304)	(164)	(294)

★ These percentages total more than 100% because respondents were active in more than one area.

Table A5.14 Basic position on nuclear weapons by partisan choice

	Conservative (%)	Alliance (%)	Labour (%)
Keep nuclear weapons	31	14	11
Keep nuclear weapons while bargaining with other nations	53	50	39
Get rid of nuclear weapons in five years	12	23	27
Get rid of nuclear weapons now	4	13	23
	100	100	100
Base for percentages	(310)	(163)	(304)

Table A5.15 The amount of help Londoners feel the emergency services might be able to give

'If London were to be attacked by nuclear weapons, how much, do you feel, would the following services be able to help those who survive?'

	Fire brigades (%)	Police (%)	Civil defence volunteers (%)	Medical services (%)
A lot of help	15	14	15	23
Some help	26	26	25	26
Only a little help	26	26	25	24
No help at all	30	31	30	24
Don't know	3	3	5	3
	100	100	100	100

Base for percentages = 1005

Table A5.16 What Londoners think their Local Authorities should be doing now to prepare for a nuclear attack, by their basic position on weapons

'What two or three things, if anything, do you think Local Authorities ought to be doing to prepare for a nuclear attack on London?'	Basic position: Keep weapons (%)	Keep weapons & negotiate (%)	Phase out in 5 years (%)	Abandon now (%)	All (%)
1. Support for individuals to build shelters	1	3	2	1	2
2. Build deep public shelters	17	23	20	11	19
3. Priority shelters for children	1	*	0	1	1
4. Build shelters, unspecified	18	14	20	16	16
5. Give grants, spend more money on shelters and preparations	2	2	1	2	2
6. Tell people what to do (unspecified)	6	6	5	5	6
7. Tell people where to go (e.g. directions to shelters)	1	4	5	2	3
8. Tell people what might happen, tell the truth, more information for survival	9	14	14	11	13
9. More specific information on how to stay alive	7	7	6	4	6

Table A5.16 (*Continued*)

'What two or three things, if anything, do you think Local Authorities ought to be doing to prepare for a nuclear attack on London?'	Basic position				
	Keep weapons (%)	Keep weapons & negotiate (%)	Phase out in 5 years (%)	Abandon now (%)	All (%)
10. Store food centrally	5	11	8	3	8
11. Information on what food to stock oneself	1	1	0	0	1
12. Safeguard water supplies	2	6	5	4	5
13. Protect food and water stocks from contamination	0	1	2	0	1
14. Retain our nuclear weapons	2	1	1	0	1
15. Prevent war	*	6	10	18	8
16. More leaflets and literature	2	3	2	3	3
17. Tell people not to panic	1	2	1	1	1
18. Safeguard power supplies	1	1	1	0	1
19. Evacuation plans	2	1	4	1	2
20. Safeguard medical services	3	7	4	1	5
21. Set up emergency command	1	2	2	0	2
22. Change the government	0	1	2	1	1
23. Safeguard sanitation system	0	1	2	1	1
24. Better warning system	0	1	1	0	1
25. Maintain emergency services	1	1	1	0	1
26. Set up good emergency communications	0	*	2	1	1
27. Educate the young	1	0	1	1	1
Other answers	5	5	4	2	5
Do nothing, 'nothing they can do'	21	16	13	29	18
Don't know, no answers	21	12	12	9	14
Base for percentages =	(184)	(451)	(205)	(140)	(980)

* Less than 0.5% but greater than 0.

Reference

Loizos, Peter, and Marsh, Alan, GLAWARS *Task 4: Concern with the Unthinkable.* London, South Bank Polytechnic, 1986, mimeo.

Appendix 6

The Weapons

Three types of weapon might be used in any future attack on London:

1 conventional;
2 chemical and biological; and
3 nuclear weapons.

This appendix reviews the chief characteristics of these weapons. Although an attack on or affecting London could include the use of all three types of weapon, the use of chemical and biological weapons currently seems very unlikely.

Conventional weapons

Since World War 2, chemical, biological and, above all, nuclear weapons have dominated public attention. The fact that conventional explosives, delivered by relatively primitive aircraft and missiles, created enormous damage during two world wars in this century is now only distantly remembered. Yet in World War 2, more than 50 million people died, dozens of cities were laid waste, and the economic effects of the war lingered on for decades (bomb craters could still be seen in London as recently as a few years ago). Even in 1945, conventional TNT and incendiary bombs were powerful weapons.

More than five million tons of TNT were used in World War 2. Only 70,000 tons were used on the UK, concentrated on such cities as Coventry, Southampton and London. Even so, social cohesion and morale broke down quickly in the attacked cities, though at the time censorship ensured that this was not widely known. Badly damaged zones had to be cordoned off by the police, and emergency services failed to cope. This was in spite of the fact that there was considerable warning of the attacks, there were pauses between the attacks, a shelter policy was in operation, and one and a half million women and children had previously been evacuated. Some 250,000 homes were damaged beyond repair and a further 3.5 million suffered reparable damage. There were some 60,000 direct casualties.

Yet raids on UK cities were not as severe as those later inflicted on such cities as Dresden, Hamburg and Tokyo. Those on Hamburg caused mass evacuation and destroyed half the city's housing. Dresden was destroyed by a firestorm which sucked in air from outside the city, producing winds of more than 300 km/h and temperatures in excess of 1000°C.

Over the past 40 years, research has produced both more sophisticated weapons and far more accurate delivery systems. In theory, at least, conventional warheads can now be delivered by air-to-ground missiles from aircraft to within tens of metres of their targets from distances of 2500 km (Kerr 1986). Whether such accuracy is achievable under wartime operating conditions is dubious. However, what is clear is that modern conventional weapons are designed primarily for destroying military targets, and that their delivery systems are sufficiently accurate to achieve that aim. Modern conventional weapons have not been developed to destroy cities, and they contain much smaller quantities of explosives than many World War 2 bombs. Incendiary weapons are likely to be far less widely used than in World War 2.

Physical effects. Conventional weapons rely for their effect on two factors: the creation of blast and of fire hazards. When TNT is ignited, the resulting detonation spreads through the material at a speed of more than 23,000 km/h. The bomb case bursts and the surrounding air is compressed, forming a blast wave, and subsequently contracts, creating a suck back. Structures near the explosion thus encounter two forces: a short but powerful force (lasting some 5 milliseconds for a 250 kg bomb) pushing them away from the blast followed by a longer (about 25 milliseconds) but much less powerful suck back. It is this combination of forces, rather than the simple effects of blast, that causes many materials to fail.

Likely areas of damage from conventional weapons are well known. A 250 kg bomb, for example, is expected to demolish brick structures up to 8 metres away, and to create serious structural damage up to 18 metres.

Secondary hazards are then created by flying splinters of material, either from the bomb case itself or from materials close to the explosion. These attain velocities of up to 10,000 km/h (3 km/s). A well known example of an explosive/fragmentation device is the French *Exocet* missile, which consists of a substantial charge of high explosive cast into a steel block. Weapons of this kind are used against machinery and electronic equipment of the type found in data processing, telecommunications, and command and control centres.

Protection against the combination of blast and flying fragments is relatively difficult. For example, protection against a direct hit from a 1 ton bomb requires about 7.5 cm of mild steel, 50 cm of reinforced concrete, 72 cm of bricks or 1.4 metres of sandbags.

Fragmentation bombs, such as the cluster bomb, are also used to hinder the activities of rescue services or repair teams. They are particularly effective when fitted with delayed action fuses. Devices also exist which detonate on mechanical contact, for example when attempts are made to clear them by bulldozer.

Sensitive military structures are protected by thick reinforced concrete. Penetrating bombs and shells are designed to create cavities in such material. Their thick cases do not fracture on impact but only after detonation, which is timed to coincide with maximum penetration. Penetrating weapons are particularly effective against structures such as roads, runways and bridges. They are designed to explode under the structures and thus destroy foundations and footings, making repair difficult. Examples of these weapons include the French *Durandal* bomb and the German *Stabo (Stammplatzbombe)*, both designed for runway destruction.

Demolition is also effected through the use of fuel/air explosives, which contain an inflammable liquid or gel. When this is dispersed into the air, it forms an explosive mixture or aerosol which is ignited by a detonating charge. Very high blast pressures are created. The US Air Force *BLU-82B* bomb is of this type.

This type of weapon creates intense fire hazards. If bombing is heavy and concentrated, a firestorm may be created in which structures burn fiercely and quickly, fuelled by air sucked in from surrounding, cooler areas. A firestorm, however, cannot spread. Conflagrations, by contrast, do. They are created by moving walls of fire, fanned by the wind, which form when fires from different explosions meet up and join. The nuclear explosions in Japan created both types of fire – a firestorm in Hiroshima and a conflagration in Nagasaki. As experience in World War 2 showed, they can also be created with conventional weapons.

Delivery systems. While conventional weapons themselves have been improved over the past 40 years, their delivery systems have undergone an even more dramatic transformation. In a modern war, conventional bombs will be guided to their targets from the launching aircraft, through the use of television, infra-red or laser-marking equipment which is capable of accuracies of a metre or two.

One disadvantage of laser guidance is that it often requires the services of a second aircraft to mark the target. For this reason, unless air defences have already been destroyed, air-to-ground missiles may well be preferred to unpowered weapons such as bombs.

The most powerful and effective missiles of this type are air-breathing cruise missiles, such as the Soviet Union's *AS-15*, carried by the *Bear-H* long-range bomber (and expected to be carried by the *Backfire* and the *Blackjack*). Maximum range is 3000 km, which means that the *AS-15* can be launched from an aircraft 2000–2500 km from its target.

The *AS-15* is probably guided by an inertial navigation system, complemented by some form of terminal guidance to offset any errors accumulated over the flight, which may last as long as three hours. US cruise missiles are equipped with terminal guidance known as TERCOM or TERPCOM (terrain contour matching and terrain profile matching). The former, installed in the US *AGM-86A* air-launched cruise missile, is claimed to be capable of placing a warhead within ten metres of its target from a range of 1900 km.

Weapons such as these have greatly improved accuracy over anything available in World War 2. They are also capable of penetrating almost any form of air defence.

Chemical and biological weapons. Chemical and biological weapons are unique in that they can be used only against living things or the processes that support them. They are thus effective only against humans, livestock and crops.

Chemical agents can be produced using standard techniques of industrial chemistry, and some are relatively simple to manufacture. They are easy to store but more difficult to dispose of. Biological agents depend on the more difficult technology of growing large numbers of infective organisms. Unless they exist as spores, which can survive in a dormant condition for many years, it is difficult to store or stockpile biological agents for lengthy periods, although a continuous production process can be used to renew supplies as necessary.

Both chemical and biological agents would normally be delivered by missile or bomber, and then dispersed as an aerosol cloud or sprayed in liquid form over the intended target. In theory, opportunities also exist for the introduction, by covert means, of either type of agent into the air-filtration systems of buildings or the water supplies of large towns and cities.

The chemical armoury. Chemical weapons, including mustard gas and phosgene, were first used on a large scale during World War 1. Although some 3000 substances were screened for use in that war, only 38 were ever actually used: 12 tear gases, 15 choking agents, 3 blood poisons, 4 blister agents and 4 vomiting gases. About 125,000 tons of these agents were dispersed, causing at least 800,000 casualties.

Mustard gas was the most effective: nine million shells were filled with it, and they produced some 400,000 casualties. On the basis of casualties produced per shell, these weapons were roughly five times more effective than either high explosive or shrapnel. On the other hand, they were considerably less lethal. The ratio of deaths to casualties from chemical weapons may have been as low as 7 per cent, roughly a quarter of the figure for conventional weapons.

The use of chemical weapons in war, except in reprisal, was subsequently outlawed in the 1925 Geneva Protocol, to which most countries in the world are currently party. Chemical weapons were not used on a large scale in World War 2 (in fact, only the Japanese used them, in repeated but small attacks against the Chinese). However, it was during World War 2 that a new generation of chemical weapons – the nerve gases – was developed in Germany.

The three best known agents were called tabun, sarin and soman (known today as GA, GB and GD respectively). About one milligramme of sarin is thought to be lethal if inhaled in one breath. Nerve gases are actually liquid at room temperature but can be dispersed as an aerosol, the liquid then evaporating very quickly. Both the gases and the liquids are lethal by either inhalation or skin contact. Furthermore, they can penetrate clothing. Most nerve agents are persistent, or can be treated to become so. This means they can be used to deny an enemy the use of terrain for considerable periods. After World War 2, the United States developed even more toxic nerve agents, including VX, and a way of producing them in which two relatively harmless chemicals were caused to react together inside the munition itself (binary munitions).

During the 1950s and 1960s, attempts were made to develop incapacitating and psychochemical weapons, the effects of which would last only a few hours and be totally reversible. At least one, code named BZ, was produced and stockpiled by the United States. However, the use of chemical agents in the field is never easy; and where they produce unpredictable effects on the mind, as did BZ, their military advantage may be highly dubious. US stocks of BZ are currently awaiting destruction.

Countries possessing chemical weapons. How many countries currently have stockpiles of chemical munitions is not accurately known. Only two NATO countries, France and the United States, possess significant quantities of chemical weapons. It is not known how many Warsaw Pact countries stock chemical weapons, although some may do so. Chemicals believed to be stockpiled by the Soviet Union include phosgene (a choking gas), hydrogen cyanide (a blood gas), mustard gas, lewisite, nitrogen mustard (blister gases), tabun, sarin and soman (nerve gases) and perhaps a toxin. The United States holds six: GB, VX, two forms of mustard gas (HD and HT), one incapacitating agent, DM, and one psychochemical, BZ (DM and BZ are awaiting destruction).

Chemical weapons have not been used on a large scale since World War 1 (excepting the use of defoliating chemicals by the United States in Viet Nam), though there is an apparently increasing number of allegations of infringements of the Geneva Protocol on a smaller scale, often in situations involving developing countries. The latest verified use of chemical weapons is by Iraq in its war against Iran.

Restrictions on the use of chemical weapons. Although chemical weapons are widely feared, their potential uses by major powers are heavily restricted by several factors. Chemical weapons are likely to be used only in situations where they can achieve a military advantage that is not possible with other weapons, or where they can achieve a military purpose more economically than other munitions. In practice, such situations are rare. Furthermore, the effects produced by chemical weapons depend greatly on prevailing weather conditions – so much so that it is extremely difficult to ensure that a chemical agent dispersed in aerosol form from a bomb or missile will produce its intended effect. The results may well affect much smaller or much larger areas than is planned. This means that surprisingly large quantities of even the most toxic chemicals would have to be used if a chemical attack were to have a high chance of success. Because of this, and because it is possible to use protective clothing effectively against CBW, conventional weapons could usually achieve the same goal more economically, more effectively and more reliably. In a war in which nuclear weapons were already being used, there would be few, if any, reasons for using chemical and not nuclear weapons.

A further limitation arises because the use of chemical agents certainly signals that an aggressor is prepared to use extreme measures, even by war-time standards, to pursue his goals. Their use therefore invites possible nuclear retaliation. In April 1985 the French Minister of Defence was quoted as saying that French forces would, in fact, respond to a chemical or biological attack by using nuclear weapons (Kerr 1986).

Biological weapons. Less need be said about biological weapons, which depend for their effect on the spread of disease through the dispersal of infective bacteria, rickettsiae and viruses which cause diseases such as anthrax, plague, typhoid and brucellosis. Although there has been a great deal of experimentation with biological agents, they have not been used in war (with only a few, still fiercely debated exceptions). It is almost certain that no country stockpiles biological weapons, though several are capable of manufacturing the infective organisms required in sufficient quantity should the need arise.

The inhibitions on the use of chemical agents apply even more strongly to biological ones. Such weapons are, by their nature, even more unpredictable in their effects than chemicals. Furthermore, their use would break infamous new ground in the evolution of modern warfare, inviting nuclear retaliation even more strongly than the use of chemicals. Their use could also be self-defeating. During biological warfare experiments in World War 2, British scientists sprayed the Scottish island of Gruinard with anthrax spores. The island is uninhabitable to this day.

Nuclear weapons

Like conventional weapons, nuclear weapons produce extensive blast and fire damage. The effects are far greater than with conventional weapons because nuclear weapons have much higher explosive power. Furthermore, the power of nuclear weapons is increased by four additional factors:

1 intense radiation emitted at the time of the explosion, lasting for a period of about one minute;
2 an intense pulse of heat and light emitted by the fireball, lasting a few seconds;
3 local radioactive fall-out which may be a health hazard for days or even weeks after the bomb is dropped; and
4 a strong pulse of electro-magnetic radiation (the EMP) which is likely to damage or destroy electronic and telecommunications devices.

The largest conventional weapon used in World War 2 contained about 10 tons of explosive. The nuclear weapons used on Hiroshima and Nagasaki were, respectively, about 1500 and 2200 times more powerful.

The smallest nuclear weapon considered in this report has an explosive power equivalent to 150,000 tons (150 kt) of explosive or 15,000 of the largest World War 2 bombs. The largest nuclear weapon considered here, equivalent to one million tons (1 Mt) of explosive, is 50 times more powerful than the bomb dropped on Nagasaki.

In fact, much greater damage can be inflicted by using several smaller weapons than by using one big one. For example, the blast effects of eight 125 kt bombs could destroy an area twice as large as that destroyed by one 1 Mt bomb. The reason why nuclear weapons have tended to become smaller over the past 15 years is that delivery systems have become more accurate. Huge yields are therefore no longer required to ensure that a nuclear weapon exploding some distance from its target still destroys it. Many inter-continental missiles now carry several small nuclear warheads, each of which can be independently aimed at a different target. Accuracy is such that each warhead has a 50 per cent chance of landing within a few hundred metres of its target. The delivery of nuclear warheads by missiles launched from aircraft can be even more accurate.

Effects of nuclear weapons exploded on Japan. Because no one knows exactly how many people were in Hiroshima and Nagasaki at the time of the nuclear explosions, the numbers of casualties (people killed or injured) are not accurately known. The most recent estimates are that in Hiroshima 130,000 people (about 40 per cent of the population) had died by November 1945; in Nagasaki, 60–70,000 (22 to 26 per cent) had died by the end of 1945. Many more died later from the long-term effects of radiation and other causes.

Almost everyone within 500 metres of the explosion and about 60 per cent of those within 2 km of it were killed. Some 13 km^2 of Hiroshima and 7 km^2 of Nagasaki were reduced first to rubble and then to ashes. All buildings in Hiroshima within 2 km of the explosion were damaged beyond repair; two-thirds of all Hiroshima's buildings were subsequently destroyed by fire. The blast produced overpressures (pressures in excess of atmospheric pressure) of about 10 pounds per square inch (psi) up to 1.3 km and of more than 4 psi up to 2 km from the explosion (Barnaby and Rotblat 1982). An overpressure of 5 psi is sufficient to demolish any brick structure.

The fireballs in both explosions grew to about 400 m in diameter within the first second. Most of those caught in the open within 1.2 km of the explosions were burned to death. Burns occurred as far as 4 km from the explosions and many people were temporarily blinded by the flash at much greater distances.

Both explosions were air bursts, which had the effect of increasing the effect of blast but reducing the amount of local fall-out. Ground bursts, or bursts in which the fireball touches the ground, produce extensive local fall-out because quantities of soil and debris are sucked up into the atmosphere together with the radioactive products of the bomb. Most of this material falls back to Earth within 24 hours.

In this report, it is assumed that ground bursts need be used only to destroy hardened military targets, which may be buried under many metres of reinforced concrete. Air bursts are considered sufficient to destroy most other types of target. This assumption has the effect of reducing the amount of fall-out produced compared to other, similar studies. Its rationale is that a potential adversary, such as the Soviet Union, that lies down wind from the UK would not wish to maximize fall-out. It would have little to gain and much to lose from doing so.

Fall-out is also produced by an air burst, but the radioactive material is usually sucked up into the stratosphere and may not return to Earth for several months. By this time, it may be thousands of kilometres from the site of the explosion. This is called global fall-out. Large air bursts produce local fall-out only if the exploding mushroom cloud encounters rain clouds, in which case radioactive material falls with the rain (as in fact happened in Hiroshima and Nagasaki). There is also some evidence that nuclear explosions may, in fact, produce these rain clouds (Rotblat, Haines and Lindop 1986); the sky above Hiroshima was clear at the time of the explosion, although rain fell shortly afterwards.

Initial radiation killed many people in Hiroshima and Nagasaki. Many of those within 1 km of the explosions in Japan are thought to have received doses of more than 10 gray (1 gray is 100 rads), which is considerably more than a lethal dose. Much controversy surrounds the issue of how large a radiation dose is sufficient to kill or injure. Among the issues that must be considered are the length of time over which the dose is absorbed, the degree to which bone marrow (which is highly sensitive to radiation damage) is protected, and the degree of medical care likely to be available. In the aftermath of a nuclear attack, of course, drugs and blood transfusions, which can greatly mitigate the effects of radiation damage, are unlikely to be widely available.

Most authorities, until recently, considered that a dose of 4 to 5 gray absorbed over a period of one week would be sufficient to kill half the people exposed to it in wartime conditions. This dose, known as the LD_{50}, was reconsidered by the Home Office in the late 1970s, with the result that the Home Office now uses higher values for LD_{50}s in its computer programmes to estimate casualty rates (Bentley 1981):

dose received in a few minutes: $LD_{50} = 6$ gray
dose received in a few hours: $LD_{50} = 8$ gray
dose received over one week: $LD_{50} = 9$ gray.

These doses appear exceptionally high on the evidence submitted to GLAWARS. Indeed, the weight of scientific opinion currently suggests that revisions of the LD_{50} may well be required in the opposite direction: an LD_{50} as low as 2.2 gray has recently been suggested (Rotblat in press). Table A6.3 gives an indication of the medical effects of radiation at varying doses.

The horrific effects of the two nuclear weapons exploded over Japan, the numbers of people killed and injured, and the damage to buildings have been described many times. The overall effects on the two cities are less well known. Since considerable emphasis is placed later in this report on the cumulative effects of nuclear explosions on London as a functioning system, it is worth describing one of the many side-effects of the Hiroshima bomb.

> . . . no fire department in the world, however well organized and trained, could have coped with the thousands of simultaneous fires in combustible

> buildings. Furthermore, wreckage blocked the streets and made operation impossible except along the perimeter of the conflagration area. Innumerable water pipes inside damaged buildings were broken, and pumping stations were disabled by the interruption of electric power. The result was that the water pressure dropped to zero immediately after the explosion, and it was therefore impossible to get water to the fires in the upper stories. Street hydrants were broken by falling wreckage or were buried in debris. Hand equipment in buildings was used very little because of numerous casualties and the resultant panic, but bucket brigades saved many dwellings along the fringe of the conflagration area. Fire walls and doors did little to prevent firespread within buildings. Interior firewalls were blown down or damaged. Many fire doors were open at the time of the explosion, and many of those that were closed were bent or displaced. Fire shutters were blown off by the blast wave, exposing interiors to heat and burning debris from nearby buildings.
>
> (Oughterson and Warren 1956)

Effects such as these – and there are many others – make civil defence against nuclear attack extremely difficult. They also add greatly to the problems of treating the injured, disposing of the dead and restoring even the most elementary functions of the city.

Effects of a 150 kt explosion. Part 2 of this report analyses the effects of five nuclear attacks on London. To provide some background to the techniques used in this analysis, the effects of a 150 kt air burst are considered below. The effects of flash burns, blast and radiation are considered in turn. It must also be remembered that many people would be blinded, temporarily or permanently, by flash.

1. Burns. The fireball from a 150 kt explosion takes only a second or two to form. Even at a distance of some 10 km, the fireball would appear about 100 times larger than the sun, and its associated flash would be correspondingly brighter.

According to the US Office of Technology Assessment (OTA), thermal radiation of 6.7 cal/cm^2 is sufficient to produce burns serious enough to kill (it is also sufficient to ignite newspapers and synthetic fabrics). Radiation of 3.4 cal/cm^2 is sufficient to cause burns requiring extensive medical treatment (OTA 1980). These figures are used in the standard assessments of casualties, although other, more complicated methods are available. An important factor in making these estimates is that burns that would injure but not kill in peace time may be lethal during a war, when medical treatment will be minimal and burns are likely to be accompanied by radiation sickness and physical injuries from blast.

The ranges at which thermal radiation levels from a 150 kt explosion reach 6.7 and 3.4 cal/cm^2 are 6.4 and 8.4 km respectively, assuming no snow or cloud cover, and good visibility (Glasstone and Dolan 1977). These ranges can be calculated for an explosion of any yield but, in practice, they depend greatly on prevailing conditions. Poor visibility reduces them considerably, while clouds and snow, because they reflect heat radiation, increase them.

Not everyone within these distances would be affected because many would be inside buildings or sheltered in other ways. All those in the open would be injured or killed, but estimating the proportion of the population likely to be exposed is difficult. At night, most people will be inside buildings. Maximum exposure would occur during the morning or evening rush hours, or during the day of a summer weekend. The OTA estimates that between 1 and 25 per cent of a city population is likely to be exposed to the heat flash. Other studies have assumed that 5 per cent of the population is likely to be exposed. Relevant factors to be considered here include whether any warning is given of the attack, and what percentage of the population heeds government advice to stay at home.

2. Blast. The effects of blast can be more accurately estimated. The technique used by the OTA is to divide the affected area into four zones: those experiencing overpressures of more than 12 psi; those experiencing 5–12 psi; those experiencing 2–5 psi; and those experiencing 1–2 psi. It is then possible to calculate the range at which each of these pressure zones occurs, both from theory and from measurements made during nuclear tests. These ranges depend on a number of factors, including the flatness of the terrain and the height at which the weapon is exploded. The ranges of the four zones, and the physical effects produced in each by both blast and the heat flash, are shown in Table A6.1 for a 150 kt explosion. It is assumed that this explosion occurs at a height designed to maximize the area subjected to a blast of 10 psi.

The human body can withstand surprisingly high overpressures. Casualties would result almost exclusively from indirect effects such as houses collapsing, people being blown against hard or sharp objects, and injuries from flying debris, including glass. Blast is initially experienced as a very strong wind, perhaps more than 200 km/h even at distances of several kilometres from the explosion, followed by stillness, followed by a suck back towards the explosion. The initial wind would be sufficiently strong to hurl people and cars down streets, collapse buildings and remove roofs.

The OTA has estimated the percentages of deaths and injuries that would arise in each overpressure zone. Figures such as these are derived from the known effects of the bombs on Hiroshima and Nagasaki, experiments with animal cadavers, and tests with dummies during nuclear weapons tests. A 150 kt bomb would therefore produce the effects shown in Table A6.2.

Table A6.1 Physical effects of blast and heat from a 150 kt air burst

Distance from ground zero (km)	Overpressure (psi)	Blast effects	Fire damage
<1.5	>12	Nearly all buildings completely destroyed; small houses reduced to rubble	Glass and many metals melt
1.5–2.4	5–12	Brick houses destroyed, other buildings damaged	Severe fire zone; wood ignites
2.4–4.1	2–5	Serious damage to houses; roofs removed and walls cracked	Clothing and shrubs ignite; severe third degree burns
4.1–6.2	1–2	Slight damage to houses, tiles removed, windows smashed, doors blown out	Lethal burns in the open

Table A6.2 Deaths and injuries from blast from a 150 kt bomb

Overpressure (psi)	Distance from ground zero (km)	Area (km^2)	Deaths (%)	Injuries (%)
> 12	< 1.5	7.07	98	2
5–12	1.5–2.4	11.03	50	40
2–5	2.4–4.1	34.71	5	45
1–2	4.1–7.8	138.32	–	25

Estimates of the percentages of people killed and injured in each zone, and the ranges at which the zones occur, have been made by many different people and institutions. The OTA describes its figures as 'conservative'. They assume, for instance, that more than half of those people whose houses are blown down on top of them (by overpressures of more than 5 psi) will survive. Figures produced by the Home Office, however, show substantially lower rates of casualties. On the evidence available to GLAWARS, the OTA figures were the best current approximations at the time this report was prepared. As mentioned in Part 2, a new method of calculating overall casualties which also includes the effects of fires has now been proposed (Daugherty, Levi and von Hippel, in press).

3. Radiation casualties. Radiation casualties are of two types: those caused by immediate radiation doses from the explosion itself; and those caused over a much longer period by local fall-out from ground bursts.

Immediate radiation effects are complicated to calculate. However, for bombs larger than about 10 kt immediate radiation doses occur only within areas already devastated by blast and heat. For example, a dose of 4.5 gray would be absorbed by most people within 2 km of the explosion. Since anyone this close to the explosion will probably have been killed by blast (or received lethal burns in the open), immediate radiation does not add greatly to the numbers of casualties (though it may produce long-term effects). The effects of varying radiation doses are presented in Table A6.3.

The effects of local fall-out over the London area are dealt with in detail in Part 2. They are difficult to calculate accurately for a number of reasons. For example, the patterns of fall-out depend greatly on prevailing wind directions and speed, and on the effects of hills and mountains on the winds. Casualty rates also depend on the total radiation dose absorbed over a period of time. Fall-out itself can take a considerable time to reach the ground, depending on such factors as the size and height of the explosion and the strength of the wind. Usually, about 60 per cent of the radioactivity from a ground burst is deposited in the first 24 hours.

The dose rate from radioactive fall-out is also complicated to calculate. As the radioactive cloud is blown over an area, fall-out is deposited. For as long as the cloud continues its passage over the affected area, more fall-out accumulates. However, the radioactivity of the fall-out decreases rapidly from the time of the explosion itself. Thus, initially, radiation levels increase as the quantity of fall-out more than offsets the effects of radioactive decay. Then, as the amount of fall-out deposited begins to decrease, the effects of decay become more important, and the dose rate begins to fall. Once local fall-out is complete, the dose rate drops rapidly as a result of radioactive decay.

The important factor for survival, however, is not the dose rate but the total dose of radiation accumulated during the time of exposure. Standard techniques exist for calculating the accumulated radiation doses over given time periods, providing the initial maximum radiation

Table A6.3 Medical effects of radiation

Dose (gray)	Symptoms	Deaths (average)
0–1	Men temporarily sterile in 0.2–0.5 gray range	–
1–2	Nausea and vomiting within 3–6 hours, no further symptoms for 2 weeks; recurrence of symptoms for further month; number of white blood cells reduced	
2–6	Nausea and vomiting for 1–2 days, later recurrence for up to 2 months; diarrhoea, severe reduction of white blood cells, blood blisters, infection; loss of hair above 3 gray; 50 per cent death rate 2–5 gray approximately	0–98 per cent in 2–12 weeks from internal bleeding or infection
6–10	Same as above but recurrence after 5–10 days, lasting 1–4 weeks	98–100 per cent from internal bleeding or infection
10–50	Same as above but recurrence with fever after about 7 days	100 per cent, within 14 days, from collapse of circulation
More than 50	Nausea and vomiting followed by convulsions, loss of control of movement and lethargy	100 per cent in 48 hours, from breathing failure or brain damage

Source: adapted from Greene *et al.* 1982.

dose rate is known. Because of radioactive decay, most of the dose that would be accumulated over, say, a two-week period would be absorbed in the first few hours. Unfortunately, it is during the first few hours that many people might venture into the open trying to evacuate, search for missing people or equip a fall-out shelter for a long stay.

Shelter provides good protection against radiation. For example, people spending most of their time indoors will accumulate only about one-third the radiation dose of those who remain outside. Those who can manage to remain in a basement shelter for one month would accumulate only about one-tenth the maximum radiation dose. In practice, of course, very few if any would be able to do that in the UK. Living in cramped quarters, with scant supplies of energy and water, primitive toilet and washing arrangements, and inadequate food would soon undermine both the morale and the health of even the most determined.

The areas affected by fall-out are much larger than those affected by blast, though they are limited mainly to downwind regions. For example, the lethal blast area from a 1 Mt explosion is about 70 km^2. The area in which a lethal radiation dose could be accumulated during the first two weeks after a 1 Mt explosion will be at least 1000 km^2, and possibly two or three times larger.

The electro-magnetic pulse. Nuclear explosions may damage or destroy a great deal of electrical and electronic equipment. The mechanisms involved are complicated; essentially, however, a nuclear explosion either at ground level or high above the atmosphere creates a very intense burst of electro-magnetic radiation known as the electro-magnetic pulse (EMP). Although the burst lasts only about one-millionth of a second, it produces very high peak powers – of the order of 6 MW/m^2, some 4000 times the radiation power of ordinary sunlight.

Some of the effects of EMP were demonstrated after a high-altitude explosion carried out on 8 July 1962 by the United States, when a 1.4 Mt bomb was exploded at a height of 400 km above Johnson Island in the Pacific. The explosion produced widespread electrical disturbances in Hawaii, some 1300 km away. Street lights went out, power lines broke down and burglar alarms started ringing.

Military planners became concerned about the effects of EMP as long ago as the early 1960s. Their fear was that computers, missile systems, military aircraft – each of which carries many thousands of electronic circuits – and defence communications networks could be knocked out by EMP. As the pulse entered sensitive electronic circuitry, disturbances of thousands of volts and amperes – perhaps a hundred times more powerful than those produced by a major lightning strike – would damage or destroy many pieces of equipment, particularly semiconductors. Electronically-controlled weapon fuses could well be triggered by EMP. It is even postulated that the first explosion in a nuclear war could be exo-atmospheric, aimed solely at knocking out electronic equipment over a wide area, perhaps a whole continent.

Since then, many billions of dollars have been spent in hardening sensitive military equipment to protect it from EMP. This can be done by protecting sensitive components with screening and using fibre optics to replace metal conductors in communications equipment. Ironically, EMP is far more damaging to modern electronic equipment than it is to old-fashioned vacuum tube valves, which are estimated to be 10 million times less vulnerable to EMP than semiconductor devices.

However, civilian equipment is not so protected. It is likely, therefore, that any nuclear attack on the UK would damage or destroy power supplies, telephone links, broadcasting networks, computing facilities and many other essential devices which depend on electronic equipment. Electronic ignition and control systems on vehicles would be damaged, and even the electronics involved in simple operations such as pumping petrol would be impaired. Domestic radio and TV sets would also be affected. Furthermore, these effects might be widespread. Although they would extend over distances of only 10–20 km from a ground explosion, an explosion above the atmosphere could damage electronic equipment over a whole continent.

Such effects might be considered relatively trivial to a population subjected to nuclear attack. Nevertheless, however horrific the attack, there will be survivors. One of the requirements of civil defence planning is to devise systems that will enable survivors to continue to survive and, as time goes on, to put together the basic elements of social and economic life. The effects of EMP are likely to make this much more difficult.

The overall effect. The danger of analysing the immediate effects of a single explosion is that the results may even appear reassuring. In practice, nuclear attacks are likely to involve many detonations, perhaps over a period of time. Such conditions are likely to produce such chaos that those who survive the actual explosions will soon face a range of new problems. They may well succumb to disease, starvation or the cold of a nuclear winter. They will also face a range of social, economic and political problems quite outside anything in their previous experience.

Damage from a nuclear attack extends far beyond the direct effects on the human population and the buildings they occupy. Medical services, hospitals, pharmacies, energy, gas and water supplies, the sewage system, food stores, roads, railways and communications, vehicles, fuel stores and fire-fighting equipment may all be damaged or destroyed. Treatment of most of the injured will probably be impossible. The movement of people out of damaged areas is likely to be possible only on foot. Hideous problems will be created by the need to dispose of huge numbers of dead bodies. Disease will become rampant, and its effects will be amplified by the damaging effect of radiation on the immune system, meaning that many more people will succumb to diseases and die from them than is normal. Food stocks will soon be exhausted, and the possibility of moving more food into London from outside areas will be very limited.

Levels of damage outside the London area are likely to be as high, if not higher, than in London itself. Much of Europe may find itself in similar plight. For these reasons, outside help after a nuclear disaster is likely to be severely limited or non-existent. Comparing the situation to World War 2, one GLAWARS researcher commented that 'the aftermath of a major nuclear war will be like Coventry trying to get help from Hamburg, while Dresden seeks help from both' (Thompson 1986).

References

Barnaby, F., and Rotblat, J., 'The effects of nuclear weapons'. In Peterson, J., and Hinrichsen, D. (eds.), *Nuclear War: the Aftermath*. Oxford, Pergamon Press, 1982.

Bentley, P. R., *Blast overpressure and fall-out radiation dose models for casualty assessment and other purposes*. London, Home Office Scientific Research and Development Branch, 1981.

Daugherty, W., Levi, B., and von Hippel, F., 'The consequences of "limited" nuclear attacks on the US'. In *International Security* (in press).

Glasstone, S., and Dolan, P., *The effects of nuclear weapons*. Washington DC, US Government Printing Office, 1977.

Greene, O., Rubin, B., Turok, N., Webber, P., and Wilkinson, G., *London After the Bomb*. Oxford, Oxford University Press, 1982.

Kerr, D. B., *GLAWARS Task 3: Conventional attack*. London, South Bank Polytechnic, 1986, mimeo.

Office of Technology Assessment, *The Effects of Nuclear War*. London, Croom Helm, 1980.

Oughterson, A. W., and Warren, S. (eds.), *Medical Effects of the Atomic Bomb in Japan*. New York, McGraw-Hill, 1956.

Perry Robinson, J., *GLAWARS Task 1: An assessment of the chemical and biological warfare threat to London*. London, South Bank Polytechnic, 1986, mimeo.

Rotblat, J., 'Acute radiation mortality in a nuclear war'. In *The Medical Implications of Nuclear War: Proceedings of the Institute of Medicine Symposium, September 1985*. Washington DC, National Academy Press, in press.

Rotblat, J., Haines, A., and Lindop, P., *GLAWARS Task 6: The health impact*. London, South Bank Polytechnic, 1986, mimeo.

Thompson, J., *GLAWARS Task 4: The behaviour of Londoners in a future major war: estimates from psychological research*. London, South Bank Polytechnic, 1986, mimeo.

Appendix 7

GLC Casualties by Borough

Standard assumptions of a 24 km/h, SSW wind apply for all the borough estimates of casualties below.

Scenario 2: total casualties from flash burns, blast and fall-out (% of total populations)

Borough	Seriously injured	Dead
City of London	0.0	0.0
Barking and Dagenham	0.0	0.0
Barnet	27.8	11.3
Bexley	0.0	0.0
Brent	32.2	16.9
Bromley	0.0	0.0
Camden	0.5	4.5
Croydon	0.0	0.0
Ealing	29.1	36.2
Enfield	0.2	0.1
Greenwich	0.0	0.0
Hackney	0.0	0.0
Hammersmith and Fulham	1.7	0.0
Haringey	0.0	1.3
Harrow	7.2	91.0
Havering	0.0	0.0
Hillingdon	0.1	99.3
Hounslow	23.9	45.1
Islington	0.0	0.0
Kensington and Chelsea	0.0	0.5
Kingston-upon-Thames	0.3	5.6
Lambeth	0.0	0.0
Lewisham	0.0	0.0
Merton	0.0	0.0

Scenario 2 (*Continued*)

Borough	Seriously injured	Dead
Newham	0.0	0.0
Redbridge	0.0	0.0
Richmond-upon-Thames	29.1	11.0
Southwark	0.0	0.0
Sutton	0.0	0.0
Tower Hamlets	0.0	0.0
Waltham Forest	0.0	0.0
Wandsworth	0.0	0.0
Westminster	0.0	0.0

Scenario 3: total casualties from flash burns, blast and fall-out (% of total populations)

Borough	Seriously injured	Dead
City of London	16.9	0.0
Barking and Dagenham	6.1	0.0
Barnet	27.0	13.0
Bexley	14.9	9.3
Brent	31.0	44.0
Bromley	9.0	17.4
Camden	32.6	32.8
Croydon	7.5	0.6
Ealing	29.9	17.5
Enfield	1.0	0.0
Greenwich	4.9	0.5
Hackney	6.9	0.0
Hammersmith and Fulham	33.4	5.3
Haringey	17.6	1.5
Harrow	11.3	81.8
Havering	0.1	0.0
Hillingdon	2.3	97.0
Hounslow	23.1	26.7
Islington	30.5	2.9
Kensington and Chelsea	35.3	9.9
Kingston-upon-Thames	0.1	0.0
Lambeth	1.1	0.0
Lewisham	0.0	0.0
Merton	0.0	0.0
Newham	0.0	0.0
Redbridge	0.4	0.0
Richmond-upon-Thames	6.1	0.8
Southwark	0.6	0.0
Sutton	0.0	0.0
Tower Hamlets	0.1	0.0
Waltham Forest	0.0	0.0
Wandsworth	2.0	0.0
Westminster	36.6	17.7

Scenario 4: total casualties from flash burns, blast and fall-out (% of total populations)

Borough	Seriously injured	Dead
City of London	0.0	98.3
Barking and Dagenham	37.2	11.1
Barnet	12.7	83.5
Bexley	25.0	28.0
Brent	11.4	85.0
Bromley	27.7	44.8
Camden	7.2	91.3
Croydon	20.7	66.4
Ealing	22.9	67.7
Enfield	23.9	62.3
Greenwich	24.4	42.7
Hackney	17.1	77.3
Hammersmith and Fulham	4.5	94.6
Haringey	10.6	87.2
Harrow	4.7	94.0
Havering	1.3	0.0
Hillingdon	1.5	98.2
Hounslow	23.5	64.9
Islington	12.4	84.3
Kensington and Chelsea	5.4	93.6
Kingston-upon-Thames	14.3	68.9
Lambeth	0.9	98.9
Lewisham	18.7	73.5
Merton	7.8	90.2
Newham	37.2	40.4
Redbridge	36.6	15.2
Richmond-upon-Thames	21.9	62.0
Southwark	0.8	99.2
Sutton	34.7	47.6
Tower Hamlets	4.3	95.0
Waltham Forest	38.1	39.7
Wandsworth	0.0	100.0
Westminster	6.9	91.7

Scenario 5: total casualties from flash burns, blast and fall-out (% of total populations)

Borough	Seriously injured	Dead
City of London	0.0	100.0
Barking and Dagenham	3.0	96.3
Barnet	5.8	92.7
Bexley	9.5	86.8
Brent	5.4	93.2
Bromley	20.7	64.1
Camden	0.0	100.0
Croydon	8.6	88.2
Ealing	14.3	81.1
Enfield	11.6	84.2
Greenwich	6.1	74.2
Hackney	0.1	99.9
Hammersmith and Fulham	0.7	99.1
Haringey	0.4	99.6
Harrow	2.9	96.4
Havering	32.3	44.9
Hillingdon	1.5	98.2
Hounslow	16.1	78.2
Islington	0.0	100.0
Kensington and Chelsea	0.3	99.7
Kingston-upon-Thames	3.5	93.5
Lambeth	0.1	99.9
Lewisham	5.4	93.3
Merton	0.9	99.0
Newham	3.0	96.4
Redbridge	9.2	88.2
Richmond-upon-Thames	15.8	76.4
Southwark	0.1	99.9
Sutton	2.5	97.2
Tower Hamlets	0.2	99.8
Waltham Forest	1.6	98.0
Wandsworth	0.0	100.0
Westminster	0.1	99.9

Index

Index by Ann Barham